The Biology of Perch and Related Fish

JOHN CRAIG

CROOM HELM
London & Sydney

TIMBER PRESS
Portland, Oregon

© 1987 John F. Craig
Croom Helm Ltd, Provident House, Burrell Row,
Beckenham, Kent, BR3 1AT
Croom Helm Australia, 44-50 Waterloo Road,
North Ryde, 2113, New South Wales

British Library Cataloguing in Publication Data

Craig, John
 The biology of perch and related fish.
 1. Percidae
 I. Title
 597'.58   QL638.P4
 ISBN 0-7099-3462-9

First published in the USA 1987 by
Timber Press,
9999 S.W. Wilshire,
Portland, OR 97225,
USA

023539

ISBN 0-88192-045-2

Printed and bound in Great Britain

CONTENTS

List of Figures
List of Tables
Preface
Acknowledgements

1. Taxonomy and Distribution 1
2. Morphology and Anatomy 14
3. Growth, Mortality and Longevity 45
4. Reproduction and Development 66
5. Food, Feeding and Energetics 94
6. Some Physiological Processes and
   Movements 122
7. Parasites and Diseases 144
8. Adaptation, Evolution and Genetics 174
9. Population Dynamics and Community
   Structure 181
10. Fisheries and Economic Importance 207
11. Other Percini 244
12. Etheostomatini 251
13. Romanichthyini 263

Bibliography and Author Index 267

Subject Index 318

LIST OF FIGURES

1.1 Suggested relationships of subfamilies, tribes and genera of the Percidae 5

1.2 Radiographs of four species of Percini and four species of Luciopercinae 6

1.3 The distribution of *Perca* species 9

1.4 The distribution of *Gymnocephalus* species 9

1.5 The distribution of *Percarina demidoffi* 10

1.6 The distribution of *Percina, Ammocrypta* and *Etheostoma* species 10

1.7 The distribution of *Stizostedion* species 11

1.8 The distribution of *Zingel* and *Romanichthys* species 12

2.1 The external appearance of *Perca fluviatilis* and the shape of its ctenoid scale 15

2.2 The external appearance of *Stizostedion lucioperca, S. marina, S. vitreum* and *S. canadense* 16

2.3 Sketches of the skeleton of *Perca* to show (a) the whole skeleton (b) dorsal view of the skull and (c) the branchial system 24

2.4 The head musculature of *Perca fluviatilis* 28

2.5 The relationship between gill surface area and body weight of *Stizostedion vitreum* 32

2.6 Lateral view of the body cavity of *Perca flavescens* to show the viscera 32

2.7 The circulatory system (a) through the gills of *Perca fluviatilis*, (b) through the viscera of *P. flavescens* and (c) the veins of the kidney region of *P. flavescens* 35

2.8 Drawings of *Perca flavescens* brain (a)
     dorsal and (b) ventral views 39
2.9 Diagram to illustrate the principles of
     the autonomic nervous system of a
     teleost 40
2.10 The ear of *Perca* 41
3.1 Diagram to illustrate the general
     metabolic system involved in growth of
     teleosts 47
3.2 Diagram to show the percentage number
     of *Perca fluviatilis* with checks laid
     down on the edge of the opercular bones
     at each month of the year 51
3.3 Photographs of *Perca fluviatilis*
     opercular bones from Windermere,
     England 52
3.4 Monthly weights of a 134 mm *Perca
     fluviatilis* from Slapton Ley,
     England 54
3.5 Monthly weights of mature *Perca
     fluviatilis* from Windermere, England .. 55
3.6 Monthly lengths of young-of-the-year
     Perca fluviatilis from Windermere,
     England and *Stizostedion vitreum* from
     Oneida Lake, USA 56
3.7 The relationship between length and age of
     female *Stizostedion vitreum* over a major
     part of their distributional range 57
3.8 Mean length at age and catch per unit
     effort at age for the 1955 and 1969
     year classes of male *Perca fluviatilis*
     from Windermere, England 58
3.9 Diagram to illustrate the effect of
     temperature and density on year class
     growth of *Perca fluviatilis* from
     Windermere, England 60
3.10 Mean length at age for *Stizostedion
     lucioperca* from three basins of Lake
     Balaton, Hungary 60
3.11 Length at age for a fast and a slow growing
     female *Stizostedion vitreum* from the 1969
     year class from Wapun Lake, Canada 61
3.12 Mean length at age of male and female
     Stizostedion vitreum from Lake Gogebic,
     USA 62
3.13 Diagram to illustrate the relationship
     between annual instantaneous mortality
     rate (Z) and the growth parameter
     (K) for different year classes of *Perca
     fluviatilis* from Windermere, England... 64

4.1 Sketch of the gravid ovary of *Perca fluviatilis* showing hyaline oocytes ... 69

4.2 Sketches of (a) spermatozoan and (b) cross-section of an egg of *Perca flavescens* 70

4.3 Plots of absolute fecundity with length for *Perca fluviatilis* from Windermere, England, *Stizostedion vitreum* from Dauphin Lake, Canada, and *S. lucioperca* from Lake Ijssel, The Netherlands 72

4.4 Plots of absolute fecundity with length for (a) *Perca fluviatilis*, from two regions of the Rybinsk Reservoir, USSR and (b) *Stizostedion vitreum* from the western and eastern basins of Lake Erie, USA 73

4.5 Drawings to illustrate embryonic development of *Perca flavescens* 83

4.6 Drawings to illustrate early embryonic development of *Stizostedion vitreum* ... 84

4.7 Drawings to illustrate late embryonic development of *Stizostedion vitreum* ... 86

4.8 The effect of temperature on the development of *Perca fluviatilis* embryos 87

4.9 The effect of temperature on the mass incubation time of *Perca fluviatilis*, *Stizostedion vitreum* and *S. lucioperca* 87

4.10 The prolarvae of (a) *Perca flavescens* and (b) *Stizostedion vitreum* 89

4.11 Sketches to show the development of the gut of *Stizostedion vitreum* 90

5.1 Diagram to illustrate metabolic pathways of ingested food 95

5.2 Prey items in the summer diet of young-of-the-year *Perca fluviatilis* from Windermere, England 96

5.3 The change in occurrence of prey items with change in length of the predator *Perca fluviatilis*, from Slapton Ley, England 97

5.4 The seasonal occurrence of various prey species in the diet of *Perca fluviatilis* from Windermere, England 98

5.5 The prey items in the diet of *Stizostedion lucioperca* from four water bodies in the USSR 100

5.6 Plot of maximum carapace width of
Daphnia hyalina and gape height of young-
of-the-year *Perca fluviatilis* from
Windermere, England 101

5.7 The relationship between the body length
of *Daphnia hyalina* eaten by *Perca
fluviatilis* and that of plankton from
Windermere, England 102

5.8 The mean daily feeling of young-of-the-year
Perca flavescens from Oneida Lake,
USA 103

5.9 Diagram to illustrate stomach "fullness" of
adult *Perca fluviatilis* at time intervals
through 24 h for each month of the year
from Windermere, England 104

5.10 Plot of dry weight of food in the
stomachs of adult *Perca fluviatilis* at
time intervals through 24 h for each
month of the year, from Windermere,
England 105

5.11 The relationships between total number of
Stizostedion vitreum caught by angling
at dusk and catch per hour with surface
illumination during the open-water period
from Shebandowan Lake, Canada 106

5.12 The gastric evacuation rate of *Gobiomorphus
cotidanus* from *Perca fluviatilis* stomachs
at 17°C 109

5.13 Semi-log plot of instantaneous gastric
evacuation rate and temperature for *Perca
fluviatilis* fed *Gammarus pulex* and fish
larvae 110

5.14 The proportions of consumed food egested
and excreted related to temperature for
Perca flavescens 117

5.15 The relationship between estimated
maintenance ratios for four weights of
Perca flavescens and temperature....... 119

5.16 The changes in specific growth rate of a
10 g *Perca flavescens* as functions of
temperature and ration level 119

5.17 Simulated growth of *Perca flavescens* for
western and eastern Lake Erie, USA 120

5.18 The seasonal energy content of wet and
dry tissues of the soma (body minus
gonads) of 225 mm male *Perca fluviatilis*
from Windermere, England.............. 121

6.1 The regulation of water and major ions
by gill and kidney action of a fresh
water teleost 123

6.2   The major rates of flux of water and ions
across the gill membrane of a fresh water
teleost and mechanisms for acid-base
regulation of products from body
metabolism 124

6.3   The structure and function of a fresh
water teleost nephron 125

6.4   Plots of lengths with age for *Perca
flavescens* held at three levels of pH
from lakes in the La Cloche Mountain
area, Canada 130

6.5   Cruising speed of *Perca flavescens*
in relation to temperature and oxygen
content 131

6.6   Ventilation volume of *Stizostedion
lucioperca* in relation to coefficient of
oxygen uptake from the water at four
temperatures 134

6.7   Ventilation volume of *Stizostedion
lucioperca* in relation to respiratory
movements at four temperatures 134

6.8   The effect of dissolved oxygen on the rate
of hatch of *Stizostedion vitreum*
eggs 136

6.9   Plots of sustained swimming speed of
larval *Perca flavescens* and *Stizostedion
vitreum* in relation to fish length 138

6.10 Plots of mean speeds of *Perca flavescens*
schools in relation to temperature
intervals measured at different times of
the year in Lake Mendota, USA 138

6.11 Plots of fish length in relation to their
ability to move 100 m in 10 min against
water velocities up to 80 cm s^{-1} for
various species of temperate fresh
water fish 139

6.12 The percentage activity every two hours over
24 h of juvenile and adult *Perca fluviatilis*
kept in experimental tanks 141

6.13 The summer activity of an ultra-sonic tagged
Perca fluviatilis from 1630 h to 0855 h the
next day in Bigland Tarn, England 142

9.1   The age group distribution of *Perca
fluviatilis* with time 184

9.2   Estimated number of mature female
Stizostedion vitreum in Oneida Lake,
USA, from 1928 to 1974 186

9.3 Simulated values of young-of-the-year
Perca flavescens biomass related to
Stizostedion vitreum biomass ranging from
10 to 30 kg ha^{-1} in June from Oneida Lake,
USA 189
9.4 Observed and simulated values of the
recruitment index (number of one
year olds per trap net lift) of
Stizostedion vitreum from 1947 to
1975 in western Lake Erie, USA 191
9.5 Observed and simulated values of abundance
(number of fish per trap net lift) of
Stizostedion vitreum from 1947 to 1975
in western Lake Erie 191
9.6 Mean catches of *Perca fluviatilis* in perch
traps in relation to time of the year in
Slapton Ley, England 193
9.7 Plots of (a) numbers of *Perca fluviatilis*
(aged two years or older) in the north and
south basins of Windermere, England, from
1941 to 1977 and (b) total numbers of
perch (1941-1976) and *Esox lucius*
(1944-1981) in the whole lake 195
9.8 Total biomass of *Perca fluviatilis*
(aged two years or older) in the north
basin of Windermere, England, from 1955 to
1976 and biomass data for year classes
1959, 1962, 1966 and 1968 contributing to
the 'total biomass' in the years where they
are represented 197
9.9 Year class strength (at age two
years) of *Perca fluviatilis* in relation to
total number of eggs laid in the north
basin of Windermere, England, from 1961 to
1974 198
9.10 Year class strength (at age two
years) of *Perca fluviatilis* in relation to
parental stock biomass (perch three years
or older) in year of hatch for the whole
lake in Windermere, England 199
9.11 Diagram to illustrate recruitment of
Perca fluviatilis (at age two years)
as a function of temperature, adult
biomass and *Esox lucius* year class
strength, in Windermere, England 200
9.12 Daytime proportional similarity in food
and thermal habitat use by Lake Michigan,
USA, fishes 203

9.13 The occurrence of prey items in the
     stomachs of *Esox lucius* and *Stizostedion
     vitreum* from Wolf Lake, Canada....... 206
10.1 Year class production for juvenile and
     adult *Perca fluviatilis* from 1955 to 1971
     in Windermere, England 208
10.2 Diagram to show relationships of fish
     stocks and yields to fishing effort ... 209
10.3 Diagram to show the simulated relation-
     ships of fish yield to fishing effort
     and age of recruitment to the fishing
     gear for *Stizostedion vitreum*, from
     Wolf Lake, Canada 210
10.4 Fishing gears used in commercial
     fisheries for *Perca fluviatilis, P.
     flavescens, Stizostedion lucioperca*
     and *S. vitreum* 212
10.5 Plots of annual commercial yields of
     the major species of fish from 1957 to
     1983 for the Canadian waters of Lake
     Erie 218
10.6 Sketch of a jigger for setting gill nets
     under the ice 220
10.7 Plots of (a) annual commercial catches of
     major fish species from 1902 to 1973 and (b)
     annual catches of *Stizostedion lucioperca*
     from commercial and sport fisheries from
     1960 to 1978 for Lake Balaton,
     Hungary 222
10.8 Diagram to illustrate hypothetical
     relationships between potential fish
     yields and environmental temperatures
     in subarctic and temperate zones 225
10.9 Plots to illustrate the relationship
     between sustainable yields of
     Stizostedion vitreum and long-term
     mean annual air temperatures 225
10.10 Estimated selectivity curves of from
     38 to 114 mm mesh gill nets to fish length
     of *Stizostedion vitreum* 227
10.11 The effect of different mortality rates
     on natural and cultured *Stizostedion
     vitreum* 232
10.12 Sketches of (a) a Zoug jar for hatching
     Stizostedion lucioperca eggs and (b) a
     jar for hatching *S. vitreum* eggs 236
11.1 The external appearance of (a) *Gymnocephalus
     cernua,* (b) *G. acerina,* (c) *G. schraetzer*
     and (d) *G. baloni* 246

11.2 Total length against age for male and female
      Gymnocephalus cernua from the Nadym River,
      USSR 248
11.3 The external appearance of *Percarina*
      demidoffi 249
12.1 The external appearance of (a) *Percina*
      maculata, (b) *Ammocrypta pellucida* and
      (c) *Etheostoma nigrum* 252
12.2 Diagram to illustrate the relationship
      between number of species for each genera
      of darters and fish length 256
12.3 Plots of length with age of male and
      female *Etheostoma perlongum* from
      Lake Waccamaw, USA 257
12.4 Genital papillae of breeding (a) male and
      (b) female *Etheostoma perlongum* 258
12.5 The annual cycle in ova differentiation in
      darters 259
12.6 Plots of embryo development time in
      relation to temperature for darters ... 260
12.7 Late yolk sac larvae of (a) *Percina*
      caprodes and (b) *Etheostoma*
      flabellare 261
13.1 The external appearance of *Romanichthys*
      valsanicola 264
13.2 The external appearance of (a) *Zingel*
      zingel, (b) *Z. asper* and (c) *Z.*
      streber 265

LIST OF TABLES

1.1 Families of the suborder Percoidei 3
2.1 Numbers of scales along the lateral line of species of *Perca* and *Stizostedion* 20
2.2 Bones of the head region of *Perca fluviatilis* 23
2.3 Numbers of spines and rays found in the dorsal and anal fins of *Perca* and *Stizostedion* species 26
2.4 Cranial nerves of *Perca flavescens* 38
3.1 Physiological optima, incipient lethal and critical thermal maxima for species of *Perca* and *Stizostedion* 48
4.1 External and histological appearances of each stage of development of the perch ovary 68
4.2 External appearances of each stage of development of the perch testes 71
5.1 Energy equations for 150 g male *Perca fluviatilis* in Windermere, England 112
5.2 Optimum and maximum temperatures for consumption and respiration for young-of-the-year and juvenile and adult *Perca flavescens* 117
6.1 The concentration of various ions in the plasma and muscle of perch placed in freshwater and 3.6, 10 and 15‰ salinities 127
6.2 Ventilation volume, coefficient of oxygen uptake and respiratory movements of *Stizostedion lucioperca* held in water of temperatures 5-20°C 133
7.1 A list of zooparasites of *Perca fluviatilis*, *P. flavescens*, *Stizostedion vitreum* and *S. lucioperca* 149

9.1 A summary of summer temperatures, growth and year class strength of perch and pike during five periods in Windermere, England 196

10.1 World yield in tonnes of *Perca fluviatilis*, *P. flavescens*, *Stizostedion vitreum* and *S. lucioperca* by country from 1980 to 1983 214

10.2 Value of recreational and commercial fisheries of central Canada, 1982-1983. 215

10.3 Estimated response of the Lake McConaughy, USA, walleye population to various length limits 231

10.4 The composition of main food items and daily consumption of young zander held in rearing ponds 236

10.5 Composition and proximate analysis of food used in the cultivation of perch 239

11.1 The number of lateral line scales and anterior dorsal fin spines in the four species of *Gymnocephalus* 245

12.1 Numbers of described species of darters in each of the major drainages of North America 254

12.2 The habitats of various species of *Etheostomatini* 255

12.3 The oxygen concentration at death for six species of *Etheostoma* held at 20°C 256

In memory of my mother, Rachel Miskin Craig

PREFACE

The perch is an attractive fish common in many lakes, rivers and canals. It is a member of the family Percidae which are fresh water fish indigenous to the north temperate zone and is a fish typical of the largest order of vertebrates, the Perciformes. Some members of the Percidae are economically important both as food and sport fish and for this reason have been extensively studied. These include the perch and zander of Eurasia and the yellow perch and walleye of North America. Other common members of the family include the ruffe, sauger and a number of species of the three genera of darters. Rarer species of which less is known are the Balkhush perch, the striped, Don and Balon's ruffes, the sea and Volga pikeperches, the zingel, streber and apron and the asprete.

The perch has been immortalised in the children's adventure book *Swallows and Amazons* by Arthur Ransome. This story was based on Windermere, in the English Lake District, the largest lake in England. The perch in Windermere have been studied continuously for over 45 years by scientists from the Freshwater Biological Association. The reason for long term studies is to determine the relationship between the fish and its environment and use this information to develop predictive models. The intent is to utilise these models in predicting responses to perturbations particularly those brought about by humans. The number of years of study devoted to this aim without its full attainment is an indicator of the complexity of the relationship between the fish and its environment. Perhaps one of the problems has been that the environments in which long term studies have been made were already perturbed. However, a great deal is known about the biology of percids and it is the aim of this book to summarise this information. Also it is hoped that it will highlight important areas for future research. Studies of fresh water fish in comparison to those of marine fish are enhanced by greater ease of sampling and also by a more precise understanding of the abiotic and biotic fresh water environment.

After an introduction on the taxonomy of the percids, the main part of the book is devoted to the biology of *Perca* and *Stizostedion* species. The anatomy and morphology of these fish, which display

many features typical of advanced teleosts, is
described in detail. Their anatomy is well adapted
to their mode of life. For example the tapetum
lucidium in the eye is extensively developed in the
walleye and slightly less well developed in the
zander. This allows these fish to actively feed in
very low light intensities such as at night or in
turbid waters. In this way they may separate themselves into different niches from other common but
day active predators such as the pike.

Temperature is an important external environmental factor which influences many processes in
cold-blooded animals. Its relevance in controlling
feeding, digestion, growth, mortality, gonad development, embryo development, parasite infections
and other functions is particularly significant in
percids which experience many differences in temperature. These differences can be encountered
over the range in latitude in which the fish live
and also with time as from season to season or year
to year. Temperature and other controlling and
limiting factors are considered in detail in
various chapters in an attempt to give a brief ex-
planation of their effect on underlying physiological processes. Percids are viewed from the perspective of the individual fish, as populations and
as part of a community of fishes. The section of
the book on perch, yellow perch, walleye and zander
is concluded with a chapter on their exploitation,
culture and vulnerability to pollution and other
perturbations. The final part of the book is
devoted to a brief synopsis of the biology of other
percids.

Attempts to make a comprehensive review of
perch and related species are not exhaustive and
the list of references although extensive is not
complete. In a number of places results from a
particular study are given in detail. The selected
study illustrates more fully the subject being discussed than a synthesis of investigations. Although each chapter commences with some fundamental
principles and aims to be complete in itself,
frequent cross references are made. For example a
knowledge of anatomy is required in understanding
how a perch captures its prey and growth cannot be
isolated from food intake and energetics.

ACKNOWLEDGEMENTS

Firstly I would like to acknowledge the late Dr J.D. Carthy of the Field Studies Council and my past colleagues at the Freshwater Biological Association, England, in particular Mr E.D. LeCren and Miss C. Kipling for stimulating my interest in the biology of perch.

I would like to thank my colleagues who read and made constructive criticisms on various chapters. These were Dr A. Bodaly, Dr J. Clayton, Dr T. Dick, Dr W. Franzin, Dr M. Giles, Dr L. Johnson, Dr R. Kelly, Dr W. Mackay, Dr J. Mathias, Dr K. Mills, Mr M.H. Papst and Dr K. Stewart. I am particularly grateful to Drew Bodaly and John Flannagan who agreed to read the whole manuscript. However any mistakes or misinterpretations in the text are solely my own.

I appreciate the efforts of the Freshwater Institute (Canada) Library staff, in particular Eric Marshall. I also acknowledge the patience of Tim Hardwick of Croom Helm who waited so long for the manuscript. Leslie Fletcher gave very useful advice and help with the word processor.

The arduous task of reading my writing and converting it into the text of this book was undertaken by Grace Decterow. I thank her for all her efforts, patience and typing efficiency.

My wife Hilary assisted in numerous ways and without her help "the book" would never have been written.

All figures were freshly drawn by the able hand of Charmaine Johnson. I also thank the Graphics Department at the Freshwater Institute, in particular Laurie Taite. I acknowledge the following for permission to reproduce their material, either in whole or in part: Academic Press Inc. for Figures 2.7a, 2.9, 3.1, 6.3, 6.5; Akademie-Verlag Berlin for Figure 13.10; the American Fisheries Society for Figures 4.2a, 4.10b, 4.11, 6.10, 12.7b and Table 10.3; the Editor of the *American Midland Naturalist* for Figure 12.7a; the Secretary of A.S.I.H. *(Copeia)* for Figures 1.2, 11.1, 12.3; the Editor of the *Journal of Animal Ecology* for Figures 3.5, 5.18, 9.7a; Dr A. von Brandt for Figures 10.4f & g; Wm C. Brown Publishers for Table 2.4; E.J. Brill, Leiden *(Netherlands Journal of Zoology)* for Figure 2.4; the *Canadian Journal of Fisheries and Aquatic*

Sciences and the *Journal of the Fisheries Research Board of Canada* for Figures 1.1, 1.5, 1.7, 1.8, 3.7, 4.4b, 5.5, 5.11, 5.14, 5.15, 5.16, 5.17, 6.9, 6.11, 9.2, 9.4, 9.5, 9.12, 10.7, 10.8, 10.9, 10.10 and Tables 3.1, 5.2; the Ecological Society of America for Table 12.3; Elsevier Science B.V. Publishers *(Aquaculture)* for Table 10.5; the Estuarine Research Federation *(Chesapeake Science)* for Figures 4.2b, 4.5, 4.6, 4.10a; the Fisheries Society of the British Isles for Figures 2.5, 3.9, 4.1, 9.7b, 9.9, 9.10, 9.11, 9.13, 10.3; the Freshwater Biological Association for Figures 3.3, 3.13, 9.8; the Editor of *Freshwater Biology* for Figures 3.2, 3.4, 3.6a, 4.8, 4.9, 5.2, 5.3, 5.4, 5.6, 5.7, 5.8, 5.10, 5.13, 9.6 and Table 5.1; the Food and Agriculture Organisation of the United Nations for Figures 1.3, 1.8, 3.6b, 3.12, 4.9, 6.8, 9.1, 10.4c,d,e,i,j, 10.6; Dr J.L. Forney for Figure 9.3; G.E.C. Gads Forlag for Figure 13.3; Hamlyn Publishing Group Ltd. for Figures 2.2a, 11.3, 13.1; Madame L. Huet-Rigo for Figure 10.12a; the Israel Program for Scientific Translations for Figure 2.2b; the *Journal Conseil Internationale pour l'Exploration de la mer* for Table 9.1; Dr W. Junk, Publishers *(Environmental Biology of Fishes)* for Figures 4.6, 4.7, 6.4, 12.2, 12.4; the Editors of *Mauri Ora* for Figure 5.12; Oxford University Press for Figure 2.3a; Pergamon Press, Ltd. for Table 6.1 42A, Lutz, P.L., taken from *Comparative Biochemistry and Physiology*, 'Ionic and body compartment responses to increasing salinity in the perch'. Copyright 1972, Pergamon Press Ltd; Dr R.A. Ryder and the Ontario Ministry of Natural Resources for Figure 5.11; Scripta Technica, John Wiley and Sons, Inc. *(Journal of Ichthyology)* for Figures 4.4a, 6.6, 6.7 and Table 6.2, 10.4; Springer-Verlag *(Naturwissenchaften)* for Figure 6.12; T.F.H. Publications, Inc. for Figures 12.1, 12.5, 12.6 and Table 12.1 and the Editor of the *Proceedings of the Fourth International Conference on Wildlife Biotelemetry* for Figure 6.13.

Chapter 1

TAXONOMY AND DISTRIBUTION

Introduction

The perch family or Percidae have the following
affinities:
      Kingdom Animalia
       Phylum Chordata
        Subphylum Vertebrata
         Superclass Gnathostomata
          Class Osteichthyes
           Subclass Actinopterygii
            Order Perciformes
             Suborder Percoidei
              Family Percidae

The Perciformes

The order Perciformes, the largest group of vertebrates, encompasses 22 suborders of fish, about
1,367 genera and over 7,800 species (Nelson 1984).
The members of this huge group of spiny-rayed fish
have a world-wide.distribution and are especially
common in tropical and subtropical seas. They are
less abundant in temperate waters but throughout
their range are found in marine, brackish and fresh
waters. The members of the Perciformes are very
varied in size and shape but in general have the
following common characteristics. They usually
have laterally compressed bodies and most have
ctenoid scales (tooth-like processes are present on
their free edge) although cycloid scales are found
in some species. The scales of *Epinephelus* Bloch
(Serranidae), above the lateral line are nearly all
ctenoid and those below it are cycloid. The
Perciformes are physoclists, that is the duct
connecting the swim bladder to the gut is closed.

There are usually two dorsal fins but never an adipose fin. The first dorsal fin is supported by spines and the second by soft rays. The anal fin has two or three spines and a series of soft rays. The caudal fin has 17 (15 are branched) or fewer principal rays. Pelvic fins, when present, are jugular or thoracic in position, each with one spine and five or fewer soft rays. The pelvic girdle is often attached to the cleithra. The pectoral fins are elevated on the sides of the fish with the base of the fins more or less vertically oriented. The skull is elongate and well ossified. The upper jaw is bordered by the premaxillae and both jaws contain well developed teeth. The post-temporal is usually forked and articulates with the skull; the orbitosphenoid and the hypocoracoid are absent. There are four to seven branchiostegal rays and gill rakers are toothed. Perciforms have 24 or more vertebrae and intermuscular bones are absent.

The order contains a widely developed assemblage of fishes and may be paraphyletic, consisting of distinct lines which evolved in parallel to a perciform grade of organisation. A thorough and detailed examination of the classification and distribution of the Perciformes is provided by Nelson (1984).

The Percoidei

The largest suborder of the Perciformes, the Percoidei, contains 73 families (Table 1.1) about 589 genera and 3,524 species. Nelson (1984) considers it to be the basic group of the Perciformes from which others evolved. Approximately 930 species live in fresh water, mainly representatives from the families Cichlidae, Percidae, Centropomidae and Percichthyidae. There is no general agreement on how the percoid families might be interrelated. Some series of families appear to be more similar to one another than to most other percoid families (e.g. Carangidae, Nematistiidae and Coryphaenidae, or Lutjanidae, Haemulidae and Sparidae) but there are no sharp morphological discontinuities demarcating such groups, nor is it clear whether the similarities are the result of families being related or from evolutionary convergence.

Table 1.1:   Families of the suborder Percoidei.
(After Nelson 1984).

Family Name	Common Name
Pomatomidae	Bluefishes
Rachycentridae	Cobia
Coryphaenidae	Dolphins
Lobotidae	Tripletails
Echeneididae	Remoras
Caritsiidae	Manefishes
Bramidae	Pomfrets
Embiotocidae	Surfperches
Nematistiidae	Roosterfish
Centrarchidae	Sunfishes
Percidae	Perches
Percichthyidae	Temperate basses
Centropomidae	Snooks, Glassfishes and Perches
Serranidae	Sea basses
Grammidae	Basslets
Pempherididae	Sweepers
Apogonidae	Cardinalfishes
Lutjanidae	Snappers
Malacanthidae	Tilefishes
Haemulidae	Grunts
Gerreidae	Mojarras
Inermiidae	Bonnetmouths
Cirrhitidae	Hawkfishes
Chaetodontidae	Butterflyfishes
Mullidae	Goatfishes
Sciaenidae	Drums or Croakers
Carangidae	Jacks and Pompanos
Sparidae	Porgies
Centracanthidae	*Centracanthus, Spicara*
Pomacentridae	Damelfishes
Coracinidae	Galjoen fishes
Cichlidae	Cichlids
Lactariidae	False trevallies
Priacanthidae	Bigeyes
Pseudochromidae	Dottybacks
Pomacanthidae	Angelfishes
Monodactylidae	Moonfishes or Fingerfishes
Leiognathidae	Ponyfishes, Slimys or Slipmouths
Grammistidae	Soapfishes
Ephippididae	Spadefishes

3

Terapomidae	Grunters or Tigerperches
Plesiopidae	Roundheads
Scatophagidae	Scats
Menidae	Moonfish
Bathyclupeidae	*Bathyclupea*
Oplegnathidae	Knifejaws
Apolectidae	*Apolectus*
Pentacerotidae	Armourheads
Owstoniidae	*Owstonia, Sphenanthias* and *Pseudocepola*
Acanthoclinidae	*Acanthoclinus, Acanthoplesiops* and *Belonepterygion*
Toxotidae	Archerfishes
Nandidae	Leaffishes
Nemipteridae	Threadfin breams
Labracoglossidae	*Bathystethus, Evistius* and *Labracoglossa*
Banjosidae	*Banjos*
Cepolidae	Bandfishes
Kuhliidae	Aholeholes
Glaucosomatidae	Pearl perch, *Glaucosoma*
Sillaginidae	Smelt-whitings
Cheilodactylidae	Morwongs
Latrididae	Trumpeters
Gadopsidae	Blackfish
Kyphosidae	Sea chubbs
Arripidae	Australian salmon
Leptobramidae	Beachsalmon
Chironemidae	Kelpfishes
Aplodactylidae	Sea carp
Enoplosidae	Oldwife
Dinolestidae	*Dinolestes*
Emmelichthyidae	Rovers
Caesionidae	Fusiliers
Lethrinidae	Scavengers or emperors
Rhinoprenidae	Threadfin scat

The Percidae

The family Percidae, unlike most of the 73 percoid families, is confined to fresh water, in the temperate and subarctic regions of North America and Eurasia (Nelson 1984). Some introductions of species of the family have been made into the southern hemisphere. Percid fossils occur as far back as the Oligocene in both landmasses (Romer 1966). The existence in eastern North America, of the endemic tribe Etheostomatini

4

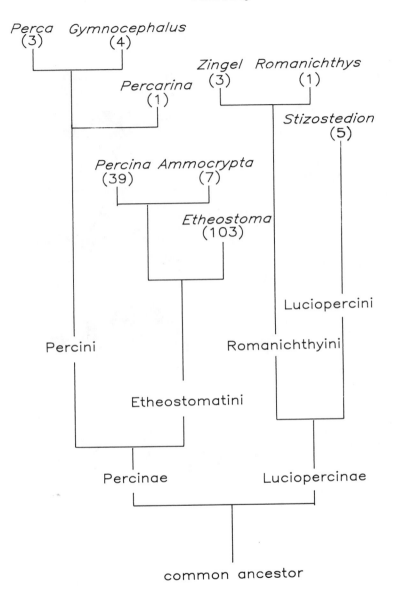

Figure 1.1: Suggested relationships of subfamilies, tribes and genera of the Percidae. The number of species of each genera are indicated in brackets. (After Collette & Bănărescu 1977).

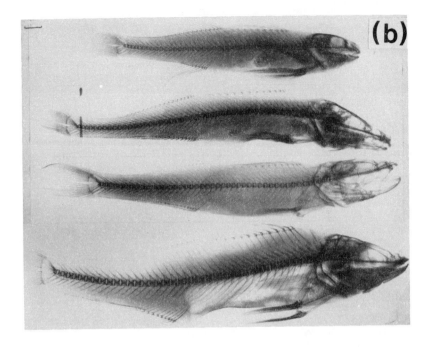

Figure 1.2: Radiographs of (a) four species of Percini, from top to bottom:
Percarina demidoffi, *Perca schrenki*, *Gymnocephalus cernua* and *G. schraetser*,
showing the enlarged anterior interhaemal bones and (b) four species of
Luciopercinae, from top to bottom: *Romanichthys valsanicola*, *Zingel zingel*,
Stizostedion canadense and *S. volgensis* with no enlargement of the interhaemal
bones. (Reproduced from the original, Collette 1963, by kind permission of
the author).

(3 genera, c. 150 species) (Kuehne & Barbour 1983)
of the subfamily Percinae is further evidence of a
long, independent history of the family in North
America. Similarly, the existence of the endemic
European genera *Zingel* (3 species) and *Romanichthys* (1 species) of the subfamily Luciopercinae
and *Gymnocephalus* (4 species) and *Percarina* (1
species) of the Percinae, tribe Percini (Collette &
Bănărescu 1977), is evidence of a long, independent
period of evolution there (Chapter 8).

Collette and Bănărescu (1977) group Percini
(Perca, Gymnocephalus and *Percarina)* and Etheostomatini *(Percina, Ammocrypta* and *Etheostoma)* into
the subfamily Percinae. *Luciopercini (Stizostedion)* and *Romanichthyini (Zingel* and *Romanichthys)*
are placed in the subfamily Luciopercinae (Figure
1.1). The Percinae have the anteriormost interhaemal bone greatly enlarged (Figure 1.2). Also
the lateral line usually does not extend onto the
caudal fin and the anal spines are large and well
developed. In the Luciopercinae, the anteriormost
interhaemal bone is not larger than the other interhaemal bones, the lateral line does extend onto
the caudal fin and the anal spines are not well developed (Collette & Bănărescu 1977).

There are three species of *Perca* Linnaeus.
P. fluviatilis Linnaeus (Eurasian perch, referred
to hereafter as perch; Russian = okuń) is widely
distributed throughout Eurasia but also has been
introduced into South Africa, Australia and New
Zealand. *P. flavescens* (Mitchill) (yellow perch)
is a North American perch and *P. schrenki* Kessler
(Balkhush perch; Russian = Balkhushskii okuń) is
found only in eastern Kazakh (USSR) (Figure 1.3).

There are four species of *Gymnocephalus* Bloch,
G. cernua (Linnaeus) (ruffe; Russian= ёrsh), *G.
schraetser* (Linnaeus) (striped ruffe; Russian =
polosatyi ёrsh), *G. acerina* (Güldenstadt) (Don
ruffe; Russian = Donskoi ёrsh) and *G. baloni*
Holčik & Hensel (Balon's ruffe; Slovak = hrebenačka
Balonova) (see Holčik & Hensel 1974). The
distribution of these four species of ruffe is
shown in Figure 1.4.

The one species of *Percarina* Nordmann, *P.
demidoffi* Nordmann (percarina; Russian = perkarina)
is distributed in the Sea of Azov and parts of the
Black Sea (Figure 1.5).

8

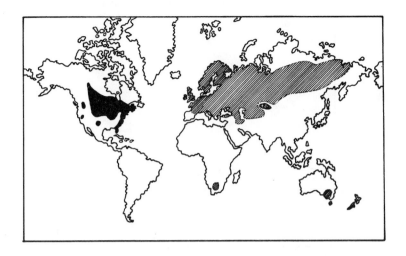

Figure 1.3: The distribution of *Perca* species. ■ = *P. flavescens*, ▨ = *P. fluviatilis* and ⊡ = *P. schrenki*. (After Thorpe 1977).

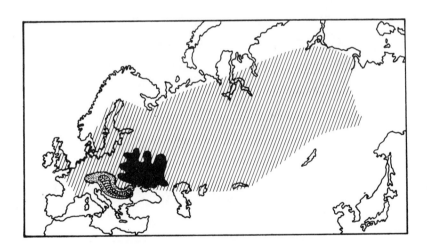

Figure 1.4: The distribution of *Gymnocephalus* species. ▨ = *G. cernua*, ⊡ = *G. schraetser*, ■ = *G. acerina* and ⊞ = *G. baloni* and *G. schraetser* combined.

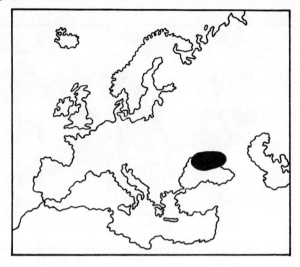

Figure 1.5: The distribution of *Percarina demidoffi* ■ (After Collette & Bănărescu 1977).

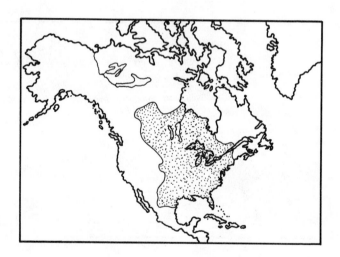

Figure 1.6: The distribution of *Percina, Ammocrypta* and *Etheostoma* species ⊡ .

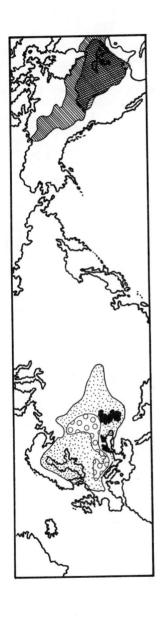

Figure 1.7: The distribution of *Stizostedion* species. ⊡ = *S. lucioperca*, = *S. marina*, ⊞ = *S. volgensis*, ▨ = *S. canadense* and ▨ = *S. vitreum*. (After Collette & Bănărescu 1977).

There are three genera of darters which are distributed solely in North America (Figure 1.6). These are *Percina* Haldeman (31 described species), *Ammocrypta* Jordon (7 species) and *Etheostoma* Rafinesque (91 described species). A thorough and well illustrated guide to the darters is given by Page (1983).

Stizostedion Rafinesque has five species, three in Europe, *S. lucioperca* (Linnaeus) (zander; Russian = śudak), *S. marina* (Cuvier) (sea pike-perch; Russian = morskoi śudak) and *S. volgensis* (Gmelin) (Volga pikeperch; Russian= bersh) and two in North America, *S. canadense* (Smith) (sauger) and *S. vitreum* (Mitchill) (walleye) (Figure 1.7).

Zingel Cloquet has three species *Z. zingel*, (Linnaeus) (zingel; Russian = tschop), *Z. streber* Siebold (streber; Russian = malyi tschop) and *Z. asper* (Linnaeus) (French = apron). Zingel and streber are found in the Danube and Vardar Rivers and apron is distributed in the Rhône River (Figure 1.8). Zingel's close relative *Romanichthys* Dumitresch, Bănărescu and Stoica, is monotypic and

Figure 1.8: The distribution of *Zingel* and *Romanichthys* species. ▨ = *Z. zingel*, ◪ = *Z. streber*, ■ = *Z. asper* and ★ = *R. valsanicola*. (After Collette & Bănărescu 1977 and EIFAC 1971).

represented by *R. valsanicola* Dumitresch, Bănărescu
and Stoica (asprete) which was found in the Arges
and Riul-Doamnei Rivers but is extinct there
(Stanescu 1971) and is now only found in the Vilsan
River (Figure 1.8).
The following chapters give a more detailed
account of the genera of the family Percidae.
Perca and *Stizostedion* are covered in Chapter 2 to
10 and the other genera in Chapters 11 to 13.
Emphasis is given to *Perca* and *Stizostedion* because
these fish are of more economic importance than the
other genera, thus the departure from the taxonomic
groupings given in this introduction.

13

Chapter 2

MORPHOLOGY AND ANATOMY

External Anatomy

The great variability in colour of *Perca* and
Stizostedion species depends on the habitat in
which they live. *Perca* species are among the most
attractively coloured fish in temperate fresh
waters. In shallow areas where light penetration
is good *Perca* tend to be darkly coloured whereas in
poorly lit areas without vegetation they are
lightly coloured. Sometimes carotinoids, derived
from Crustacea in the diet make the perch deeply
reddish-yellow. Usually the dorsal surface is
bright green to olive and this colour is extended
down the sides in seven tapering bars (Figure
2.1a). The sides of the body are yellow to yellow-
green and the ventral surface grey to white. The
eyes are green to yellow in colour as are the dorsal and caudal fins. The first spine of the dorsal
fin is often black and there is black colouration
on the membrane between spines one and two and on
the membranes between the last four or five
spines. The pectoral fins are amber and transparent and the pelvic and anal fins are silver
white to yellow and opaque. The body of the
Balkhush perch is usually light coloured and the
dark transverse bands are absent (Berg 1965). Some
perch have been found with perfectly black bodies.
All species of *Stizostedion* are highly variable in colour. Their eyes are always silvery due
to the reflective nature of the tapetum lucidum
which will be discussed later in this chapter. The
zander is coloured brownish to brownish-black on
the dorsal surface and this extends onto the flanks
in eight to twelve characteristic bands which are
most apparent in juveniles. The sides of the fish
are greenish to blue grey and the ventral surface

14

(a)

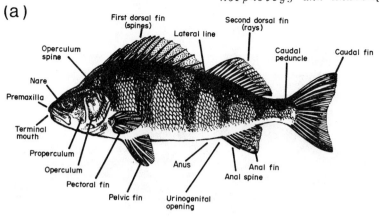

First dorsal fin
(spines)

Lateral line

Second dorsal fin
(rays)

Caudal
peduncle

Caudal fin

Operculum
spine

Nare

Premaxilla

Terminal
mouth

Properculum

Operculum

Pectoral fin

Pelvic fin

Anus

Urinogenital
opening

Anal fin

Anal spine

(b)

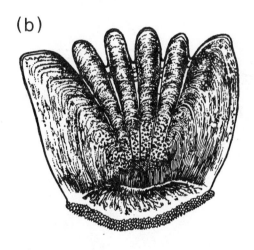

Figure 2.1: The (a) external appearance of *Perca fluviatilis* and (b) the shape of its ctenoid scale.

15

(a)

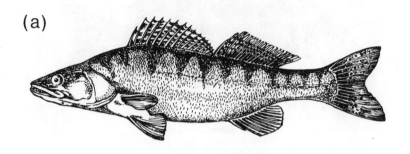

(b)

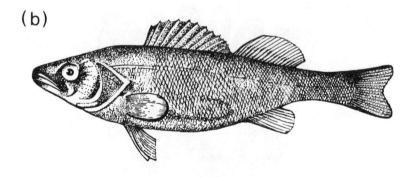

(c)

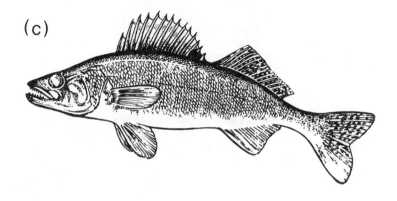

(d)

Figure 2.2: The external appearance of (a) *Stizostedion lucioperca* (after Holčík & Mihálik 1970), (b) *S. marina* (after Berg 1965), (c) *S. vitreum* and (d) *S. canadense*.

is a silvery to dirty white. During spawning this
surface becomes marbled blue in the males and pure
white in the females (Holčik & Mihalik 1970). Both
dorsal fins have irregular rows of black spots on
the membranes between spines (Figure 2.2a) and the
caudal fin is spotted in transverse rows. Other
fins are yellowish grey, the pectoral and pelvic
fins being almost transparent. The head has numerous shining blue to brass coloured zones on a
marbled brown to grey green background. Colouration of the Volga pikeperch is similar to the zander but the sea pikeperch is lighter than the other
two species (Berg 1965) (Figure 2.2b). The back of
the sea pikeperch is light grey with 12 to 13
transverse dark bars on the body. Quite often
these bars are indistinct. The first dorsal fin is
usually without spots, dark grey or black in
colour. The other fins are grey. The walleye is
paler in turbid waters but in clear waters it is
more vividly marked (Scott & Crossman 1973). The
body is olive-brown to golden brown to yellow. The
dorsal surface is darker and the flanks paler with
golden flecks on the scales. The ventral surface
is yellow white to milk white. The first dorsal
fin is dusky, clear or vaguely speckled and has a
characteristic black blotch at the base of the last
few membranes (Figure 2.2c). The second dorsal and
caudal fins have small dots of pigment in regular
rows. The lower lobe of the caudal fin and the tip
of the anal fin are milk white in colour. The
pectoral fins are olive with black dots at the
bases and the pelvic fins are yellow or orange-
yellow. The sauger is sandy to dull brown. The
dorsal surface is usually brown with three or four
brown stripes expanding onto the flanks. There are
also several large round spots on the sides (Figure
2.2d). The ventral surface is milk white. The
first dorsal fin has dark pigment on the edge of
the membranes and rows of distinct spots below
this. There is no black blotch at the base of the
posterior membranes as in the walleye. The second
dorsal fin of the sauger has two bands of dark
spots on the membranes and the caudal fin also has
rows of dark brown bars. The lower lobe of the
caudal fin sometimes has a white tip as does the
anal fin which is white with small spots of pigment. The pelvic fins are also white and speckled
with pigment. The pectoral fins are almost transparent and amber with a dark spot at the base of
each fin.

The skin of percids is similar to other

teleosts consisting of a thin epidermis and a thicker dermis (Greenwood 1975). The epidermis, derived from the ectoderm, is composed entirely of living cells. The cells nearest the dermis are cuboidal and generate new cells which migrate towards the surface becoming flattened as they progress and then finally being sloughed off. The epidermis contains mucous, a product of decomposed epidermal cells. The dermis, developed from mesenchyne, is made up of connective tissue and also contains nerves, blood vessels, smooth muscle, chromatophores and scales.

The colours of fish are mostly due to cells called chromatophores which contain pigment (Fujii 1969). These thin walled cells have many branches and they can contract the pigment into small spots or expand the pigment over a relatively large area. The pigments of chromatophores are either red, orange, yellow (carotenoids or flavines) or black (melanin). Iridocytes in the skin are made up of opaque crystals of guanin which reflect light and in the absence of chromatophores give a white or silvery appearance. When the iridocytes are located within the scales the colours appear irridescent. The physiological control of colour changes is still not fully understood. Quick responses are certainly under nervous control (Figure 2.9) but longer term changes are also influenced by hormones (Pickford & Atz 1957).

Ctenoid (Figure 2.1b) and cycloid scales are distinguished on the basis of their surface sculpture but their origin and development are similar. Ctenoid scales are so called because of the numerous teeth or cteni at the posterior end. These cteni may number up to 70 in zander (Linfield & Rickards 1979). Percidae do not produce a lot of mucous so the body often feels rough to touch due to the presence of these cteni on the scales. Scales consist of two layers, a hyalodentine (bony) layer deposited over a fibrous sheet called the fibrillar plate (Simkiss 1974). The scales are derived from osteoblasts and fibroblasts in the dermal papillae. The bony layer only grows along its edge depositing rings (circuli). The fibrillar plate deposits sheets beneath the scale so that this layer is thickest at the centre and thinnest at the margins. It has been suggested (Simkiss 1974) that scales may be reabsorbed to provide calcium during periods of deficiency such as when the fish is developing gametes. Apparent differences in the spaces between circuli on scales have been thought to relate to different seasonal rates of growth of temperate water fish (reduction or reabsorption of mineral deposits would make the circuli closer together) and thus have been used in ageing the fish. Van Utrecht (1979) disputes this interpretation. In the scales of zander he studied the circuli in the bony layer were very regular and no groups of narrowly interspaced circuli could be found. Ring-like structures were also found in the fibrillar plate which were 3-5 μm closer together than the circuli. These rings on the two layers of the scale were said to create an interference pattern and bear no relation to the development of the two layers (Van Utrecht 1979). This questions very seriously the validity of using scales in fish ageing. Another problem in using scales to age fish (ageing will be more fully discussed in Chapter 3) is that scales are not fully developed until sometime after hatching. For example the walleye is not completely scaled until it is about 45 mm in length (Priegel 1964). Attempts have been made to discriminate between stocks of walleye by using scale shape but with mixed success (Chapter 8). Jarvis, Klodowski & Sheldon (1978) were able to use scale shape to distinguish between two stocks in eastern Lake Erie, North America. However Riley and Carline (1982) found that variability within stocks masked any between stock differences in western Lake Erie.

The number of scales along the lateral line varies between and within species. The range for the different species of *Perca* and *Stizostedion* are given in Table 2.1.

Table 2.1. Numbers of scales along the lateral line of species of *Perca* and *Stizostedion*.

P. *schrenki*	41-54	S. *volgensis*	70-83
P. *flavescens*	51-61	S. *marina*	75-88
P. *fluviatilis*	56-77	S. *lucioperca*	80-97
		S. *canadense*	82-100
		S. *vitreum*	83-104

The Skeleton

The skeleton of *Perca* is a compact, sturdy structure (Figure 2.3a). The outer layer of the skull is made up of dermal bone (bone formed from the embryonic cells of the dermis). The inner skull and other skeletal structures are subdermal in origin and their formation is usually preceded by the development of cartilage (endochrondral bones). A thorough review and study of the functional morphology of the head of perch has been given by Osse (1966). The following brief description is based on this work and that of Chiasson (1966) for yellow perch. A summary of the bones of the skull (neurocranium) is given in Table 2.2. The elongated nasal bones are located anteriorly in the olfactory region (Figure 2.3b). The paired frontal bones form most of the anterior roof of the skull and also the dorsal border of the orbits. The lateral ethmoids are attached to the sides of the frontals and form the anterior edge of the orbits. The lacrimal bones also border the orbit anteriorly and the suborbital bones (four on each side of the head) extend from them around the orbit to the frontal and dermosphenotic bones. In the dorsal median, the large supraoccipital crest lies posteriorly and the mesethmoid lies anteriorly. The parietal bones are small and lie posteriorly to the frontals. They are separated in the midline by the dorsal spine of the supraoccipital. In the palate of the mouth, the narrow median parasphenoid extends from the vomer to the basioccipital (Figure 2.4d). The narrow palatines also articulate with the vomer posteriorly and laterally and extend back to meet the ectopterygoids. Most of the roof of the mouth is formed by the pterygoid bones. The premaxillae and maxillae are both paired bones of the upper jaw. The premaxillae are curved bones which are connected posteriorly and ventrally to the maxillae and the mesethmoid. The maxillae also articulate with the vomer and lacrimal bones. Each side of the lower jaw consists of three bones, the dentary, the articular and the angular which are connected together by cartilage and connective tissue. The articular forms the caudal portion of the lower jaw and at its thickened posterior end it articulates with the quadrate. The articular bone is developed from part of Meckel's cartilage (the primary lower jaw). The angular bone is situated in the posterior-ventral angle of the lower jaw and forms the

retro-articular process. The jaw is suspended from
the neurocranium by means of the suspensorium. The
suspensorium consists of a number of bones forming
a V-shaped complex. The bones comprise the palatine, ectopterygoid, metapterygoid, symplectic,
preopercular, hyomandibular, quadrate and
pterygoid. The hyomandibular is located between
the quadrate and cranium. It is connected to the
cranium by means of the anterior-dorsal ball and
socket joint (formed with the splenotic and
prootic) and a dorsal ridge-like articulating surface formed partly with the pterotic. The epiotic,
opisthotic, prootic and sphenotic contain semicircular canals (Figure 2.10). The hyomandibular
is also jointed with the opercular posteriorly and
the interhyal bone at its most ventro-posterior
tip. Teeth, villiform and in bands, are located on
the premaxilla, palatine, ectopterygoid, dentary
and vomer bones (Table 2.2). *Perca* have no
canines. In *Stizostedion* teeth are located on the
same bones and some canines are present (except in
adult Volga pikeperch).

The opercular series consists of the preopercular, the opercular, the subopercular and the
interopercular. The vertical limb of the L-shaped
preopercular is firmly connected to the hyomandibular along most of its length and forms part of
the suspensorium already described. The horizontal
limb of the bone bears seven spines and the
posterior vertical part is serrated. The opercular
is a large flat triangular bone which has been used
as an ageing structure (Chapter 3). Anteriorly it
is connected by skin to the preopercular and in the
ventral posterior region the opercular is joined to
the subopercular by connective tissue. Dorsally it
lies close to the pectoral girdle. The subopercular is a flat elongated bone which forms the
border of the gill flap. It is connected to the
interopercular by connective tissue.

The hyoid arch is located behind the lower jaw
in the floor of the buccal cavity. It bears the
six branchiostegal rays. The ceratohyals form the
main part of the apparatus and are separated in the
anterior midline by the hypohyal. The interhyal
suspends the apparatus from the hyomandibular and
symplectic.

The five branchial arches form the gill apparatus which is dorsally attached to the ventral
side of the skull and ventrally to the copulae.
Except for the fifth, each branchial arch bears two
gills. The bones are covered on the medial sides

Table 2.2. Bones of the head region of *Perca fluviatilis*. Dermal bones are in italics and endochondral bones are in normal print. (* = bears teeth).

SYNCRANIUM
NEUROCRANIUM

Olfactory region	Orbital region	Otic region	Basicranial region
Nasal	*Frontal*	*Parietal*	Parasphenoid
Lateral ethmoid	*Lacrimal*	Epiotic	Basioccipital
Mesethmoid	*Suborbital*	*Scale bone*	
*Vomer**	*Dermosphenotic*	*Post temporal*	
		Pterotic	
		Exocipital	
		Supraoccipital	
		Epiotic	
		Opisthotic	
		Sphenotic	
		Prootic	

BRANCHIOCRANIUM

Oromandibular region	Hyoid region	Branchial region
Quadrate	Hyomandibular	Epibranchial
Articular	Symplectic	Hypobranchial*
*Premaxilla**	*Preopercular*	Ceratobranchial
Maxilla	*Opercular*	Pharyngobranchial
Angular	*Interopercular*	complex*
*Dentary**	*Subopercular*	
Articular	Ceratohyal	
*Palatine**	Epihyal	
*Ectopterygoid**	Interhyal	
Metapterygoid	*Branchiostegal ray* (6)	
Pterygoid	*Urohyal*	

with two rows of bony plates each plate bearing numerous recurved teeth. The second and third branchial arches are complete (hypobranchial, ceratobranchial, epibranchial and pharyngobranchial) but the first lacks a pharyngobranchial, the fourth a hypobranchial and the fifth consists only of a ceratobranchial which forms the dentigerous plate (Figure 2.3c). The pharyngobranchials lie close together in the posterior region of the buccal cavity forming a complex. They are also covered with recurved teeth.

The pectoral girdle forms the posterior section of the opercular chamber. It consists of

five pairs of bones: the post temporal, the supra-
cleithrum, the cleithrum, the scapula and the coracoid which join in the ventral midline. The cleithrum is the largest bone of the girdle and of the
head region. Anteriorly it is attached to the sup-
racleithrum which in turn articulates with the
skull at the post temporal. The pelvic girdle is
simple in structure made up of paired pelvic plates
or basipterygia which are fused in the midline.
The bones are connected to the cleithra by ligaments. The median fins are dermal in origin and
are made up of fin rays each of which is supported
by a pterygiophore (except the caudal fin) (Figure
2.3a). There are some variations in the number of
spines and rays found in the fins of different
species of *Perca* and *Stizostedion* and these are
given in Table 2.3. The anterior pterygiophores
are fused together in the anal fin to form a base
for the first two fin rays. The internal spine of
this fused structure is connected to the ribs of
the vertebral column and the first true haemal arch
is just behind this spine.

The vertebral column of *Perca* is made up of
from 36 to 40 vertebrae. The notochord passes

(a)

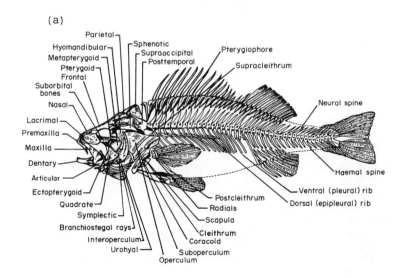

(b)

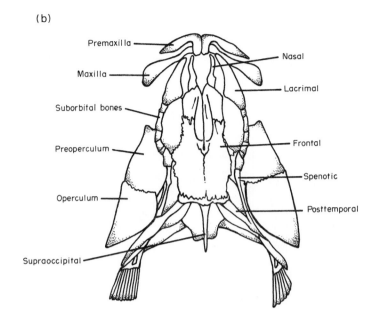

(c)

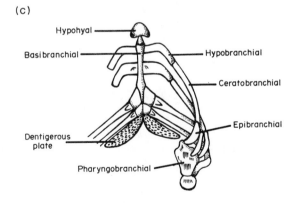

Figure 2.3: Sketches of the skeleton of *Perca* to show (a) the whole skeleton (after Young 1962), (b) dorsal view of skull and (c) the branchial system.

Table 2.3. Numbers of spines and rays found in the dorsal and anal fins of *Perca* and *Stizostedion* species (after Scott & Crossman 1973 and Berg 1965).

	P. schrenki	P. fluviatilis	P. flavescens	S. marina	S. volgensis	S. lucioperca	S. vitreum	S. canadense
1st dorsal spines	12-13	12-13	13-15	13-14	12-16	13-17	12-16	13-15
2nd dorsal spines	2-3	1-3	1-2	2-4	1-2	1-3	1-2	1-2
2nd dorsal rays	12-13	13-15	12-15	15-18	20-22	19-27	17-22	16-21
anal spines	2	2	2	2-3	2	2-3	2	2
anal rays	7-9	7-10	6-8	10-22	9-10	11-13	11-14	11-14

through the notochordal canal in the middle of the
centrum and the spinal cord passes through the neural arch. The ribs are of two types, ventral
(pleural) and dorsal (epipleural) (Figure 2.3a).
The dorsal ribs are attached to the posterior surfaces of the ventral ribs by ligaments but the last
seven ventral ribs do not have dorsal ribs attached
to them. In the tail region the vertebrae contain
haemal arches through which blood vessels pass.
The base of the caudal fin consists of compressed
neural spines called epurals. The last vertebrae
forms a plate called the urostyle below which lies
a modified haemal arch called the hypural.

Musculature

The head and body muscles of perch contain
four main fibre types, two red and two white
(Akster & Osse 1978). These muscle types can be
distinguished by ATPase activity, pH stability of
ATPase and reactions with specific antisera. White
and red muscles are associated with anaerobic and
aerobic metabolism respectively. White muscles in
the head are only active during rigorous and rapid
movements such as eating and coughing. Each type
of red muscle can be divided further into two sub-
types. In the head, red muscles with a comparatively high ATPase (energy requiring enzymes)
activity are functional during rapid respiratory
movements. Red muscles with low ATPase are
associated with little movement and quiet respiration. The myotomes consist mainly of white
muscle (an adaptation to sudden movement such as
darting at prey) and there is no extensive development of red muscle. Red muscle in the body of
teleosts is usually associated with sustained swimmers and in percids may function in the less stren-
uous aspects of normal activity such as maintaining
position or searching behaviour. Akster (1981) has
determined that there is a decrease in contraction
velocity of muscle fibres from white through to
deep red which is in agreement with the activities
already described.
Cranial muscles can be divided into jaw
muscles, suspensorum muscles, opercular muscles,
ventral head muscles and muscles of the branchial
arches (Figure 2.4a-d). The muscles of the
branchial arches are part of the pharyngeal jaw
apparatus (Lauder 1983). The adductor mandibulae
is the most complicated muscle in *Perca*. It is a

27

(a)

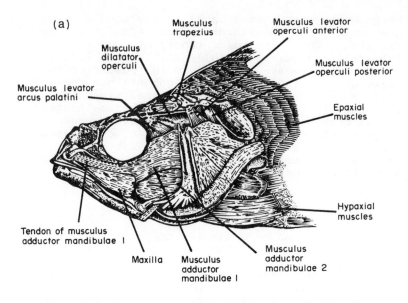

Musculus trapezius

Musculus levator operculi anterior

Musculus dilatator operculi

Musculus levator operculi posterior

Musculus levator arcus palatini

Epaxial muscles

Hypaxial muscles

Tendon of musculus adductor mandibulae I

Maxilla

Musculus adductor mandibulae I

Musculus adductor mandibulae 2

(b)

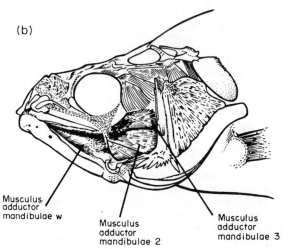

Musculus adductor mandibulae w

Musculus adductor mandibulae 2

Musculus adductor mandibulae 3

(C)

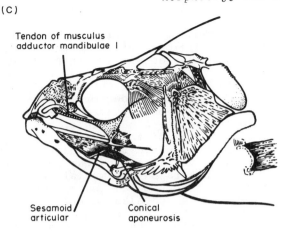

Tendon of musculus
adductor mandibulae I

Sesamoid
articular

Conical
aponeurosis

(d)

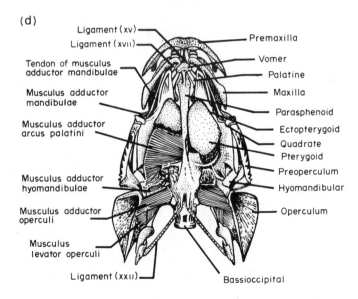

Ligament (xv)
Ligament (xvii)

Tendon of musculus
adductor mandibulae

Musculus adductor
mandibulae

Musculus adductor
arcus palatini

Musculus adductor
hyomandibulae

Musculus adductor
operculi

Musculus
levator operculi

Ligament (xxii)

Premaxilla

Vomer

Palatine

Maxilla

Parasphenoid

Ectopterygoid

Quadrate

Pterygoid

Preoperculum

Hyomandibular

Operculum

Bassioccipital

Figure 2.4: The head musculature of *Perca fluviatilis*. (a) Side view of the
left superficial head muscles, (b) side view of the head muscles with the musculus adductor mandibulae 1 removed, (c) side view of the aponeurotic system
of the left musculus adductor mandibulae and (d) ventral view of the skull
showing the adductor muscles (lower jaw, hyoid and branchial arches have been
removed). (After Osse 1969).

29

large triangular muscle covering most of the suspensorium and is divided into four parts (Figure
2.4a). The head muscles are important in changing
the shape of the head when *Perca* is capturing prey
(see Chapter 5). Muscles of the paired fins comprise both adductors and abductors. The pectoral
fin muscles originate on the scapula and coracoid
bones and insert on the fin radials, the adductors
on the anterior faces of the bones and the abductors medially. The pelvic fin muscles originate on
the pelvic plates and insert on the pelvic fin
radials, the adductors on the medial region of the
bones and the abductors on the outer surfaces. The
median fin movements are also controlled by two
sets of muscles. The first set are superficial and
are found in the skin. They originate in the connective tissue and insert on the base of the fin
spines. The second group of muscles run between
the pterygiophores. The most anterior of these
muscles is attached to the posterior edge of the
supraoccipital bones. The caudal fin is controlled
by the trunk myomeres. The body musculature is
made up of W-shaped myotomes with the two bottom
points of the W facing to the posterior (Chiasson
1966).

Gills

The pharynx wall is pierced by five pairs of
gill slits (Figure 2.7a), the first between the
last branchiostegal rays and the first branchial
arches, the last between the last branchial arches
and the dentigerous plate and the rest between the
branchial arches. The gills are attached to the
four branchial arches and are covered laterally by
the opercular shield. Each gill is composed of two
hemibranchs, one anterior and one posterior making
up a holobranch (Hughes 1984). Each hemibranch is
made up of gill filaments (supported by gill rays)
which in turn support lamellae which increase the
surface area of the gill (Chapter 6). Niimi and
Morgan (1980) found that the first two gill arches
in walleye contained both the highest number of
filaments and lamellae and the largest gill and
lamellae surface areas. The gill surface area increased significantly with body weight (Figure
2.5). The epithelum of the filaments contain
mucous, chloride and rodlet cells (Leino 1982;
Matei 1984). The distribution and quantity of

these cells may vary depending on the environment in which the fish lives (Matei 1984). The branchial arches bear gill rakers on their inner anterior surfaces. The numbers of these gill rakers varies according to species and there is considerable variation in the number within species. These comb-like rakers prevent material passing from the mouth to the delicate lamellae of the filaments and thereby aid in feeding on small particles.

Gut

The cavities of the percids include the peritoneal cavity containing the gut, glands, kidneys, gonads and swim bladder and the pericardial cavity containing the heart. The gut of yellow perch is illustrated in Figure 2.6. The oesophagus is short and connects the pharynx with the stomach. The stomach ends posteriorly as a blind sac and the intestine joins the pyloric region of the stomach in a dorsal position. The first section of the intestine is S-shaped, the bottom of the S running to the straight intestine which ends at the anus. At the anterior end of the intestine are blind sacs called intestinal (pyloric) caecae. There are 3 of these caecae in *Perca* species (there are also 3 in walleye and Volga pikeperch but zander has 4 to 9 and sea pikeperch has 5 to 7). The anterior dorsal region of the intestine receives 4 to 6 bile ducts from the gall bladder which in turn is fed by a system of tubules from the liver. The spleen is positioned posteriorly on the dorsal surface of the stomach and the pancreas is located on the ventral side of the anterior part of the intestine. The swim bladder is found dorsally in the peritoneal cavity below the kidneys. It is connected to the oesphagus by the pneumatic duct which is closed in adult percids. The swim bladder acts as a hydrostatic organ.

The gut wall is made up of an inner mucosa layer and an outer submucosa layer. The mucosa layer contains various secretory and absorptive cells and submucosa is made up of blood vessels, nerves, muscle fibres and connective tissue (Kapoor, Smit & Verighina 1975). The mucosa of the oesphagus contains basal epithelial, surface epithelial and mucous cells. The muscle of the submucosa is composed of an inner layer of longitudinal striated muscle fibres surrounded by an outer layer of circular muscle containing both

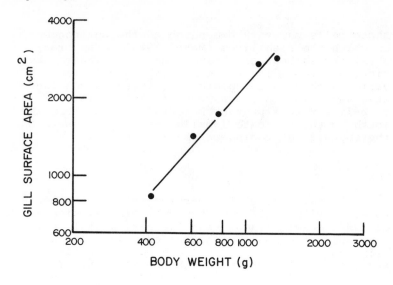

Figure 2.5: The relationship between gill surface area and body weight of-
Stizostedion vitreum. (After Niimi & Morgan 1980).

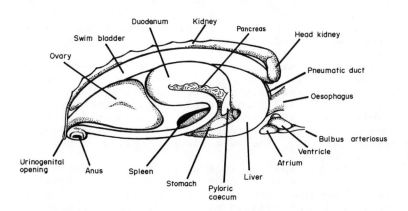

Figure 2.6: Lateral view of the body cavity of *Perca flavescens* to show the
viscera.

striated and smooth fibres (Hirji 1983). Towards
the stomach the longitudinal muscles cease and the
muscle layer is represented solely by circular
muscle. The stomach is lined by circular muscle
with an outer narrow layer of longitudinal muscle.
The intestine is surrounded by an inner circular
and an outer longitudinal muscle layer. The cytology of the gastric mucosa, occurring in the
stomach, has been described by Noaillac-Depeyre
and Gas (1978). Cell types include mucous, mucous
neck, oxytic and endocrine. The endocrine cells
found between the mucoid cells are of three types
distinguished by the type of secretory granules
they produce (Noaillac-Depeyre & Gas 1982). The
intestine can be divided up into three segments
based on the nature of the absorptive epithelium
(Noaillac-Depeyre & Gas 1979). Enterocytes concerned with lipid absorption occur in the proximal
section while those in the middle section undertake
pinocytosis of exogenous proteins. The distal
segment contains absorptive cells with short micro-
villi (see Chapter 5).

Rodlet cells are pear-shaped secretory cells
found in the epithelium of various organs in
teleosts. They are of interest to histologists because no one is quite sure of their function (Leino
1982). In the gut of perch rodlet cells are found
in the mucosa of the stomach, intestinal caecae and
anterior region of the intestine (Hirji & Courtney
1979).

Circulatory system

The circulatory system of teleosts is described in many standard texts (Randall 1970). This description as for the musculature will therefore be
brief. A full description for yellow perch is
given by Chiasson (1966).

The heart is located in the pericardial cavity
and consists of four chambers: the sinus venosus,
atrium, ventricle and bulbus arteriosus (Figures
2.6 and 2.7c). Blood passes from the bulbus arteriosus to the ventral aorta and is distributed to
the gills via the afferent branchial arteries
(Figure 2.7a). These arteries divide up to form
capillaries within the gill filaments. Oxygenated
blood is then passed to the dorsal aorta from the
efferent branchial arteries. The internal carotoid
arteries, serving the brain, extend from the first
efferent branchial arches. The dorsal aorta passes

along the trunk of the fish and through the haemal
arches into the tail where it becomes the caudal
artery. The dorsal aorta and caudal artery serve
the viscera (Figure 2.7b) and body muscles with
oxygenated blood. The anterior, cranial cardinal
veins drain blood from the head and the two posterior, caudal cardinal veins from the muscle,
backbone and kidneys. These veins empty into the
two common cardinal veins (duct of Cuvier) which
with the hepatic veins (two pairs) drain into the
sinus venosus (Figure 2.7c). The liver receives
blood from the gut via the hepatic portal vein.

Excretory and Reproductive Systems

The kidneys of percids are paired and elongated and lie pressed against the dorsal body wall in
the peritoneal cavity (Figure 2.6). The kidneys
are separated anteriorly by the dorsal aorta but
posteriorly they are fused in the midline. Each
kidney is in two parts, the head kidney at the
anterior end and the trunk kidney posterior to it.
The head kidney is not directly concerned with ion
or water regulation. It contains lymphoid,
hematopoietic, interrenal and suprarenal tissue
(see under endocrine system). The trunk region of
the kidney is directly involved with excretion and
osmotic regulation (Chapter 6). Distributed
throughout the trunk region are clusters of
nephrons each cluster fed by an artery and drained
by a vein. The nephron consists of (a) a renal
corpuscle containing a well-vascularised glo-
merulus, (b) a ciliated neck region, (c) an
initial proximal segment with prominent brush
border and numerous prominent lysosomes, (d) a
second proximal segment with numerous mitochrondria
but less well developed brush border, (e) a narrow
ciliated intermediate segment, (f) a distal segment
with elongate mitochondria and (g) a collecting
duct (Figure 6.3) (Hickman & Trump 1969). The collecting ducts (nephronic ducts) empty into branches
of the ureter. Each ureter (Wolffian duct) runs
ventrally in the trunk kidney and opens into the
urinary bladder. In the female perch the urinary
bladder is fused with the oviduct to form a urogenital sinus. There is no cloaca in adult perch.
Externally there is a urogenital papilla which in
the male is an obvious extension of the urinary
bladder. Excretions are passed through a urinary
pore in the papilla. The testes of the male are

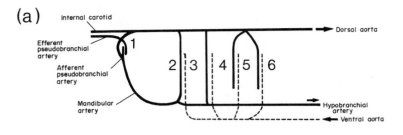

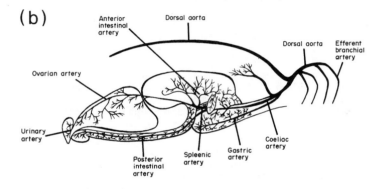

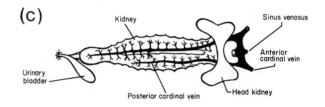

Figure 2.7: The circulatory system (a) through the gills of *Perca fluviatilis* (after Laurent 1984), (b) through the viscera of *P. flavescens* and (c) the veins of the kidney region of *P. flavescens*. The branchial slits (2.7a) are 1, spiracle, 2, hyoidean and 3-6 aortic.

paired and are located in the midline of the peritoneal cavity between the gut and swim bladder. For about one third of their length at the posterior end, the testes are united by a septum. The testes have a number of longitudinal folds and the vasa deferentia run from these folds and eventually join at the posterior midline. The single duct from the two testes empties at the base of the urinary bladder. The sperm is produced in a zone of the testes composed of numerous tubules. The tubules consist of a layer of germinal epithelial cells and an outer layer of connective tissue. The spermatic artery lies in a dorsal groove of the testes. The ovaries of *Perca* and *Stizostedion* species are also paired but during development in *Perca* these ovaries fuse together leaving a single ovary (Figure 2.6). This ovary is located in a similar position to the testes. At the anterior end the ovary is blunt and rounded and posteriorly it is tapered. In *Stizostedion* species the paired ovaries unite posteriorly. Often one ovary is larger than the other (usually the right) (Eschmeyer 1950). The ovary and oviduct are enveloped in a fold from the peritoneum. The ovary wall consists of three parts: an outer epithelial layer (peritoneum), a layer of connective tissue and an inner germinal epithelium which give rise to the ova (Chapter 4). There are transverse blood vessels throughout the length of the ovaries of *Perca* and *Stizostedion* species which becomes more conspicuous with maturity. Hermaphrodites have been reported for species of both *Perca* (Chevey 1922; Turner 1927; Brunelli & Rizzo 1928; Jellyman 1976) and *Stizostedion* (Dence 1938).

The Nervous System

The nervous system of teleosts consists of the central (brain and spinal cord), the peripheral (cranial and spinal nerves) and the autonomic (parasympathetic and sympathetic) nervous systems and sensory organs (nose, ear, eye and lateral line). The brain is divided up into the fore-brain (prosencephalon), the mid-brain (mesencephalon) and the hind-brain (rhombencephalon). The fore-brain consists of the telencephalon and diencephalon. The paired olfactory bulbs are distinct posteriorly from the telencephalon but anteriorly they blend with the telencephalon to form the olfactory nerves (Figure 2.8a). The telencephalon contains the two

most anterior ventricles. The diencephalon consists of the epithalmus, thalmus (divided into dorsal thalmus and ventral thalmus) and the hypothalmus. The floor of the diencephalon is formed by
the hypothalmus which is connected to the well developed pituitary (Figure 2.8b). The thalmus of
the diencephalon is joined to the telencephalon,
hypothalmus and mid- and hind-brains (Dodd & Kerr
1963). The epithalmus is made up of the pineal
organ and the habenular nuclei. The mid-brain is
composed of the optic lobes and is divided into the
optic tectum and tegmentum. The optic tectum forms
the roof of the third ventricle and the tegmentum
the base of the ventricle. A channel runs forward
in the midline to connect with the telencephalon
ventricles and posteriorly through the aqueduct of
Sylvias to the fourth ventricle. The hind-brain
consists of the cerebellum and medullar oblongata.
The latter merges into the spinal cord. The fourth
ventricle is located dorsally in the rhombencephalon. The cranial nerves and their functions are
listed in Table 2.4. The spinal cord runs the
length of the body of the fish through the neural
arches of the vertebrae and ends in the urophysis,
a neuroendocrine organ which has an osmoregulatory
function. The spinal nerves are paired and pass
from the spinal cord through foraminae in the vertebrae. The first three spinal nerves run to the
muscles of the pectoral and pelvic girdles. The
first spinal nerve also has a dorsal branch which
serves the back of the cranium and a ventro-
anterior branch which innervates the hyoid muscles
(Chiasson 1966).

Percids like other teleosts have a ganglionat-
ed sympathetic nerve chain. This is found medial
to the ribs within the body cavity extending cau-
dally to the tail. The ganglia, two per spinal
segment, are connected with the spinal nerves by
both grey and white rami communicantes after the
dorsal and ventral roots of the nerve have joined.
Both afferent and efferent sympathetic fibres pass
through the ventral root. The major part of the
parasympathetic system is represented by the vagus
nerve and to a lesser extent by the oculomotor. A
diagram to summarise the function of the autonomic
nervous system is given in Figure 2.9.

Chemoreception is achieved by taste, olfaction
and an overall 'body sense' (Hara 1971). Taste is
carried out through receptors in the mouth,
pharynx, gill cavity and gill arches. The olfactory organs of yellow perch innervated by the first

37

Table 2.4. Cranial nerves of *Perca flavescens*. (From Chiasson, Robert, Laboratory Anatomy of the Perch, 3rd ed. (c) 1966, 1974, 1980. Wm. C. Brown Publishers, Dubuque, Iowa. All rights reserved. Reprinted by permission).

Name	Origin	Function	Serving
0. Nervus terminalis	Ventral border of olfactory bulb	Sensory	Sense endings of snout and olfactory epithelium.
I. Olfactory	Anterior end of olfactory bulb	Sensory	Nasal epithelium.
II. Optic	Optic lobes, ventral to telencephalon	Sensory	Retina of eye.
III. Oculomotor	Posterior ventral end of medulla, between optic lobes and cerebellum.	Motor	Superior and inferior rectus and inferior oblique muscles.
IV. Trochlear	Dorso-lateral anterior surface of medulla.	Motor	Superior oblique muscle.
V. Trigeminal	Anterior lateral border of medulla oblongata.	Motor and Sensory	Jaw muscles, tactile endings in skin of the head.
VI. Abducens	Anterior ventral end of medulla oblongata.	Motor	Lateral rectus muscle and retractor bulbi muscles in part.
VII. Facial portion of Acoustico-facialis	Lateral border of medulla oblongata just posterior to Trigeminal and with Acoustic.	Motor and Sensory	Skin of the head, taste endings and lateral line organs.
VIII. Acoustic portion of Acoustico-facialis	With Facial from lateral border of medulla oblongata.	Sensory	Inner ear and lateral line organ.
IX. Glossopharyngeal	Posterior lateral border of medulla with Vagus.	Motor and Sensory	Gill muscles and lateral line organ.
X. Vagus	Posterior lateral border of medulla with Glossopharyngeal.	Motor and Sensory	Gills, heart, lateral line organ and anterior alimentary tract.

(a)   (b)

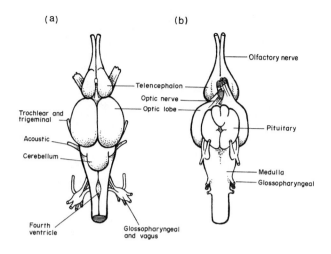

Figure 2.8: Drawings of *Perca flavescens* brain (a) dorsal and (b) ventral views.

cranial nerve are oval and rosette shaped and nearly fill two cartilaginous chambers just under the rostrodorsal surface of the head (Lyons 1983). The rosette consists of a number of neuroepithelial lamellae radiating from a midline raphe. There are 14 to 16 of these primary lamellae. The olfactory epithelium is developed best in the proximal portions of the lamellae and consist of basal, sensory and ciliated sustentacular cells. The distal section of the lamellae are made up of mucous cells and undifferentiated epithelium. This structure is similar to that of perch (Teichmann 1954). Water is drawn in and out of the nasal cavities by normal respiratory movements (Bannister 1965).

The ear of percids as in all fish consists of the labyrinth or inner ear only (Figure 2.10) (Lowenstein 1971). The anterior vertical semicircular canal, utriculus and sacculus are located inside the cranial cavity and the horizontal and posterior vertical semicircular canals are embedded in the skeleton (prootic, opisthotic and epiotic). The laybrinth is served by branches of the VIIIth nerve (Table 2.4). The semicircular canals are tubes filled with labyrinthine fluid. At one end the canals enlarge to form the spherical ampulla

39

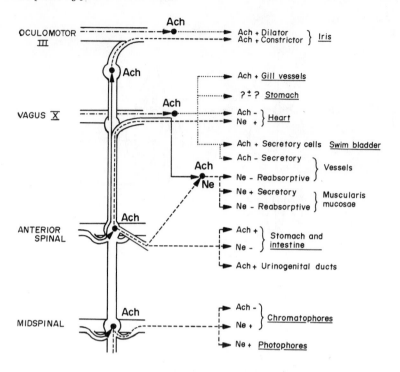

Figure 2.9: Diagram to illustrate the principles of the autonomic nervous system of a teleost. Nerve types shown are —— = preganglionic sympathetic, ---- = postganglionic sympathetic, -··- = preganglionic parasympathetic and ····· = postganglionic parasympathetic. ● = ganglionic synapses and transmitter substances are acetlycholine (Ach) and norepinephrine (NE). Nerve action causing excitation of muscle and gland and concentration of chromatophores is represented by + or relaxation of the same by -. (After Campbell 1970).

which contain a sensory apparatus. This apparatus consists of the crista ampullaris which is covered by an epithelium containing sensory cells. Otoliths are found in the utriculus, sacculus and lagena. The otoliths, composed of calcium salts, are heavier than the surrounding endolymph and lie above a sensory epithelium. When the epithelium deviates from the horizontal plane the otolith will slide along it and activate the sensory cells. The otolith from the sacculus is used to determine the age of many species of fish but has not been used extensively for percids. The labyrinth functions as a sound receptor (in conjunction with the swim bladder), as a gravity receptor, as a receptor for angular accelerations and in the maintenance and regulation of muscle tone.

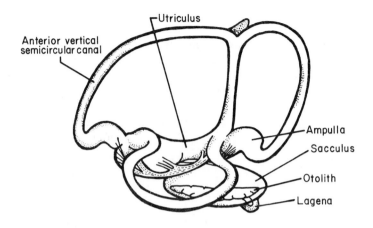

Figure 2.10: Lateral view of the *Perca* ear.

The eye of species of *Perca* and *Stizostedion* have received considerable attention. The eye is located within the orbit and moved by the inferior, superior, lateral and medial recti muscles and the superior and inferior oblique muscles. The eyeball is covered by the sclera which is thin and transparent in the anterior region to form the cornea. The choroid layer which forms the heavily pigmented iris proximal to the cornea is inside the sclera coat. The lens is spherical and suspended from the anterior edge of the retina by a suspensory ligament. The visual acuity of perch increases exponentially with age mainly as a result of lens development and increase in focal length (Guma'a 1982). The pupil of the perch is egg-shaped (the point directed forward). The eyeball is filled with vitreous humor. The retina lines the inside of the eyeball in the posterior region. The organisational structure of the retina varies between *Perca* and *Stizostedion* species. The former are active during the day while the latter are mainly nocturnal. Before metamorphosis the retina of perch contains only cones, rods appear at or after this stage (Guma'a 1982). The adult fish has a retina of the duplex type made up of eight

41

layers of cells and membranes (Blaxter 1968). The distribution of cones in the retina indicates the importance of acute vision in perch (Ahlbert 1969). The cones are arranged in a regular square pattern. This pattern is made up of single, double and triple cones. The highest density of cones are to be found in a region temporal to the optic nerve. The cones of zander are arranged for increased sensitivity rather than visual acuity and are organized in a predominantly row-like pattern with single, double and triple cone types. Only single cones are present in zander smaller than 8 mm (Ahlbert 1969). There are two types of cones in the retina of adult walleye, midwave and longwave with maximum sensitivity at 533 and 605 nm respectively (Burkhardt & Hassin 1983). The rods of *Perca* species are relatively large and evenly spaced while those of *Stizostedion* species are relatively small and grouped (Ali, Ryder & Anctil 1977). The tapetum lucidum is a distinctive feature of the eye of *Stizostedion*. It was first described in detail for North American species by Moore (1944) and further investigations have been carried out by Ali and Anctil (1968; 1977) and Zyznar and Ali (1975). The tapetum lucidum is a reflective layer found in the pigmented epithelium layer of the retina. The reflecting material in the cells is a reduced pteridine, 7, 8-dihydroxan-thopterin. In dark-adapted eyes the rods are in groups optically isolated from each other by the tapetal processes. Light can be reflected back and forth between the tapetal processes with additional absorption by the rods after each reflection (Zyznar & Ali 1975). European species of *Stizostedion* have a relatively smaller effective area for reflection by the tapetum lucidum than North American species.

The lateral line system is of considerable importance as a sensory organ to teleosts in general (Disler 1950; Flock 1971; Disler & Smirnov 1977). Its main function is that of a tactile receptor for the detection of water displacements. It acts as a near field receptor operating at low frequencies and can be considered as an acoustic sense organ. Sensory hairs from a receptor cell are attached to a cupular which rests upon a sensory epithelium. The sensory cells or neuromasts may either be at the bottom of the canal sunk below the skin (these are particularly concentrated in the head region) or as epidermal organs situated at the skin surface with the cupula extending into the water. The

lateral line runs from behind the head to the base
of the caudal fin and extends over the scale portion of the fin in *Stizostedion* species. In members of both *Perca* and *Stizostedion* it is curved
upwards following the line of the back. The acoustic nerve VIII acts as the peripheral sensory
supply to the lateral line (Pearson 1936). It is
also served by nerves VII, IX and X (Table 2.4).

The Endocrine System

The endocrine system of teleosts is discussed
by Hoar and Randall (1969) and an enlightening
account of endocrine control of metabolic processes
is given by Baker and Wigham (1979). Endocrine
glands of teleosts include the pituitary, pancreas,
thyroid, adrenal, ultimobranchial, pineal body,
urophysis, ovary and testes. Through a feedback
system the large pituitary gland, found attached to
the hypothalmus below the brain, controls other endocrine glands and with its close contact with the
nervous system is probably the most important
gland. The pituitary consists of two parts, the
neurohypothesis, formed from a down growth of the
floor of the diencephalon and the adenohypophysis
originating embryonically from epidermal tissue in
the buccal cavity. The pancreas is concentrated
into islets bearing three types of endocrine
cells. Type A produce glucagan, type B insulin and
type C a third as yet unidentified substance (Epple
1969). The thyroid gland reacts to levels of
pituitary thyrotrophic hormone (TSH). It
accumulates iodine and produces the tyrosine-
derived hormone, thyroxine. Thyroxine is manu-
factured by secretory follicles which are scattered
in connective tissue throughout the pharyngeal
region. The adrenal gland is closely associated
with the kidney and is made up of interenal, suprarenal (chromaffin tissue) and stannius corpuscle
components. The interrenal organ produces
steroids. The interrenal and suprarenal glands are
found in the head kidney and develop from
coelomic epithelum. The interenal tissue of zander
is located as two clusters around each posterior
cardinal vein. Suprarenal tissue is also found
near the posterior cardinal vein and its branches,
usually where there is no interrenal tissue. With
a few minor exceptions the same system is found in
perch and other percids (Mezhnin 1972). Stannius
corpuscles are developed from outgrowths of the

43

walls of Wolffian ducts. Three to five corpuscles
lie in the zander trunk kidney close to its
connection with the head kidney. In the Volga
pikeperch, three corpuscles lie in the caudal
region of the trunk kidney and in perch two corpuscles lie in a similar region (Mezhnin 1979).
The adrenal tissue undergoes changes with the reproductive cycle in perch (Mezhnin 1977) although
its main function is water and ion balance. The
ultimobranchial gland found in the last gill arch
is responsible for calcium regulation.

Cytology

There has been some dispute over the number of
chromosomes in the cells of *Perca* and *Stizostedion* species. Nygren, Edlund, Hirsch and Åhsgren
(1968) found a variable diploid number (2n) of
chromosomes. The majority of cells from the testes
of perch and zander had 2n = 48 and this diploid
number has been confirmed for several other percids
including yellow perch and walleye (Danzmann
1979). Although zander kidneys were not examined,
polyploid mitotic cells occurred in testes tissue
of both species and also in the kidney cells of
perch (Nygren *et al.* 1968).

Chapter 3

GROWTH, MORTALITY AND LONGEVITY

Introduction

The fundamentals of growth and mortality will be
examined in this chapter. In the introduction the
hormonal control of growth and the external factors
which influence hormonal production will be discussed. Secondly, the techniques for measuring
growth and condition will be described. Thirdly,
the scope for growth in percids within their range
is given. This growth will be related to mortality
and longevity in the fourth and fifth sections.
Since feeding has a major influence on growth, this
chapter should be read in conjunction with Chapter
5.
    Growth studies of fish populations, in the
form of measuring increases in length or weight,
are common in the literature but the underlying
processes of growth are complex. Growth starts
from division of the fertilised oocyte and continues through the absorption of the yolk sac
(Chapter 4), exogenous feeding (Chapter 5) and in
many fish throughout life. Several stages occur
between feeding and eventual tissue deposition and
these stages are under physiological control which
in turn are influenced by internal and external
factors (Figure 3.1). For example in the spring,
rising water temperatures and increasing day
lengths may stimulate increased activity of the
pituitary gland which produces both thyrotropic
(promotes thyroxine) and gonadotropic hormones.
Pituitary growth, anabolic steroid and thyroid
hormones and possibly insulins stimulate growth
(Donaldson, Fagerlund, Higgs & McBride 1979).
Swift and Pickford (1965) studied the seasonal
effects on growth of the hormones secreted by the
perch pituitary gland. An assay technique was used

in which male *Fundulus heteroclitus* (Linnaeus) were injected with a hormone preparation. In the winter months when there was little growth, the level of the hormone was low but with the onset of growth in the spring the amount of hormone increased ten-fold to a peak in June. It then declined to a minimum in August, which was well below the winter minimum value. Unfortunately the interactions of the external environment and the hormone system and their effect on growth processes are not fully understood.

Growth responses to the growth hormone produced by α cells in the pars distalis of the pituitary gland are dependent on temperature. The most important external influence on percids is undoubtedly temperature. Not only does it affect hormone production but it affects all body processes by its direct influence on enzymes. Essentially it controls growth, feeding, reproduction, activity, survival and distribution. An excellent account on the temperature requirements of percids has been given by Hokanson (1977). He classifies this group as temperate (able to withstand near freezing temperatures) mesotherms. Pike, *Esox lucius* Linnaeus, having a physiological optimum temperature of 26°C close to that of percids (Table 3.1) also belong to this group. Other temperate fish are either stenotherms, for example the rainbow trout, *Salmo gairdneri* Richardson, with a physiological optimum temperature of 17°C, or eurytherms, for example the carp, *Cyprinus carpio* Linnaeus, with a physiological optimum temperature of 32°C. The ability of the major *Perca* and *Stizostedion* species to tolerate high temperatures is reduced in the order zander, perch, yellow perch, walleye and sauger (Table 3.1). The upper lethal temperatures derived for percids show some variation in the literature due to the methods and the size of fish used in their derivation. The critical thermal maximum is obtained by gradually increasing the temperature until death and is usually several degrees above the incipient lethal temperature which is determined from sudden exposure of the fish to increased temperature (Fry 1947). Thermal tolerance is minimal at embryogenesis, maximal during fry development and then gradually declines in adults (Lapkin, Svirskij & Golovanov 1981).

There has been recent interest in the effect of power plant heated effluent on fish populations. Depending on the temperature the effluent can be

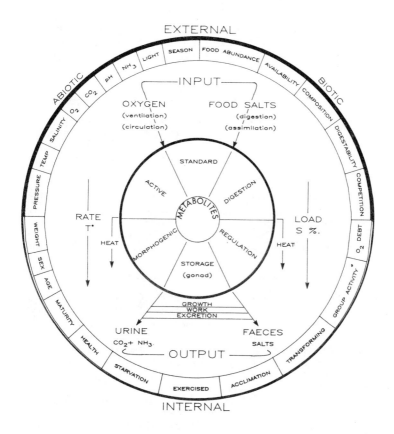

Figure 3.1: Diagram to illustrate the general metabolic system involved in growth of teleosts. External and internal factors affecting the system including both input (food and oxygen) and output products (growth, work and excretion) are shown. Specific dynamic action, SDA (Chapter 5) is part of the heat released. Morphogenic metabolism applies to internal work energy required to produce body substance. Temperature is shown as the major factor controlling metabolic rate and salinity as the main energy-demanding factor in regulation. (After Brett 1979).

lethal, sublethal (harmful over a period of time), or near the physiological optimum. Willemsen (1977a) found that perch and zander congregated

Table 3.1 Physiological optima, incipient lethal and critical thermal maxima (°C) for species of *Perca* and *Stizostedion*. (*not determined). (After Hokanson 1977).

Species	Physiological optimum (°C)	Incipient lethal (°C)	Critical thermal maximum (°C)
S. canadense	22.0	30.4	*
S. vitreum	22.6	31.6	*
P. flavescens	24.7	29.2-34.0	33.4
P. fluviatilis	25.4	31.4-33.5	35.5-35.9
S. lucioperca	27.0	34.3-35.0	37.0

near the cooling water discharge of the Flevo power plant on Lake Ijssel in the Netherlands. Experiments showed that the fish were able to feed at these high temperatures although in the case of perch they were near to the upper lethal limits. Willemsen recorded only a mortality of five percent at 29°C and eight percent at 30.5°C for perch and no mortalities for zander below 32°C. Although these fish were able to feed and survive at such temperatures it is probable that they were in a state of stress and more vulnerable to disease. Weatherley (1963) found that interrenal tissue in perch kidney underwent atrophy when the fish were exposed to temperatures reaching 30-31°C. The interrenal tissue functions in a similar way to the adrenocortical tissue of mammals in opposing stress. Recent studies using telemetry have shown that percids, as a rule, do not make use of these artificial warmed areas in their environment (Ross & Siniff 1980; 1982; Maclean, Teleki & Polak 1982). In Lake Monona, USA, maximum temperatures in the outflow from the power plant reached 35°C in the summer and 14°C in the winter. The unheated parts of the lake rarely exceeded 29°C in the summer (Neill & Magnuson 1974). Yellow perch avoided the

heated effluent and those caught had a body temperature below 29°C. There is evidence that at extremes of temperature the avoidance of the temperature overrides other factors such as food availability or hunger of the fish (Neill & Magnuson 1974).
Percids thus show the ability to select out preferred temperatures for growth and reproduction.
This ability to thermoregulate has been demonstrated experimentally by Reynolds and Casterline
(1979). In their experiment yellow perch exhibited
diel patterns of behaviour selecting a maximum of
16.7°C at predawn and 23.8°C at dusk. The overall
mean for 24 h was 20.2°C. Although these
experiments were held in April under natural
photoperiod and the yellow perch would be unlikely
to encounter such temperatures at this time, the
selected temperature values are close to the
physiological optimum for yellow perch (Table 3.1).

Light has an important influence on the body
mechanisms and organisation in nearly all
organisms. It is probably, apart from temperature,
ration size and size of fish (see Chapter 5) the
most important factor governing metabolic activity,
feeding, growth and reproduction (Ryder 1977). The
effect of light on hormones in teleosts has not
been well studied and there is little information
for percids. Seasonal differences in the mobilisa-
tion or deposition of food stores depends on the
nutritional status of the fish and the action of
individual hormones such as growth hormone, thyroxine and insulin. It is also important to have
synergistic cooperation between hormones which is,
theoretically, brought about as a result of environmental influences (Baker & Wigham 1979). Hormones such as prolactin, cortisol and thyroxine
fluctuate diurnally. Additionally, peaks of activity for these hormones are brought in and out of
phase at different times of the year. Hormone
levels may increase in the blood plasma in response
to photoperiod as well as to temperature.

Certain cells of the body may only become
sensitive to external stimuli during specific
phases in a cycle. Light cannot have a direct
effect on hormone production as does temperature
but must act through a transducing process. In the
hypothalmus-pituitary complex (Chapter 2) gonado-
trophic hormones are secreted in the mesoadeno-
hypophysis and prolactin and adrenocorticotropin in
the proadenohypophysis. Thyrotropin and somato-
tropin secreting cells occur in both. Pituitary
activity is controlled by neurosecretory cells in

the hypothalmus with major concentrations in the
nucleus lateralis tuberis and the nucleus
preopticus (Peter & Nagahama 1974). These cells
are neurally controlled by appropriate receptors
for environmental stimuli (Scott 1979). Part of
this complex is the pineal body or epiphysis which
contains photoreceptive cells. Thus the pineal
body may be affected by light conditions and act as
a neuroendocrine transducer for photoperiod
information. However, little is known for teleosts
in general and work on specific species is required. Hopefully this work can be conducted on
percids since they live under conditions which have
pronounced environmental cycles.

Techniques for Measuring Age and Growth

The usual method of measuring growth in fish
investigations relies on ageing the fish and de-
scribing yearly, sometimes monthly, increments in
length or weight. The ability to determine the age
of fish is undoubtedly one of the most useful
skills of the fish biologist and the ability is
particularly applicable to temperate fish where
well defined seasons result in annual marks or
checks being laid down on various calcified body
structures. By knowing the age of the fish many
different statistics about the individual and the
population as a whole may be determined including
growth rates, age at maturity and longevity.
Perca and *Stizostedion* species have been aged by a
variety of body structures. Before an ageing
method can be adopted it is essential that it is
validated, a factor often omitted. This can be
achieved by a number of methods (Bagenal & Tesch
1978). Craig (1974b) examined monthly samples of
perch opercular bones throughout the year, from
Slapton Ley, England, and counted the number of
bones with checks on the outer edge. As can be
seen in Figure 3.2 the checks on the bone are
annual and the majority are laid down in May when
perch growth in Slapton Ley is resumed. The use of
opercular bones for ageing perch was well established by Le Cren (1947). A broad opaque zone on
the bone represents summer growth (Figure 3.3). As
growth diminishes with the onset of autumn and then
winter, this zone gradually becomes transparent.
The narrow transparent zone abruptly changes to the
opaque zone in late spring. If growth is interrupted in the summer, a false check may be laid

down but this usually starts and ends sharply. The presence of a strong year class or cohort also aids in verifying an ageing technique. For example the number of perch hatched in 1959 in Windermere, England, was particularly large whereas year classes that followed were weak. This 1959 year class could be distinguished in the following years in annual samples. Other methods of age verification include keeping fish in ponds so they are of known age when recaught. Ageing of walleye by use of the opercular bone has been verified by applying tetracycline antibiotic (Babaluk & Campbell, in press). Fish in Wapun Lake, Canada, were injected with tetracycline in the summer and then tagged and released into the lake. Tagged fish were recaught one or two years later with one or two checks respectively outside the tetracycline layer (which fluoresces under ultraviolet light).

Although opercular bones have been found by many biologists to be satisfactory ageing structures for *Perca* and *Stizostedion* species other methods have been used including the examination of cleithra, otoliths and vertebrae (Belanger & Hogler 1982; Campbell & Babaluk 1979; Erickson 1983; Schmitt & Hubert 1982). The use of structures such as scales and fins do not require sacrificing the fish (Abdu-Nabi 1983; Belanger & Hogler 1982; Campbell & Babaluk 1979; Carlander 1961; Sterns 1981). Scales are not usually a satisfactory method of ageing, although they have been used fairly extensively, because checks are often

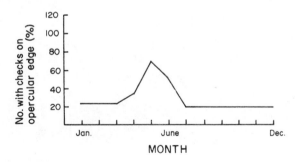

Figure 3.2: Diagram to show the percentage number of *Perca fluviatilis* with checks laid down on the edge of the opercular bones at each month of the year. (After Craig 1974b).

(a)

(b)

1 cm

Figure 3.3: Photographs of *Perca fluviatilis* opercular bones from Windermere, England. (a) Seven year old perch of the 1968 year class and (b) sixteen year old perch of the 1959 year class. (Kindly provided by T. Furnass, Freshwater Biological Association).

indistinct and there is some doubt as to their validity (Chapter 2).

The growth of the opercular bone can be related to the growth of the fish in body length. This relationship can be used to determine the length of the fish at each year of its life (and thus its growth) and is referred to as back calculation (Le Cren 1947; Duncan 1980). As a rule the body length (L) and opercular width (B) relationship is allometric and can be expressed by:

$$L = aB^b$$

where a and b are constants. The value of the exponent b can vary between different groups of fish within the same population. For example Craig (1980a) found that perch from Windermere b = 0.814 for immatures of both sexes and for mature males but b = 0.723 for mature females.

In many populations of fish faster growing individuals die earlier than slow growing ones. Thus a sample of older fish may represent slow growers and back calculations from these fish may underestimate growth of the population. This is referred to as Lee's phenomenon (Bryuzgin 1963).

In a field situation it is often more convenient to measure the length of a fish than its weight. Weights (W) can be determined from these lengths (L) by estimating length-weight relationships from samples of fish. These relationships usually take the form:

$$W = aL^b \hspace{4em} \text{Equation 3.1}$$

where a and b are constants. Neither a or b remain the same between or within populations. Variations can be caused by sex, maturity, season and even time of day. These differences are tested by analysis of covariance before data are pooled (Le Cren 1951). For a given group an average value of b is calculated which remains the same throughout the year. Craig (1974b) calculated the monthly weights of a 134 mm (this was the mean size of the population) perch for each maturity group using a pooled value for b and monthly values of a. These weights were used to compare seasonal changes in condition between the different maturity groups (Figure 3.4). Immature females rapidly increased in weight from April to May but this increase was

53

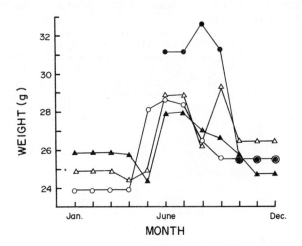

Figure 3.4: Theoretical monthly weights (g) of a 134 mm (total length) *Perca fluviatilis* from Slapton Ley, England. ● = young-of-the-year, o = immature females, ▲ = mature females and △ = mature males. (After Craig 1974b).

delayed in mature fish from May to June due to spawning. After spawning fish quickly put on weight as is also illustrated by Windermere mature male and female perch (Figure 3.5). As b is often close to 3 this value has been applied in many studies. However this can lead to error if b is significantly different from 3 and fish are of different lengths (Bagenal & Tesch 1978). The condition factor (K) is commonly used to determine the "fatness" or the well being of the fish and can be empirically calculated by:

$$K = \frac{W}{aL^b}$$

(values as for Equation 3.1)

Le Cren (1951) carried out an extensive study of the condition factors of Windermere perch using this equation. Condition expressed by these methods of calculation relies on the assumption that an increase in wet weight is an increase in energy content. There may be instances where an increase in weight is caused by an uptake of water and the fish although heavy is not in good condition. This can be determined by measuring water

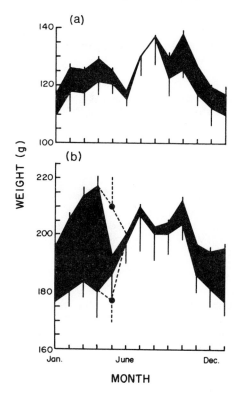

Figure 3.5: Theoretical monthly weights (g) of mature *Perca fluviatilis* from Windermere, England. (a) Male 225 mm and (b) female 260 mm (both total length). The lower line represents somatic weight, the upper line represents total weight and the solid black represents gonad weight. Upper limits of 95% confidence limits are given for gonad weights and lower limits for the somatic weights. The dotted line represents females still ripe in May. (After Craig 1977a).

or fat or energy content of the fish tissue (Craig 1977a).

Growth

Percid fish show extensive plasticity in their growth. Variations in growth are caused by differences in abiotic and biotic factors. These variations can be illustrated from comparisons between mean growth of different populations, between mean growth of year classes within the same population and between individual growth from the same year class.

Perch and yellow perch hatch at a length of about 5 mm (range 4 to 7 mm) (Konstantinov 1957;

Hokanson & Kleiner 1974). Zander hatches at about 4 mm (Woynarovich 1960), sauger at 4 to 6 mm and walleye slightly larger at 7 mm (range 6 to 9 mm) (Scott & Crossman 1973). The growth of both genera can be sigmoidal in the first year of life and a logistic curve can be fitted to growth data (Figure 3.6). The equation for this curve is as follows:

$$L_t = L\infty/(1+e^{(a-bt)})$$ Equation 3.2

where L_t = length at time t, $L\infty$ is the value of L when $\Delta L/\Delta t$ = 0 and a and b are constants. On an annual basis empirical data on yearly growth of adult fish can be described in many cases by the Von Bertalanffy (1938) growth model:

$$L_t = L\infty(1-e^{-K(t-t_o)})$$ Equation 3.3

where K = the rate at which the growth curve approaches the asymptote ($L\infty$), t_o = the theoretical age at which L = 0 and other symbols are as for Equation 3.2.

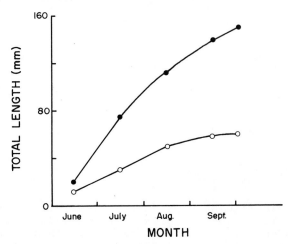

Figure 3.6: Monthly lengths (mm) of young-of-the-year *Perca fluviatilis* from Windermere, England (o) (after Guma'a 1978a) and *Stizostedion vitreum* from Oneida Lake, USA (●). (After Colby, McNicol & Ryder 1979).

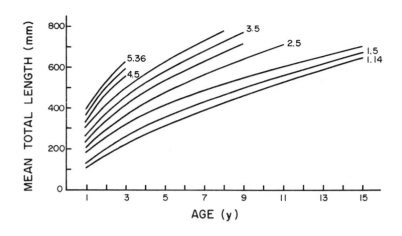

Figure 3.7: The relationship between length (mm) and age (years) of female *Stizostedion vitreum* over a major part of their distributional range. Numbers adjacent to growth curves represent 'growing degree days' >5°C x 10^{-3}. (After Colby & Nepszy 1981).

Species of *Perca* and *Stizostedion* populations in the northern hemisphere grow more slowly the further north they live. This is a reflection of reduction in mean annual temperatures with latitude (Figure 3.7) (Colby & Nepszy 1981).

Often there are differences in growth rate within a population, between different year classes. Figure 3.8 illustrates the mean population growth of male perch for the 1959 and 1968 year classes in Windermere based on back calculations from opercular bones (Figure 3.3). Equation 3.3 was applied to these data. Between year fluctuations within populations may be partly the result of summer (main feeding period) temperature differences (Figure 3.9). Le Cren (1958) found that two-thirds of the variation in the yearly growth of perch in Windermere could be accounted for by temperature (above 14°C) in the growing period. Other factors which control the growth of Windermere perch include the negative effect of density (Figure 3.9). In this situation the availability of food may become limiting on growth. Craig (1980a) also suggested that the type of food available to the fish was important and perch achieved faster growth from a diet of fish than from inver-

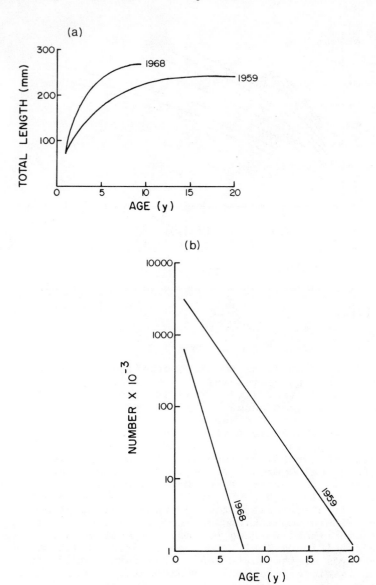

Figure 3.8: Mean length (mm) at age (a) and catch per unit effort (numbers) at age (b) for the 1959 and 1968 year classes of male *Perca fluviatilis* from Windermere, England.

tebrates. Forney (1966) found that the early summer growth of young-of-the-year walleye (range in size from 36 to 64 mm on 1 July from 1958 to 1962) in Oneida Lake, USA, was significantly correlated with water temperature. Serns (1982) also showed that first year growth of walleye in Escanaba Lake, USA, was related to early summer (June) temperatures. Later in the summer in Oneida Lake, variations in growth (range in size from 118 to 163 mm on 11 October from 1956 to 1964) were related to the availability of forage fish. Walleye fingerlings grew faster on a diet of fish than on a diet of invertebrates. In Lake Balaton, Hungary, zander grew at different rates in the three basins (Figure 3.10). The initial growth was higher in the southwest basin but was reduced in older fish which were more abundant in this region. Genetic differences as well as competition within a group (year class or cohort) leads to differences in growth rate between individuals and these factors may be critical in the first year of life (Figure 3.11). Productivity of a water system and the number of fish in that system competing for the available food will influence growth.

Many *Perca* and *Stizostedion* populations exhibit sexual dimorphism in which females grow faster and reach a greater ultimate size than the males (Figure 3.12). Artificially reared female yellow perch were observed to start growing faster than the males at 110 mm length (Schott, Kayes, & Calbert 1978).

There is no evidence in *Perca* species that populations are stunted because of genetic factors (Alm 1946; Hoestlands 1979). Recent developments in the identification of distinct stocks by electrophoretic techniques may distinguish differences in genetic growth potential between the stocks.

Growth is an anabolic process and only occurs when catabolic processes have been satisfied (Chapter 5). Growth may be an increase in somatic tissue or energy may be directed towards the development of gonads (Figure 3.5). In some situations energy stored in somatic tissue is later transferred to gonad tissue (Craig 1977a). Age of maturity will play an important role in continued somatic growth as development of the gonad takes up some of the available energy. Craig (1977a) found that the amount of stored energy decreased (or inversely the amount of water increased) as perch grew older. Thus the drain of surplus energy to reproductive processes will slow down somatic

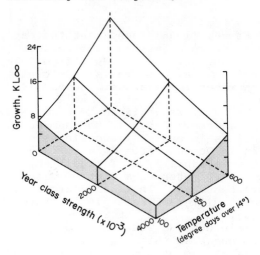

Figure 3.9: Diagram to illustrate the effect of temperature (degree days >14°C) and density (year class strength at age 2 y X10^{-3}) on year class growth (KL$_{\infty}$) of *Perca fluviatilis* from Windermere, England. (After Craig & Kipling 1983).

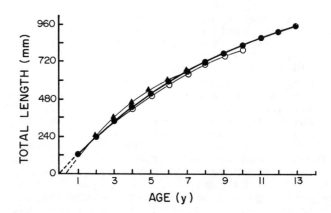

Figure 3.10: Mean length (mm) at age for *Stizostedion lucioperca* from the three basins of Lake Balaton, Hungary. (●) Northeast basin, (o) central basin and (▲) southwest basin. (After Biró 1985).

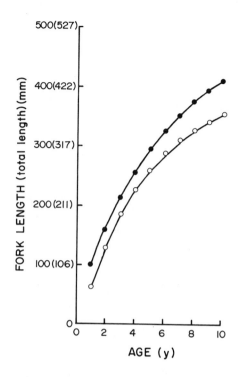

Figure 3.11: Length (mm) at age for a fast (●)and a slow (o) growing female *Stizostedion vitreum* from the 1969 year class from Wapun Lake, Canada. (Data provided by J. Babaluk).

growth and possibly lead to eventual senescence and death. Populations which are slow growing tend to be late maturers. Female perch and yellow perch mature between two and four years and males in the same water body usually mature one year earlier. Walleye show more disparity between ages of maturity in different localities and like growth, differences can be related to temperature (Colby & Nepszy 1981). Maturity of females ranges from two years in the southern states of the USA to ten years in the Northwest Territories, Canada. Zander mature at between two and five years.

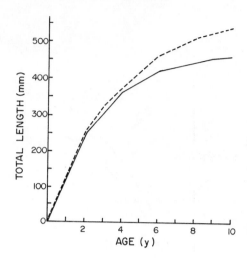

Figure 3.12: Mean length (mm) at age of male —— and female — —
Stizostedion vitreum from Lake Gogebic, USA. (After Colby *et al.* 1979).

Mortality

The life of a fish population takes it through
a succession of different stages in which the
mortality rates of the population vary. At the
juvenile stage when mortality is usually the result
of predation or competition for food, faster
growing fish will have an advantage over slower
growers (Craig 1985). Later in life faster growing
fish will often have a higher natural mortality
rate than slow growing fish. This is the reason
that slow growing populations in northern latitudes
live longer than faster growing populations situated further south (Figure 3.7). Mortality rates,
especially juvenile mortality rates, will be discussed further in Chapter 9 on population dynamics.
However to make the following account com-
prehensible a few definitions are necessary. The
total mortality rate of a population of fish may be
expressed in two ways (Ricker 1975):(i) annual mortality rate (A) expressed as a fraction or percentage and (ii) the instantaneous mortality rate (Z)

where the number at age t+1, N_{t+1}, depends upon the number at age t, N_t. Thus

$$N_{t+1} = N_t e^{-Z}$$

(t is often measured as 1 year).
The annual survival rate = $1-A = N_1/N_0$ and $Z = -\ln(1-A)$.

Forney (1967) calculated annual mortality rates of adult walleye in Oneida Lake, USA, by marking the fish when spawning and recapturing marked fish during the following summer and autumn. The annual mortality rate, A, is the sum of rate of death from angling (rate of exploitation = u) and from natural causes (the expectation of natural death = v) where A = u+v. For the years 1957-8, 1958-9 and 1959-60 values for u from angling were 0.14, 0.10 and 0.47 and values for v were 0.06, 0.01 and 0.07 respectively. From these values the total instantaneous mortality rate, Z, could be calculated and also the instantaneous fishing mortality, F, and instantaneous natural mortality, M, rates where Z = F+M. For the three years given above for Oneida Lake, M = 0.07, 0.01 and 0.10 respectively. Forney (1967) considered that adult natural mortality probably remained fairly constant with time and M=0.06 was a best estimate of the population's natural mortality rate. Fluctuations from this were caused by errors in population statistic estimates. However studies on perch in Windermere, England, have shown that M can be very variable in a population and can also vary considerably between year classes and between sexes (Craig, Kipling, Le Cren & McCormack 1979; Craig & Kipling 1983). Before a major fishery for perch was started in 1941 the adult population M was probably stable at about 0.41. After the fishery ceased M continued approximately at this level until about 1969 when between 1969 and 1975 the rate increased and varied from 0.65 to 1.28. This was a time of rapid growth in year classes in the population. Values of Z (Z = M since F was negligible) were calculated for each year class of mature perch from 1955 to 1972. Values for males ranged from 0.25 to 1.11 (Craig *et al.* 1979). The mortality rates for males for the 1959 and 1968 year classes are illustrated in Figure 3.8. These mortality rates were estimated from catch curves and relate to fish three years or older since younger fish were not fully recruited by the fishing gear.

Adult mortality rate remains remarkably constant throughout nearly all the life span of each year class. M is usually greater for males than females.

Longevity

Perch and yellow perch longevity can range from six to about 21 years, walleye from three to 19 years and zander from six to 17 years. Mortality and thus maximum age is related to temperature. In the northern limits of distribution, slower growing percids have a longer life expectancy than those living further south.

It will be apparent from the foregoing account that growth and mortality are closely related. Craig (1980a; 1982), in the Windermere study, has shown that M and K (equation 3.3) are linearly related for year classes of perch from recent years (Figure 3.13). The reasons for the relationship are not yet fully clear. It has already been suggested that percids, and fish in general, are very plastic in their response to environmental cues (especially temperature). Genetical

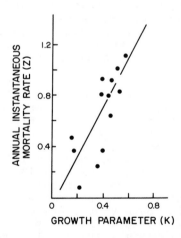

Figure 3.13: Diagram to illustrate the relationship between annual instantaneous mortality rate (Z) and the growth parameter (K) for different year classes of *Perca fluviatilis* from Windermere, England. (After Craig 1982).

variations have always been difficult to elucidate. Alm (1946) found that stunted perch improved their growth rate when transplanted to a more favourable environment and fertilized eggs from the stunted population grew equally well compared to a normal population.

Both M and K are correlated with temperature (Pauly 1980). Craig (1985) suggests that in perch (and fish in general) longevity is controlled by physiological processes which are genetically determined but are controlled by a biological clock. Thus a speeding up of these physiological processes may induce the release of immune responses and resultant early death. External factors influence these internal systems.

Chapter 4

REPRODUCTION AND DEVELOPMENT

Introduction

The development of the gonad requires energy which
is in excess of maintenance or catabolic energy.
This concept was discussed in Chapter 3. The chapter also gave information on ages of maturity and
seasonal changes in the weight and energy value of
the gonads and soma (body minus the gonad). In
adult perch in Windermere, England, the ovary develops during the winter months at the expense of
the soma (Figure 3.5). The cost of egg production
is high. For example the energy lost in eggs by a
260 mm female perch would amount to 168.4 kJ which
is equal to 87% of the energy stored by the soma in
a year (Craig 1977a). The energy lost by the
testes in milt is much less and for a 225 mm male
perch would amount to 32.5 kJ which is equal to
about 10% of the energy stored by the somatic
tissues in the year. Percid growth is sexually di-
morphic (Chapter 3), the female growing to a larger
size than the male. Recent studies on yellow perch
have shown that sex steroids have a profound effect
on growth (Malison, Kayes, Best, Amundson &
Wentworth 1986). It appears that attainment of a
specific body size (80-100 mm) and maturation of
specific hormone receptors may be necessary for
these growth responses to hormones. Similar conditions appear to control spermatogenesis and
vitellogenesis. Oestradiol-17β injections
stimulated yellow perch growth by affecting
appetite but not metabolism. Androgens retarded
growth probably by altering metabolism. When gona-
dectomies were performed on yellow perch, it was
found that males had reduced blood levels of testo-
sterone and growth improved. Castrated female fish
had reduced blood levels of oestradiol-17β but

growth was poorer. The direct effect of these
hormones on metabolism is still unclear. From an
evolutionary perspective, the female may have developed a system to take in more energy to compensate for the large outlay of energy in egg production.

Gonads

The sex of *Perca* and *Stizostedion* species is
not easy to identify from external appearances except at spawning time when the gravid female is
more rounded and the male expels milt on handling.
Internal examination often combined with histological investigations is necessary to study changes in
maturity. The primary sex cells are present at the
time of hatching and they migrate into the region
of the prerenal ducts. The female is probably the
homogenetic sex and this has been demonstrated in
the yellow perch (Malison *et al.* 1986). Sex differentiation begins in the perch at a length of 10
to 12 mm (Mezhnin 1978; Zelenkov 1982). Oogenesis
in hatchery reared yellow perch proceeded at 35 mm
and vitellogenesis and spermatogenesis at 85 mm
(Malison *et al.* 1986). The single ovary of the
female is formed by fusion of two rudiments and it
has no external oviduct (Chapter 2). A summary of
the stages of the developing ovary is given in
Table 4.1. The ovary of the gravid perch contains
hyaline oocytes which are filled with yolk (Figure
4.1). The cells of post ovulatory follicles of
perch undergo disintegration and autophagocytosis.
Cell debris is reabsorbed and the size of the
follicle is reduced. Other cells of the follicular
epithelium become synthetically active cells and
take on a secretory function (Lang 1981).
The paired ovaries of walleye are small and
not well developed up to a fish length of about 75
mm. They are heavily pigmented by melanophores
(Eschmeyer 1950). As the fish increases in size
the pigment becomes more scattered over the ovaries
until in adults it is confined to a few areas in
the anterior dorsal region. Large, immature
females have transparent ovaries which are cylin-
drical in shape although the anterior end is
rounded. Transverse blood vessels become more conspicuous as the fish matures. The dorsal longitudinal blood vessels lie on the surface of the ovaries. As in perch (Figure 3.4) the ovaries of
walleye develop through an annual cycle. In

Table 4.1. External and histological appearances of each stage of development of the perch ovary. (After Treasurer & Holliday 1981).

Maturity stage	External	Histological
Virgin	Small thread-like transparent organ lying underneath the bladder; no oocytes visible.	Two primordial ovaries separated by an epithelian layer; connective tissue matrix containing primary germ cells (3.3-6.7 µm), oogonia (13.3-20.0 µm) and primary oocytes (13.3-60.0 µm); ovary wall 4.2-10.4 µg thick.
Maturing virgin	Small pear-shaped pink organ; oocytes not yet visible.	Internal organisation advanced: ovary traversed by ovigerous lamellae; primary oocytes have increased to 20.0 - 116.6 µm diameter; ovary wall is 13.3 - 30.0 µm.
Developing (early)	Ovary is opaque and reddish with blood capillaries; occupies about half of body cavity; eggs visible to the eye are whitish and granular.	Developing oocytes 162 - 346 µm; follicle comprises theca externa and granulosa; chorion comprising tunica propria, a loose network, and the inner striated zona radiata; formation of yolk vesicles; ovarian wall is 40-97 µm thick.
Developing (late)	Ovary reddish and opaque eggs clearly discernible; ovary occupies about two thirds of body cavity.	Distinct size separation between developing and resting oocytes, the latter forming distinct groupings; oocytes up to 773 µm diameter, cytoplasm almost filled with yolk vesicles; chorion much wider.
Gravid	Ovary fills ventral cavity; eggs completely round and only appear translucent a few days prior to spawning.	Hyaline oocytes present (these usually collapse in histological sectioning); at best the yolk appears as a homogeneous mass filling the interior of the oocyte.
Spawning	Roe runs with slight pressure; most eggs translucent with few opaque eggs left in ovary.	Histologically similar to gravid stage; intense vasodilation; oviduct wall is thinner.
Spent	Ovary empty, flaccid and red, occupying about two-thirds of the body cavity; ovary wall thick and tough; a few residual occtyes may be visible.	Ovigerous lamellae disorganized; follicles contracted and folded; tunica wall is folded with an increase in diameter; occasional residual oocytes undergoing reabsorption.
Resting	Ovary grey-red; firmer than spent stage; length about half that of the body cavity; occasional residual oocytes may be visible.	Varying rates of recovery but normally organisation of lamellae is advanced; follicular remains arranged on outer edge of ovigerous lamellae; increase in number of small oocytes; advanced oocytes developing a granulosa layer.

68

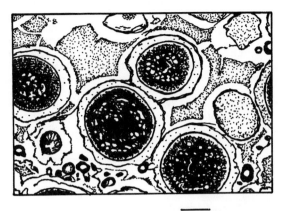

246 μm

Figure 4.1: Sketch of the gravid ovary of *Perca fluviatilis* showing hyaline oocytes. (After Treasurer & Holliday 1981).

Lake Gogebic, USA, the percentage ovary weight to total body weight increased from 0.7 in August to 4.7 in October and to 16.3 in May of the following year when spawning took place (Eschmeyer 1950). The maturation stages of *Stizostedion* are very similar to those of *Perca* (Table 4.1).

A summary of gross anatomical changes of the *Perca* testes is given in Table 4.2. The spermatozoa are of the primitive-type found in other teleosts (Figure 4.2a) (Koenig, Kayes & Calbert 1978). The number of sperm per unit volume varied from 1.14×10^{10} to 3.02×10^{10} sperm ml^{-1} in the sample of 10 yellow perch studied by Koenig *et al.* (1978). This compared to 3.7×10^{10} to 12.74×10^{10} sperm ml^{-1} (mean 7.62 sperm ml^{-1}) for 42 perch studied by Piironen and Hyvaerinen (1983). Up to a fish length of about 75 mm, walleye testes are thread-like with little or no pigment and are smaller in cross section than ovaries from fish of a similar size. Testes of larger immature males are elongate and uniform in diameter along their length. The transverse blood vessels are not very apparent in the testes although they are conspicuous in the ovaries. Testes in a resting phase are greyish-white in colour. In Lake Gogebic, walleye testes had this appearance during July

69

and August but by mid-October they were large, soft and milky-white. They reached a similar size and weight to the ovaries of the female at this time (Eschmeyer 1950). The testes became firmer through the winter months until the spawning season when milt was produced. The spent testes were similar in appearance to resting gonads. The percentage weight of testes to body weight varied from 0.2 in July and August to 4.3 in October. It remained at about 4% until spawning then declined to 0.4%, in late June.

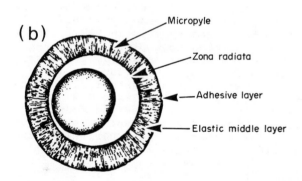

Figure 4.2: Sketches of (a) spermatozoan (After Koenig *et al.* 1978) and (b) cross-section of an egg (after Mansueti 1964) of *Perca flavescens* .

Table 4.2. External appearances of each stage of development of the perch testes.

Maturity Stage	External
Virgin	Very small paired organs close under the vertebral column. Transparent.
Maturing virgin	Translucent. Length about half of the ventral cavity.
Early development	Opaque and reddish with blood capillaries. They occupy about half of the ventral cavity.
Late development	Reddish-white in colour. The testes occupy about two-thirds of the ventral cavity. No milt is produced with pressure.
Gravid	The testes occupy the length of the ventral cavity. They are white and produce milt with pressure.
Running	As for gravid but milt is produced with only slight pressure.
Spent	The testes start to shrink. Some milt apparent in testes. They are reddish in colour.
Resting	Translucent. Length less than half of the ventral cavity.

The number of eggs laid by a fish is described by the total number (the absolute fecundity) or by the number of eggs produced per unit weight of fish (the relative fecundity). The absolute fecundity (F) can usually be related to another variable of the fish by a simple relationship such as

$$F = ax^b$$ Equation 4.1

where X = length, weight or age and a and b are constants (Bagenal & Braum 1978). Figure 4.3 illustrates some absolute fecundity and body length relationships for perch, walleye and zander. All species lay a large number of eggs but for a given size, zander is more fecund than walleye. Within a species, for a given length, the absolute fecundity can vary widely between fish from different areas although this is not necessarily a function of latitude. Thorpe (1977) for example could find no significant relationship between relative fecundity and latitude in different perch populations. Fecundity can vary between different populations in the same body of water as is illustrated by two perch populations in the Rybinsk Reservoir, USSR, and by walleye populations in the two main basins of Lake Erie (Figure 4.4). The number of eggs laid by a female is influenced, as is growth and age of maturity, by food supply or energy intake of the fish. Differences in fecundity can occur in the same population with time as differences in food

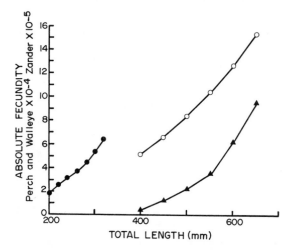

Figure 4.3: Plots of absolute fecundity with length (mm) for *Perca fluviatilis* (●) from Windermere, England, *Stizostedion vitreum* (○) from Dauphin Lake, Canada and *S. lucioperca* (▲) from Lake Ijssel, the Netherlands.

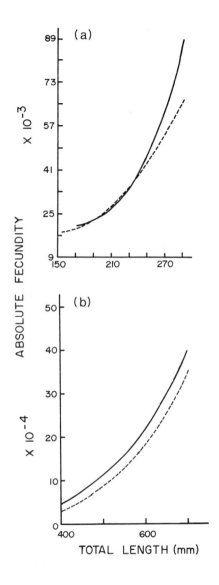

Figure 4.4: Plots of absolute fecundity with length (mm) for (a) *Perca fluviatilis*, from two regions ▬ and - - of the Rybinsk Reservoir USSR (after Volodin 1980) and (b) *Stizostedion vitreum* from the western ▬ and eastern - - basins of Lake Erie, USA (after Wolfert 1969).

availability occur. Kuznetsov (1982) noted that
Volga pikeperch produced more eggs with higher fat
content following a year of good feeding conditions
compared to a year of poor food supply. Deficiency
of food and poor growth in a preceding summer can
have a marked effect on reproduction in the following spring. Poor conditions delay the reabsorbing processes after spawning and delay oocyte development so that the females may miss the next
spawning period. Insufficient energy stored in the
soma during the summer for translocation to the
ovaries as they develop in the winter may cause the
death of female *Perca* as illustrated for yellow
perch by Newsome and Leduc (1975).

There is still speculation on the effect of
age on egg production. Evidence suggests that as
perch females grow older the number of eggs per
unit weight (relative fecundity) declines but the
size of the egg increases (Volodin 1980; Craig
1974b). Absolute fecundity and age follow a power
law relationship (Equation 4.1) until the age when
senescence causes egg numbers to decline.

Environmental Cues and Hormonal Changes

The reproductive cycle can be divided into two
main phases, gametogenesis and spawning. During
gametogenesis highly specialised gametes (oocytes
or spermatozoa) are formed from simple germ cells
(oogonia or spermatogonia). The duration of gametogenesis varies according to species and temperature. Spawning involves a sequence of events which
are complex and more variable in duration than
gametogenesis. This leads to liberation of
gametes, meiosis resumption, oocyte maturation,
ovulation and oviposition in females and spermiation and sperm release in males. Endocrine changes
during the reproductive cycle include variations in
the levels of pituitary and plasma gonadotrophin
(GTH) and plasma sex steroids. There is strong
evidence for a gonadotrophin-releasing hormone
(GnRH) in the teleost brain and probably a
gonadotrophin release-inhibiting factor (GRIF)
(Stacey 1984). GTH release appears to be controlled by the interaction of these two hormones.
There are possibly two types of GTH, one with a low
carbohydrate content which stimulates vitellogenin
uptake in the oocytes and one with a high carbohydrate content which stimulates steroid oogenesis,
oocyte maturation, ovulation and spermiation. GTH

increases in the blood during the preovulatory
stage. The effects of GTH and steroids varies between percid species. GTH induces final maturation
of the oocyte indirectly in yellow perch by stimulating the production of steroids. In this species
the most potent steroid for this function is 17α
-hydroxy-20β-dihydroxyprogesterone (Goetz &
Theofan 1979). Steroids produced by yellow perch
are also responsible for inducing germinal vesicle
breakdown (Theofan & Goetz 1983). Germinal vesicle
breakdown in walleye can be directly influenced by
GTH. *In vitro* effects of various GTH preparations
on yellow perch and walleye germinal vesicles
caused breakdown in walleye but no significant
effects in yellow perch (Goetz & Bergman 1978). The
direct effect of GTH on ovulation in walleye was
demonstrated by Lessman (1978). Preparations of
carp and human GTH induced ovulation in prespawning
walleye but cortisone and progesterone were in-
effective. Ovulation, the expulsion of the oocyte
from the follicle may be controlled by prostaglan-
dins (Stacey 1984). In males, just before spermiation, there is an increase in androgens (testoste-
rone and 11-ketotestosterone).

Perca and *Stizostedion* spawn once a year in
the spring. This annual rhythm is controlled by
exogenous factors which are difficult to quantify.
Indeed little is known about how these factors control spermiation and ovulation in teleosts as a
whole. Some possible environmental conditions
which influence this reproductive cycle include
temperature, photoperiod, substrate conditions,
water levels and velocity and social interactions
(including the possible production of pheromones).
Temperature probably plays the major role and the
following examples emphasise its importance. Experiments on temperature effects demonstrated that
optimal conditions for yellow perch maturation
occurred when fish were held at a water temperature
of 6°C or lower for 185 days from 30 October. The
number of maturing females declined as the holding
temperature increased (Hokanson 1977). In the
southern USA yellow perch is at the limit of its
range. Warm winter temperatures (8 to 10°C) may
impair reproductive success (Clugston, Oliver &
Ruelle 1978). When walleye were introduced into
California reservoirs where the winter temperature
ranged from 10 to 12.5°C, they failed to reproduce
(Miller 1967). The timing of spawning is also influenced by temperature, both by absolute
temperature and by temperature change with time.

Perca species in the northern hemisphere spawn from February to July depending on latitude and intro- duced populations in the southern hemisphere spawn from August to October. Walleye in the southern limits of their range spawn early in the year, for example they migrate up the Pearl River, Mississippi, USA, to spawn in late January or early February (Cook 1959), whereas those in northern Canada spawn in late June (Scott & Crossman 1973). Zander spawn from February to early July (Deelder & Willemsen 1964) depending on latitude and water temperature. Two populations of zander in Turkey, living in the same latitude, spawn at different times due to the temperature disparities between two lakes. Zander spawn in the warmer lake in late February or March and in May or June in the colder lake (Aksiray 1961). An accelerating temperature appears to be the major factor inducing spawning (Thorpe 1977; Hokanson 1977) and photoperiod may only play a minor role (Kayes & Calbert 1979). An interruption of this temperature acceleration by a cold period may cause oocytes to be reabsorbed and spawning is missed. This has been noted in perch at Windermere, England, where many perch failed to spawn and females were found to be reabsorbing their eggs after a severe winter in 1962-63 (Le Cren 1965; Kipling 1976). However some races of perch are exposed to ice conditions annually and perch have been noted to spawn under the ice at 4°C in the Aral Sea (Filatov & Duplakov 1926). An in- terrupted spawning season caused by cold weather induced walleye females to reabsorb their eggs in Heming Lake, Canada (Derback 1947). In the Don River, USSR, a cold spring delays the migration of zander and many of those entering the river in May are in the process of reabsorbing their eggs (Golovanenko, Shuvatova, Putina, Fedorova & Arakelova 1970).

Spawning Behaviour

Usually spawning migrations of *Perca* species are short-ranged. In a lake system this involves movement from deep water where the fish have over- wintered to shallow water spawning areas. Other movements may be from lakes into rivers or from brackish areas into rivers. Male *Perca* arrive on the spawning grounds earlier than the females. Male yellow perch in southeastern Lake Michigan, USA, concentrate in water depths of 6 to

12 m in early May. Females stay in deep water (>18 m) until late May when they join the males and spawning takes place (Dorr 1982). The duration of spawning varies. In southeastern Lake Michigan yellow perch spawning lasts for about two weeks compared to Slapton Ley, England where spawning of perch occurs over about an eight week period (Craig 1974b).

Perch and yellow perch will spawn over a wide variety of substrates including boulders and gravel, aquatic macrophytes, roots of trees, dead branches and other materials normally in water depths from 0.5 to 8 m. Spawning can take place throughout the day and night and the fish lose their normal diel behaviour patterns during the spawning season (Craig 1977b).

A single female *Perca* is accompanied by a number of males, usually four or five but sometimes two or three. The female swims in a non-directional manner through, over and around the spawning substrate. She often pauses between these movements. Some movements are circular (anti-clockwise and clockwise) others are spiral and up-ward. As a rule one male follows the female in these movements swimming alongside and slightly be-neath her, the other males remaining stationary. The active male often touches the vent of the female with its snout. If the female swims to another site the group of males follow her. Some-times the male following the movements of the female may break away and be replaced by another individual. In vegetation this type of behaviour can go on for about 30 min with frequency of move-ments and swimming speed increasing until ovulation (Treasurer 1981). The egg strand is released as the female swims in a spiral clockwise movement flexing herself into a U-shape. All the eggs are released in this egg strand which becomes twisted around and attached to the spawning substrate. Treasurer (1981) noted that at least two males, one following and another swimming in the opposite direction release milt. Egg and sperm release takes about five seconds (Treasurer 1981; Fabricius 1956; Hergenrader 1969). The sperm of perch is only viable for a few minutes after release (Lindroth 1947) probably less than two minutes (Piironen & Hyvaerinen 1983). There is little if any protection of the eggs. After spawning females and males show signs of loss of equilibrium which may take up to one hour to regain.

Walleye will start spawning migrations before

the ice has melted from a lake, particularly into
an inflowing stream which has a higher water temperature than the lake. Spawning migrations can be
blocked if the streams are colder than the lake
water (Forney 1967). Walleye have been observed to
spawn in lakes under ice (Eschmeyer 1950). In
Southern Indian Lake, Canada, walleye commenced
spawning migrations into streams when the lake was
still covered in ice but the streams had reached a
temperature of 5°C (Bodaly 1980). Should the temperature drop below this value the upstream movements ceased. The size of stream discharges did
not have a direct effect on these upstream migrations. Movements only take place at night and in
Southern Indian Lake occurred over 10 to 18 days in
May. The time of spawning migrations depends on
latitude but in general occurs from April to May.
In some extreme situations, on the southern limits
of walleye distribution, spawning occurs earlier.
For example in the Canton Reservoir, USA, the peak
of spawning occurs in mid-March (Grinstead 1971).
Walleye do appear to return to the same general
vicinity to spawn each year. Bodaly (1980) found
that 20% of the spawning population returned to the
same stream whereas 62% exhibited homing to the
same general vicinity. Although more studies are
needed, there is evidence that distinct stocks of
walleye use different areas of a lake to spawn
(Chapter 8). In Southern Indian Lake stocks of
walleye with identifiable phenotypic differences
spawned in streams 75 km apart (Bodaly 1980). As
in *Perca* species, male walleye arrive at the
spawning areas before the females and will remain
there for a few days after the females have left.
Males always predominate in numbers and at peak of
spawning can reach a ratio of male to female of 52
to 1 (Bodaly 1980).

Walleye will spawn in streams or lakes in
depths ranging from 0.1 m to 4.6 m (Colby *et al*.
1979). Spawning areas include river and stream
mouths, shallow shoreline areas and gravel reefs of
lakes and riffle regions in tributary streams.
Eggs are laid over a substrate of rock, rubble or
gravel although if these are not available spawning
may occur over sand or silt. Submerged twigs or
branches or vegetation in flooded marshy areas may
sometimes be used.

Spawning of walleye unlike *Perca* species is
normally nocturnal and shows a diel pattern (Ellis
& Giles 1965). Activity increases in the evening
when illumination falls below about 0.172 lx.

Courtship involves approaches by males or females
to fish of the opposite sex either from behind or
laterally and pushing the other fish. Sometimes a
fish will drift back into another one pushing it
backwards. The dorsal fins are alternately raised
and lowered during these activities and in shallow
water the fins will appear above the surface.
Courtship may last up to one to two minutes before
the release of eggs and milt. There is no pairing
or territorial behaviour and courtship is promis-
cuous. This courtship activity increases with time
and one or more females start to make forward and
upward movements which culminate in a sudden rush
to the surface by the females followed by one or
more males. At the surface this group swims around
vigorously releasing eggs and milt (Ellis & Giles
1965). This rush to the surface, release of sexual
products and return to the bottom may last only for
about five seconds. An individual female may spawn
in this way up to three times in one minute. Ellis
and Giles (1965) observed sizes of spawning groups
ranged from one female with one or two males to two
females with 6 males but the average is about 7
fish (Eschmeyer 1950).

Walleye exhibit no parental care. Eggs are
adhesive and stick to rocks and gravel.

Zander spawn in April and May with extremes
from February to July normally at a temperature of
about 12°C but spawning can occur at 8°C. The
faster the water warms the earlier the time of
spawning. Specific nursery areas are chosen and
spawning migrations occur within lakes, from lakes
into rivers and from brackish areas to rivers.
Zander in the Sea of Azov spawn in the Kubon River,
in the Kubon estuary, in the river flood plain and
in lower sections of the river's tributaries. Over
a period of 50 years' study the spawning behaviour
of these fish has changed and this is thought to be
due to increased salinity in the Sea of Azov
(Troitskiy & Tsunikova 1976). More adult zander
now approach the Kubon coast in the autumn. The
main spawning run takes place in late March or
early April over 20 to 27 days. Fifty years ago
spawning took place about one month later and could
last over a duration of 43 days. A protracted
period of spawning may increase the survival potential of the young as it increases the chances that
some larvae will hatch at an optimum period.

In rivers, zander spawn in depths from 0.5 to
1.0 m usually in water velocities of 0.1 to 0.2 m
s^{-1} (Deelder & Willemsen 1964). This water

velocity helps to remove silt from the eggs. In lakes, spawning sites are selected in depths from 0.5 to 17 m (far deeper than the 4.5 m maximum depth of walleye). The substrate selected is sand or stones in which male fish build nests. The male, while nest building, exposes plant roots on which the eggs are later deposited and where they stick. Female and male zander are monogamous as the female lays all eggs simultaneously and the male stays to protect the eggs and young fry.

Spawning of zander occurs at dawn. The female remains stationary over a nest while the male circles rapidly around her at a distance of about one metre. The male then assumes a vertical position. This behaviour continues for 20 to 25 min until both fish swim around very energetically, the water becomes very turbid and during this time eggs and milt are released. The female then moves away and the male remains to aerate the eggs with his pectoral fins (Botsjarnikowa 1952). The sea pike-perch in the Caspian Sea has rather a similar reproductive biology to zander. Spawning occurs in the sea at depths from 3 to 12 m in nests built by the males in a sandy substrate (Guseva 1974). Spawning takes place from mid-April to mid-May at a temperature range of 10 to 17°C. All the eggs of one female are laid in one nest and the male guards these eggs.

Balon (1975) separates walleye and zander into two divergent ecoethological guilds based on their reproductive behaviour. Thus walleye belong to the non-guarding, open-substrate spawning lithophil guild while zander are members of the guarding, nest-spawning, phytophil guild.

Development of the embryo

Perca species produce a unique transparent gelatinous accordion-folded egg strand which can be up to 2.1 m long and 51 to 102 mm wide (Scott & Crossman 1973). This egg strand formed in the ovary is slightly heavier than water and becomes entangled in debris, submerged vegetation or attached to the lake or river bottom. Eggs are individually connected to the mucilaginous sheath which withstands mechanical shock and provides protection from predators and disease. Water can circulate and aerate the eggs between the outside and the central canal through spaces between the eggs. Milt also has to penetrate through these gaps into the

centre as the spermatozoa enter the eggs through
the micropyles (Figure 4.2a) which face inwards
(Thorpe 1977).

The egg of perch is clear, pale amber in
colour and has a thick membrane which consists of
an outer adhesive layer, a wide middle area composed of fine radially arranged fibres and an inner
layer called the zona radiata (Figure 4.2b). Before hardening, the diameters of the fertilised
egg, yolk and the single oil droplet are 1.0 to 2.0
mm, 1.3 mm and 0.6 mm respectively (Thorpe 1977).
Within three minutes after fertilisation the membrane swells and loses its adhesive properties and
the egg reaches a diameter of 1.9 to 2.8 mm. The
eggs of walleye and zander are both spherical,
translucent and pale yellow in colour (Colby *et
al.* 1979; Deelder & Willemsen 1964). The mean egg
diameter of walleye is 1.5 to 2.0 mm and it contains an oil droplet about 0.8 mm in diameter at
the vegetative pole. The egg of zander is slightly
smaller, 1.0 to 1.5 mm, and contains an oil globule
of 0.4 mm. Both species lay adhesive eggs which
clump together and to the substrate. The eggs
swell after fertilisation due to uptake of water.

Embryonic development depends on water
temperature, the effect of which will be discussed
later. Mansueti (1964) studied the development of
yellow perch eggs at an incubation temperature of
8.5 to 12°C (Figure 4.5). The time intervals given
here are based on Mansueti's studies. However, the
incubation time to hatching of 25 to 27 days is
longer than normal, 8 to 10 days for yellow perch
recorded by Scott and Crossman (1973). The oil
droplet in the fertilised egg shifts to one side
after 14 min pulling yolk material with it.
Frequently an indentation in the yolk appears in
the area of the oil droplet. Within 30 min the
transparent colourless blastodermal tissue grows
over the oil droplet which continues to bulge from
the yolk. Cleavage of the egg occurs within five
hours into a two-cell stage. The late blastula has
a peripheral germ ring and a blastocoel at about 21
h. The gastrula stage is reached in 29 h and the
germ ring has grown one-third of the way around the
yolk by this time. The embryo develops slightly
off centre and up to six days no chromatophores are
found. By the sixth day the tip of the tail becomes freed from the yolk. Between days 6 to 11
body melanophores appear and auditory vesicles,
pectoral buds and caudal finfolds form. From days
14 to 16, pigment appears in the eyes, the

pectorals are well developed and the myotomes are
nearly complete. Melanophores cover most of the
yolk and the vent is visible at the junction of the
tail and the yolk. Primitive gill structures and
the mouth are present at this stage. The structure
of the heart and auditory vesicles can be plainly
seen and the tail is extended in a curve over the
head. At about 24 days the egg case beings to sof-
ten and hatching occurs from day 25 to 27. Emerging
fry range in length from 4.1 to 6.6 mm (Thorpe
1977).

Embryonic development in *Stizostedion* species
is similar to those of *Perca*. A detailed account
of walleye development under laboratory conditions
where the eggs were held at 15°C has been given by
McElman and Balon (1979). The following description, based on that of McElman and Balon (1979), is
probably a very close approximation to development
in other *Stizostedion* species.

Cleavage starts after 2.5 h and ends just
after 48 h (Figure 4.6a-d). Cleavage of the blastodisc brings about reduction in blastomere size
but an increase in their numbers. At just under 14
h the periblast is discernible on the margins of
the blastodisc. The blastodisc assumes a dome
shape and becomes compressed. Cells become individually indistinguishable and the translucent cell
mass becomes dark and opaque. At nearly 29 h the
embryonic shield and germ ring appear in the
thicker areas of the blastoderm and by about 31 h
the blastoderm envelopes about 50% of the surface
area of the yolk (Figure 4.6e).

The embryonic phase lasts from 46 h to 9 days
when hatching occurs. It is separated from the
cleavage phase by the formation of primordial optic
vesicles. The first step is the differentiation of
head and trunk by 2 days 22 h. At this time the
germ ring closes around the top of the oil globule
forming a trunk-tail mound (Figure 4.6f). The body
undergoes a 90° anterior translocation during this
step. By 2 days 1.5 h the trunk-tail has moved off
the top of the large oil globule, six somite pairs
appear in the mid-body region and a notochord becomes visible. Small oil globules accumulate
around and below the posterior half of the body especially in the trunk-tail region. At 2 days 6 h
the head is elevated to 0.25 mm above the yolk
blastoderm and has a maximum width of 0.55 mm at
the optic vesicles. Somites total 9 to 11. By 2
days 10 h the head is 0.30 mm above the yolk
blastoderm and three slight constrictions of the

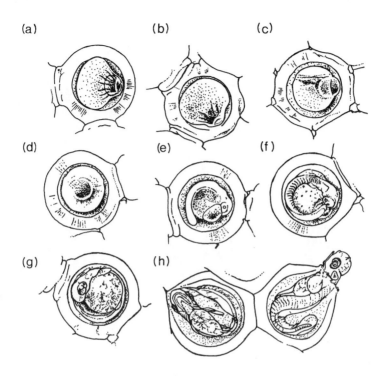

Figure 4.5: Drawings to illustrate embryonic development of *Perca flavescens*. (a) Prior to blastula formation (14 min), (b) blastula (22 min), (c) early gastrula (21 h 25 min), (d) gastrula (29 h 9 min), (e) tail-free (144 h), (f) formation of myotomes and pectoral buds (11 days), (g) pigmentation of the eyes and development of the pectoral fins (16 days) and (h) hatching (27 days). Diameter of eggs c.2 mm. (After Mansueti 1964).

hind-brain are apparent. Optic stalks develop between the brain and each optic vesicle. Optic cups form from these vesicles by just over 2 days 16 h, but due to expansion of the fore- and mid-brain regions, they are not connected to the brain. The trunk-tail is now below the lower margin of the oil globule and the head is above. By 2 days 17.25 h, the embryo restablishes its bilateral symmetry with respect to the yolk and large oil globule. It has a total length of 3.20 mm and 17 to 19 pairs of somites. The small oil globules have disappeared from the trunk-tail area and the yolk starts to diminish from the lower half of the large oil globule. The trunk-tail region becomes elevated. Development up to nearly 3 days 7 h (Figure 4.6g) includes formation of spherical lenses and olfactory

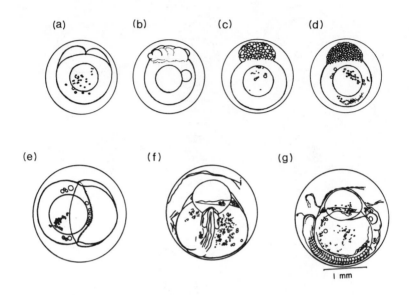

Figure 4.6: Drawings to illustrate early embryonic development of *Stizostedion vitreum*. (a) Two blastomere stage (3 h 47 min), (b) 8 to 16 blastomeres (6 h 41 min), (c) late cleavage vertical view (9 h 20 min), (d) as for (c) (13 h), (e) mid epiboly vertical view (1 day 7 h 10 min), (f) head and trunk development (2 days 22 h) and (g) left side view of embryo (3 days 50 min). (After McElman & Balon 1979).

and auditory vesicles. The trunk-tail becomes elevated to 0.25 mm. The dorsal median fin fold is apparent anterior to the tip of the trunk-tail band and posterior to the 29 to 31 pairs of somites most of which are slightly V-shaped. The cerebellum is discernable due to lateral expansion and the hindbrain becomes split by a midline cleft.

From 3 days 7 h to 4 days 10 h melanophores form, contraction of the primordial skeletal and cardiac musculature (heart rate contractions are about 87 min^{-1}) occurs, otoliths appear and there is a rapid increase in length up to 4 mm (Figure 4.7a). Somites total 45 pairs. During the next stage up to 5 days 10 h, somite segmentation is completed (52 pairs), eye pigments develop and a simple blood flow occurs in a subintestinal vitel-

line circulatory system. The embryo reaches a
total length of 5.5 mm. It becomes more mobile and
a thickening of tissues in the ventral finfold posterior to the yolk indicates the position of a primordial rectal region. Hatching cells appear on
all exposed surfaces of the head to just behind the
auditory vesicles. Heart contraction rate increases up to 7 days 4 h of development (the
highest mean value was 164 min^{-1} observed by
McElman & Balon 1979). New blood vessels form increasing areas of circulation (Figure 4.7b).
Blood circulates to head, liver and myomeres
(somites become differentiated into muscle fibres)
and haemoglobin is synthesised. The urinary
bladder develops, adjacent and posterior to the
lower half of the rectum. Melanophores concentrate
on the lateral and ventral yolk surfaces and along
the ventral surface of the caudal fin. They
eventually form a continuous series on the ventrum
of the postanal myomeres. The head continues to
lift away from the large oil globule and mouth formation becomes noticeable as do the otoliths. Eggs
appear black and opaque. The final stage to time
of hatching at about 9 days (Figure 4.7c) includes
an increase in liver size. Heart rate contractions
decrease to around 106 min^{-1} and vitelline blood
circulation reaches a maximum. Cartilage forms in
the head. The embryo shows movements within the
egg membranes and there is a straightening of head
and trunk.

As in perch and walleye, zander hatch with
well developed eyes but with little pigment in the
eyes or on the yolk sac. Sauger also hatch with
only a few chromatophores. Walleye hatch at a
length of 6.0 to 8.6 mm and zander hatch at a
length of 4.0 to 5.0 mm.

Eggs of perch were exposed to 10 incubation
temperatures (range from 6 to 22°C) by Guma'a
(1978b). He found that the time to develop from
one stage to another decreased with increasing
temperature (Figure 4.8). This was also
demonstrated for yellow perch by Hokanson and
Kleiner (1974). The relationship between speed of
embryonic development and incubation temperature is
exponential (Figure 4.9). However the sum of heat
in degree-days required by perch for 10, 50 and 90%
of the eggs to hatch was found to be a constant regardless of the incubation temperature. These
(with range of 95% confidence limits) amounted to
91.4 (83.3-102.0) degree-days above 4.6°C for 10%
hatch, 97.1 (90.9-104.2) degree days above 4.9°C

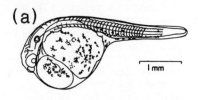

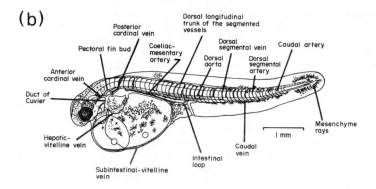

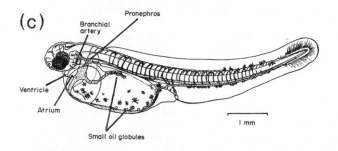

Figure 4.7: Drawings to illustrate late embryonic development of *Stizostedion vitreum*. (a) Embryo at age 4 days 5 h 15 min (right side view after removal from egg membranes, (b) embryo at age 6 days 18 h 10 min (left side view after removal from egg membranes and (c) embryo at 8 days 1 h 35 min immediately after hatching (left side view). (After McElman & Balon 1979).

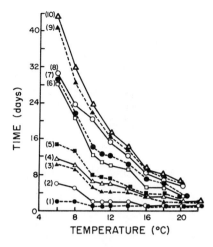

Figure 4.8: The effect of temperature on the development of *Perca fluviatilis* embryos. The time taken to develop from one stage to another is given as a mean from six observations. Stages observed are (1) complete blastula, (2) complete gastrula, (3) early embryo, (4) free tail, (5) embryo moving but eyes still unpigmented, (6) eye-pigment developed, (7) hatching started, (8) 10% hatched, (9) 50% hatched and (10) 90% hatched. (After Guma'a 1978b).

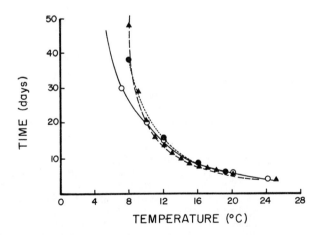

Figure 4.9: The effect of temperature on the mass incubation time of *Perca fluviatilis* (●), *Stizostedion vitreum* (o) and *S. lucioperca* (▲). (After Guma'a 1978b, Colby *et al.* 1979 and Deelder & Willemsen 1964).

for 50% hatch and 101.0 (94.3-108.7) degree days
above 5.0°C for 90% hatch. Guma'a (1978b) found
that the largest and healthiest larvae hatched at
14°C. Kokurewicz (1969) also demonstrated this as
an optimum temperature for incubation of both perch
and zander. The highest viability of yellow perch
and walleye embryos are produced by parents accli-
matised at 6 to 9°C and incubation of the embryos
at 9 to 15°C.

The viability of spawned eggs ranges from 3.4
to 100% in walleye (Colby *et al.* 1979). In a study
of perch Treasurer (1983) found <2.0% of eggs were
infertile, <2.4% were moribund and <1.8% had defor-
mities in early embryonic development. Later in
development up to 10% of the embryos were deformed.
A number of environmental factors affect the mortality of fertile eggs. Higher temperature causes
higher mortality especially at late stages of development (Guma'a 1978b; Hurley 1972). In the walleye three to five percent of walleye mortality
occurred from fertilisation to eyed stage, compared
to 23 to 44% from the eyed stage to hatching
(Hurley 1972). Oxygen concentration is important
but levels down to 3.4 mg l^{-1} show no significant
effects on developing embryos. Below this value
larvae are smaller at hatching (Siefert & Spoor
1974). In streams and rivers, currents remove
debris which might cover the eggs and reduce oxygen
concentration. Death of embryos may occur when
eggs spawned in flooded marshy areas become exposed
to air when there is a drop in water level. Eggs
laid in lakes may be destroyed by high winds which
cause the eggs to be washed ashore. Clady and
Hutchinson (1975) estimated that 0.8% of the total
eggs laid by yellow perch in one area of Oneida
Lake, USA, perished for this reason.

Mortality of eggs increases with a lowering in
pH. Perch eggs develop normally above pH 5.5
(Runn, Johansson & Milbrink 1977). At pH 5.0 mortality is still <10% but incubation time increases
(Rask 1984). The mortality at pH 4.0 is 59% and
development time is increased by 29%. At pH 3.5 no
eggs hatch. Walleye eggs are more sensitive to low
pH than perch. The 90.5% mortality of walleye eggs
from fertilisation to eyed stage occurs at pH 5.4
(Hulsman, Powles & Gunn 1983) although mortality is
comparatively low (25.5 to 33.5%) at pH 6.0.

Development of Larva

At the start of exogenous feeding most of the yolk has been absorbed. The larva from the time of hatching until this stage is referred to as a prolarva. As yolk absorption continues, the mouth becomes fully developed (Figure 4.10). Larvae of *Perca* and *Stizostedion* species develop large mouths, well-developed jaws, teeth and eyes. At the end of the prolarva stage the gut is a simple straight tube and the larva has teeth, buccal cavity, oesophagus, stomach, liver and gall bladder. Blood vessels develop in the gills and gut as the importance of gill respiration increases and with the onset of feeding. At 7.0 mm the yellow perch operculum can be distinguished behind the pre-operculum and four gill arches can be identified (Mansueti 1964). At this length the larva begins active feeding although food is still gained from the yolk sac. At 7.2 mm the head is more elongate. There is more extensive development of chromatophores particularly over the head, auditory vesicles and developing air bladder. In the postlarva phase pigmentation increases on the head and body. The vertical bands on yellow perch appear at about

(a)

(b)

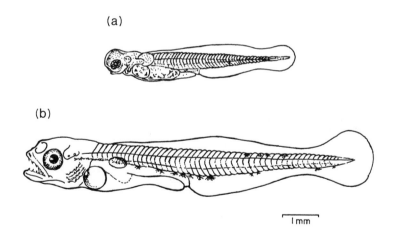

I mm

Figure 4.10: The prolarvae of (a) *Perca flavescens* and (b) *Stizostedion vitreum*. (After Mansueti 1964 and Li & Mathias 1982).

20 mm length. In this species all fins are
differentiated at a fish length of 14 mm but not
all are fully formed with spines and rays until
fish are 21 to 27 mm. The scales appear on the
caudal peduncle at a fish length of about 20 mm and
scalation proceeds along the lateral line (Pycha &
Smith 1955). Perch are fully scaled at 36 to 37
mm. One or two scales are present on walleye at 24
mm. Scale development proceeds in a similar
fashion to perch and is complete at 45 mm (Priegel
1964). Adult walleye coloration is reached at 35
mm (Nelson 1968).

Li and Mathias (1982) divided the postlarva
phase of walleye into two stages. Stage I postlarva has an oil globule but no yolk. The gut is
very similar to that of the prolarva although a
sphincter divides the gut into intestine and
rectum. Some exogenous feeding occurs combined
with an endogenous energy source from the oil
globule. Stage II of the larval development
commences when the oil globule is fully absorbed.
The stomach wall thickens and expands and the first
loop appears in the intestine (Figure 4.11). The
gill filaments increase in size and the gill rakers

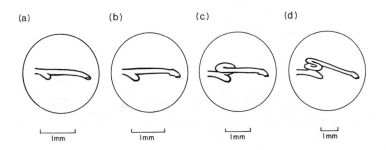

(a)   (b)   (c)   (d)

Imm   Imm   Imm   Imm

Figure 4.11: Sketches to show the development of the gut of *Stizostedion
vitreum*. (a) Prolarva, (b) postlarva-I, (c) postlarva-II and (d) juvenile.
(After Li & Mathias 1982).

begin to differentiate. At the end of Stage II the
larva is 16 to 19 mm in total length. During the
juvenile stage the gut develops further with
expansion of the stomach and the formation of pyloric caecae. Three caecae are formed at 19 mm.
Gill rakers continue to differentiate and take on a
filtering function.

Newly hatched *Perca* larvae tolerate a
temperature range from 3 to 28°C but are inactive
below 5.3°C (Hokanson 1977). The optimum survival
occurs when temperature is raised 1°C day^{-1} from
initial incubation temperature to reach 16 to 18°C
at the prolarvae stage. For *Stizostedion* species
this optimum temperature lies between 14 to 23°C.
During the postlarval feeding stage the optimum
temperature is 21°C for *Perca* species rising to a
physiological optimum of 25°C for juveniles. No
postlarvae survive at temperatures of 10°C or
below. These values are probably near optimum for
Stizostedion species although zander juveniles and
adults have a higher physiological optimum temperature of about 27°C. Smith and Koenst (1975) found
that no walleye or sauger postlarvae survived at
temperatures of 15°C or less compared to 8% at
21°C. Critical levels of oxygen concentrations for
the larvae are those below 50% (4.8 mg l^{-1} at 17°C)
(Siefert & Spoor 1974). Growth and survival of
larvae and juveniles will be strongly influenced by
other factors such as food availability and predators. Li and Mathias (1982) identify the critical
period for walleye larvae to occur at the commencement of exogenous feeding when food density and
availability need to be at an optimum. Both *Perca*
and *Stizostedion* larvae are cannabalistic on their
siblings (Smyly 1952; Li & Mathias 1982).
Cannabalism by adults also takes place in both
species when larvae are >18 mm. Other predators
include fish, in particular pike, and invertebrates. A cyclopoid, *Diacyclops thomasi* Forbes has
been found to prey heavily on yellow perch larvae
(Hartig & Jude 1984).

Behaviour of Larvae and Fry

The embryos of *Perca* and *Stizostedion* species
show some movement to the surface and they have
been observed to do so with the egg membrane still
attached to the head (Belyi 1972; Reighard 1890).
The larva eventually escapes from this membrane by
energetic movements. The prolarva swims upwards at

an angle of about 30° to the vertical and then
sinks passively head down at an angle of about
80°. The oil globule gives some buoyancy at this
stage since the swim bladder is not fully formed
and inflated (Ross, Powles & Berrill 1977; Li &
Mathias 1982; Belyi 1972; Guseva 1974). Usually
the movement upwards is directed towards the surface film. Belyi (1972) noted that zander larvae
spent about 7 s in active movement followed by
sinking for 8.6 s. The active movement occurred
for 46% of a 24 h period over the first four days
from hatch. In a fluvial system the larvae are
carried passively by currents usually in the middle
layer of the flowing water. At the postlarvae
stage the fish become stronger swimmers and swim
almost continuously at 30° to the horizontal near
the surface. They find areas of little flow and
cease to move downstream. Many populations of walleye and zander have larvae which migrate passively
from a fluvial to a lacustrine environment. The
latter environment will, as a rule, have a more
suitable food supply. Larvae of *Perca* and
Stizostedion species are positively phototactic.
One to eight week old walleye larvae (9 to 32 mm in
length) were attracted to the highest light intensity (7800 lx) used under experimental conditions
(Bulkowski & Meade 1983). Fish >8 weeks (32 to 40
mm) were attracted to the lowest light intensity (2
to 4 lx). Fingerlings of zander migrate downstream
over 24 h in turbid rivers but at dusk or in the
night in clear water.

Most studies of lake *Perca* species have shown
that after hatching the larvae become limnetic
(Whiteside, Swindoll & Doolittle 1985; Coles 1981;
Guma'a 1978c; Chirkova 1955). They are distributed
over the lake by currents controlled by wind
action. They remain pelagic until full development
of fins which varies according to water temperature. This may be June in Llyn Tegid, North Wales
(Coles 1981) or mid-July in Windermere, England
(Guma'a 1978c). The fingerlings then move inshore
to the littoral zone, in depths usually <3 m, and
form shoals. At the end of the summer (end of
August in Llyn Tegid and end of September in
Windermere) the perch move to deeper water to overwinter.

Walleye prolarvae in the lake are transported
by lake bottom currents. Older larvae are transported by surface currents generated by wind
action. In Oneida Lake, USA, Houde (1969a) found
that larval yellow perch and walleye were distri-

buted according to prevailing winds. Most of the
yellow perch were in 2 m depth but the walleye were
in 2 m depths when the winds were light and in 3 m
depth when winds were stronger (>5 m sec^{-1}).
Walleye are able to distribute themselves more
actively by this behaviour at an earlier stage,
within one to two weeks after hatching, than yellow
perch (Colby *et al.* 1979). In Lake Gogebic, USA,
walleye fry move inshore at a length of 25 mm in
late June or early July (Eschmeyer 1950). This
compares to a length of about 35 mm attained by
Oneida Lake walleye before they migrate to inshore
areas (Forney 1976).

Chapter 5

FOOD, FEEDING AND ENERGETICS

Introduction

Production in a biological system involves energy
supply, metabolism and growth (Figure 5.1). As
well as obtaining energy from its food, mainly from
lipids and proteins and sometimes lesser amounts
from carbohydrates, a fish must take in essential
vitamins and mineral salts (Ketola 1978; Milliken
1982; Chapter 10). This whole process is very complex and involves many interactions between the external environment and the internal system of the
fish (Figure 3.1). This chapter describes the type
of foods eaten, prey selection, food consumption,
digestion and allocation of energy intake. In many
cases there are scanty data for percids and some
details are based on other teleosts, in particular
salmonids.

Food Items in the Diet

Percids tend to be opportunistic feeders utilising available prey although in young fish prey
size may be limiting. The larvae of *Perca* and
Stizostedion species commence exogenous feeding on
immature copepods and cladocerans and sometimes
rotifers (Smyly 1952; Whiteside *et al.* 1985; Belyi
1972; Kukuradze 1974; Mathias & Li 1982). Guma'a
(1978c) found algal cells and ciliates in the
stomachs of larval perch (Figure 5.2). As the fish
increase in length they consume larger members of
the plankton. In a detailed study of the food of
perch fry in Windermere, England, Smyly (1952) observed that zooplankton were the dominant prey from
May to September. Some benthic organisms were
eaten after the fry had reached the age of one

94

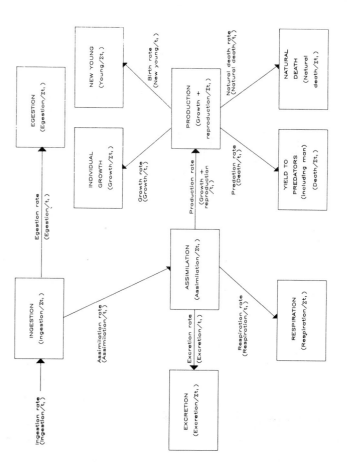

Figure 5.1: Diagram to illustrate metabolic pathways of ingested food.

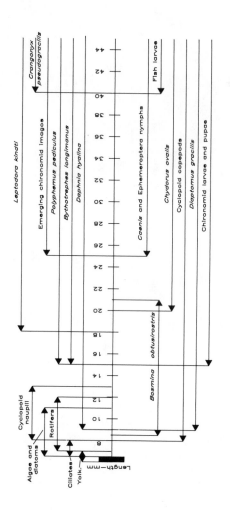

Figure 5.2: Prey items in the summer diet of young-of-the-year *Perca fluviatilis* from Windermere, England. (After Guma'a 1978c).

month and cannibalism by larger fry on smaller siblings took place only in mid-July. In ponds,
young walleye feeding progressed from zooplankton
to *Chaoborus* sp. Lichtenstein and Ephemeroptera
nymphs, then to *Gammarus lacustris* Sars and finally
to fish (Mathias & Li 1982). In many lakes young
walleye are piscivorous by midsummer. For example
Swenson and Smith (1976) found that by August in
Lake of the Woods, USA, walleye fry fed predominantly on young-of-the-year yellow perch.
Zander in their first year show similar trends to
walleye. Early in the summer the fry feed on large
Crustacea such as Mysidacea and on the young of
other fish (for example *Clupeonella* sp. Kessler and
roach, *Rutilus rutilus* (Linnaeus)).

Perca eat a wide range of organisms in all
stages of their life (Figure 5.3) and they are cannibalistic when young-of-the-year are abundant.
Slapton Ley, England, perch became piscivorous when
they were >150 mm in length (Craig 1974a).
Windermere, England, perch over a large size range
(32 to 311 g) fed on organisms ranging from zooplankton to perch fry, but there was little relationship betwen size of fish and the type of food
organism eaten (Craig 1978). Differences in prey

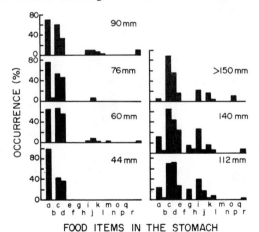

FOOD ITEMS IN THE STOMACH

Figure 5.3: The change in occurrence of prey items with change in length of
the predator, *Perca fluviatilis* from Slapton Ley, England (After Craig 1974a).
(a) = Plankton, (b) = *Chaoborus*, (c) = chironomid larvae (d) chironomid pupae,
(e) = *Asellus*, (f) = *Sialis*, (g) = tricopteran larvae, (h) = *Hydroporus*, (i) =
ephemeropteran nymphs, (j) = *Corixa*, (k) = others, (l) = insect remains, (m) =
Hirudinea, (n) = tubificids, (o) = *Perca*, (p) = *Scardinius/Rutilus*, (q) = fish
remains and (r) = empty.

97

can usually be explained more by seasonal vulnerability than by size of predator (Figure 5.4).

Juvenile and adult walleye consume a wide range of fish species depending on what is available. In many lakes invertebrates are also eaten by all size classes, especially in late spring and early summer. These include Ephemeroptera nymphs, chironomids, amphipods and leeches (Colby *et al.* 1979). In the central and northern areas of walleye distribution, yellow perch are the most common prey. Walleye food items in western Lake Erie changed seasonally but remained fairly consistent

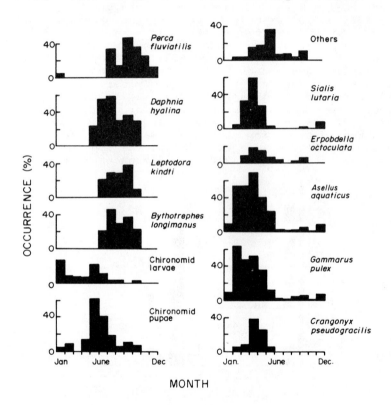

Figure 5.4: Diagram to illustrate the seasonal occurrence of various prey species in the diet of *Perca fluviatilis* from Windermere, England. (After Craig 1978).

from year to year (Knight, Margraf & Carline 1984). Walleye aged one year or older were almost entirely pisciverous. In the spring they fed on yearling emerald shiners, *Notropis atherinoides* Rafinesque, and spottail shiners, *N. hudsonius* (Clinton), but changed to young-of-the-year gizzard shad, *Dorosoma cepedianum* (LeSueur), and alewife, *Alosa pseudoharengus* (Wilson), in late July. In the autumn both shiners and clupeids were eaten. Spiny-rayed fish such as other percids and trout-perch, *Percopsis omiscomaycus* (Walbaum), were less important than shiners and clupeids in the diet. Invertebrates, mainly chironomids, were only found in the stomachs of one year old walleye, chiefly in the spring. From this study Knight *et al.* (1984) concluded that yellow perch were more opportunistic feeders than walleye in western Lake Erie, a view supported by others for these species generally in North America (Ney 1978).

Zander up to two years of age may continue to eat mysids and gammarids if these are abundant and forage fish are scarce. Zander eat mainly, shoaling fish including their own young (Biró 1973). Typical foods include roach, ruffe and perch. In the northern portion of the zander range, smelt, *Osmerus eperlanus* (Linnaeus), and vendace, *Coregonus albula* (Linnaeus), are fre-quently eaten while in the south gobiid fishes are preferred (Figure 5.5). Like other percids they exhibit extensive plasticity in prey selection. When smelt were low in abundance in the Baltic Sea the zander switched to the ruffe (Samokhvalova 1982). In the Danube Delta, zander consumed white bream, *Blicca bjoerkna* (Linnaeus), Crucian carp, *Carassius carassius* (Linnaeus), Gobiidae and rudd, *Scardinius erythrophthalmus* (Linnaeus), (Kukuradze 1974). They fed away from the Delta from May to August when the brackish water was diluted with fresh water and prey included anchovy, *Engraulis encrasicolus* (Linnaeus), sprat, *Sprattus sprattus* (Linnaeus), silverside, *Atherina presbyter* Valen-ciennes, and scad, *Trachurus trachurus* (Linnaeus).

Food Selection

Size and availability of prey are important in food selection but a more difficult factor to mea-sure is the acceptability of the prey. The size of the mouth gape in young percids determines the size of the prey eaten. Guma'a (1978c) related perch

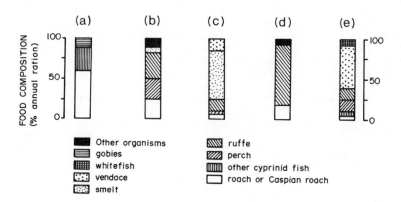

Figure 5.5: Prey items in the diet of *Stizostedion lucioperca* from four water bodies in the USSR. (a) = Volga Delta, (b) = Rybinsk Reservoir, (c) = Pskov-Chudskoy Lake with high smelt abundance, (d) = Pskov-Chudskoy Lake with low smelt abundance and (e) = Syam Lake. Food composition is expressed as a percentage of the annual ration. (After Popova & Sytina 1977).

mouth gape-height to the maximum carapace width of *Daphnia hyalina* Leydig found in the stomach of the perch from Windermere, England (Figure 5.6). Before August fry could not take *D. hyalina* with a carapace width greater than 0.8 mm, but from August onwards, rapid growth in the gape of perch enabled even the largest *D. hyalina* in the population (Figure 5.7) to be consumed. The perch selected the larger prey; the mean length of the prey in the perch stomachs was greater than the mean in the surrounding water. Before mid-July yellow perch were eating small (<1.3 mm length) *Daphnia pulicaria* Brandl in West Blue Lake, Canada. An increase in gape size allowed the yellow perch fry to eat all sizes of the cladocerans present after this time (Wong & Ward 1972) although these fry did not always eat the largest available cladocerans. Young yellow perch at a size of 30 to 35 mm in Oneida Lake, USA, shifted their preference for prey from *Diaptomus minutus* Lilljeborg to *Daphnia pulex* Leydig (Mills, Confer & Ready 1984). They were capable of consuming the largest *D. pulex* but did not preferentially select them.

Perch fry may show a preference for particular prey. Furnass (1979) demonstrated that as long as the preferred prey *Eudiaptomus gracilis* Sars were

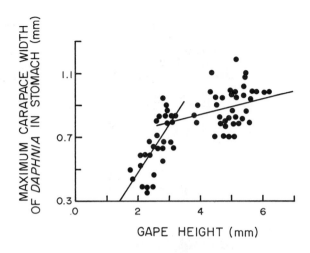

Figure 5.6: Plot of maximum carapace width of *Daphnia hyalina* and gape height of young-of-the-year *Perca fluviatilis* from Windermere, England. (After Guma'a 1978c).

visible, the perch would continue to strike at these species even though another prey species *Daphnia hyalina var galatea* Sars of similar size was more abundant. Movement of the prey is an important factor in the feeding of both *Perca* and *Stizostedion* species. Under experimental conditions both perch and walleye strike at glass containers holding live food organisms (Furnass 1979; Rottiers & Lemm 1985). Both species also respond to certain odours in the water. For example walleye reacts positively to washings from live *Daphnia* sp. Müller and *Artemia* sp. Leach (Rottiers & Lemm 1985).

Perch and yellow perch are shoaling predators although some become ambush predators living a solitary life and having a home range. They are active in the daytime. In the early morning the stomachs of demersal young-of-the-year yellow perch in Oneida Lake, USA, were empty (Noble 1972). The fish then fed on zooplankton and the stomachs quickly filled. The stomachs remained full until about 1600 h when the volume of stomach contents declined. Feeding can be summarised as a bell-shaped curve in which the stomach was fullest from 1200 to 1600 h (Figure 5.8). For most of the year,

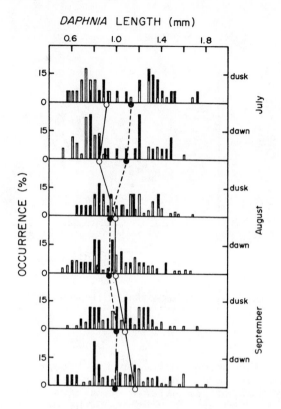

Figure 5.7: The relationship between the body length of *Daphnia hyalina* eaten by young-of-the-year *Perca fluviatilis* □ and that of the plankton ■ from Windermere, England. The solid and broken lines represent the mean lengths of *D. hyalina* in perch stomachs (o) and in the plankton (●) respectively. (Afer Guma'a 1978c).

peaks of activity of adult *Perca* occur at sunrise and sunset (Craig 1977b; Eriksson 1978; Helfman 1979; Hubert & Sandheinrich 1983). There are some indications that maximum feeding coincides with these peaks although there is so much variⁿ ability that this is not easy to establish (Figure 5.9). At any point in time during the day the stomach contents of individuals within a sample of Windermere perch could range from being empty to full (Craig 1978). A number of regression equations were determined for each state of stomach fullness apart from those which were empty (using a scale from 1 to 4, where 4 was full). These equations related the total dry weight of the stomach contents to the total wet weight of the fish. By determining the proportion of stomach fullness for

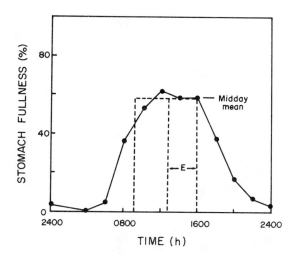

Figure 5.8: The mean daily feeding period of young-of-the-year *Perca flavescens* from Oneida Lake, USA. E = stomach evacuation time: the time taken for a particle of food to pass through the stomach regardless of its type and amount of food already in the stomach. (After Noble 1972).

individuals in the sample population, it was possible to determine the mean weight of stomach contents for a given length of fish at three-hour intervals (Figure 5.10). Although the perch population fed throughout the day, maximum intake occurred in the late afternoon or evening in most of the months of the year. A small peak occurred in the early morning. Similar patterns of morning and evening feeding have been observed in different lakes for both perch and yellow perch (Thorpe 1977; Manteifel, Girsa, Leshcheva & Pavlov 1965; Ward & Robinson 1974). During the night, both species remain relatively inactive on the lake floor in shallow water (Hasler & Villemonte 1953; Scott 1955; Helfman 1979). At dawn they move offshore and feed in the open water on plankton and fish and some will feed on the benthos. During the winter *Perca* normally stay in deep water although they continue to capture some benthic prey (Figure 5.4) and may make some inshore movements to capture these. *Perca* in early stages are strongly positively phototactic (Chapter 4). A light shown over the water at night in early July at Windermere, England, attracted large numbers of perch fry. This response would enable the fry to feed con-

103

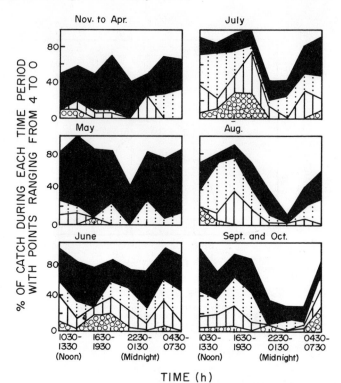

Figure 5.9: Diagram to illustrate stomach "fullness" of adult *Perca fluviatilis* at time intervals through 24 h for each month of the year from Windermere, England. Coefficients of stomach fullness are: ▣ = 4 (full), ▥ = 3, ▦ = 2, ■ = 1 and □ = 0 (empty). (After Craig 1978).

tinually during the day on zooplankton. Older perch become more sensitive to high light intensity (Figure 6.12) and confine their feeding activities to dawn and dusk (Chapter 6).

The shoaling of *Perca* may aid them in prey capture. If a prey fish species can swim as fast as the predator, in an initial attack the prey will often escape, but the prey has a good chance of swimming into another member of the shoal. This type of behaviour among a group of perch has been observed in aquaria by Deelder (1951) who used roach as prey.

Walleye normally feed from the evening until the early morning but will feed in the daytime, especially during the winter when food consumption is low. Maximum feeding is apparently associated with

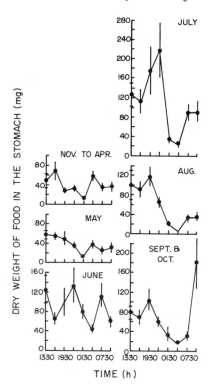

Figure 5.10: Plot of dry weight of food (with 95% confidence limits) in the stomachs of adult *Perca fluviatilis* at time intervals through 24 h for each month of the year, from Windermere, England. (After Craig 1978).

optimum light intensity and occurs towards the early morning (Colby *et al*. 1979). In turbid lakes, walleye will continue to feed through the day (Ryder 1977). Similarly, feeding occurs in daytime during winter if light is reduced. Ryder (1977) studied the response of walleye to light (surface illumination) by recording the number of fish caught by angling. He found an inverse relationship between catch per unit effort and surface illumination (Figure 5.11). Walleye may actively select optimum conditions of light. Scherer (1976) demonstrated that walleye positioned themselves in aquaria in an inverse relationship to the light intensity. At 2 lx they were near the top and at 200 lx they were at the bottom of the tank. Underwater SCUBA observations show that

during the day walleye inhabit turbid regions of
the lake but in clear water areas they remain near
the bottom and find some physical shelter so that
the ambient light level is reduced (Ryder 1977).
The development of the tapetum lucidium (Chapter 2)
in *Stizostedion* species has enabled this group to
utilise dim light conditions. Young-of-the-year
walleye like *Perca* are positively phototactic
enabling them to feed during the day on zooplankton. This positive reaction to light lasts
from hatching to the postlarvae phase and then pro-
gresses gradually with age to a negative reaction
(Chapter 4). This response is an adaptation to
their change in feeding habits. Walleye primarily
hunt by vision but hearing, taste and smell
probably also play a part in prey detection. Walleye normally hunt near the bottom and may enter
shallow water to feed. They feed over macrophyte
beds or rocky areas. Walleye shoal and form large
schools even when they become piscivorous and this
behaviour continues as adults. Zander also are
shoaling as young fish when they feed on plankton
but as they become piscivorous they are solitary
(Woynarovich 1962).

Zander hunt prey in the open water, on the

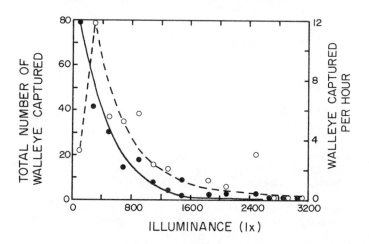

Figure 5.11: The relationships between total number of *Stizostedion vitreum*
caught by angling at dusk ● and catch per hour o with surface illumination
during the open-water period from Shebandowan Lake, Canada. (After Ryder
1977).

bottom and amongst vegetation. Like walleye they feed at low light intensities, mainly during twilight periods. The tapetum lucidum of zander is well developed although the tapetal area is not as extensive as in walleye. Thus the zander are less well adapted to water of high turbidity than the walleye but they can feed more easily during the daytime at higher levels of illumination (Jovanovic 1970). In Lake Ladoga, USSR, which has clear water, zander ingested most prey in the early morning (0500-0600 h) from June to August (Fedorova & Drozzhina 1982). In September two peaks of feeding activity occurred, 2100-2200 h and 0500-0600 h. There was virtually no feeding during the day due to strong light intensity and very little during the middle of the night when there was insufficient light.

After chasing their prey, walleye and zander seize them sideways. The prey fish is turned around so that it can be swallowed head first by walleye (Colby *et al.* 1979) and tail first by zander (Neuhaus 1934; Steffens 1960). Cannibalistic walleye fry also tend to try to swallow their siblings tail first (Mathias & Li 1982).

In teleosts, the mechanics of feeding based on hydrodynamic principles have been extensively studied (Osse 1969; Elshoud-Oldenhave 1979; Van Leeuwen & Müller 1984a; 1984b; Müller & Osse 1984). When a perch senses the presence of prey it erects its dorsal spines and gently swims towards the prey, and when close the prey is captured (Osse 1969). As the prey is approached the buccal and opercular cavities of the perch are greatly enlarged and the mouth is opened. This produces a considerable localised reduction in water pressure which lessens the speed of the prey and increases the speed of the predator. This 'suction' causes water surrounding the prey to be drawn into the enlarged mouth. Osse (1969) describes the sequence of head expansion as follows. Lowering of the lower jaw is combined with dorsal movements of the opercula. There is caudal movement of the shoulder girdle, dorsal movement of the neurocranium, abduction of the suspensoria and protrusion of the upper jaw (Chapter 2). This opening movement takes about 0.04 to 0.15 s. For adult perch (250-300 mm) at 0.04 s the volume of water sucked into the mouth is 500 cm^3 at a velocity of 200 $cm\ s^{-1}$. If the prey is separated from the predator by a distance equal to or less than the latter's head length it will be sucked in by the predator. The head returns to normal shape more slowly than during pre-feeding expansion. The mouth is closed during this phase, although the upper jaw still protrudes and there are ventral movements of the opercula. Adduction of the suspensora occurs and the opercula start to adduct. The branchiostegal rays move dorsally and the neurocranium moves ventrally into its normal position. Adduction of the gill covers and of the suspensoria continues, the hyoid symphysis moves rostrally and the angle between the hyoid bars diminishes. The symphysis of the pectoral girdle moves dorsally and rostrally. Eventually, the adduction of the gill covers and suspensoria is complete. During these later stages the pectoral fins are brought forward, probably to stabilise the fish's position. If the prey is small, this cycle is sufficient to bring the prey to the oesophagus. If the prey is large the cycle may be repeated several times but the amplitude is reduced in each subsequent cycle. The prey is prevented from escaping by teeth in the mouth and on the branchial arches and pharynogobranchial plates (Table 2.2) (Osse 1969).

The zander uses both 'suction' and grasping to capture its prey (Elshoud-Oldenhave 1979). As it approaches the prey it accelerates and when the prey is within reach, it opens its mouth and seizes the prey. If the food particle is small it is sucked in. A larger particle is drawn towards the buccal cavity and is normally grasped crosswise. It is turned loose by the zander and drawn in by reduced pressure in the mouth and buccal cavity caused by rapid expansion of the head. The expansion of the head involves 24 muscles of the head including the branchial basket, and the anterior body muscles (Figure 2.4 illustrates the head muscles of the perch). The main muscular action in head expansion involves the epaxial and hypaxial body muscles which bring about movements of the neurocranium, pectoral girdle and hyoid arch (Elshoud-Oldenhave 1979). The neurocranium can be moved in a number of directions so that the 'suction' can be aimed toward the prey. Head muscles regulate head expansion and contraction. The successful capture of prey depends on predator velocity and the timing of head enlargement.

Food Consumption

The amount of food eaten by percids is controlled by temperature, prey density, physiological state of the fish and other factors. A number of methods have been used to calculate daily ration for percids in various bodies of water. The method described below is given in some detail since it quantifies food intake more precisely than the other methods. The appetite of a perch is dependent on the quantity of prey already in its stomach and intestines. This is determined by the rate of gastric evacuation, the time taken for a given weight of food to pass through the fish's stomach. This rate is usually measured from laboratory experiments and for many fish species including perch (Griffiths 1976; Thorpe 1977; Persson 1981) the rate is exponential (Figure 5.12). The formula to describe the amount of matter in a fish's stomach is given by:

$$Y_X = Y_O e^{-RX}$$

where X is time (h), Y_O is the weight of a meal (mg), Y_X is weight of food present in the

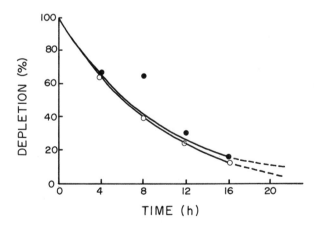

Figure 5.12: The gastric evacuation rate of *Gobiomorphus cotidanus* from *Perca fluviatilis* stomachs at 17°C. Percentage depletion is plotted with time. (●) Perch were force fed and (o) perch were voluntarily fed. (After Griffiths 1976).

stomach (mg) at time X and R is the instantaneous rate of gastric evacuation.

The rate (R) is dependent on temperature (T, °C) and the relationship between the R and T is usually positively exponential (Figure 5.13):

$$R = ae^{bT}$$

where a and b are constants.

Different types of invertebrate prey do not appear to affect the rate of gastric evacuation in perch. This was tested by Persson (1979) using *Gammarus pulex* (Linnaeus), *Chaoborus* sp., chironomids and zooplankton as prey. In a later experiment, Persson (1981) found that the rate of gastric evacuation of prey such as fish larvae was slower than that of the invertebrates. Generally meal size, meal frequency and predator size do not affect the rates of gastric evacuation. However, Persson (1981) found the first phase of digestion was slower for fish eaten when perch were almost satiated. The ration at which this occurred was lower for smaller perch. Swenson and Smith (1973) applied linear models to their walleye data from gastric evacuation experiments. Meal size affected

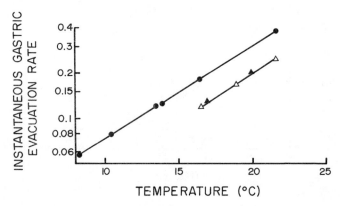

Figure 5.13: Semi-log plot of instantaneous gastric evacuation rate and temperature for *Perca fluviatilis* fed *Gammarus pulex* (●) and fish larvae (▲). (●) and (▲) are single values and (△) are geometric means. (After Persson 1981).

the rate. At small meal sizes (<10 mg g^{-1} wet weight of predator) the rate appeared to fit the exponential model. At greater meal sizes (>10 mg g^{-1} fish wet weight) a linear model applied. When walleye were nearly satiated, the first part of digestion took longer than when the stomachs were only partly filled.

If the rate of gastric evacuation is exponential and the rate of food consumption is constant, then the amount of food consumed in t hours (C_t) is given by

$$C_t = \frac{(S_t - S_o e^{-Rt})\ Rt}{1 - e^{-Rt}} \qquad \text{Equation 5.1}$$

where S_o and S_t are the stomach contents at the start and end of sampling respectively (Elliott & Persson 1978; Craig 1979). Modifications to this equation were made by Craig (1978). Samples were taken at fixed time intervals (three hours) over 24 h so that S_o, S_t in equation 5.1 are estimated by S_0 and S_1 for the first sampling interval, S_1, S_2 for the second interval and up to S_{m-1} and S_m for the last sampling interval. If the food in the stomach is the same at the beginning and end of the 24 h period so that $S_o = S_m$, daily food consumption (ΣC_t) is then given by

$$\Sigma C_t = \frac{Rt}{1 - e^{-Rt}} \cdot \sum_{i=1}^{i=m} S_i (1 - e^{-Rt})$$

Therefore

$$\Sigma C_t = R t_m \overline{S}$$

where $\overline{S} = \dfrac{\Sigma S_i}{m}$

and in 24 h

$$\Sigma C_t = 24\ \overline{S}R \qquad \text{Equation 5.2}$$

Craig (1978) used Equation 5.2 to calculate the daily consumption of perch for each month in Windermere, England. Energy intake values (C_t, joules day^{-1}) for male perch are listed in Table 5.1.

Prey density affects food consumption. In a laboratory study on larval perch and zander, Kudrinskaya (1970) found a reduction of zooplankton prey from densities of 3.0-6.0 mg l^{-1} to 0.1-0.5 mg l^{-1} at 19.3°C caused 70% of the larvae to cease feeding and predator food consumption was reduced by a factor of 3 for perch and 2.6 for zander larvae. A reduction in temperature to 16.0°C increased the number of non-feeding fish to 80-90% and also reduced food consumption at all levels of prey density. Swenson and Smith (1976) found that food consumption of adult walleye increased with density of prey up to about a density of 400 mg m^{-3} when it levelled off at 3% of body weight.

Most of the measurements of daily food consumption of percids have been recorded as percentages of body weights. These are not very precise as the proportion of food intake will decrease as fish weight increases. The following examples give only approximate consumption values but are useful in making comparisons.

Table 5.1: Energy equations for 150 g male *Perca fluviatilis* in Windermere, England, where Q_c = energy of consumed food calculated from the components which are Q_w = energy lost from egestion and excretion, Q_r = energy of resting metabolism, Q_a = energy expended in activity, Q_g soma = energy changes in the soma and Q_g gonad = energy changes in the gonad. Also given are energy values for consumption based on field measurements Q_{cst} and calculated by Equation 5.2 (see text). All values are in joules and calculated on a daily (24 h) basis. (Modified from Craig 1978).

Month	Q_{cst}	Q_c	Q_w	Q_r	Q_a	$Q_{g soma}$	Q_g gonad
Nov-April	5785	5590	1118	2384	2384	− 201	− 95
May	4581	8694	1739	3716	3716	247	−724
June	11456	9350	1870	5441	5441	−3063	−339
July	32501	24845	4969	6794	6794	6623	−335
August	15141	19046	3809	8334	8334	−1456	25
Sept-Oct	10404	14439	2888	5547	5547	−466	923

As the foregoing discussion implies, the daily consumption of juvenile fish is higher than that of adults. In Oneida Lake, USA, yellow perch fry consumed from 14 to 43% of their body weight per day (Mills & Forney 1981) during June and July when they fed almost exclusively on *Daphnia pulex*. In the Mozhaisky and Uchinsky reservoirs, USSR, perch fry fed on a daily ration of 12 to 16% body weight in June when *Daphnia* were the chief prey item (Spanovskaya & Grygorash 1977). Many of the studies on both adult perch and yellow perch have shown that these two species exhibit similar seasonal trends in daily food intake. In the study already described for Windermere (Craig 1978), daily food intake per body weight rose from 0.7% in May to 5.2% in July and declined to 2.4% in August and 1.6% in September and October. The perch of Loch Leven, Scotland consumed 6.5% in June and July declining to 3.2% in September (Thorpe 1977). Three year old perch from Sövdeborgssjön, Sweden, had a maximum food intake of 3% body weight in July declining to 0.1% in November (Persson 1983a). In two small lakes further north in Sweden, Nyberg (1979) found the highest percentages (4-6%) from May to August falling to 1% in September. Yellow perch in Lake Memphremagog on the Canada and USA border, consumed 6.1% of their body weight in July which then declined to 3.7% in August, 1.6% in September and 2.4% in October (Nakashima & Leggett 1978).

Food consumption of walleye is usually greatest in the autumn. In Lake of the Woods, USA, walleye consumed 1% of their body weight in June, 2% in July and 3% in August and September. Although the water temperatures were the same in June and September, more food was available in the latter month (Swenson & Smith 1973).

Zander in the Volga Delta had the highest food intake in April (Orlova 1976), amounting to 2.6% body weight. Consumption then declined to about 0.5% during the summer.

Digestion

The breakdown of food consumed by the fish takes place in a number of stages in the stomach and along the intestine. The prey of percids tend to be swallowed whole. Acid gastric fluids are secreted in the stomach and in perch pH of stomach fluids ranges from 3.0 to 5.0 (Fish 1960). The

acidity increases after food intake. Several proteases are present in the gastric fluids, the most
important being pepsin. This is secreted by the
gastric gland cells (Chapter 2) in the form of pep-
sinogen which is activated in an acid environment
(Fänge & Grove 1979).

Little is known about the composition of pancreatic secretions in the intestine. They contain
enzymes involved in the digestion of proteins, carbohydrates, fat, and nucleotides and probably bi-
carbonates to neutralise acids entering the intestine (Fänge & Grove 1979). Many of the intestinal
enzymes are most active at a neutral or slightly
alkaline pH. Proteases from the pancreas include
trypsin, chymotrypsin, elastase and carboxypepti-
dase. Amylase has been isolated from the diffuse
pancreas of perch (Fish 1960). Chitinase is
probably produced in *Perca* species because these
fish feed extensively on insect larvae and
Crustacea. This chitinase will come mainly from
the pancreas although some may be produced by
bacteria in the intestine. The pancreas is
probably also the main source of lipases.

Secretions into the intestines from the gall
bladder are similar to those in mammals. Bile contains bile salts, cholesterol, phospholipids, bile
pigments, glycoproteins, organic anions and inorganic ions (Fänge & Grove 1979). The secretion
is weakly alkaline and has a high sodium and a low
chloride concentration.

Some enzymes are secreted by the brush border
cells of the intestinal epithelium although most
enzyme activity is brought about by secretions from
the pancreas. Enzymes thought to be produced by
the intestinal mucosa include aminopeptidases, di-
and tripeptidases, acid and alkaline nucleosidases,
polynucleotidases, lecithinase, lipase and other
esterases and various carbohydrate digesting
enzymes (Fange & Grove 1979). Activity of enzymes
in the intestinal lumen is low especially in the
middle and posterior regions and most breakdown
occurs at the intestinal mucosa brush border. α
amylase, which works at an optimum pH of 6.7 (Fish
1960), is less active and probably less abundant in
perch and zander intestine than more omnivorous
species. Kuzmina (1984a) found the enzyme to be
more active in the intestinal mucosa (54-59%) than
in the gut lumen of zander but there was no significant difference in activity between the two areas
in perch. Significantly more maltase activity
(66-77%) was found in extracts of mucosa than in

the luminal fluid of perch and saccharase was found
to be active only in extracts from the intestinal
mucosa of perch.

Kuzmina (1984b) discovered that the phosphatase activity from the intestinal mucosa of zander
had two pH optima (5.0 and 9.0-10.0) at 0° and
20°C. When the seasonal activity of zander alkaline phosphates was examined, Gelman, Mokady and
Cogan (1984) found that it was much higher in the
summer than in the winter and the thermal stability
of the enzyme declined in the winter.

Absorption in the intestine has already been
discussed in Chapter 2. Absorption is carried out
by both diffusion and active transport. Amino
acids are absorbed against a concentration gradient
and some proteins and peptides are absorbed by
pinocytosis in the middle section of the intestine. Fats are absorbed by epithelial cells in the
anterior part of the intestine including in perch,
mucosal cells of the pyloric caeca (Jansson &
Olsson 1960).

Energetics

Food consumption of perch, yellow perch, walleye and zander have aleady been described for
field situations. The basic equation which
summarises the fate of the energy intake is as
follows:

$$C = R + \Delta B + F + U \qquad \text{Equation 5.3}$$

where in energy units, C=food consumption,
R=metabolism, ΔB=growth, F=egested loss and
U=excreted loss. R may be divided up into a number
of components: $R = R_s + R_a + R_d$, where R_s = the
energy used for standard metabolism in a resting
non-feeding fish, R_a = the energy used in activity,
such as swimming and R_d = the energy used in the
digestion, movement and deposition of food
materials including specific dynamic action.
Specific dynamic action is the energy released from
the hydrolysis of the peptide bonds between amino
acids of proteins and other conversion processes.

The most complete studies on fish energetics
have been performed on salmonids (Elliott 1979),
but few data exist for percids. If for con-
venience, we assume similar processes for teleosts
as a whole, some general principles derived from
salmonids can be extrapolated to percids. This was
was the approach taken by Kitchell, Stewart and
Weininger (1977) in their paper on yellow perch and

walleye. They used data derived by Solomon and
Brafield (1972) for perch and Kelso (1972) and
Swenson and Smith (1973) for walleye as a basis and
applied other data, including those from other species especially salmonids (Brett 1971; Brett,
Shelbourn & Shoop 1969; Elliott 1976a; 1976b) to
fill in gaps necessary for their model.

A few basic principles in energetics may make
the rest of this chapter more understandable. The
satiation ration (C_{max}) can be related to fish
weight (W) and temperature (T) by:

$$C_{max} = aW^{b_1} e^{b_2 T}$$

where a, b_1 and b_2 are constants in certain
temperature ranges (Elliott 1975a;b;c).

The maintenance energy intake (C_{main}) allows a
fish to maintain its body weight ($\Delta B=0$). When the
energy intake is below C_{main}, then ΔB is negative.
The range where ΔB is positive between C_{main} and
C_{max}, is the 'scope for growth' or 'anabolic
scope'. The optimum energy intake (C_{opt}) produces
the greatest increase in the energy content of the
fish for the least intake. In this situation the
gross efficiency ($\Delta B/C$) is maximised. Net
efficiency can be described by $\Delta B/(C-C_{main})$.
This is the increase in energy or growth derived
from excess energy over that required for
maintenance. As for C_{max}, both C_{main} and C_{opt} are
affected by fish weight and temperature. In the
model produced by Kitchell *et al.* (1977)
temperatures used in the simulations were taken
from Hokanson (1977). These are given in Table
5.2. The specific dynamic action was considered to
remain constant at 15% of the food consumed.

Faeces contain small quantities of secretions
from the fish and some nitrogenous waste products
as well as undigested food. Solomon and Brafield
(1972) kept perch at a fixed temperature (14°C) and
found that the percentage loss in faeces increased
with ration increase. Elliott (1976b) demonstrated
that percentage loss decreases with increase in
temperature in the brown trout *(Salmo trutta*
Linnaeus). Faecal loss was also affected by fish
size but when faecal loss was expressed as a proportion of fish size, it remained fairly constant
for different sized fish. Simulating this in the
model for percids produced a curve which is shown
in Figure 5.14. The main excretory product of
teleosts is ammonia lost through the gills. Other

Table 5.2: Optimum and maximum temperatures (°C) for consumption and respiration for young-of-the-year, juvenile and adult *Perca flavescens*. Derived from Hokanson (1977) and utilised in the bioenergetics model of Kitchell *et al.* (1977).

		T(°C)
Optimum temperature for consumption	Young of the year	29
	Juveniles and adults	23
Maximum temperature for consumption	Young of the year	32
	Juveniles and aduts	28
Optimum temperature for standard respiration	Young of the year	32
	Juveniles and adults	28
Maximum temperature for standard respiration	Young of the year	35
	Juveniles and adults	33

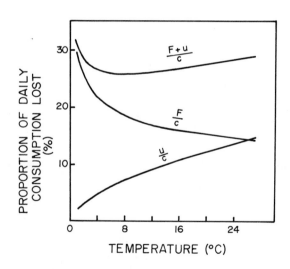

Figure 5.14: The proportions of consumed food egested (F/C) and excreted (U/C) and their sums ((F+U)/C) in relation to temperature for *Perca flavescens*. (After Kitchell *et al.* 1977).

excretory products include urea, uric acid, crea-
tine, creatinine, amines and amino acids (Elliott
1979) but in energetic terms losses from these products are minimal. Elliott found that losses from
excretory products increased with fish size, water
temperature and ration size. However like egestion, the proportion of the daily ration lost in
excretion remains faily constant. The simulation
for percids is given in Figure 5.14. The net loss
from both egestion and excretion remains fairly
constant at 26-32%.

The total energy for metabolism is sometimes
directly measured by holding fish in respirometers
and recording oxygen uptake. In teleosts, the
metabolism is affected by fish size (W) and water
temperature. Oxygen consumption (Q) is usually
derived from:

$$Q = aW^b$$

where a is dependent on temperature and b is a constant with a value of about 0.8 (Winberg 1956).

The model of Kitchell *et al*. (1977) shows
the highest maintenance values for yellow perch of
all sizes at 27°C (Figure 5.15). A more difficult
energy expenditure to measure is that used in
activity (R_a). The best method might be to use
telemetry on free living percids. Winberg (1956)
made the assumption that energy used by fish in
activity was roughly equal to that used in resting
metabolism $(R_a = R_s)$. It is surprising that although this is a perilous assumption it is consistent with many calculated energy budgets (Elliott
1979). The model of Kitchell *et al*. (1977) was
also used to simulate specific growth rates which
were related to water temperature and ration size.
These are given in Figure 5.16 for a 10 g yellow
perch. Growth rates decline with increasing
temperatures at all ration levels. Maintenance
rations (g g^{-1} day^{-1}) range from 1% at 8°C to 4% at
27°C. The figure also shows the effect of temperature and ration size on gross and net efficiency.
Using the highest rations the gross efficiency exceed 45% in the temperature range 4-20°C. In a
field situation, young-of-the-year yellow perch in
Oneida Lake, USA, had a gross conversion efficiency
of 27% (Mills & Forney 1981). The simulated model
illustrates that net efficiency exceeds 64% in the
yellow perch at low ration levels and temperatures
below 10°C.

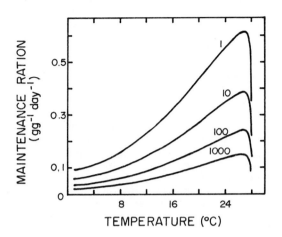

Figure 5.15: The relationship between estimated maintenance rations for four weights (1-1,000 g) of *Perca flavescens* and temperature. (After Kitchell *et al.* 1977).

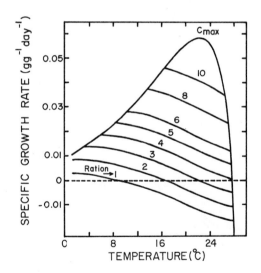

Figure 5.16: Changes in specific growth rate of a 10 g *Perca flavescens* as functions of temperature and ration level (expressed as percentage body weight ranging from one percent to maximum, C_{max}). (After Kitchell *et al.* 1977).

Kitchell *et al.* (1977) illustrate how well the model simulates growth by comparing the derivations from temperature data for Lake Erie with observed growth data (Figure 5.17). The model serves a useful purpose not only in deriving values for an energy budget for percids but also highlighting areas where research is urgently required. Further research would result in more empirical data and thus fewer assumptions would need to be made.

The energy that is available for growth can be used to increase the energy content of the soma or for gonad development in mature fish (Chapters 3 and 4). As perch in Windermere, England, get older, a greater proportion of available energy is directed towards gonad development (Craig unpublished data). Most studies on energetics have been performed on immature fish because the growth component of the energy budget is easy to determine as a result of high somatic growth rates. However, Craig (1978) calculated the energy budgets for large mature perch and details are given in Table 5.1 for male Windermere perch. Consumption values are based on field data already described earlier in the chapter (C_{st}) and summation of the com-

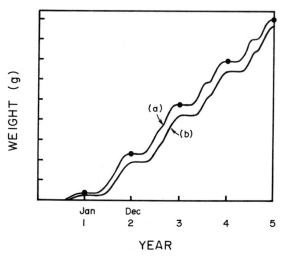

Figure 5.17: Simulated growth of *Perca flavescens* for (a) western and (b) eastern Lake Erie, USA and Canada, based on the bioenergetics model of Kitchell *et al.* (1977). (●) are observed values.

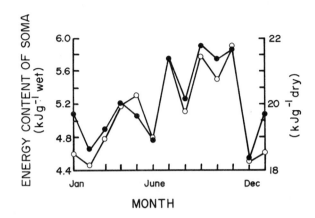

Figure 5.18: The seasonal energy content of wet (●) and dry (o) tissues of the soma (body minus gonads) of 225 mm male *Perca fluviatilis* from Windermere, England. (After Craig 1977a).

ponents of the budget (C). There was no significant difference (P>0.05) between these two values and they are reasonably similar. This is reassuring because of the assumptions and approximations which had to be made in their derivation. In male and female perch, energy was stored in the soma in July. Energy was transferred to the testes in the late summer and autumn and to the ovary during the winter. Spawning behaviour may have accounted for the large amount of energy lost in June from the male soma (it was lost through Q_a).

The energy value of the tissues does not remain constant but varies with energy intake and requirements of the fish. Perch fed on fish have a higher calorific value per unit weight than those fed on invertebrates (Jezierska 1974). The energy content of perch tissue in Windermere improves during the period of increased feeding in July, declines in August and improves again during the autumn before it declines once again in the winter (Figure 5.18). Care should always be taken in converting weights to energy values as the conversion factor will not always remain constant because of these seasonal changes.

Chapter 6

SOME PHYSIOLOGICAL PROCESSES AND MOVEMENTS

Ionic and Water Balance

Percids are essentially fresh water fish although
they venture into brackish waters. When in fresh
water the blood and body fluids are hypertonic to
the external medium. That is they contain a greater concentration of ions and a greater osmotic
pressure than the surrounding medium. The osmotic
and ion concentration gradient favours the influx
of water and the loss of inorganic salts. In
brackish water exceeding 10‰ the reverse occurs,
the body fluids are hypotonic to the surrounding
medium and without control, there is a loss in
water and a gain in inorganic salts. The control
is brought about mainly by action of gills and kidneys (Figure 6.1). Since the gills are concerned
with oxygen uptake from the water to the blood they
must have a large surface area. This large area
also provides a surface for water and ion transfer.
There may be a 'trade-off' between maximum permeability to oxygen and minimum fluxes of water and
ions. The epithelium of the gill contains a respiratory component, mainly the secondary lamellae,
and a non-respiratory epithelium containing
chloride cells. The former makes up 96% of the
epithelium surface area compared to 4% for the
latter (Isaia 1984). Water fluxes take place
through the respiratory cells. Over 90% of diffu-
sional water exchange takes place at the gill surface. The non-respiratory epithelium provides a
surface for ion transfer. The number of chloride
cells in the epithelium increase with increase in
salinity of the external environment. These
chloride cells contain numerous mitochondria and a
well developed endoplasmic reticulum. They are
concerned with the regulation of salt uptake either

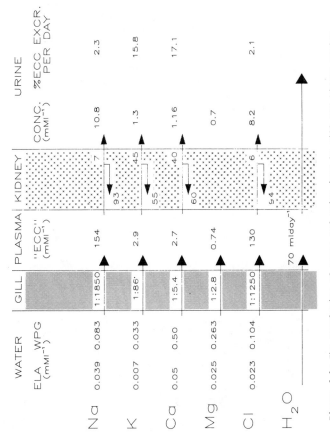

Figure 6.1: The regulation of water and major ions by gill and kidney action of a fresh water teleost. Water intake is for 1,000 g fish. Fish were held in Experimental Lakes Area (ELA) or Winnipeg (Wpg), (Canada), water. ECC = extra cellular compartment. (Data kindly provided by M. Giles).

123

in taking up or secreting ions and use energy in the process. The energy required for osmo-regulation is not clearly understood. In some teleosts held in isosmotic solutions oxygen con-sumption has been shown to be reduced (Rao 1968; Farmer & Beamish 1969). In fresh water the gills absorb Na^+ and Cl^- replacing those lost by renal action. Sodium ions are exchanged with ammonium or hydrogen ions and chloride ions with bicarbonate ions (Figure 6.2) (Payan, Girard & Mayer-Gostan 1984). Transfer is linked to acid-base equilibrium and elimination of ammonium from deamination of proteins. The ionic transfer across membranes of Na^+, K^+ and Ca^{2+} involves ATPases. Calcium regulates H^+ uptake and the resulting loss in Na^+. In acid water Na^+ is lost. The kidneys can modify the glomerular

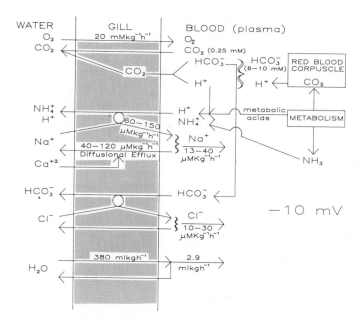

Figure 6.2: The major rates of flux of water and ions across the gill membrane of a fresh water teleost and mechanisms for acid-base regulation of products from body metabolism. (Data kindly provided by M. Giles).

filtrate depending on the external medium (Figure 6.3). The kidney conserves filtered electrolytes. It reabsorbs Na^+ and Cl^- ions from the plasma ultrafiltrate. The urine of fresh water fish is dilute and nearly free of Na^+ and Cl^- (Figure 6.1) (Hickman & Trump 1969). In fresh water the primary role of the kidney is to retain electrolytes while excreting the net osmotic gain of water via production of a dilute hypotonic urine. In brackish water urine production is much reduced. The gut may be involved to a lesser extent in water and ion exchange and some salts may be lost in the faeces. Percids are thought to drink little water in contrast to many marine fish. Water and ion transfer are influenced by hormones. These are produced principally by the pituitary and head kidney.

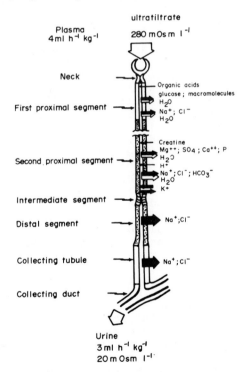

Figure 6.3: The structure and function of a fresh water teleost nephron. Solid arrows indicate active and open arrows passive movements. The width of the arrows is proportional to the rate of movement of substances across the tubular epithelium. (After Hickman & Trump 1969).

Hypophysectomy of fresh water fish reduces the rate of water turnover which is restored with prolactin injection (Rankin & Bolis 1984). Paralactin, an equivalent to prolactin of mammals, was isolated in cyprinodont fish by Ball (1969). In the head kidney (Chapter 2) interrenal tissue contains corticosteroid producing cells. Cortisol increases water fluxes and its production is controlled by pituitary adrenocorticotrophic hormone. The head kidney also contains chromaffin tissue consisting of catecholamine producing cells. The production of adrenaline from this tissue causes an increase in oxygen uptake and a disequilibrium effect on water balance. The result is an increase in gill permeability to water.

Perca living in water with a high sodium ion concentration tend to have a higher concentration of Na^+ in their blood serum compared to *Perca* living in waters with lower concentrations of sodium ions. The Volga River has a sodium concentration of 1.07 (meq) l^{-1} and the blood serum of perch living in the river contains sodium ions at 150 ± 8 (meq) l^{-1}. In Lake Baikal, USSR, where the sodium concentration is 0.18 (meq) l^{-1} the sodium in the blood serum of the resident perch amounts to 114 ± 6 (meq) l^{-1} (Natochin & Lavrova 1974). Experiments were conducted by Lutz (1972) to test the tolerance of perch to increasing concentrations of salinity. The results of his experiments, in which he subjected the perch to concentrations ranging from fresh water to 15‰ salinity, half the concentration of seawater, and measured the concentrations of major inorganic ions in the blood plasma and muscle are given in Table 6.1. Perch survived well in concentrations up to and including 10‰ sea water concentration (most fresh water fish are isotonic at this concentration) but did not survive 15‰ sea water. All ion levels increased in the blood plasma at the 15‰ concentration level and there was a large invasion of sodium and chloride ions into the muscle. The whole body lost water although the liver remained fairly resistant to water loss and chloride ion invasion. The water content of the muscle was significantly lower than that of perch held in fresh water. In the Aral Sea, perch inhabit waters with a salinity of 10‰ (Letichevskii 1946) and in prairie saline lakes in Manitoba, Canada, yellow perch live in salinities of 10.3‰ (Driver & Garside 1966). *Perca* are able to live in other areas where the salinity does not exceed about 10‰. This includes the Baltic Sea where both perch and zander feed in salinities ranging from fresh water to 8‰(Berzins 1949). Yellow perch are found in Chesapeake Bay, USA, at salinities ranging from 5 to 7‰(Muncy 1962) and in the Neuse River, USA, in salinities up to 12.2‰but preferring areas of 1.8 to 3.5‰(Keup & Bayless 1964).

The sudden transfer from fresh water to high saline concentrations can cause damage to the tissues and often death. Zander transferred in this manner are unable to keep ions in equilibrium and hydration of the cells leads to death. Sodium ions increase in the cells and potassium and calcium ions are lost (Neacsu, Craciun & Craciun 1981). The sudden transfer causes an initial reduction in ATPase activity followed by recovery and the intense osmotic claim may cause the death. Zander are able to tolerate high salinities if transferred gradually. This results in increased ATPase activity to pump out salts to meet the new osmotic equilibrium (Craciun, Craciun, Neacsu & Trandafirescu 1982). The fish does appear to tolerate a sudden change back to fresh water and can control and regain ionic equilibrium. Zander

Table 6.1. The concentration (mM 1^{-1}) of various ions in the plasma and muscle of perch placed in fresh water (FW) and 3.6, 10 and 15‰salinities. Also given are the water concentrations (g water per g dry weight) of the muscle. (After Lutz 1972).

		Concentrations (mM 1^{-1})					
		Na	K	Ca	Mg	Cl	Water (g water per g dry wt)
Plasma	FW	154	3.6	4.4	1.5	120	
	3.6‰	155	3.7	4.8	1.5	136	
	10‰	156	5.3	4.0	2.7	138	
	15‰	210	6.0	7.3	7.7	196	
Muscle	FW	19.9	143	2.6	15.2	10.3	4.2
	3.6‰	19.3	149	3.5	16.3	11.5	3.9
	10‰	20.6	162	3.4	16.6	12.1	4.0
	15‰	47.8	173	3.7	21.9	32.6	3.4*

*significantly different from FW (P < 0.05)

tolerates salinities of 12‰ although this is about the upper limit. An increase in salinity from 10.6 to 12.7‰ in the Sea of Azov has restricted zander to low salinity areas in the Bay of Taganrog and has also caused a decline in growth (Avedikova & D'Yakova 1979). The optimum salinity is probably about 6‰. Zander fingerlings have the best growth rates at this salinity and mortality declines in salinities ranging from 3.5 to 11‰ compared to controls held in fresh water (Zhmurova & Somkina 1976). Optimum salinities for walleye are similar to those of zander and lie in the range of 4 to 8 ‰. They have been found to live in waters of much higher salinity than this such as saline prairie lakes of 15‰ salinity where they were introduced (Rawson 1946). They are apparently unable to reproduce in these lakes.

The acid-base balance in the body of fish relates to the maintenance of pH in the body fluids. Acid stands for the sum of all anions except hydroxyl ion and base stands for the sum of all cations except the hydrogen ion (Albers 1970). Enzymes which control metabolic reactions are pH sensitive thus it is important to maintain an optimum pH for normal body functioning.

Carbon dioxide produced from catabolic processes in the tissues diffuses into the blood and reacts with water to form carbonic acid (Figure 6.2). The process is a slow one in the plasma but is speeded up in the red cells by the enzyme carbonic anhydrase (Albers 1970). Carbonic acid dissociates into hydrogen ions, bicarbonate ions and to a small extent carbonate ions. Hydrogen ions recombine with the plasma proteins and haemoglobin which represent the buffer agents. Temperature affects disassociation constants of the buffer agents as well as the solubility of carbon dioxide. In a steady state the production of surplus hydrogen ions are excreted at the same rate as they are produced. Temperature increase and stress cause an increase in H^+ and OH^- ion production which upsets the acid-base balance. The buffering mechanisms of the body and changes in gill ventilation are limited in their ability to deal with this increase. An increase in gill ventilation is restrained by physical limitations in the energy supply for long-term hyperventilation in a water medium (Heisler 1984). Excretion plays the main role in maintaining a steady state and adjusting pH and acid-base balance during a time of stress. Bicarbonate may be directly excreted through the

gills. Also the excretion of ammonia causes an influx in Na^+ ions. As a consequence of the high
degree of solubility of CO_2 in water and its high
permeability coefficient through the gill, fish are
unable to regulate acid-base balance by adjusting
the CO_2 concentration in the blood. Fish regulate
blood pH therefore by controlling plasma bicarbonate levels.

Acid stress in the external medium interferes
with permeability and electrolyte transport at the
gill surface with the resultant loss of electrolytes, especially sodium. A series of adjustments
are made in gill permeability and electrolyte
transport and also in acid-base balance. Some
waters are naturally acidic and contain populations
of *Perca*. Perch and yellow perch are more hardy to
low pH than walleye which are not normally found in
these lakes. Perch and yellow perch naturally
occurring in acidic lakes have a higher tolerance
to low pH than those living in non-acidic lakes.
This is in part, a genetic characteristic (Rahel
1983). *Perca* inhabiting naturally acid waters also
have gills with lower permeability to hydrogen and
sodium ions (McWilliams 1982). Rahel (1983) found
that the yellow perch in an acidic Wisconsin brown
water lake which had a low salinity (pH 4.6, Na 13
(meq) l^{-1} and K 11 (meq) l^{-1}) had only slightly
lower sodium and potassium levels in the blood than
those yellow perch from non acidic, high salinity
lakes (pH 7.6, Na 70 (meq) l^{-1} and K 18 (meq) l^{-1}).

Many lakes are now becoming acidic due to acid
precipitation from the burning of fossil fuels and
the roasting of sulphide ores. Oxides of nitrogen
and sulphur are released into the atmosphere and
return as acid snow and rain. Surface waters
running into lakes increase the hydrogen ion concentration and reduce the buffering capacity. In
the Sudbury area of Ontario, Canada, the pH of many
of the lakes is 5.0-5.5. In these lakes the walleye populations are more sensitive to the low pH
than the yellow perch. This may in part be due to
the sensitivity of eggs and embryos. The snowmelt
into the streams where walleye spawn may decrease
the pH considerably (Gunn 1982). Female *Perca*
living and laying eggs in an acid environment may
lay eggs which produce fry more tolerant to low pH
than normal (Rask 1984). In the Lac Cloche
Mountain lakes, Canada, young yellow perch grow
faster than normal and older yellow perch grow
slower (Ryan & Harvey 1980). The reversal in
growth occurs at about 140 mm (Figure 6.4). The

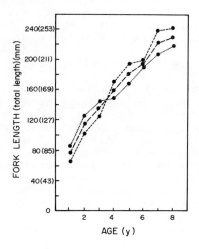

Figure 6.4: Plots of lengths with age for *Perca flavescens* held at three levels of pH (••••• = pH 4.5, — — = pH 5.5 and ---- = pH 6.5) from lakes in the La Cloche Mountain area, Canada. (After Ryan & Harvey 1980).

young yellow perch have a high mortality rate and may grow faster due to more food being available for the survivors.

Respiration

Oxygen is essential in the metabolism of all living cells where it is involved in aerobic respiration. In fish the demand for oxygen or oxygen consumption is dependent on temperature and fish weight (Chapter 5). The demand for energy and thus oxygen also increases with activity. Lowered oxygen concentrations can restrict activity (Figure 6.5). Oxygen is taken up from the surrounding water through the gills. The flow of water over the gill surface is rhythmic or continuous depending on activity and brought about by movements of the walls and floor of the oral cavity, the gill covers and the branchiostegal apparatus. A hydrostatic pressure difference exists between the oral cavity and the opercular region. Occasionally the flow will be reversed by a 'coughing' reflex which cleans the gills of foreign matter. Very little oxygen is taken up by the skin and in *Perca* it is insufficient to meet cutaneous demands let alone supply other organs (Nonnotte 1981). Oxygen is absorbed through the surface of the epithelium lining the gill lamellae into the blood capillaries over a diffusion gradient. The exchange of gases is limited by the surface area of the gill, A, the permeability of the gill surface to gases, K, the distance from the water to the blood, d, and the mean difference in oxygen partial pressure between water and blood, ΔPg. Thus:

$$\text{Oxygen uptake} = \frac{KA\,(\Delta P_g)}{d}$$

(after Jones & Randall 1978). For a full account of oxygen and carbon dioxide exchange in fishes readers should consult Randall and Daxboeck (1984).
  There is extensive variability between species in their response to oxygen concentrations in the external medium. At one extreme, fish in fresh water sometimes encounter supersaturation of oxygen in the water and this can lead to their death. Gas supersaturation in Lake Waubesca, USA, in 1940 was due to extensive algal blooms (Woodbury 1942). Concentrations of 30-32 mg 1^{-1} were recorded and large numbers of walleye died in the lake. This

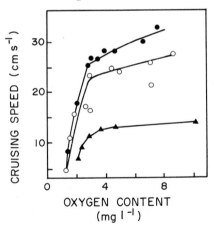

Figure 6.5: Cruising speed of *Perca flavescens* in relation to temperature (• = 25°C, ○ = 15°C and ▲ = 10°C) and oxygen content. (After Fry 1957).

was caused by gas emboli which blocked circulation
of blood through the gill capillaries and led to
death through respiratory failure. A detailed
study on the response of three fresh water fish,
including zander, to reduction in oxygen concentration in the water was made by Dolinin (1974).
He conducted two experiments, one for fish at rest
and one in which the fish induced to be active. He
carried out his tests at four temperatures 5, 10,
15 and 20°C covering a range normally encountered
by the fish. Dolinin (1974) defined three important levels of oxygen concentration. When oxygen
concentration is reduced in the water the rate of
gas exchange by the fish remains unaltered until a
'critical' concentration is reached when the amount
of oxygen taken up by the fish declines. This critical level varies with temperature and from 5°C to
20°C increases by a factor of 1.7 in zander. At
5°C the critical concentration is 4.18 ± 0.29 mg 1^{-1}
($\pm$S.E.) rising to 6.93 ± 0.81 mg 1^{-1} at 20°C. The
point where the rate of decline starts to increase
is called the 'threshold' concentration. This concentration remains fairly constant with temperature
and has a value of 4.23 ± 0.22 mg 1^{-1}. At the
'limiting' concentration of 1.41 ± 0.14 mg 1^{-1} ex-
traction of oxygen ceases. The amount of water
pumped through the gill apparatus increases
gradually as the oxygen concentration is reduced
and then falls sharply when the 'threshold' value
of 4.23 mg 1^{-1} is reached. The maximum amount of
water pumped through the gills increases with a
rise in temperature, as does the coefficient of
oxygen uptake and the number of respiratory movements in fish held at the 'threshold' oxygen
concentration (Table 6.2). Coefficient of oxygen
uptake is equivalent to the transfer factor (TO_2):

$$TO_2 = \frac{O_2 \text{ uptake} \times 100}{PO_2 \text{ water} - PO_2 \text{ blood}}$$

where PO_2 is the partial pressure of oxygen (Jones
& Randall 1978). A reduction in oxygen concentration below the 'threshold' value causes the coefficient of oxygen uptake to fall to zero. There
is also a reduction in ventilation volume. In concentrations above the 'threshold' value the oxygen
uptake coefficient is inversely related to the ventilation volume (Figure 6.6). Respiratory movements are linearly related to ventilation volume

Table 6.2. Ventilation volume (ml min^{-1} Kg^{-1}), coefficient of oxygen uptake (%) and respiratory movements (min^{-1}) of *S. lucioperca* held in water of temperatures 5-20°C. (After Dolinin 1974).

	Temperature (°C)			
	5	10	15	20
Ventilation volume (ml min^{-1} Kg^{-1})	400.0±20.6	489.1±18.3	581.6±42.0	634±18.3
Coefficient of oxygen uptake (%)	29.4± 2.6	39.3± 2.2	44.0± 4.8	54.8± 2.3
Respiratory movements (min^{-1})	25 ± 2	33 ± 2	42 ± 4	50 ± 3

(Figure 6.7) and as the temperature increases the intercept of the line relating the two factors increases although the slope remains the same. There appears to be no difference in the relationship for active or non-active fish. In active fish the changes in gas exchange are similar in nature to those of a resting fish and oxygen consumption halts at about a concentration of 1.47 mg l^{-1}. However the alteration of ventilation volume varies from that of resting fish. The maximum ventilation is not reached at the 'threshold' value as in a resting fish but at the 'critical' one. The ventilation volume remains constant below the 'critical' value until it begins to fall at a similar value to that for a resting fish. The relationship between ventilation volume and oxygen uptake coefficients remain the same in active and resting fish above the 'threshold' value. A reduction in ventilation volume from 400 to 200 ml min^{-1} kg^{-1} results in an increase in the coefficient from 52.3 to 71.5% in active zander held in water containing oxygen above the 'threshold' value. However, below 'threshold' concentrations there is a decline in the coefficient from 38.6 to 17.1%.

Studies of the tolerance of other percids to reduction in oxygen are not as complete as the one described for zander. Jones (1964) suggested that the 'limiting' oxygen concentrations for perch were 1.1-1.3 mg l^{-1} at 16°C and 2.25 mg l^{-1} at 20-26°C. Activity is reduced at 7 mg l^{-1} in yellow perch at a summer temperature of 20°C (Fry 1957). Yellow perch can survive in oxygen concentrations down to 0.25 mg l^{-1} at 2.5-4°C, conditions often ex-

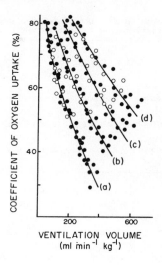

Figure 6.6: Ventilation volume of *Stizostedion lucioperca* in relation to co-efficient of oxygen uptake from the water at four temperatures (a) 5°C, (b) 10°C, (c) 15°C and (d) 20°C. ● & o results obtained with no motor activity and induced motor activity respectively. (After Dolinen 1974).

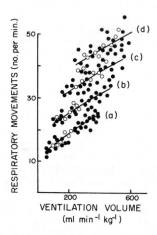

Figure 6.7: Ventilation volume of *Stizostedion lucioperca* in relation to res-piratory movements at four temperatures (a) 5°C, (b) 10°C, (c) 15°C and (d) 20°C. ● & o results obtained with no motor activity and induced motor activity respectively. (After Dolinen 1974).

perienced under the ice in northern lakes of North
America. Ventilation of the gills increases as
oxygen is reduced from 4 to 1 mg l^{-1}. Maximum ventilation occurs at 0.5 mg l^{-1} at 2.5-4°C (Petrosky
& Magnuson 1973). The yellow perch were observed
to swim up and nose at the underside of the ice at
0.25 mg l^{-1} oxygen. Walleye held in the laboratory can survive low levels of oxygen (2.0 mg l^{-1})
without showing ill effect. At an oxygen concentration of 1.0 to 1.5 mg l^{-1} at a temperature of
22°C walleye rise to the surface and at 0.6 mg l^{-1}
they lose coordination and equilibrium (Scherer
1971). Unlike yellow perch, walleye are not able
to obtain oxygen from the surface film and are
thus less able to withstand hypoxic conditions
sometimes experienced in lakes during the summer
(Gee, Tallman & Smart 1978). Walleye tend to inhabit waters with oxygen concentration >3 mg l^{-1}.
Oxygen depletion causes a reduction in negative
phototactic behaviour in walleye. There is no
negative response to light at oxygen concentrations
of 1-2 mg l^{-1} which still allow the walleye to be
mobile. Scherer (1971) using aquaria over which
lights were shone, found that walleye remained in
their shelters down to an oxygen concentration of 5
mg l^{-1}. Below this level they moved in and out
from the shelters but at 1-2 mg l^{-1} they swam to
the surface. At optimum oxygen concentrations the
walleye remained in their shelters if carbon
dioxide tension was kept below 5 mm Hg, whereas if
the carbon dioxide level was raised the fish were
more active in the light and exhibited upward movements. No light avoidance was shown at 14-18 mm Hg
(30-40 mg l^{-1}). Free carbon dioxide in the water
suppresses oxygen uptake.

Good quantitative data on the oxygen requirements of eggs and young stages are lacking. At low
oxygen concentrations walleye eggs take longer to
hatch (Figure 6.8). Oseid and Smith (1971) found
that there was no difference in mortality of eggs
held at constant temperature in the range of 2 to 7
mg l^{-1} of oxygen. However, low levels of oxygen
reduced the size of larvae at hatching and retarded
larval growth. Walleye larvae raised at 2.4 mg l^{-1}
oxygen were found to be weaker swimmers than those
reared at normal oxygen levels.

Percids in general have a well developed respiratory apparatus and they live in oxygen rich environments. They are not a very active and mobile
species and thus their demands are low. When exposed to low levels of oxygen they can show

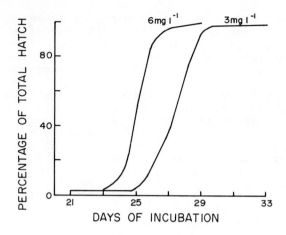

Figure 6.8: The effect of dissovled oxygen on the rate of hatch of-
Stizostedion vitreum eggs. Two oxygen concentrations were used, 3 and 6
mgl^{-1}, temperature was 4-5°C for the first 21 days and 12.3°C thereafter and
flow rate of water through the eggs was 300 ml min^{-1}. (After Colby *et al*.
1979 from Oseid & Smith 1971).

considerable tolerance.

Movements

  The movement of a fish in its environment is a
response to both endogenous and external factors
enabling it to feed, escape predators, escape hos-
tile areas and reproduce. It involves the maximum
interaction between the physiological make up of
the fish and its external environment.
  Compared to many other species of fish *Perca*
is a poor swimmer. In experiments on fast-start
performance, yellow perch were shown to be poor
accelerators. Maximum acceleration rate ±2 S.E. =
23.9 ± 12.4 m s^{-2} compared for example to pike with
maximum acceleration = 39.4 ± 8.5 m s^{-2} (Webb
1978). *Perca* may overcome poor swimming ability by
schooling, which provides protection for the young
fish and social hunting in older fish (Chapter 5).
The swimming speed of larval yellow perch and walleye is fairly similar and increases with size
(Figure 6.9). Walleye swim more slowly than yellow
perch in the size range 7-9 mm since they contain
more yolk than the yellow perch. Swimming ability
improves from 8 to 9.5 mm as the yolk sac is

absorbed and from 9.5 to 14.5 mm they swim equally well.

Temperature plays a major role in swimming speed. Hergenrader and Hasler (1967) measured the swimming speed of yellow perch at different times of the year using sonar. Slowest movements were in the winter at water temperatures of 0-5°C and they increased with a rise in temperature to a maximum in the summer when the water temperature reached 20-25°C. Swimming speeds were found to be linearly related to water temperature (Figure 6.10). The greatest variation among individuals was found in the summer. The tracking of individual fish showed that these swam on average at half the speed of schools. The annual variation in swimming ability of perch was demonstrated by Sandstroem (1983) in a unique experiment. He used a rotary flow technique in which the critical revolutions per minute in the apparatus were the maximum the fish could withstand. This critical value increased in summer and declined during the autumn. Laboratory tests with perch held under constant conditions showed that the response was endogenous and not temperature dependent. It suggests an economic use of stored energy so that, for example during winter months when energy intake is limited, the perch will not use up energy reserves. Thus swimming ability appears to be endogenous with temperature acting as an external control.

Walleye have the ability to swim against strong currents (Figure 6.11). Jones, Kiceniuk and Bamford (1974) derived a relationship between length (L, cm) of fish and water velocity (V, cm sec^{-1}):

$$V = KL^e$$

where the constant K = 13.07 and exponent e = 0.51 for walleye. The calculated velocity is that which can be maintained for 10 minutes. The relationship is unaffected by acclimatisation to different temperatures or temperature shock of ±7°C. There does not appear to be any differences between sexes.

Swimming in fish is well described in standard texts (e.g. Webb 1975; Hoar & Randall 1978). The swim bladder plays an important role in this activity. The swim bladder counteracts the negative buoyancy of the fish. The swim bladder pressure of yellow perch and walleye living in running water is reduced compared to that of fish

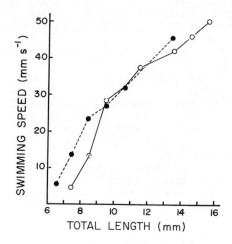

Figure 5.9: Plots of sustained swimming speed of larval *Perca flavescens* (●) and *Stizostedion vitreum* (o) in relation to fish length. (After Houde 1969b).

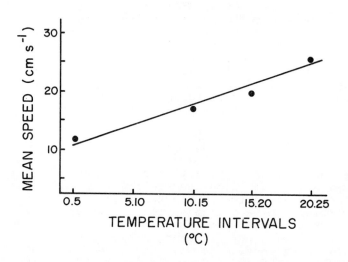

Figure 6.10: Plots of mean speeds of *Perca flavescens* schools in relation to temperature intervals measured at different times of the year in Lake Mendota, USA. (After Hergenrader & Hasler 1967).

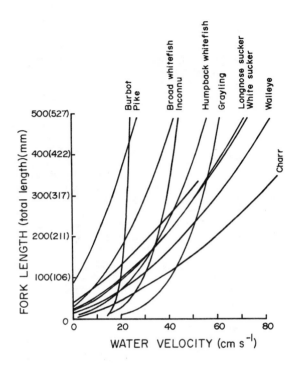

Figure 6.11: Plots of fish length in relation to their ability to move 100 m in 10 min against water velocities up to 80 cm s^{-1} for various species of temperate fresh water fish. (After Jones *et al*. 1974).

held in still water (Gee, Machniak & Chalanchuk 1974). The control of the swim bladder is not well understood. It is probably under secretory cholinergic nervous control. In perch and other physoclists the swim bladder has a postganglionic innervation which exhibits acetyl choline esterase activity (Figure 2.9) (Fänge & Holmgren 1982).

Both *Perca* and *Stizostedion* species are schooling fish although adult zander tend to become solitary. Some very large perch in Windermere, England, which become solely pisciverous are also solitary. Vision is important in schooling behaviour (Breder 1959) and perch and yellow perch schools break up at twilight and the fish settle to the bottom (Hasler & Villemonte 1953). From mark and recapture data Craig (1973) found that fish

marked at the same place and time could be recaught
together at a different location up to 18 months
later. It was also interesting to note that male
and female perch often were in separate schools.
Helfman (1984) describes school fidelity as the co-
hesiveness of social aggregations over time as
measured by the repeatability with which individuals reoccur as members of a school. He found
yellow perch in Cazenovia Lake, USA, to be facul-
tative schoolers with individual differences between fish in schooling tendency (percentage of
time in the schools).

Hergenrader and Hasler (1968) established a
high negative correlation between yellow perch
school size, in terms of space, and light transmission properties of the water. In the summer the
spaces between individuals was less than about 0.6
m and the distance from top to bottom of the school
was 2.5 m. In the winter the distance between individuals was greater than about 0.6 m and the
height of the school was 6.7 m. In the winter the
yellow perch is not very active and loses some of
its tendency to school.

Both *Perca* and walleye show distinct patterns
of diel activity. As a rule perch and yellow perch
are more active during the day in contrast to walleye which are more active at night. This can vary
among age groups. In some instances juvenile
Perca have been found to be active at night. In
West Blue Lake, Canada, young yellow perch were
active at night and were vunerable to predation by
walleye (Kelso 1976). However, Johnson and Müller
(1978) suggest that young perch were active at
night when they migrated down the River Ångeran in
northern Sweden, to avoid predation by pike and
adult perch which were diurnally active (Figure
6.12). Increased activity at dawn and dusk is a
common feature of perch, yellow perch and walleye
behaviour (Chapter 5) (Craig 1977b; Eriksson 1978;
Hasler & Bardach 1949; Kelso 1976; Lind, Ellonen,
Keranen, Kukko & Tenhunen 1973; McConville & Fossum
1981). The extent of this activity increases with
rise in water temperature. As daylength shortens
and light intensity decreases during the onset of
winter perch and yellow perch become active during
the day (Hergenrader & Hasler 1966; Lind *et al.*
1973). Perch also become active during the day in
the summer on dull days (Svirskii, Malinin &
Ovchinnikov 1976) or when the water is turbid or
light penetration is reduced by algal blooms
(Thorpe 1977; Craig 1977b). Hasler and Bardach

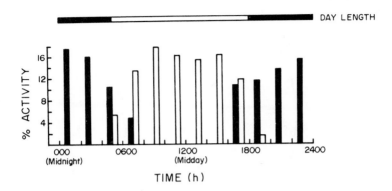

Figure 6.12: The percentage activity every two hours over 24 h of juvenile (■) and adult (□) *Perca fluviatilis* kept in experimental tanks. (After Johnson & Müller 1978).

(1949) noted that in the summer yellow perch moved inshore one hour before sunset and cruised parallel to the shore at the 6 m contour feeding until after the sun disappeared. Carlander and Cleary (1949) also observed that walleye came into shallow water to feed at dusk although Einhouse and Winter (1981) and Holt, Grant, Oberstar, Oakes and Bradt (1977) found no such activity. Two types of behaviour have been noted in the daily movements of perch and walleye (Mackay & Craig 1983; McConville & Fossum 1981). Firstly, a variable meandering movement in which the direction changes rapidly and often. This type of movement commonly occurs at sunrise and sunset and may be associated with feeding (Figure 6.13). Secondly, movements in a relatively straight line suggesting cruising which can occur at any time during the normal activity period of the fish. This latter movement may be a movement from one feeding area to another.

Distances moved by perch over the year are not extensive and most are localised (Smith & Van Oosten 1939; Craig 1974a). It is not clear if perch return to 'home' areas to spawn although this has been demonstrated by some tagged fish in Windermere (Kipling & Le Cren 1984). There is

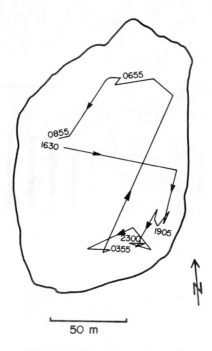

Figure 6.13: The summer activity of an ultra-sonic tagged *Perca fluviatilis* from 1630 to 0855 h the next day in Bigland Tarn, England. (After Mackay & Craig 1983).

convincing evidence that walleye 'home' to spawning areas. Olson, Schupp and Macins (1978) put forward the theory that this is adult learned behaviour and is strengthened by repeated migrations. Since eggs and larvae of walleye are often carried substantial distances in river currents from areas of egg deposition, natal conditioning is unlikely. In Oneida Lake, USA, three distinct walleye populations return to their own specific spawning grounds in successive years (Forney 1963). After spawning, the population gradually disperse from the spawning grounds and there is some mixing between the populations. Widest distribution occurs in the late summer. However evidence suggests that like perch, the movement of walleye except at spawning time is confined to a limited area. Daily migrations of walleye of the Nipigon Bay region of Lake Superior,

North America even at spawning time are not often greater than 3 km day^{-1} and usually about 0.8 km day^{-1} (Ryder 1968). Apart from individual exceptions (Colby *et al*. 1979) the majority of walleye populations migrate less than 16 km between spawning and feeding areas. In large areas of water, mixing between different stocks during summer feeding periods may not occur. Tagged walleye in eastern Lake Erie were released on spawning grounds near Barcelona, USA (Wolfert & Van Meter 1978). They moved northeast along the shore to the summer feeding area near the Buffalo-Niagara River inlet. During late summer and the autumn the fish moved back towards the spawning grounds near Barcelona. There were no indications of westward movements which might have brought them in contact with other stocks.

Zander undertake major migrations for spawning. Other movements are fairly localised. There is also some evidence that this species has a 'home' area for spawning and members of the same population return to this area year after year (Puke 1952).

Chapter 7

PARASITES AND DISEASES

Introduction

When a parasite has established itself on or within a fish, it can cause the death of the fish, develop an equilibrium state with no evident disease symptoms or be eliminated by the defence system of the fish.

Perca and *Stizostedion* species are host to a large number of parasites but many of these parasites, as far as is known, do not cause harm to the fish. However all parasites must deprive the fish of some anabolic energy. In an extreme case, Pitt and Grundman (1957) found that *Ligula intestinalis* reduced the growth of yellow perch by 50% over a five year period. Host-parasite relationships appear to be evolutionary adaptive and in some parasites morphological and physiological adaptations are remarkable. Disease outbreaks occur when there is an imbalance between the fish host, the pathogen or disease agent and the environment. Fish respond significantly to ecological variables, as explained in other chapters, so outbreaks of disease are strongly affected by environmental conditions. The parasitic fauna can be influenced by abiotic and biotic factors including temperature, light, salinity, pH, oxygen concentration, water velocity, the diversity of the local aquatic fauna, the diversity of fish-eating birds, the history and geographic isolation of the fish environment, the size, age and physiological state of the fish host, the size of the host population and the season of the year. Fish can be intermediate or definitive hosts of parasites. When a fish is an intermediate host it must be eaten before the parasite can be transmitted to the definitive host. The parasite

can escape from the definitive host from the body
surface (ectoparasite) or through body openings
(endoparasite).

Few reports of genetic defects in percids have
been made. A skeletal muscle abnormality observed
in walleye in some lakes of Minnesota and North
Dakota may be genetical but there certainly is an
environmental component in the disease expression
since disease prevalence is higher in walleye from
more eutrophic lakes (Economon 1978; Holloway &
Smith 1982). Economon (1978) suggested that the
disease could be likened to muscular dystrophy
found in man. The disease causes pronounced degeneration of the lateral trunk musculature.
Affected tissue is yellowish-brown and coarsely
fibrous. Histological investigation shows muscle
fibres in various stages of degeneration.

Yellow perch have been observed to suffer from
tumours (abnormal growths) in the testes, ovaries,
ganglia and epithelial tissue of the lower jaw,
urinary bladder and thyroid (Budd, Schroder & Dukes
1975). The study of neoplasia in fish is not extensive (Mawdesley-Thomas 1972) and other tumours
of percids have gone unrecorded.

In this chapter the authorities for parasite
species are not given. These can be found in the
references cited.

Causative agents

Percids can show severe disease symptoms
caused by viruses, bacteria and fungi. Fish
virology is currently in a phase of rapid development but additional tissue culture systems need to
be developed for the specific testing of viruses.
This has been achieved for walleye (Kelly & Miller
1978) and for zander (Lartseva & Zubkova 1981).
Walker (1969a) detected three viruses from skin
lesions in Oneida Lake, USA, walleye. These
viruses were associated with lymphocystis which was
common and with dermal sarcoma and epidermal hyperplasia which were locally common in the walleye
from Oneida Lake. The incidence of these viruses
extends into central and western regions of Canada
and may be widespread throughout walleye populations in North America (Yamamoto, MacDonald,
Gillespie & Kelly 1976; Yamamoto, Kelly & Nielsen
1985). In central Canada a fourth virus
(Herpesvirus vitreum) associated with a different
form of epidermal hyperplasia has been isolated

(Kelly, Nielsen, Mitchell & Yamamoto 1983).
Lymphocystis is a common viral disease of walleye.
Afflicted fish exhibit wart-like protuberances on
the fins, jaws and opercula. It was first
recognized in the ruffe, *Gymnocephalus cernua*,
(Weissenberg 1965) and is probably widespread in
many of the percids (Walker & Weissenberg 1965;
Amin 1979; Sonstegard personal communication).
Dermal sarcoma tumours are similar in gross
appearance to those of lymphocystis. They are
large, white growths often tinged with red. On
more careful observation, they have a smooth
appearance in contrast to the granular nature of
the enlarged cells of lymphocystis. Epidermal
hyperplasia may be associated either with a retro-
virus or a herpesvirus and has a clear slime-like
appearance. However the lesion with the associated
herpesvirus has a more diffuse character and there
is often a swelling of the underlying tissue
(Yamamoto *et al*. 1985). Epidermal hyperplasia was
identified by Walker (1969b) in yellow perch but no
viruses were detected. Virus-containing skin
lesions in walleye show some seasonality in incidence and are frequently common during the spawning
period. Lymphocystis and dermal sarcoma appear to
have the most effect on adult fish causing open
wounds and loss of blood.

Walleye fry and fingerlings are susceptible to
infectious pancreatic necrosis virus (IPNV) and infectious haematopoietic necrosis virus (IHNV), two
viruses that cause severe diseases in salmonids
(Schat & Carlisle 1980). Problems of cross infection may occur if walleye and infected salmonids
are stocked together in the same pond.

A cytopathic viral agent, Nillahcootie redfin
virus has been isolated from the viscera of a population of perch in Victoria, Australia (Langdon,
Humphrey, Williams, Hyatt & Westbury 1986). Many
fish showed signs of focal hepatocellular and
haematopoietic necrosis. The origin of the virus
is unclear since the perch were originally introduced from England (Cadwallader & Backhouse 1983)
and no isolation of the virus nor similar disease
symptoms have been recorded in Europe.

Bacterial infections appear to be less important than viral infections in fish. There are only
a few recorded cases where bacteria have been identified as being the primary cause of a disease outbreak in percids. In many cases diseases have been
aggravated by secondary bacterial infections
(Bauer, Musselius & Strelkov 1973). Nordstrom,

Bailey & Heaton (1960) isolated gram negative ba-
cilli which were similar to *Pseudomonas* from yellow
perch found dead in large numbers in Dailey Lake,
USA. The disease, which produced symptoms of multiple petechiae present in the skin and dorsal musculature and inflammation of the peritoneal cavity,
appeared to be specific to the yellow perch. A
well recorded high mortality of perch occurred in
Windermere, England (Bucke, Cawley, Craig,
Pickering & Willoughby 1979). The perch population
has been studied over many years (Chapter 9) so it
was possible to estimate that over 98% of the population, over one million fish, were killed by
'perch disease'. A wide variety of common water
bacteria were isolated from both healthy and
diseased fish. The bacteria included *Aeromonas*,
Pseudomonas and some flexibacteria. The commonest
bacterium found in infected fish was *A. hydrophila*
subspecies *hydrophila*. These bacteria were considered to be secondary in nature and the causative
organism was not isolated. However symptoms
resembled those of furunculosis and a form of
Aeromonas not identified may have been the cause of
the disease. This disease was specific to perch
and no other species in the lake seemed to be
affected, although the decline in the perch population had a dramatic affect on other species, particularly pike, the main predator of perch. Tenta-
tively, a subspecies of *Aeromonas salmonicida*
specific to perch may be the cause of a form of
furunculosis which is normally found in salmonids.
Furunculosis has been identified in perch by
McCarthy (1975) and is probably more widespread
than is realised.

The diseased Windermere perch also had
secondary infections of fungi. These were mainly
species from the family Saprolegniaceae. Six
genera were isolated, *Achlya*, *Aphanomyces*,
Leptolegnia, *Leptomitus*, *Pythiopsis* and
Saprolegnia (Bucke *et al*. 1979). The occurrence of
fungi was higher in the winter than in the summer.
The seasonal differences may be caused by the preference of the fungi for lower temperatures compared to the bacteria found in the perch lesions.
In both winter and summer up to four different
species of fungi could be found on a single
lesion. Spores of fungi are present in the water
but infection of the fish does not occur until
there is a break in the skin. It is of interest
that a year before the outbreak of perch disease in
Windermere, the parasitic branchiuran, *Argulus*

147

foliaceus, (see later in this chapter) was discovered for the first time in the lake. The
acquisition and growth of fungi appeared to be
fairly unselective. This was also the case when
young-of-the-year perch in Windermere were found to
be infected by fungi in an earlier study
(Willoughby 1970). *Saprolegnia ferax*, common in
Windermere water samples, did not occur on the
perch in either study. Secondary infections of
Saprolegniaceae fungi on damaged eggs can also
cause serious losses in all species of percids.
Disease inducing fungi are composed of branched
hyphae without septa and form dense sometimes
cottonlike growths in severe cases. The sporangia
are located at the end of the hyphae, separated by
septa, and in the sporangia large numbers of zoo-
spores are formed. These spores are liberated into
the water when ripe.

The number of zooparasite species associated
with perch, yellow perch, walleye and zander is
extensive; a comprehensive list is given in Table
7.1. Protozoa and Myxosporida are parasites of the
skin, gills, gut, eye, urinary system and blood.
Many species of these groups are limited to a
specific host of percid. However, *Icthyophirius
multifiliis* is a common parasite found under the
epidermis of perch, yellow perch and walleye. When
suitable conditions occur it can become an
epizootic and cause mass mortality. The mature
trophonts break away from the host, sink to the
bottom and attach to plants or other substrate.
Each cyst divides into 1,000-2,000 daughter cells
which are released into the water (Bauer *et al.*
1973). These mobile ciliates then search for a new
host, penetrate the skin, grow and mature. If a
new host is not found within two to three days the
parasite dies.

Monogenea and Trematoda are common parasites
of percids. Monogeneans are ectoparasites of
gills, skin and body orifices and trematodes infect
many of the body organs (Table 7.1). The monogeneans have a direct life cycle with a single
host. For example *Urocleidus adspectus* lives on
the gills of yellow perch. Its eggs may overwinter
away from the host on the lake bottom (Tedla &
Fernando 1969). Free swimming larvae hatch from
these eggs and infect a new host when contact is
made. Trematodes may need one or two intermediate
hosts for development and the definitive host can
be a fish, bird or mammal. Apart from a few
exceptions such as *Sanguinicola occidentalis*, it is

Table 7.1. A list of zooparasites of *Perca fluviatilis* (P), *P. flavescens* (YP), *Stizostedion vitreum* (W) and *S. lucioperca* (Z). (For authorities see the references given).

Parasite	Host	Site	Author
PROTOZOA AND MYXOSPORIDA			
Apiosoma sp.	P		Kennedy 1974
Balantidium sp.	YP	Intestine	Hoffman 1967; Margolis & Arthur 1979
Dermocystidium percae	P	Skin	Bykhovskaya – Pavlovskaya *et al.* 1964
Eimeria laureleus	YP	Intestine	Margolis & Arthur 1979; Molnar *et al.* 1974
E. percae	P		Bykhovskaya – Pavlovskaya *et al.* 1964
E. rivierei	P	Liver	Markevich 1963
E. tedlai	YP	Intestine	Margolis & Arthur 1979
Glossatella campanulata	P		Bykhovskaya – Pavlovskaya *et al.* 1964
Glossatella sp.	P		Campbell 1974
Henneguya acerinae	Z	Gills	Markevich 1963
H. creplini	Z	Gills	Petrusherskii 1963
H. cutanea forma nanum	Z	Gills	Markevich 1963
H. doori	YP	Gills	Hoffman 1967; Margolis & Arthur 1979
H. percae	YP	Gills	Hoffman 1967; Margolis & Arthur 1979
H. psorospermica	P	Gills	Bykhovskaya – Pavlovskaya *et al.* 1964
H. wisconsinensis	YP		Hoffman 1967
H. zschokkei	P		Bykhovskaya – Pavlovskaya *et al.* 1964
Henneguya sp.	P,YP	Gills	Kennedy 1974: Margolis & Arthur 1979
Icthyophthirius multifiliis	P,YP,W	Skin, fins, gills	Bauer 1962; Hoffman 1967; Margolis & Arthur 1979
Myxidium percae	YP	Subdermal	Hoffman 1967
Myxobilatus asymmetricus	W	Urinary bladder	Hoffman 1967
Myxobolus carassi	P	Body cavity, liver, intestine, gills	Markevich 1963
M. dispar	P		Bykhovskaya – Pavlovskaya *et al.* 1964
M. ellipsoides	P	Gills, body cavity, gall bladder	Bykhovskaya – Pavlovskaya *et al.* 1964; Markevich 1963

Parasite	Host	Site	Author
M. macrocapsularis	Z		Petrusherskii 1963
M. minutus	P		Bykhovskaya – Pavlovskaya *et al.* 1964
M. mulleri	P	Gills	Kennedy 1974
M. percae	YP	Fin base, eye	Hoffman 1967; Margolis & Arthur 1979
M. permagnus	P	Gills	Markevich 1963
M. phyriformis	YP		Hoffman 1967
M. volgensis	Z	Gills, eye (cornea), skin, fins, muscle	Markevich 1963
M. wegeneri	P		Bykhkovskaya – Pavlovskaya *et al.* 1964
Myxobolus sp.	YP,W		Hoffman 1967
Myxosoma anurus	P		Bykhovskaya – Pavlovskaya *et al.* 1964
M. branchialis	P	Gills	Markevich 1963
M. dujardini	P	Gills	Markevich 1963
M. neurophila	YP	Optic tectum	Hoffman 1967
M. scleroperca	YP	Sclera of eye	Hoffman 1967; Margolis & Arthur 1979
Myxosporidia gen. sp.	W,Z	Various	Margolis & Arthur 1979
Spironucleus sp.	YP	Intestine	Molnar *et al.* 1974; Margolis & Arthur 1979
Thelohanellus piriformis	YP	Spleen	Hoffman 1967
Trichodina domerguei	P,Z	Gills	Bykhovskaya – Pavlovskaya *et al.* 1964
T. megamicronucleata	Z	Gills	Bykhovskaya – Pavlovskaya *et al.* 1964
T. meridionalis	P		Bykhovskaya – Pavlovskaya *et al.* 1964
T. nigra	P,Z	Gills	Bykhovskaya – Pavlovskaya *et al.* 1964
T. urinaria	P	Urinary bladder ureters	Bykhovskaya – Pavlovskaya *et al.* 1964; Markevich 1963
Trichodina sp.	YP,W	Gills, urinary bladder,ureters	Hoffman 1967; Margolis & Arthur 1979
Trichodinella epizootica	P		Bykhovskaya– Pavlovskaya *et al.* 1964
Tricophyra intermedia	P		Bykhovskaya – Pavlovskaya *et al.* 1964
T. piscium	YP		Hoffman 1967
Trypanosoma acerinae	P		Jastrzebski 1984
T. luciopercae	Z	Blood	Markevich 1963

Parasite	Host	Site	Author
T. percae	P,YP	Blood	Bykhovskaya - Pavlovskaya *et al*. 1964; Hoffman 1967; Markevich 1963; Margolis & Arthur 1979

MONOGENEA AND TREMATODA

Parasite	Host	Site	Author
Allocreadium isoporum	P		Bykhovskaya - Pavlovskaya *et al*. 1964
A. lobatum	W	Stomach	Hoffman 1967; Fischthal 1952
Ancyrocephalus creplin	P	Gills	Markevich 1963
A. percae	P		Chubb 1977
A. paradoxus	P,Z	Gills	Bykhovskaya - Pavlovskaya *et al*. 1964; Markevich 1963
Ancyrocephalus sp.	YP		Hoffman 1967
Apophallus americanus	YP,W		Hoffman 1967
A. brevis	YP	skin, fins, gills, musculature	Noble 1970a; Margolis & Arthur 1979
A. itascensis	YP		Hoffman 1967
A. müehlingi	P,Z		Bykhovskaya - Pavlovskaya *et al*. 1964; Chubb 1979
A. venustus	YP,W	Musculature	Hoffman 1967; Margolis & Arthur 1979
Apophallus sp.	YP		Hoffman 1967
Ascocotyle coleostoma	P		Bykhovskaya - Pavlovskaya *et al*. 1964
Aspidogaster limacoides	P		Bykhovskaya - Pavlovskaya *et al*. 1964
Asymphylodora sp.	YP		Hoffman 1967
Azygia acuminata	YP,W		Hoffman 1967
A. angusticauda	YP,W	Stomach, intestine	Hoffman 1967
A. bulboa	W		Hoffman 1967
A. longa	YP,W	Stomach, intestine	Hoffman 1967
A. lucii	P,Z	Stomach, intestine	Bykhovskaya - Pavlovskaya *et al*. 1964; Markevich 1963
A. sebago	YP		Hoffman 1967
Azygia sp.	YP,W		Hoffman 1967; Margolis & Arthur 1979

151

Parasite	Host	Site	Author
Bolboforus confusus	P		Bykhovskaya – Pavlovskaya *et al.* 1964
Bucephaloides pusilla	W		Hoffman 1967
Bucephalopsis pusillum	YP		Hoffman 1967
Bucephalus elegans	YP	Gut (pyloric caecae)	Hoffman 1967; Margolis & Arthur 1979
B. markewitschi	Z	Intestine	Markevich 1963
B. polymorphus	P,Z	Intestine	Bykhovskaya – Pavlovskaya *et al.* 1964; Markevich 1963
Bunocotyle cingulata	P,Z	Intestine	Bykhovskaya – Pavlovskaya *et al.* 1964; Markevich 1963
B. luciopercae	YP,W	Intestine	Dechtiar 1972a; Margolis & Arthur 1979
B. nodulosum	YP		Hoffman 1967
Bunodera sp.	YP		Margolis & Arthur 1979
Bunoderina sacculata	YP,W	Intestine	Hoffman 1967; Margolis & Arthur 1979
Centrovarium lobotes	YP,W	Intestine, pyloric caecae	Hoffman 1967; Margolis & Arthur 1979
Cleidodiscus aculeatus	W		Hoffman 1967
Cleidodiscus sp.	YP,W	Gills	Hoffman 1967; Margolis & Arthur 1979
Clinostomum complanatum	P,YP,W	Gills, musculature	Bykhovskaya – Pavlovskaya *et al.* 1964; Margolis & Arthur 1979; Markevich 1963
C. marginatum	YP,W	Gill cavity, musculature, fins, mesenteries	Hoffman 1967; Margolis & Arthur 1979
Clinostomum sp.	YP,W	Musculature, viscera	Margolis & Arthur 1979
Coitocoecum skrjabini	P,Z	Intestine	Markevich 1963
Cotylurus communis	W	Mesenteries, liver	Hoffman 1967; Margolis & Arthur 1979
C. pileatus	P		Bykhovskaya – Pavlovskaya *et al.* 1964
Crassiphiala bulboglossa	YP,W	Musculature, skin	Hoffman 1967; Margolis & Arthur 1979
Crepidostomum cooperi	YP,W	Intestine, pyloric caecae, gall bladder	Hoffman 1967; Margolis & Arthur 1979
C. farionis	P,YP	Intestine, pyloric caecae, gall bladder	Hoffman 1967; Kennedy 1974; Margolis & Arthur 1979

Parasite	Host	Site	Author
C. isotomum	YP	Intestine	Margolis & Arthur 1979
C. laureatum	YP		Hoffman 1967
Crepidostomum sp.	YP,W	Intestine, gall bladder	Hoffman 1967 Margolis & Arthur 1979
Crowcrocoecum skrjabini	P		Bykhovskaya – Pavlovskaya *et al.* 1964
Cryptogonimus chili	YP	Intestine, pyloric caecae, stomach	Hoffman 1967; Margolis & Arthur 1979
Gyrodactylus longiradix	P		Bykhovskaya – Pavlovskaya *et al.* 1964
Dactylogyrus tenuis	P	Gills	Bykhovskaya – Pavlovskaya *et al.* 1964
Digenea gen. sp	W	Skin, fins, eye, viscera, musculature	Margolis & Arthur 1979
Diplostomulum clavatum	P	Eye (vitreous humour and lens)	Bykhovskaya – Pavlovskaya *et al.* 1964 Markevich 1963
D. huronense	YP	Eye (vitreous humour & lens)	Hoffman 1967
D. scheuringi	YP,W	Eye (vitreous humour)	Hoffman 1967; Margolis & Arthur 1979
Diplostomulum sp.	YP,W	Eye (vitreous humour), brain, pharynx	Hoffman 1967; Margolis & Arthur 1979
Diplostomum adamsi	YP	Eye (retina)	Margolis & Arthur 1979
D. gasterostei	P		Kennedy 1981
D. spathaceum	P,YP,Z	Eye (vitreous humour, lens)	Bykhovskaya – Pavlovskaya *et al.* 1964; Margolis & Arthur 1979; Molnar *et al.* 1974; Chubb 1979
D. spathaceum huronense	YP	Eye	Margolis & Arthur 1979
D. volvens	P		Deufel 1961
Diplostomum sp.	P		Kennedy 1974
Distomum nodulosum	YP		Hoffman 1967
Echinochasmus donaldsoni	YP	Gills	Hoffman 1967
Euclinostomum heterostomum	P		Bykhovskaya – Pavlovskaya *et al.* 1964
Euparyphium melis	YP	Nares, urinary bladder	Hoffman 1967
Gyrodactylidae gen. sp.	YP	Gills	Margolis & Arthur 1979
Gyrodactyloidea gen. sp.	YP,W	Skin, gills	Margolis & Arthur 1979
Gyrodactylus freemani	YP	Fins	Margolis & Arthur 1979
Gyroactylus sp.	P,YP	Skin, fins, gills	Hoffman 1967; Kennedy 1974

153

Parasite	Host	Site	Author
Hemiurus appendiculatus	P		Bykhovskaya – Pavlovskaya *et al.* 1964
Hysteromorpha triloba	P		Bykhovskaya – Pavlovskaya *et al.* 1964
Ichthyocotylurus cucullus	P		Kennedy 1974
I. pileatus	P,Z		Chubb 1979
I. platycephalus	P		Chubb 1979
Ichthyocotylurus sp.	P		Kennedy 1974
Leuceruthrus sp.	YP	Gut	Hoffman 1967 Margolis & Arthur 1979
Maritrema medium	YP		Hoffman 1967
Metagonimus yokogawai	P,Z		Bykhovskaya – Pavlovskaya *et al.* 1964; Chubb 1979
Metorchis conjunctus	YP	Musculature	Margolis & Arthur 1979
Microphallidae gen. sp.	YP		Margolis & Arthur 1979
Microphallus medius	YP		Hoffman 1967
M. opacus	YP	Intestine	Hoffman 1967; Margolis & Arthur 1979
Neascus brevicaudatus	P	Eye (vitreous humour and iris)	Bykhovskaya – Pavlovskaya *et al.* 1964; Markevich 1963
N. ellipticus	YP	Muscle	Hoffman 1967
N. longicollis	YP	Skin	Hoffman 1967
N. oneidensis	YP		Hoffman 1967
N. pyriformis	YP	Skin, fins	Hoffman 1967; Margolis & Arthur 1979
Neascus sp.	YP,W	Mesenteries, gills, skin	Hoffman 1967; Margolis & Arthur 1979
Paracoenogonimus ovatus	P,Z		Bykhovskaya – Pavlovskaya *et al.* 1964; Chubb 1979
Petasiger nitidus	YP		Hoffman 1967
Phyllodistomum americanum	YP		Hoffman 1967
P. angulatum	P,Z	Urinary bladder	Bykhovskaya – Pavlovskaya *et al.* 1964; Markevich 1963;
P. folium	P		Bykhovskaya – Pavlovskaya *et al.* 1964
P. pseudofolium	P		Bykhovskaya – Pavlovskaya *et al.* 1964
P. superbum	YP,W	Ureters, urinary bladder	Hoffman 1967; Margolis & Arthur 1979
Posthodiplostomum brevicaudatum	P		Chubb 1979
P. cuticola	P		Bykhovskaya – Pavlovskaya *et al.* 1964

Parasite	Host	Site	Author
P. minimum	P,YP,W	Kidney, liver mesenteries, spleen	Hoffman 1967; Margolis & Arthur 1979
P. minimum centrarchi	YP	Liver	Margolis & Arthur 1979
Prosorhynchoides pusilla	W	Stomach, pyloric caecae, intestine	Margolis & Arthur 1979
Ptychogonimus fontanus	YP	Stomach	Hoffman 1967; Margolis & Arthur 1979
Rhipidocotyle illense	P		Kennedy 1974
R. papillosa	YP	Musculature	Margolis & Arthur 1979
Rossicotrema donicum	P		Bykhovskaya – Pavlovskaya *et al.* 1964
Sanguinicola occidentalis	YP,W	Blood	Hoffman 1967; Margolis & Arthur 1979
Sphaerostoma bramae	P	Intestine	Bykhovskaya – Pavlovskaya *et al.* 1964; Markevich 1963
Stephanophiala farionis	YP		Hoffman 1967
Striegeidae gen. sp.	YP	Mesenteries	Margolis & Arthur 1979
Tetracotyle diminuti	YP	Mesenteries	Margolis & Arthur 1979
T. echinata	P	Peritoneum	Bykhovskaya – Pavlovskaya *et al.* 1964
T. intermedia	YP	Heart, mesenteries	Margolis & Arthur 1979
T. percafluviatilis	P	Peritoneum, walls of swim bladder and surface of various body cavity organs	Bykhovskaya – Pavlovskaya *et al.* 1964; Markevich 1963
T. variegatus	P,Z	Peritoneal epithelium, walls of swim bladder and other body cavity organs	Markevich 1963
Tetracotyle sp.	P,YP,Z	Heart, pericardium, kidney, wall of swim and urinary bladders, mesenteries, musculature	Hoffman 1967; Kennedy 1974; Margolis & Arthur 1979; Petrushevskii 1963

155

Parasite	Host	Site	Author
Tylodelphys clavata	P,Z		Kennedy 1974; Chubb 1979
T. podicipina	P		Kennedy 1974
Urocleidus aculeatus	W	Gills	Margolis & Arthur 1979; Suriano & Beverley-Burton 1981
U. adspectus	YP	Gills	Hoffman 1967; Margolis & Arthur 1979
Uvulifer ambloplitis	YP,W	Skin, musculature, fins, gills	Hoffman 1967; Margolis & Arthur 1979

CESTODA

Parasite	Host	Site	Author
Abothrium crassium	W		Cross 1938
Bothriocephalus cuspidatus	YP,W	Pyloric caecae; intestine	Hoffman 1967; Margolis & Arthur 1979
Bothriocephalus sp.	P,YP	Pyloric caecae, intestine	Kennedy 1974; Margolis & Athur 1979
Cestoda gen. sp.	YP	Musculature, mesenteries, viscera, intestine	Margolis & Arthur 1979
Corallobothrium sp.	YP	Intestine	Margolis & Arthur 1979; Molnar *et al.* 1974
Cyathocephalus truncatus	P,YP,Z	Pyloric caecae, intestine	Bykhovskaya – Pavlovskaya *et al.* 1964 Dechtiar & Loftus 1965; Deufel 1961; Margolis & Arthur 1979
Cysticercus Gryporhynchus cheilancristrotus	P		Bykhovskaya – Pavlovskaya *et al.* 1964
Diphyllobothrium latum	P,YP,W	Musculature, body cavity	Bykhovskaya – Pavlovskaya *et al.* 1964; Hoffman 1967; Margolis & Arthur 1979
Diphyllobothrium sp.	P,YP,W	Viscera, musculature, body cavity, blood vessels of heart	Kennedy 1974; Margolis & Arthur 1979

Parasite	Host	Site	Author
Eubothrium crassum	P	Gut	Bykhovskaya - Pavlovskaya *et al.* 1979
Eubothrium sp.	P		Kennedy 1974
Ligula intestinalis	P,YP,Z	Body cavity	Hoffman 1967; Margolis & Arthur 1979; Markevich 1963
Proteocephalus ambloplitis	YP,W	Viscera	Hoffman 1967; Margolis & Arthur 1979
P. cernuae	P	Intestine	Bykhovskaya - Pavlovskaya *et al.* 1964; Markevich 1963
P. dubius	P	Intestine	Bykhovskaya - Pavlovskaya *et al.* 1964; Markevich 1963
P. luciopercae	W	Intestine	Hoffman 1967; Margolis & Arthur 1979
P. pearsei	YP,W	Intestine	Hoffman 1967; Margolis & Arthur 1979
P. percae	P,Z	Intestine	Markevich 1963
P. pinguis	YP,W	Intestine	Hoffman 1967; Margolis & Arthur 1979
P. stizostethi	W	Intestine	Hoffman 1967; Margolis & Arthur 1979
P. torulosus	P	Intestine	Markevich 1963
Proteocephalus sp.	P,W	Intestine pyloric caecae	Hoffman 1967; Kennedy 1974; Margolis & Arthur 1979
Schistocephalus solidus	YP	Abdominal cavity	Margolis & Arthur 1979; Molnar *et al.* 1974
Triaenophorus crassus	W	Intestine	Margolis & Arthur 1979
T. nodulosus	P,YP W,Z	Liver and gut	Bykhovskaya - Pavlovskaya *et al.* 1964; Hoffman 1967; Margolis & Arthur 1979; Markevich 1963
T. stizostedionis	W	Intestine	Hoffman 1967; Margolis & Arthur 1979
T. tricuspidatus	YP		Hoffman 1967
Triaenophorus sp.	YP,W	Musculature	Margolis & Arthur 1979

Parasite	Host	Site	Author
NEMATODA			
Agamospirura sp.	Z		Chubb 1980
Anisakis sp.	Z		Eslami & Mokhayer 1977
Camallanus lacustris	P,Z	Intestine	Bykhovskaya – Pavlovskaya *et al.* 1964; Markevich 1963
C. oxycephallus	YP,W	Intestine	Hoffman 1967; Margolis & Arthur 1979
C. truncatus	P,Z	Intestine	Bykhovskaya – Pavlovskaya *et al.* 1964; Markevich 1963
Camallanus sp.	YP		Hoffman 1967; Margolis & Arthur 1979
Capillaria catenata	YP,W	Intestine	Hoffman 1967
C. salvelina	P	Intestine	Kennedy 1974
Contracaecum aduncum	P		Bykhovskaya – Pavlovskaya *et al.* 1964
C. brachyurum	YP,W	Stomach, intestine	Hoffman 1967
C. rudolphii	YP		Chubb 1980
C. spiculigerum	YP	Liver, mesenteries	Hoffman 1967; Margolis & Arthur 1979
C. squalii	P	Body cavity	Bykhovskaya – Pavlovskaya *et al.* 1964
Contracaecum sp.	YP,W	Intestine, stomach, viscera, mesenteries, musculature	Hoffman 1967; Margolis & Arthur 1979
Cucullanellus cotylophora	YP,W	Intestine	Margolis & Arthur 1979
Cucullanus marinus	Z	Intestine	Markevich 1963
C. truttae	P	Intestine	Kennedy 1974
Dactinitoides cotylophora	YP,W		Hoffman 1967
Desmidocercella numidica	P		Chubb 1980
Desmidocercella sp.	P,Z		Bykhovskaya – Pavlovskaya *et al.* 1964; Chubb 1980
Diohelyne sp.	YP		Bangham 1955
Eustrongylides excisus	P,Z		Bykhovskaya – Pavlovskaya *et al.* 1964; Chubb 1980
E. mergorum	P		Bykhovskaya – Pavlovskaya *et al.* 1964
E. tubifex	YP		Chubb 1980

158

Parasite	Host	Site	Author
Eustrongylides sp.	P,YP W,Z	Viscera, musculature, body cavity, ovary	Hoffman 1967; Kennedy 1974; Margolis & Arthur 1979; Petrushevskii 1963; Chubb 1980
Gnathostoma sp.	P		Bykhovskaya - Pavlovskaya *et al.* 1964
Ichthyobronema conoura	P	Intestine	Markevich 1963
I. gnedini	P		Bykhovskaya - Pavlovskaya *et al.* 1964
I. tenuissima	P	Stomach	Markevich 1963
Nematoda gen. sp.	YP	Viscera, musculature, intestine, stomach	Margolis & Arthur 1979
Philometra abdominalis	Z		Chubb 1982
P. cylindracea	YP,W	Peritoneum, abdomen, swim bladder	Hoffman 1967; Margolis & Arthur 1979
Philometra sp.	YP	Body cavity, intestine	Margolis & Arthur 1979
Porrocaecum reticulatum	P		Bykhovskaya - Pavlovskaya *et al.* 1964
Raphidascaris acus	P,W,Z	Intestine	Bykhovskaya - Pavlovskaya *et al.* 1964; Margolis & Arthur 1979; Markevich 1963; Chubb 1980
R. cristata	P		Kennedy 1974
Raphidascaris sp.	YP,W	Liver, gut	Margolis & Arthur 1979
Rhabdochona canadensis	W	Intestine	Margolis & Arthur 1979
R. cascadilla	YP	Intestine	Margolis & Arthur 1979
R. ovifilament	YP	Intestine	Hoffman 1967; Margolis & Arthur 1979
Rhabdochona sp.	YP	Intestine	Hoffman 1967; Margolis & Arthur 1979
Spinitectus carolini	YP,W		Hoffman 1967
S. gracilis	YP,W	Intestine	Hoffman 1967; Margolis & Arthur 1979
Spinitectus sp.	YP,W	Gut	Hoffman 1967; Margolis & Arthur 1979
Spiroxys contortus	YP	Intestinal serosa	Margolis & Arthur 1979; Molnar *et al.* 1974
Spiroxys sp.	YP	Viscera, mesenteries, digestive tract	Hoffman 1967; Margolis & Arthur 1979

Parasite	Host	Site	Author
Thynnascaris brachyura	W		Margolis & Arthur 1979

ACANTHOCEPHALA

Parasite	Host	Site	Author
Acanthcephalus anguillae	P	Intestine	Bykhovskaya - Pavlovskaya *et al.* 1964
A. clavula	P		Kennedy 1974
A. jacksoni	YP		Hoffman 1967; Margolis & Arthur 1979
A. lucii	P,Z	Intestine	Bykhovskaya - Pavlovskaya *et al.* 1964; Markevich 1963
Corynosoma semerme	P,Z	Body cavity	Bykhovskaya - Pavlovskaya *et al.* 1964; Petrushevskii 1963
C. strumosum	P,Z	Intestine	Bykhovskaya - Pavlovskaya *et al.* 1964; Petrushevskii 1963
Echinorhynchus clavula	P,Z	Intestine	Markevich 1951
E. coregoni	YP		Hoffman 1967
E. lateralis	YP		Hoffman 1967
E. salmonis	YP	Intestine	Hoffman 1967
E. salvelini	YP		Hoffman 1967
E. truttae	P	Intestine	Campbell 1974
Echinorhynus sp.	P		Kennedy 1974
Leptorhynchoides thecatus	YP,W	Intestine	Hoffman 1967; Margolis & Arthur 1979
Metechinorhynchus lateralis	YP	Intestine, mesenteries	Margolis & Athur 1979
M. salmonis	P,YP,W	Intestine	Bykhovskaya - Pavlovskaya *et al.* 1964; Dechtiar 1972a; Margolis & Arthur 1979; Oliver 1960
Metechinorhynchus sp.	W		Margolis & Arthur 1979
Neoechinrhynchus crassus	W	Intestine	Margolis & Arthur 1979
N. cylindratus	YP,W	Intestine	Hoffman 1967; Margolis & Arthur 1979
N. pungitius	YP	Intestine, stomach	Margolis & Arthur 1979
N. rutili	P,YP	Intestine	Bangham 1955; Margolis & Arthur 1979; Bykhovskaya - Pavlovskaya *et al.* 1964

Parasite	Host	Site	Author
N. tenellus	W		Hoffman 1967; Margolis & Arthur 1979
Neoechinrhynchus sp.	YP,W	Intestine	Margolis & Arthur 1979
Pomphorhynchus bulbocolli	YP,W	Intestine, mesenteries	Hoffman 1967; Margolis & Arthur 1979
P. laevis	P	Intestine	Kennedy 1974
Pomphorhynchus sp.	W	Intestine	Margolis & Arthur 1979
Pseudoechinorhynchus clavula	P		Bykhovskaya - Pavlovskaya *et al.* 1964

HIRUDINOIDEA

Actinobdella sp.	YP		Hoffman 1967; Margolis & Arthur 1979
Cystobrunchus verrilli	W		Hoffman 1967
Hemiclepsis marginata	P		Bykhovskaya - Pavlovskaya *et al.* 1964
Illinobdella alba	YP	Skin	Hoffman 1967; Margolis & Arthur 1979
I. moorei	YP,W		Hoffman 1967
Illinobdella sp.	YP	Fins	Hoffman 1967; Margolis & Arthur 1979
Macrobdella decora	W	Skin	Margolis & Arthur 1979
Myzobdella moorei	YP,W	Fins	Margolis & Arthur 1979
Percymoorensis marmorata	W	Skin	Margolis & Arthur 1979
Piscicola geometra	P,W	Skin	Bykhovskaya - Pavlovskaya *et al.* 1964; Markevich 1963; Rawson 1957
P. punctata	YP,W	Skin, gills	Margolis & Arthur 1979; Oliver 1960
Piscicola sp.	YP	Skin	Hoffman 1967; Margolis & Arthur 1979
Placobdella parasitica	YP	Skin	Hoffman 1967; Margolis & Arthur 1979
P. picta	YP		

MOLLUSCA

Anodonta anatina	P.		Campbell 1974
Anodonta sp.	YP	Gills	Margolis & Arthur 1979
Elliptio complanata	YP	Gills	Margolis & Arthur 1979
Lampsilis radiata	YP	Gills	Margolis & Arthur 1979
Unionidae gen. sp.	YP,W	Fins, gills, skin	Margolis & Arthur 1979

Parasite	Host	Site	Author
CRUSTACEA			
Achtheres lacae	YP	Gills	Hoffman 1967
A. percarum	P,Z	Gills, mouth	Bykhovskaya – Pavlovskaya *et al.* 1964 Markevich 1963
Argulus appendiculosus	YP		Hoffman 1967
A. biramosus	YP,W		Hoffman 1967
A. canadensis	W		Dechtiar 1972b
A. catostomi	YP		Hoffman 1967
A. foliaceus	P,Z	Oral and gill cavities, body surface	Bykhovskaya – Pavlovskaya *et al.* 1964
A. stizostethii	YP,W	Skin, fins	Hoffman 1967; Margolis & Arthur 1979
A. versicolor	YP,W	Fins	Dechtiar 1972a; Hoffman 1967; Margolis & Arthur 1979
Caligus lacustris	P	Gills, skin	Bykhovskaya – Pavlovskaya *et al.* 1964
Copepoda gen. sp.	W.	Gills, fins, mouth	Margolis & Arthur 1979
Ergasilus briani	P	Gills	Bykhovskaya – Pavlovskaya *et al.* 1964
E. caeruleus	YP,W	Gills	Hoffman 1967; Margolis & Arthur 1979
E. centrarchidarum	YP,W	Gills	Hoffman 1967; Margolis & Arthur 1979
E. confusus	YP,W		Hoffman 1967
E. luciopercarum	YP,W	Gills	Hoffman 1967; Margolis & Arthur 1979
E. sieboldi	P,Z	Gills	Bykhovskaya – Pavlovskaya *et al.* 1964
Ergosilus sp.	YP,W	Gills	Margolis & Arthur 1979
Lernaea cyprinacea	P	Skin	Bykhovskaya – Pavlovskaya *et al.* 1964
L. esocina	P,Z	Skin and gills	Bykhovskaya – Pavlovskaya *et al.* 1964; Markevich 1963
Thersitina gasterostei	P	Skin	Bykhovskaya – Pavlovskaya *et al.* 1964
ACARINA			
Hydrachna sp.	YP	Gills	Margolis & Arthur 1979

usually the larval stage of the parasite which
causes disease in fish. The adult parasite of *S.
occidentalis* lives in the blood vessels of yellow
perch and walleye, and a snail, belonging to the
family Limnaeidae, acts as the single intermediate
host. *Diplostomum spathaceum* infects the eye of
perch, yellow perch and zander. These fish are the
second intermediate host to the parasite, the
definitive host is a bird, often a gull. Eggs from
the adult worm in the gut of the gull are released
in the faeces and motile miracidia which develop
from these eggs infect the first intermediate host,
a limnaeid snail. Cercaria are released from the
snail, penetrate the skin of the percid and reach
the eyes through the blood system. Here the parasites develop into metacercaria and the life cycle
is complete when the fish is eaten by a bird.

Many cestodes are parasitic on percids. The
adult tapeworms live in the gut of the definitive
host but encyst in the body organs and muscle of
fish which act as intermediate hosts. Adult
Triaenophorus nodulosus for example live in the gut
of pike. Coracidia which develop from the eggs released in the faeces of the pike infect copepods
such as *Cyclops bicuspidatus* Claus. Here they
develop into infective procercoids and when eaten
by a percid, penetrate the intestine of the fish.
They enter the body cavity and eventually encyst as
plerocercoids in the liver. If the percid is not
eaten by a pike the parasites will eventually die
and degenerate.

Adult worms of Nematoda are found in the gut
of percids and encysted larval stages often inhabit
the liver. Adult *Raphidascaris acus* occur in the
pyloric caecae and anterior regions of the intestine. The main definitive host appears to be pike
although gravid female worms have also been found
in the intestines of walleye (Poole & Dick 1986).
Fertilised eggs are released with the host's
faeces. The eggs may be eaten by a fish host
directly or larvae hatching from the eggs may be
eaten by a fish or an invertebrate. In the latter
situation, the fish becomes infected when the
invertebrate is eaten. After the larvae are
ingested by the perch they penetrate the intestine
wall and enter the body cavity. They migrate to
the liver where they encyst. The parasite is
transmitted to the definitive host when the perch
is eaten. Walleye can also carry larval worms in
the liver and thus act as an intermediate host
(Poole & Dick 1986).

Acanthocephala adult and larval worms live in the intestine. Mature worms produce shelled acanthors which are liberated into the water and are ingested by the intermediate host which is usually an invertebrate. *Acanthcephalus lucii* is a common parasite of perch and zander, the intermediate host is normally the isopod, *Asellus aquaticus* (Linnaeus). Infection of the fish host occurs when *A. aquaticus* is eaten. Pike have been reported to become infected with the parasite by eating perch which acts in this situation as an intermediate host (Moravec 1979).

Several leeches (Hirudinoidea) are external parasites living on the skin and gills of fish. *Piscicola geometra* commonly occurs on these sites particularly at the base of the fins and in the mouth of perch. It has been introduced into North America and has been identified on walleye. It is probably a parasite of yellow perch but no record has been seen. When a fish swims within range of a leech attached to the substratum the leech moves onto the surface of the fish and finds a suitable location. Blood is drawn from the host by insertion of a proboscis and when engorged the leech drops from the fish. Sexual reproduction takes place away from the host on the river or lake bottom. The cocoons each containing one egg are produced in large numbers and are deposited on stones.

Larval stages of some molluscs are also ectoparasites of fish including percids. The fresh water clam, *Lampsilis radiata,* has a life cycle which is partly parasitic. The early development of the clam takes place within the marsupium of the female. Glochidia, released by the females in late spring and early summer, burrow into the gills of fish including yellow perch and encyst. In this stage they develop adult organs and eventually break away and settle to the bottom as young clams.

Some copepod and branchiuran crustacea are parasitic on the body, gills and oral cavity of percids. The copepod, *Ergasilus sieboldi,* is a common gill parasite of perch and zander. The mature female is the parasitic phase of the life cycle. Embryonic development takes place in egg sacs which are paired and contain about 100 eggs each. There are three nauplius and four copepodid free living stages each proceeded by a moult. Differentiation of the sexes and copulation occur at the fourth copepodid stage. The males die and

the females enter the gill cavity and finally
attach themselves to the gill filaments where they
live for about one year (Bauer *et al.* 1973). Some
parasitic species of copepod are found on a number
of fresh water fish groups, for example *Lernaea
cyprinacea* is common in cyprinids as well as percids. Others, such as *Actheres percarum*, have
specific hosts, perch and zander (Fryer 1982).
Branchiurans, unlike copepods, moult several times
after reaching sexual maturity and adults can be
found in a wide range of sizes (Fryer 1982). Eggs
of *Argulus foliaceus* are laid in clumps or rows on
stones or other suitable substrate and vary in
number but are usually in the range 250-300 per
clutch. Those laid in the summer hatch in that
year while those laid in the autumn may overwinter
as eggs. Larvae hatch as late nauplii (Fryer 1982)
and must find a host fish within about 48 h. All
stages, other than the egg, are free swimming thus
the parasite can move from host to host. The
maxillules are elaborate hook-like structures in
the larval stage which are used to cling onto the
host. After several moults the maxillules are
transformed into suckers. On attaching itself to
the host, *A. foliaceus* pierces the skin with its
proboscis and sucks blood.

The last group of parasites to be considered
belong to the Acarina. Their life cycle is not
completely clear. Eggs of water mites are usually
laid on stones, vegetation or debris but in the
case of *Hydrachna* they are deposited in the tissues
of aquatic plants. Free swimming larvae emerge
which eventually become attached to aquatic
insects. A species of *Hydrachna* has been found on
the gills of yellow perch (Tedla & Fernando 1969).
The parasitic larvae develop into inactive nymphs
called nymphophans. Nymphs break from the host and
after an active free living period, pupate on
rooted vegetation or bottom debris. This second
pupal stage is called a teleiophan, from it emerges
the sexually mature adult which is also free
living.

Abiotic and Biotic Factors

As outlined in the introduction to this
chapter, abiotic and biotic conditions of the environment play a major part in the population
dynamics of parasites and the outbreak of disease.
Abiotic factors not only influence ectoparasites

and free living stages of endoparasites directly, but through their control of the physiological and or hormonal state of the host (invertebrate or vertebrate), affect all parasites indirectly. Temperature is probably the single most important abiotic controlling factor (Bauer 1962; Chubb 1982). This is particularly the case with ectoparasites. In monogeneans for example, temperature is significant in all stages of life including rate of oviposition, speed of development of embryo, length of life of oncomiracidium, the speed of maturation of the juvenile and the longevity of the adult. An increase in temperature can increase activity and decrease longevity of these parasites. It can shorten embryonic development time and in some cases promote synchronised hatching. Larvae of *Ichthyophthirius multifiliis* hatch faster from the ciliospores at higher temperatures although they tend to be smaller (Bauer 1962). The optimum temperature for embryonic development is characteristic for a given species of parasite and these may be different for two or more parasites living off the same host. *Triaenophorus nodulosus* and *Diphyllobothrium latum* eggs can develop at 0°C but the optimum is 20°C and death of the embryos occurs at 35°C. These types of parasites with wide thermal limits are called eurythermic by Bauer (1962). Eggs of *Argulus foliaceus* will not develop below 10°C and optimum temperature is 25-26°C. This is the same optimum temperature for *Ichthyophthirius multifiliis, Ergasilus sieboldi, Lernaea cyprinacea, Ligula intestinalis* and others. This latter group will not develop below 14°C. Temperature limits restrict the distribution of parasites. The trematode *Clinostomum complanatum* is normally located within the annual 10°C isotherm and warmer regions. It has been found in a colder area where its host existed in warmed waters from a cooling plant and the artificially raised temperatures allowed the eggs of the parasite to develop (Grabda-Kazubska 1974). Temperature increases may not always benefit egg production. *Bunodera lucioperca* matures during the winter, is gravid in the spring and releases eggs in the summer. A cool period through the winter is required for their development (Andrews 1977). Egg release at an optimum temperature can produce epizootics in a number of species which cause fish kills at the hottest time of the year. This has been reported

for *Ichthyophthirius multifiliis* and *Diphyllobothrium latum* and probably occurs in many other
disease inducing parasites. Temperature influences
such fish-parasite active invasive phases as protozoan ciliospores, monogenean free swimming larvae,
digenetic trematode miracidia and cercaria, cestode
coracidia and various stages of crustaceans. The
seasonal changes in prevalence and intensity of
parasites (Margolis, Esch, Holmes, Kuris & Schad
1982) are in many cases a reflection of temperature. The subject of seasonality of helminth
parasites has been extensively reviewed by Chubb
(1977; 1979; 1980; 1982) but the complex underlying
controlling factors are still not elucidated. A
study conducted on the helminths found in the
intestine of yellow perch of Lake Opeongo, Canada,
illustrates the complexity of seasonal abundance of
parasites in the host (Cannon 1973). Two trematodes, *Bunodera sacculata* and *B. lucioperca*, and
one cestode, *Proteocephalus pearsei*, showed their
lowest incidence in the summer. One trematode,
Crepidostomum cooperi, and one nematode, *Dactinitoides cotylophora*, were highest in incidence in
the summer. The cestode *Bothriocephalus* sp., the
nematode *Spinitectus gracilis* and the acanthocephalan *Leptorhynchoides thecatus* showed no
seasonality. Some parasites may not show any
seasonality in their overall abundance although the
maturation state of the parasite may show marked
seasonality. Larvae and adults of the nematode,
Camallanus lacustris, are found in the intestine of
perch throughout the year and their abundance is
non-seasonal (Skorping 1980). However the number
of gravid females shows marked seasonality. The
parasite is mainly found in the pylorus region of
the intestine from May to October, but from
December to March most of the worms are found in
the posterior region.

Light, oxygen concentration, pH, salinity and
possibly water current and water chemistry help
control the life cycle of parasites but have less
influence than temperature. Only a few experiments
have been carried out to test the importance of
light. The eggs of *Triaenophorus nodulosus* were
found to take longer to develop in the dark compared to those kept in diffuse light (Mikhailov
1951). The coracidia of this parasite are
positively phototactic and thus, like the cyclo-
poids which ingest them, are active in the daytime. Although light may be important in the
development of larvae from eggs, it can reduce the

time of the free living larval stage in some
species. The ciliospores of *Ichthyophthirius multifiliis* die two to four times faster in diffuse
light than in the dark (Bauer 1962). Light
probably plays an important role in the seasonality
of parasites. This influence can be direct, such
as on ectoparasites and free living stages of endoparasites, or indirectly, through hormonal response
of the host to light. This may be an area of
future productive research.

Many ectoparasites and free living stages of
endoparasites show considerable variability in
their tolerance to different concentrations of
oxygen in the water. *Piscicola geometra* for
example has a high oxygen demand and when it is
free living, it is found on wave-washed shores of
lakes or in fast-flowing streams and rivers
(Elliott & Mann 1979). At the other extreme,
Argulus foliaceus appears to be intolerant of high
levels of oxygen and can carry out all stages of
its life cycle at low oxygen concentrations. It is
best suited to living in stagnant water. Oxygen
dependence of parasites living in the fish will be
determined by the physiological state of the fish.
Those parasites living in oxygen rich areas of the
body, for example the blood, heart and swim
bladder, may carry out more aerobic respiration
than those living in oxygen poor areas, such as the
gut, where anaerobic respiration is probably manda-
tory. Endoparasites live in a fairly constant pH
environment of 7.2 to 7.8. Ectoparasites and free
living developmental stages will normally tolerate
pH limits over a similar range to their fish hosts
(Chapter 6). *Icthyophthirius multifiliis* has a
tolerance range from pH 5.5 to 10.1. Above or
below these values the parasite cannot attach
itself to the host and cysts are not formed (Bauer
1962). The coracidia of *Triaenophorus crassus* die
at pH 5.0.

Many of the parasites found on percids are
also tolerant to the same salinity ranges as their
hosts (Chapter 6). *Triaenophorus nodulosus* is
euryhaline and its eggs can develop in salinities
up to 6‰ and coracidia can live in salinities not
exceeding 7‰. This parasite exists on perch and
zander which live in brackish areas such as the
Baltic Sea. They appear to be able to tolerate the
transition between fresh and brackish water. Some
ectoparasites, including leeches, molluscs and
crustacean larvae, are sensitive to increases in
salinity.

Other living organisms in the environment have a major influence on the abundance of fish parasites. Parasite transmission is influenced by the diet and rate of food intake of the fish host. If the incidence of the parasite in the infective stage can reach a peak at the same time as maximum feeding in the host then transmission of the parasite will be greatly enhanced. Chubb (1964) showed that the low incidence of *Triaenophorus nodulosus* in perch at Llyn Tegid, Wales, was caused by the absence of copepods, first intermediate hosts, in the diet of perch at the main period of infection. In a long term study at Heming Lake, Canada, on the occurrence of *T. nodulosus* in yellow perch and pike which were subjected to heavy fishing, Lawler (1969) discovered some interesting aspects concerning parasite loading and the state of the fish host populations. Young yellow perch had a higher prevalence of the parasite than the older and larger yellow perch because cyclopods were far more important in the diet of young fish. If the yellow perch were not eaten by the definitive host, in this case the pike, the encysted plerocercoids degenerated. This occurs after one and a half to three years in perch (Chubb 1964). At Heming Lake the reduction in the size of the yellow perch population by fishing allowed the remaining yellow perch to grow more quickly but the fishing also reduced the numbers of large old pike which formed a reservoir for *T. nodulosus* eggs. The smaller pike were not able to feed on the larger yellow perch and a reduction in the prevalence of the parasite took place. After fishing stopped *T. nodulosus* again became common in the yellow perch (Poole & Dick 1985).

A number of parasites may be eaten by predators. For example some copepods feed on *Icthyophthirius multifiliis* and the coracidia of *Ligula intestinalis* (Bauer 1962) and perch feed on *Piscicola geometra* (Bauer 1962) and *Argulus* sp. (Craig 1974a). Bauer (1962) suggests that considerable numbers of eggs of helminth parasites may be eaten and digested by detritus feeders and this could have a significant effect on parasite abundance. Little is known about this.

Some species of parasite may compete for similar sites of infection. The metacercariae of *Diplostomum gasterostei*, *Tylodelphys clavata* and *T. podicipina* are found in the eyes of perch, usually in the vitreous humour, although *D. gasterostei* is occasionally found in the lens.

T. clavata was accidentally introduced in Slapton
Ley, England, where previously the only eyefluke
observed in perch had been *D. gasterostei*. The
population of *T. clavata* in the perch host and its
interactions with other eyeflukes were studied over
the next seven years (Kennedy 1981). During the
study *T. podicipina* was introduced into the system.
The definitive host of the *Tylodelphys* species is
the great crested grebe, *Podiceps cristatus*
Linnaeus, which started a breeding population and
is believed to have introduced the parasites. All
three parasites infect the snail, *Lymnaea peregra*
Müller, as the first intermediate host. The population of *T. clavata* increased slowly at first then
rapidly and finally declined as the population
level reached an equilibrium. Kennedy (1981) considers a decline in the population of *D.
gasterostei* was due to two independent events.
Firstly the numbers of the perch host carrying
heavy infections declined and secondly the recruitment of the parasites into young perch was reduced.
It was suggested by Kennedy that these processes
related to changes in the population density of the
other eyeflukes. The decline in the number of fish
heavily infected with *D. gasterostei* was
significantly related to the increase in *T.
clavata* and the decrease in the recruitment into
the young fish was related to the increase in *T.
podicipina* in the eyes of the young perch. Kennedy
(1981) suggests that the two species of *Tylodephys*
interact negatively with *D. gasterostei* and in
Slapton Ley are presently partitioning the perch
habitat between themselves. There are probably
many other examples of competition between
parasites and antagonistic relationships between
them.

In many cases the density of the fish host
population controls the abundance of the parasite.
A large host population increases the chance of
success at the invasive phase of the parasite.
When the fish is living at the extreme of its range
and densities are low the number of species and
density of parasites is minimal compared with the
host in its normal range (Bauer 1962). Outbreaks
of disease often occur when fish populations con-
gregate together during spawning which enhances the
chances of infection although fish may be more vulnerable to invasion by the parasite at this time
due to their physiological state. The condition or
fat content of the fish host may influence the
susceptibility of the fish to infection. At the

time of spawning the condition of the fish is usually poor. The life cycle of parasites may be linked to the hormonal condition of the fish. The actions of host hormones on the parasite are probably indirect though there is no real indication of the mechanisms involved. Some parasites make some selection in the sex of the host. In Lake Opeongo, Canada, no species of parasite was more prevalent in the male than in the female yellow perch but the cestode, *Proteocephalus pearsei*, and the acanthocephalan, *Leptorhynchoides thecatus* were more prevalent in female fish (Cannon 1973). Prevalence of parasites increased with size of the yellow perch although the increase in some parasites was influenced by sex. For example *Bunodera lucioperca*, *Bothriocephalus* sp., *Spinitectus gracilis* and *L. thecatus* only increased in abundance with increase in size of female yellow perch.

Long term climatic and biotic changes in the environment can lead to alterations in the parasitic fauna. During the period 1928 to 1936, 26 parasites were recorded in yellow perch from Oneida Lake, USA. In 1966, 24 parasites were found (Noble 1970a). Some rare or accidental parasites identified in the earlier period were not recorded in 1966. The only common species in 1928-31 not found in the yellow perch in 1966 was the trematode, *Clinostomum marginatum*. The trematodes, *Tetracotyle* sp., *Apophallus brevis* and *Urocleidus adspectus* appeared for the first time in the 1966 investigation. Cooper, Ashmead and Crites (1977) compared the long term changes in the helminth parasites of yellow perch in western Lake Erie between the period 1927-9 and the 1970s. They discovered that some parasites had increased in prevalence (*Triaenophorus nodulosus* and *Eustrongylides tubifex*), some had decreased in prevalence (*Crepidostomum cooperi*, *Bothriocephalus* sp., *Proteocephalus* sp. and *Dacnitoides cotylophora*) and some remained about the same (*Philometra cylindracea* and *Camallanus oxycephalus*). Care should be taken in interpreting the results of long term studies since different methods are often used over the time span.

Disease and Mortality

The effect of parasites and diseases on the mortality of the host is not easy to quantify and

mortality is usually only recorded when it is
dramatic. An area of future research must be the
part played by parasites in the natural mortality
of fish populations. Sublethal effects of parasites need further investigation. Do cysts of
flukes in the eye of percids cause vision impair-
ment? Do gut parasites reduce absorption in the
gut and thus reduce feeding efficiency? How do
parasites affect oxygen uptake and ion balance? Do
some of these effects make the host more susceptible to predation? When large kills of percids
have been recorded it has usually been difficult to
identify the causal agent and often little is known
about the fish populations which have died. It has
long been recognised by fish culturists that transfer of fish between ponds or from one hatchery to
another could induce outbreaks of disease often
leading to heavy mortalities. Water quality was
and is considered of fundamental importance in the
successful rearing of fish. It has also been observed that the resistance of fish to disease is a
function of their age, and exposure of fish to an
epizootic results in more resistance to subsequent
attacks.

Immunology is the study of the host's ability
to make itself exempt from a disease by defending
itself against attack (Anderson 1974). It is a
discipline that has been poorly researched in fish
other than those being cultured such as salmonids
and carps (cyprinids). We need to know much more
about the ability of fish to withstand invasion by
viruses, bacteria, protozoan and metazoan
parasites. The most effective defence against
pathogens, other than against those entering the
gut after ingestion, is the skin. The protective
layers include the mucous, scales, epidermis and
dermis. The constant sloughing of the mucous re-
moves foreign particles attached to it. The mucous
may also contain antibodies. A break in this protective barrier by wounding, including penetration
by parasites such as leeches and branchiurans,
allows entrance of bacteria, viruses and fungi.
Inflammation may occur at the wound. Inflammation
allows repairs to tissue damage and prevents
further harm by the accumulation of polymorpho-
nuclear leucocytes and lymphocytes. This reaction
and other immune responses of fishes are controlled
by environmental factors, in particular
temperature. Those fish living near an optimum
temperature will have better responses to parasite
invasion and disease than those living in colder or

warmer areas.

Although there has been some recent development of intensive percid culture, the future of re-
liable sources of fish for consumption must lie in
the enhancement and rehabilitation of their natural
habitat (Chapter 10). One method of doing this is
by planting reared larvae and fry into the water
body. Little is known about the rate of recruitment of the indigenous parasitic fauna by the
introduced fish and whether mortality occurs as a
result. This has been discussed by Poole and Dick
(1985). Walleye fry introduced into Heming Lake,
Canada rapidly acquired parasites that were non-
specific and common to indigenous populations of
walleye and yellow perch. Some parasites, in
particular *Raphidascaris acus* and *Ergasilus
luciopercarum*, were acquired at a higher prevalence
and mean intensity than those found in the indigenous stocks of walleye. These two parasites are
known to be pathogenic. This type of study is
clearly important in any introductions of fish and
must become necessary procedure in the future if
successful management of percid stocks is to be
achieved.

Chapter 8

ADAPTATION, EVOLUTION AND GENETICS

The percids, as described in previous chapters, are
hardy species tolerating a wide range of environments. Some factors of these environments may be
limiting. For example, water temperature limits
their distribution through its effects on metabolic
processes. The upper limit for *Perca* species is a
summer air isotherm of about 31°C which is reached
on the edge of their range in Italy, Greece, the
USA and Australia. The lower limits of the
temperature range may influence reproductive
success rather than the survival of the adults.
The northern distributional limit of walleye to
about the summer air isotherm of 13°C probably is
more a reflection of temperatures required for
maturation and spawning success on a seasonal
cyclic basis than limitations to metabolism.
Perca eggs and young stages can tolerate low pH and
have intermediate requirements in terms of temperature and oxygen concentrations when compared to
other temperate fresh water fish. High production,
growth and survival of percids requires appropriate
food such as zooplankton, littoral invertebrates
and prey fish, at the correct stage in the life
cycle. *Perca* are very successful animals within
the limits of tolerable environmental conditions.
They have relatively high fecundity, fairly un-
specific spawning requirements and can expand
rapidly in numbers when they are introduced to new
bodies of water such as reservoirs and canals. The
same criteria apply to *Stizostedion* species although zander appears to tolerate higher summer
maxima than walleye; it may also be better adapted
to spawning than walleye. Nest building and
guarding leads to better fertilisation and hatching
rate and to lower mortality of eggs and larvae. In
addition the zander is more fecund than the walleye

(Figure 4.3). These factors probably enable zander to spawn more successfully under stressed conditions and to flourish in areas where it has been introduced. Both zander and walleye are particularly successful in lakes with low mean depth, where the water is mixed and there is no thermal stratification. *Stizostedion* species also may compete successfully with other predators because their activities are usually confined to twilight and night.

The plastic nature of percid adaptation to the environment undoubtedly has enabled them to expand within their niche both naturally and as a result of human influence. Specialisation often leads to the end of an evolutionary line. The amount of DNA in teleost haploid cells ranges from 0.4 to 4.4 x 10^{-12} g. It tends to decline the more specialised the fish becomes (Hinegardner 1968; Hinegardner & Rosen 1972). The Percoidei are a fairly specialised group of fish but within the group, members of the Percidae family are of a generalised form. Thus *P. flavescens* has a DNA content of 1.2 x 10^{-12} g compared to a more specialised species such as *Chaetodon ocellatus* Bloch (Chaetodontidae, butterfly fishes) which has a DNA content of 0.87 x 10^{-12} g. Specialisation usually means the loss of structures and possibly an evolutionary 'dead-end'. The generalised form of the percids makes them radially adaptive. However they have certainly not been as successful as Cyprinidae. Up to the Miocene period the Percidae probably played a major role in the fish fauna in Europe. But the appearance of cyprinids at this time may have prevented diversification of the percids. This was not the case in North America where only one fairly primitive cyprinid appeared during the Miocene. Thus some groups of percids were able to diversify leading to the present day extensive *Etheostoma* fauna (Collette & Bănărescu 1977).

A *Perca* ancestor probably evolved from an anadromous offshoot of the Serranidae during the Cenozoic. The basic form of the family Percidae is found in Europe. Fossils of *P. fluviatilis* have been found in Miocene deposits in USSR (Lebedev 1952; Yakovlev 1960), Pliocene deposits in USSR, Austria and Belgium (Sychevskaya & Devyatkin 1960; Weinfurter 1950; Newton 1908) and Pleistocene deposits in USSR and Germany (Svetovidov & Dorofeeva 1963; Gripp & Beyle 1937; Weiler 1933). Fossils of *P. flavescens* have been found from Pleistocene deposits in Oklahoma, USA. These

deposits contain fossils of animals which inhabited
the Great Plains at that time (Smith 1954).
     Although it is generally accepted that *Perca*
and *Stizostedion* species invaded North America by a
north Pacific route (Yakovlev 1961; Collette &
Bănărescu 1977) a number of scientists believe that
the route was from Europe across the Atlantic.
Čihăr (1975) suggests that perch moved from Europe
to North America during the late Pleistocene
glacial Würm period 13-15,000 BP, through brackish
water along the foot of the receding ice sheet.
Their advance in North America was stopped by the
Rocky Mountains in the west and the MacKenzie
mountains in the north west. The spread eastwards
in Asia was halted by the Kolyma and Anadyr
mountains. Čihăr (1975) draws these conclusions
from the fact that perch are not found in north
Siberian rivers (the furthest east is the Kolyma
River, USSR) nor the yellow perch in North American
rivers running into the Bering Sea and Pacific
Ocean. Recently (nineteenth century), yellow perch
have been introduced by humans into water basins
flowing into the Pacific Ocean. Initially, the
yellow perch was distributed in eastern and central
parts of North America from Labrador to Georgia.
Its range in the west was bounded by the
Mississippi River basin and Lesser Slave Lake in
the Mackenzie River system. However Metcalf (1966)
believes, from fossil evidence, that *Perca* were
present in North America 300,000 BP but were
limited to the south of the Great Plains. After
the Wisconsonian glaciation (10,000 BP) they spread
northwest.
     The Balkhash perch, *P. schrenki*, has developed
in isolation since the Tertiary period, unaffected
by glacial activity. However when *P. schrenki* has
been introduced into waters containing *P.
fluviatilis*, hybridisation has occurred and the resulting populations exhibit convergence of morphological characteristics from the two species
(Dukravets & Biryukov 1976). *P. fluviatilis* and
P. flavescens evolution is closely connected and
their similarities in morphology, physiology and
behaviour would indicate that their divergence has
been very recent and their similarities are a result of a common ancestor rather than convergent
evolution. They are limited in their distribution
by similar factors such as salinity, current speed
and oxygen concentration. There has been much con-
troversy over their taxonomy. Mitchill (1818),
Gunther (1859), Steindachner (1878), Day (1880;

1886) Sterba (1962), Scott and Crossman (1973) and
Collette and Bănărescu (1977) have classified *P.
fluviatilis* and *P. flavescens* as separate species.
Jordon and Gilbert (1877), Smith (1892), Berg
(1905; 1949), Pokrovskii (1951) and Čihăr (1975)
have made *P. flavescens* a subspecies of *P.
fluviatilis*, *P. fluviatilis flavescens*. Thorpe
(1977) compared many aspects of the morphology and
biology of the two animals and found them very
similar. Collette and Bănărescu (1977) have
pointed out that there is a difference in the position of the predorsal bone. In *P. fluviatilis* the
bone is anterior to the first neural spine but
in *P. flavescens* the bone is inserted between the
first and second neural spines. On this evidence,
Thorpe (1977) bowed to the opinion of Collette and
Bănărescu (1977) and considered the perch and
yellow perch as two separate species. The contro-
versy will continue until more convincing evidence
is produced. Molecular methods may provide this
evidence although this, as yet, has not been done.
There is no doubt that *P. fluviatilis* and *P.
flavescens* are very closely related.

   S. vitreum has been represented by two subspecies, *S. vitreum vitreum* (Mitchill) and the blue
pike, *S. vitreum glaucum* (Hubbs 1926). The blue
pike inhabited Lake Erie and Lake Ontario but is
now extinct (McAllister 1970). As well as
competition from stocked exotic fish and selective
fishing (Chapter 10), the gene pool of the blue
pike may have become mixed with that of *S. vitreum
vitreum* by hybridisation and the subspecies lost
(Regier, Applegate & Ryder 1969).

   The environmental requirements of walleye are
similar to those of yellow perch although the
walleye extends further north than the yellow
perch. Their niches are closely connected and
probably these species have evolved together. Thus
yellow perch is the chief food of walleye in many
waterbodies and predation may play a part in controlling recruitment both for the predator and prey
(Chapter 9).

   S. lucioperca originated in the Elbe River and
the drainage basins of the Black, Baltic, Caspian
and Aral seas. It has spread throughout Europe as
a result of human introductions. It also now
occurs in western Turkey (Aksiray 1961) and Morocco
(Brunet 1957). Many of the introductions have been
recent and well monitored. The zander did not
appear in French waters until the 1900s. In 1910
it inhabited the Rhine River and the canal

connecting the Rhine and Rhône Rivers (Gagne 1977).
By 1915 it was found in Doubs River, by 1920 in
Sâone River and by 1932 in the Rhône basin (Vivier
1951). In 1948 it inhabited the brackish waters of
Etang du Vaccares, France, where it has now become
very abundant. The zander spread through numerous
introductions into canals, rivers and ponds. Today
it is found in all river basins and a large number
of lakes in France.

The zander was first introduced into England,
by the Duke of Bedford in 1878 (Sachs 1878). He
stocked the lakes on his Woburn estate with them.
Several introductions were made and by 1910 a
breeding population was established (Fitter 1959).
After several unsuccessful attempts at introductions, zander became established in the Great
Ouse Relief Channel, England, in 1963 from the
Woburn stocks (Wheeler & Maitland 1973; Linfield &
Rickards 1979). The zander has spread uncon-
trollably from this open water system to many of
the canals and rivers of East Anglia.

S. volgensis is an eastern European species
while *S. marina,* a partially marine species, is
found in the Black and Caspian seas and the lower
reaches of the River Bug and River Dneiper. Both
species probably have evolved in partial isolation.

Within a percid species there are a number of
races and stocks but the extensive variation in
morphological characteristics within even a population makes it often difficult, if not impossible,
to differentiate between these stocks. Some
attempts have been made in this direction, for
example in comparing scale shape and brain weight
to body weight ratio between populations. The
latter was shown to vary between three populations
of perch in the USSR (Yakovleva, Amstislavskiy &
Baymuratov 1976). The most exciting work being
carried out on stock identification in recent years
has been the use of biochemical techniques. For
example two stocks of perch were identified in one
lake by separation of their blood proteins
(Kirsipuu 1967). This would be consistent with the
theory that two forms of perch live in the same
body of water, a predatory deep water form and a
littoral form living off invertebrates and small
fish. These two forms are certainly present in
Windermere, England, and have been observed else-
where (Starmach 1983). Care should be taken to
ensure that blood protein comparisons have a
genetic basis (Kirsipuu 1971).

Examination of 19 enzymatic loci using starch

gel electrophoresis failed to show any differences
in samples of yellow perch from Green Bay, Lake
Michigan or nearby Keyes Lake, USA (Leary & Booke
1982). All of the loci were effectively monomorphic. Significant differences were found at
four loci between the pooled Lake Michigan yellow
perch and a sample from Lake Champlain, Vermont.
However the reasons for the differences are con-
fusing and do not give any indication of the evolution of these stocks. Starch gel electrophoresis
of muscle myogens demonstrated a polymorphism of
three patterns in walleye, A, B and AB from lakes
in central Canada (Uthe, Roberts, Clarke & Tsuyuki
1966; Uthe & Ryder 1970). The distribution of
these patterns within populations was related by
the authors to the glacial isolation proposed for
walleye, one Atlantic and one Mississippi with a
later mixing as may have occurred in the Great
Lakes. All three forms of polymorphism occur in
the Great Lakes. However the extent of walleye
sampling was not extensive enough to derive
definite conclusions about continental-scale zoo-
geographic events, although of course it is
supported by work on other animals.

In many walleye populations in North America
three alleles are known from one of the supernatant
(cytoplasmic) malate dehydrogenase loci, MDH
(s-mdhB-1, s-mdhB-2 and s-mdhB-3) taken from white
muscle (Clayton, Tretiak & Kooyman 1971; Murphy,
Nielson & Turner 1983). The protein subunits
specified by these alleles produce isozymes that
can be recognised by starch gel electrophoresis.
Other polymorphic loci known in walleye include
mitochondrial isocitrate dehydrogenase, s-idh,
superoxide dismutase, SOD, alcohol dehydrogenase,
ADH, and sorbitol dehydrogenase from the liver and
phosphoglucamutase, PGM, and phosphoglucose
isomerase, PGI, from the muscle myogen (Clayton
personal communication).

In Saskatchewan, walleye populations in two
headwater lakes have a high frequency of one MDH
allele. The frequency of this allele declines a
short distance downstream (Clayton, Harris &
Tretiak 1974). The authors considered that there
was insufficient data to draw any definite conclusions from these population differences.
However the presence of dissimilar genetic groups
has been used in determining the success of
stocking walleye into waters which contain indigenous populations (Schweigert, Ward & Clayton
1977; Murphy, Nielson & Turner 1983; Chapter 10).

The differences between the frequencies of MDH
alleles can be used as 'genetic tags' in the
absence of other suitable marks or morphological
discriminators.

Walleye, sauger and their suspected hybrid
have been distinguished by mitochondrial MDH isozymes (Clayton, Harris & Tretiak 1973). Sauger is
monomorphic containing only s—mdhB—3 compared to
the three alleles in walleye which have already
been described. Hybridisation between these two
species has been recorded and they probably
diverged in recent time. Lynch, Johnson and Schell
(1982) have bred 'saugeye' from female walleye
crossed with male sauger. These 'saugeye' grew and
developed satisfactorily and by the end of the
third year they had reached an average length of
350 to 400 mm. Other attempts at hybridisation
between different species have met with less
success. In cases where the embryo developed, such
as a cross between *P. fluviatilis* and *S.
lucioperca*, the larvae died after hatching
(Kammerer 1907; Balon 1956). In a cross
between *P. fluviatilis* and *Gymnocephalus
schraetser* embryos developed but did not hatch
(Kammerer 1907). Hubbs (1971) tried to cross *P.
flavescens* with a number of percids including *S.
vitreum*, *Percina sciera* (Swain) and *Etheostoma
spectabile* (Agassiz) but the progeny failed to
develop or died after hatching. Closely related
species can breed and produce hybrids but this is
not possible between more widely separated species.
Success with crosses is mainly achieved between
species of the same genera.

The separation of subpopulations of percid
species by investigating morphological or biochemical differences has had only limited success.
There may be some evidence for discrete stocks but
main differences between stocks appear to be in
factors such as growth, age of maturity and
fecundity which are fundamentally influenced by the
environment.

Continued studies on the adaptation, evolution
and genetics of percid species will not only help
in better management of stocks under severe pressure from perturbations brought about by humans but
will give some insight into the processes of
natural selection in a successful vertebrate group.

Chapter 9

POPULATION DYNAMICS AND COMMUNITY STRUCTURE

Introduction

Population dynamic analysis involves numbers of
organisms and the rates at which these numbers
change. Essentially it is involved with birth and
death rates and indirectly with somatic growth
since growth has a direct influence on both rates.
Birth rate is the number of offspring produced per
female per unit of time. As soon as eggs are laid,
they and the resulting offspring are subject to a
mortality rate which will normally vary at
different life stages of the fish. As a rule mortality will be most intense in the early stages,
declining as age and size increase. Mortality is
usually measured over a period of one year. The
annual instantaneous rate, Z, is normally used
where the number at age t+1, N_{t+1}, depends upon the
number at t, N_t. Thus

$$N_{t+1} = N_t e^{-Z}$$

Z can represent two components, natural mortality,
M, and fishing mortality, F, where $Z = F+M$. Fishing
mortality is an important factor in the overall
mortality of exploited fish. In order for populations to remain in a steady state, a balance must
exist between birth and mortality rates. These
rates depend on the density of the population.
Thus as the population increases, the death rate
will tend to increase and the birth rate will tend
to decrease. This is an example of density dependence and may result from factors such as shortage
of food, from predation by other species or from
cannibalism. The effect of environmental factors
such as temperature and oxygen concentration on
birth and death rates does not depend on the size

181

of the population and thus is density independent.
Both density dependent and density independent factors influence the abundance of a population.
These concepts are the basis of population dynamics. The extent of our knowledge about population
dynamics of percid fishes will be illustrated by
some case histories. Since many percids are important commercial fishes (Chapter 10) population
dynamic studies have, in some cases, been quite
detailed. Also, percid populations, unlike marine
species, are confined within limited areas which
makes sampling and analysis a little easier. The
case histories will attempt to illustrate the
effects of density dependent and density independent factors operating on population dynamics.

Lake Tyulen

Thorpe (1977) has interpreted the model of
Menshutkin and Zhakov (1964) which was based on
their studies of perch in Lake Tyulen, Karelia,
USSR. It was a simple model and thus helps to
explain the concepts of population dynamics. The
lake contained only one species, the perch, but
from year to year perch recruitment to the population varied considerably. The variations in the
strengths of these year classes (all fish of a
species that hatch in a particular year are
referred to as a year class for that year) was explained by Menshutkin and Zhakov (1964) on the
basis of cannibalism. Other environmental factors
such as temperature were assumed to be constant in
the model and the overall limiting factor was
considered to be the maximum supply of
zooplankton. A number of other assumptions
were made. These included: perch ages 0 to 5
years were cannibalised by fish aged 1 to 8 years;
a proportion of perch in their first year and ages
from 4 to 8 years died as a result of starvation;
perch from ages 6 to 8 years died as a result of
old age, disease and other causes; and female perch
became sexually mature at age 4 years and
reproduced in that and future years. The
probability of death of any one individual due to
cannibalism was determined on the basis of year
class strengths of predator and prey and the
electivity of the predator (Ivlev 1955). Changes
due to starvation were based on the available
planktonic food which could support a maximum
amount of perch fry. If the fry exceeded this

maximum amount they all died with consequent effects on older fish who depended on them. Natural deaths were considered to be 80% at ages 6 and 7 years and 100% at age 8 years.

The number of perch of age t, N_t, surviving to the next year, t+1, was calculated from:

$$N_{t+1} = N_t(1-\mu_t)(1-\eta_t)(1-v_t)$$

where μ_t, η_t and v_t were the probability of deaths due to cannibalism, starvation and natural causes respectively. The number of prey of an age group, K, ΔN_k, available for predators was given by:

$$\Delta N_k = \mu_k \cdot N_k$$

The number taken by a particular age group of predators was dependent on their electivity value, E, and their relative density. The relationship between actual (r) and maximal (R) ration was derived as follows:

$$r_i = \overset{k}{\Sigma} \mu_k \cdot N_k = \overset{k}{\Sigma} \frac{1}{m_k}(1-e^{-m_k})$$

where $m_k = \dfrac{N_k}{\Delta maxN_k} = \dfrac{1}{R_tK}$, N_k was the number of prey

of age k and $\Delta maxN_k$ was the number taken at maximum ration.

Mortality due to starvation was related to actual and maximum ration so that:

$$L_t = \frac{r_t}{R_t}$$

and $\eta_t = 1 - L_t^n$

When natural mortality occurred in the older year classes v = 0.8 or 1.0 as explained above.

Two further sets of assumptions were made in fitting the model. In the first, the quantity of food which a perch could consume at an unrestricted prey density was taken as 20 times the annual average increment in weight for each age group over 3 years and slightly less for younger fish which did not rely entirely on cannibalism for food. In

this set the fecundity of a female perch was taken
as 2,400 yr^{-1} from age 4 years onwards. In the
second set the maximum ration was increased
progressively to allow for increased intensity of
cannibalism with age. A female perch was assumed
to lay 2,000 eggs at age 4 years increasing by
1,000 eggs per year. In both sets of computation
the sex ratio was kept constant at 1:1 and egg and
fry survival from egg and larvae to reach the
designated 0+ years age group was taken as five
percent.
     Computations using this model showed that
fluctuations in year class strengths and dominance
over several years by the year class were predicted
well (Figure 9.1). It illustrated the cyclic
nature of these population characteristics and the

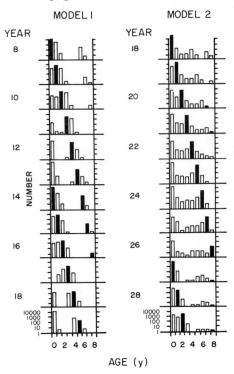

Figure 9.1: The age group distribution of *Perca fluviatilis* with time according to the two models of Menshutkin and Zhakov (1964). Solid columns represent dominant year classes. (After Thorpe 1977).

long-term stability of the population. The next example demonstrates how stability in populations may be brought about by a simple predator-prey relationship between two different percids. In Oneida Lake, New York, USA, walleye prey on yellow perch fry, that is, yellow perch in their first year.

Oneida Lake

Oneida Lake is situated in New York state, USA. It is a relatively eutrophic lake and in recent years has been used extensively by sports fishermen. The lake has been studied for many years and the following account will deal with the period from 1900 to 1975. It is of particular interest because of the relationship between yellow perch and walleye (Forney 1977a). From 1900 to 1975 the pike and eel, *Anguilla rostrata* (Lesueur), have declined and the chain pickerel, *Esox niger* Lesueur, has become nearly extinct. The walleye is now the main predator in the lake. In surveys carried out from 1915 to 1927 and from 1960 to 1970 the yellow perch was found to be the most abundant species in the littoral regions of the lake. The lake is now dominated by these two percids and in the period 1958 to 1973 they made up 85% of the catch in experimental gill nets. The reduction of other predators in the lake resulted in increased numbers of walleye (Figure 9.2) but not an increase in their size (Forney 1977a). Thus although recruitment of walleye was improved there was increased intraspecific competition for food as growth is a function of prey density. This was illustrated by Forney (1977a) who found a close relationship between yellow perch abundance and length increments of one to four year old walleye. In 1971, first year yellow perch were abundant and weights of three year old walleye increased rapidly in July and slowed towards September. The walleye fed on invertebrates from spring until mid June when yellow perch fry were about 18 mm and acceptable in size to the walleye. The invertebrate diet gave no anabolic energy for growth but the yellow perch diet gave excess energy for growth above that required for catabolic processes. In 1973 the yellow perch were less abundant and there were insufficient of these even for maintenance diet required by the walleye. This was particularly apparent in five year old walleye which

decreased in weight in July. The walleye started
to gain weight in August and this gain was rapid
through September and October. During this time
the consumption of white perch, *Morone
americana* (Gmelin), increased. The white perch
year class in 1973 had been more successful than
that of the yellow perch but the walleye did not
prey on them until the white perch changed from a
pelagic to a demersal habit. The walleye consumes
a high proportion of the prey production and the
stable size of the adult stock is brought about by
equilibrium with the prey. Thus growth and
recruitment in the walleye stock changes in
response to prey abundance. High prey density
increases walleye growth and recruitment and it
also reduces cannibalism. The year class produced
in this situation soon increases its biomass
through rapid growth and eventually this leads to
intraspecific competition and reduction in growth.
The large year class, both in number and individual
size intensifies cannibalism and suppresses
succeeding year classes, a similar situation to
large year classes of perch in Windermere, England
(see later in this chapter).
   The yellow perch have improved their growth

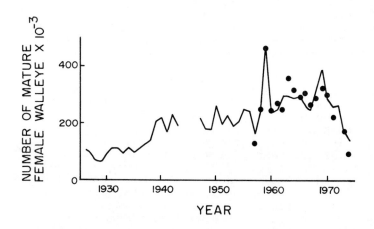

Figure 9.2: Estimated number of mature female *Stizostedion vitreum* in Oneida
Lake, USA, from 1928 to 1974. ● are values based on mark-recapture data.
(After Forney 1977a).

over the period of study in Oneida Lake due to
reduced competition with other prey species. The
populations of walleye and yellow perch were less
varied in abundance in the 1930s when other predators were present in the system. The walleye may
have been able to feed on several age groups rather
than relying merely on the abundance of first year
yellow perch as the yellow perch were smaller at
that time. The present single predator and prey
relationship is probably less stable than a mixed
one.

Older yellow perch in Oneida Lake are cannibalistic on yellow perch fry but the walleye affect
the mortality of the yellow perch to a much greater
degree. The density of yellow perch fry declines
exponentially through the late summer and autumn.
The number of yellow perch consumed by walleye was
estimated from examination of walleye stomachs
caught by otter trawls (Forney 1977b). The
abundance of pelagic yellow perch fry was estimated
by Miller samplers (Noble 1970b) in June and demersal yellow perch were estimated by trawls. Numbers
of yellow perch consumed by walleye between mid-
June and October ranged from 18,000 ha^{-1} in 1973 to
243,000 ha^{-1} in 1971. The number eaten was found
to be approximately proportional to the fish
available. The numbers eaten by three year and
older yellow perch were 56,000 ha^{-1} in 1971, 24,000
ha^{-1} in 1975 and was negligible in other years.

A predator-prey model was formulated by Forney
(1977c) to predict the effect of different levels
of walleye biomass on year class strengths of
yellow perch (in their first year). Assumptions on
which the model was based were: (1) all mortality
of young yellow perch was caused by walleye
predation and (2) mortality of yellow perch was
proportional to walleye biomass on days when ration
size was less than the satiation ration.

Number of yellow perch (P) on day t was
described by:

$$P_t = P_O - \sum_{t=1}^{t_i} 0.000186\ (9.5)\ B_t$$

where P_O was the initial density of yellow perch
ha^{-1} and B_t was the biomass of walleye in kg ha^{-1}.
The daily mortality of yellow perch, 9.5, was described by the product of average attack and average duration of nocturnal feeding. The ration, R,

consumed kg^{-1} by walleye was given by:

$$R_t = P_t \bar{w}_t \ 0.00176$$

where $\bar{w}_t$ was the mean weight of yellow perch on day
t. The ration to satiate walleye was assumed to be
0.06 body weight. Biomass of walleye (B_t) was calculated from the product of average weight and
numbers of individuals. The numbers declined at a
exponential rate Z and individual daily weight increment was calculated as 0.14 of the ration in
excess of 0.01 body weight.

$$B_t = N_o e^{zt} \ [\bar{w}_o + \sum_{1}^{t} (R-0.01w)(0.14)]$$

The model was used for predicting yellow perch
fry biomass using an initial density of 240,000 and
growth data collected by weekly sampling from June
to October 1971 (Figure 9.3). A biomass of 22 kg
ha^{-1} was estimated for the walleye in the spring of
1971. Yellow perch biomass at a walleye biomass
between 18 and 30 kg ha^{-1} peaked in late June and
early July and declined in the late summer. The
predicted values did not fit the observed values
very accurately. Forney (1977b) suggested that the
rate of walleye predation may have been lower or
biomass of yellow perch was sufficient to satiate
walleye and thus the effective rate of predation
was reduced. Observed rate of predation did not
exceed 0.06 body weight but in practice it may have
been lower than this due to physiological factors.
A minimum biomass of walleye of 10 to 18 kg ha^{-1} is
needed to control the year class strengths of
yellow perch otherwise the amount of available food
must limit yellow perch recruitment. Recruitment
is probably a function of parental stock size. The
resulting curve has been derived by Ricker (1954;
1975) thus

$$R = \alpha \ Pe^{-\beta P} \qquad \qquad \text{Equation 9.1}$$

where R is the number of recruits, P is the size of
the parental stock, α is a dimensionless parameter
and β a parameter with dimensions 1/P. In the next
case history the recruitment of walleye is
described as a function of parental stock and
spring temperatures when the walleye are spawning.

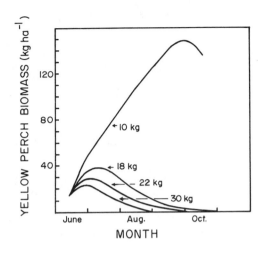

Figure 9.3: Simulated values of young-of-the-year *Perca flavescens* biomass related to *Stizostedion vitreum* biomass ranging from 10 to 30 kg ha^{-1} in June from Oneida Lake, USA. (After Forney 1977c).

Western Lake Erie

Lake Erie has a long history of commercial fishing (Chapter 10). The walleye has been a major species exploited in this fishery. Over the last hundred years there have been many habitat changes brought about by man's influence. Particularly important to the walleye has been the reduction in spawning areas. The walleye has also been overexploited and fishing probably exceeded sustainable yields in the mid-1950s (Shuter & Koonce 1977). A reduction in walleye density over the period of observation was apparent from catch per unit effort data and year class strengths were found to decline. In response to this reduction in numbers, younger fish increased in growth and some walleye became sexually mature earlier. Shuter and Koonce (1977) showed that growth was related to population density which implies that forage density was the controlling factor. In 1927 about 40% of three year old female walleye were mature and this increased to about 80% by 1965. Recruitment (R) was related to stock size (S) and spring temperature (Δt, the rate of water temperature increase in the spring during spawning) by:

$$\log R = \alpha + \beta \log S + \delta \Delta t$$

where α, β and δ are constants. The number of yearlings (R_i) were related to the adult spawning stock and spring temperature in the year before ($i-1$). There were indications that these stock and recruitment relationships were working in the period 1947 to 1967.

From these basic principles, a model for the walleye population was developed (Shuter & Koonce 1977; Shuter, Koonce & Regier 1979). An assumption was made that the annual natural mortality was 20% and this acted on all ages from one to eight years. A minimum length of 152 mm at age one year was used in the modelling. Different regimes of fishing mortality were used. The resultant predictions are very close to the observed values for both recruitment (Figure 9.4) and stock abundance (Figure 9.5). Thus information on relative abundance, year class strength and growth can be combined into a model which appears to be a good predictor for western Lake Erie walleye.

Lake Ijssel

The importance of temperature in growth and recruitment of percids is illustrated by the zander in Lake Ijssel. Lake Ijssel is a shallow eutrophic rather turbid lake in the Netherlands (Willemsen 1977b). It was created in 1932 by damming a marine bay and forming a fresh water lake. The lake contains mainly zander, perch, pike, ruffe, smelt, bream, *Abramis brama* (Linnaeus), roach, *Rutilus rutilus* (Linnaeus), and eel, *Anguilla anguilla* (Linnaeus). Up till 1970 an eel trawl was used in the lake but this was discontinued when it was realised that it caused heavy mortality on other desirable species. Willemsen (1977b) found that the food of perch and zander was very similar and there was little predation or competition for food between or within species and growth did not appear to be limited by food availability. Smelt were the most important food for both zander and perch when zander were >50 mm and perch >100 mm. Cannibalism was only slight, 0.14% in zander and 2.00% in perch. However, there were marked differences between years in year class strengths, by a factor of times 20 in the zander and times 100 in the perch. The year class strength of the zander was significantly correlated with summer temperature (degree days over 14°C) but correlation between

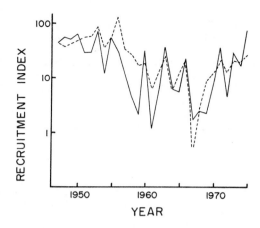

Figure 9.4: Observed —— and simulated --- values of the recruitment index (number of 1 year olds per trap net lift) of *Stizostedion vitreum* from 1947 to 1975 in western Lake Erie, USA and Canada. (After Shuter & Koonce 1977).

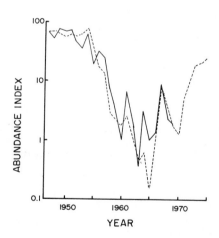

Figure 9.5: Observed —— and simulated --- values of abundance (number of fish per trap net lift) of *Stizostedion vitreum* from 1947 to 1975 in western Lake Erie, USA and Canada. (After Shuter & Koonce 1977).

perch year class strength and temperature was not significant. There were insufficient data to explain fluctuations in perch year class strengths and the processes await elucidation. The final case history illustrates a more complex system where both density independent factors, particularly temperature, and the density dependent factors, predation and cannibalism, have controlled recruitment and stock abundance. These factors, however, have had variable importance over the time span the populations have been studied.

Windermere

Windermere, the largest lake in England, is a lake formed by glaciation and is situated in the English Lake District. It is divided into a north and a south basin, by a series of islands and shallows. Windermere contains a relatively simple fish fauna consisting mainly of perch, pike, charr, *Salvelinus alpinus* (Linnaeus), brown trout, and eels. The fish in this lake have undergone intensive investigation for over 45 years. Particular emphasis has been placed on factors which control the abundance of perch and pike. Historically the lake was fished commercially, although, apart from a small plumb-line fishery for charr, no commercial fisheries are in operation today. The sport fishery, unlike Oneida Lake, is not extensive.

In a wartime fishery from 1941 to 1947 over 90 tonnes of perch were removed from the lake reducing the biomass of the perch from 136 tonnes to 55 tonnes. Large scale removal of perch continued in the north basin of Windermere until 1948 and in the south basin until 1964. Unbaited fish traps were used to catch fish for the fishery and these traps have continued to be used for sampling the population ever since. The pike depends on the perch as its main source of food, a similar, single predator-prey relationship to that found in Oneida Lake. There were fears that the large scale removal of perch would alter the feeding habits of the pike, specifically that the pike would feed heavily on more desirable species such as charr. In 1944 an experimental winter gill net fishery was started to remove large pike (>550 mm) and this fishery has continued on an annual basis until the present. About one third of the pike population >550 mm is removed by the fishery yearly.

Both types of fishing gear used to sample perch and pike are selective. Windermere perch traps, for example, catch perch equally well between the sizes of 90 and 300 mm, but more males than females are trapped during the spawning time as found by Craig (1975) in Slapton Ley, England (Figure 9.6). Variances between catches in individual traps can be considerable (Bagenal 1972a). For example using 30 traps the confidence limits to the geometric mean would still be ± 1.5. Perch vulnerability to traps also varies from year to year. Likewise gill nets can be highly selective for such factors as size and condition (Kipling 1957; Hamley 1980) and, gillnet catches also are highly variable (Bagenal 1972b; Craig, Sharma & Smiley 1986). These factors were considered in the Windermere study, and where necessary adjustments were made. Tag and recapture experiments showed that the perch populations in each basin were quite discrete so they were treated separately. Estimates made were quantitative despite the problems in sampling gear (Le Cren, Kipling & McCormack 1977; Craig *et al.* 1979; Kipling & Frost 1970).

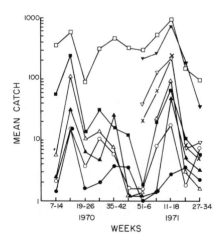

Figure 9.6: Mean catches of *Perca fluviatilis* in perch traps in relation to time of the year in Slapton Ley, England (1970-1971). Mean catch is expressed as Log_{10} (x+1) where x is for 8 lifts. Symbols represent trap (12.5 mm mesh) settings in various parts of the lake or trap modifications (▼ = 6 mm mesh, ∇ = trap covered over except for the ends and x = trap covered except at the tunnel end. (After Craig 1975).

193

Numbers of perch and pike in Windermere from 1941 to 1976 are shown in Figure 9.7. It can be seen that trends in the perch population were closely followed by that of pike; similar trends occurred in both basins. There was an initial fall in number as a result of the fisheries and numbers of perch remained low until 1957 in the south basin and until 1961 in the north basin. Pike recovered more quickly although they were still being fished. From 1949 to 1971 there were more pike than before the fishery, but these were younger fish. After 1971 the pike population declined. Kipling (1984) describes five stages of population changes during the study (Table 9.1). Up to the end of the 1950s, year classes of perch and pike were very dependent on summer temperatures in their first year of life. The slow growth of perch made them available as food for both young-of-the-year and older pike. In the early-1960s the populations were dominated by the very strong 1955 and 1959 year classes of both species. Year classes of perch produced during this period were heavily preyed upon by pike and also by older perch. The year classes were already weak as a result of cold summers in the years of hatch. The very poor growth of old pike at this time indicate that they were short of food. In the late-1960s the summers were warmer and perch year classes were stronger and they grew faster. Perch in this period were seven or eight times heavier than they had been at the start of the fishery. They rapidly outgrew the size at which young pike could feed on them. Pike became more cannibalistic which reduced their numbers, although growth improved. In 1976 a disease killed over 98% of the perch population and the pike had lost almost completely their previous main source of food. The pike continued to decrease in numbers, growing fast and obtaining their food from cannibalism and probably charr. Large pike were no longer found in the summer in the littoral zone but they were caught from time to time by charr fishermen in deep water. Since the disease the perch have shown signs of recovery.

Although numbers of perch declined as a result of the fishery, the perch biomass did not decline proportionally because the growth rate increased. In the south basin numbers and biomass increased in the mid-1950s, due to the strong 1955 year class, but did not start to increase in the north basin until the late-1950s when the 1959 year class made a major contribution to the population. This year

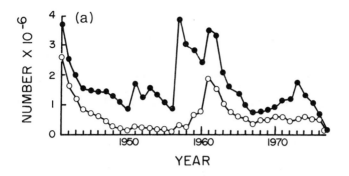

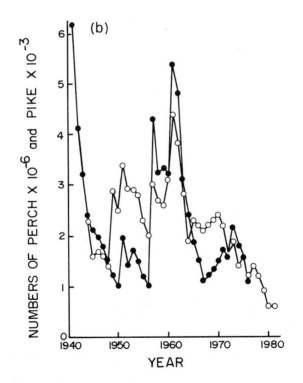

Figure 9.7: Plots of (a) numbers of *Perca fluviatilis* (aged two years or older) in the north (o) and south (●) basins of Windermere, England from 1941 to 1977 and (b) total numbers of perch (●)(1941-1976) and *Esox lucius* (o) (1944-1981) in the whole lake. (After Craig *et al.* 1979 and Craig & Kipling 1983).

Table 9.1. A summary of summer temperatures, growth and year class strengths of perch and pike during five periods in Windermere, England. (After Kipling 1984).

Period	Summer temperature	Growth Perch	Pike	Year class strengths Perch	Pike
Pre-exploitation	variable	very slow	slow	not known	
Late 1940s and 1950s	variable	increasing	variable	variable	variable
Early 1960s	low	slow	slow	weak	medium
Late 1960s and early 1970s	high	fast	fast	strong	weak
1976-1982	variable	fast	fast	weak	weak

class dominated the population in the north basin for most of the 1960s and it made up most of the adult biomass (Figure 9.8). After reaching a peak in 1962 the 'total biomass' in the north basin fell slightly until 1964 but then remained almost constant (49 ± 3 tonnes) until the disease of 1976. Year classes from the early-1960s made little contribution to the 'total biomass' (note ordinate in Figure 9.8 is on a logarithmic scale). As the 1959 year class declined, later year classes made an increasing contribution to the biomass. It may be that the warm summers of the mid- and late-1960s and early-1970s allowed stability in the population through density dependent factors. However, it is unlikely that this population, with its rapid growth and high mortality, was as stable as pre-1941 (before the fishery).

Some of the causes for the changes described above can be elucidated. From the principles of population dynamics an increase in mortality rate, either natural or fishing with resulting decrease in population density, should result in increased birth rate. Perch responded to decrease in numbers by increasing their rate of egg production. In the period 1944 to 1960 a female perch of 200 mm length

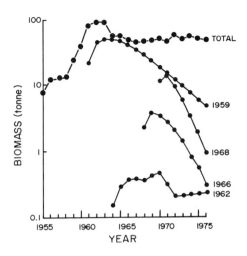

Figure 9.8: Total biomass of *Perca fluviatilis* (aged two years or older) in the north basin of Windermere, England, from 1955 to 1976 and biomass data for year classes 1959, 1962, 1966 and 1968 contributing to the 'total biomass' in the years where they are represented. (After Craig 1982).

spawned on average 13,100 ± 700 eggs compared to the period 1979 to 1981 when a female of the same length laid 19,300 ± 1,800 eggs, a 47% increase. Before the disease the youngest age of sexual maturity in the female perch had been three years but after 1976, some mature two year old fish were found. However egg numbers laid had no correlation with the number being recruited into the population at age two years (Figure 9.9). A stock-recruitment curve (based on Equation 9.1) for perch indicate that adult population egg production has never limited the number of recruits (Figure 9.10). In fact one of the lowest adult stocks produced one of the largest year classes. Therefore the factors controlling year class strengths must be affecting the survival of perch in the first two years of life. The chief factors have been found to be summer water temperature in the year of hatch, the biomass of adult perch and the year class strength of pike of the same year. Not all these factors have been significant throughout the whole study.

During the period from 1961 to 1975, 73% of the variation in year class strength of perch could be accounted for by summer water temperatures. Over the whole period from 1942 to 1975 the

197

Figure 9.9

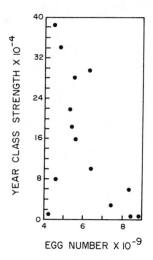

EGG NUMBER X 10^{-9}

Figure 9.9: Year class strength (at age two years) of *Perca fluviatilis* in relation to total number of eggs laid in the north basin of Windermere, England,
from 1961 to 1974. (After Craig & Kipling 1983).

correlation between year class strength and summer
water temperature was still significant but only
accounted for 28% of the variability. Between 1959
and 1974 there was a significant negative
correlation between year class strength and the
biomass of adult perch in the year of hatch. This
would explain the downward trend of the stock-
recruitment curve at high levels of adult biomass
(Figure 9.10). Before 1959 the intensity of predation by pike on young perch may have made cannibalism by adult perch insignificant. From 1959 to
1974 the negative correlation between perch year
class strength and pike year class strength in the
year of hatch continued to be highly significant.
From these relationships a simple model could be
produced to predict recruitment from 1959 to 1974.
This model took the form:

$$\ln R = C_0 + C_1 \, T + C_2 \, P + C_3 \, \ln Y \qquad \text{Equation 9.2}$$

where R was the year class strength at age two
years, T was temperature measured in degree days
over 14°C, P was biomass of the adult stock in
tonnes and Y was the year class strength of pike.
C_0, C_1, C_2 and C_3 are all constants, C_2 and C_3 are

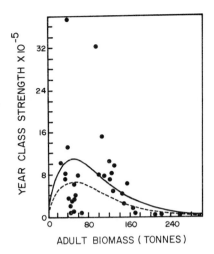

Figure 9.10: Year class strength (at age two years) of *Perca fluviatilis* in relation to parental stock biomass (perch three years of older) in year of hatch for the whole lake in Windermere, England. Both arithmetic (——) and geometric (---) Ricker curves have been fitted to the data. (Equation 9.1). (After Craig & Kipling 1983).

negative. This model is illustrated in Figure 9.11. For the period 1959 to 1971 this model could explain 87% of the variance in year class strength in the north basin and 90% of the variance in the south basin. The model clearly shows how an increase in temperature, a density independent factor, increases year class strength but an increase in predation both by cannibalism and predation by pike, density dependent factors, decreases year class strength. The model does not allow for much variability caused by competition between fish of the same year class but perhaps this is not important in Windermere except at extreme density levels.

Although temperature has played a major role in determining year class strengths its direct influence has not been elucidated. It certainly affects growth and survival but not directly. It is probably involved in the control of timing of food production in the food chain. The correct timing of this production, especially the optimum food particle size at the right time, is critical to the survival of the young fish. This is an area where much research is required.

In unexploited percid populations oscillations

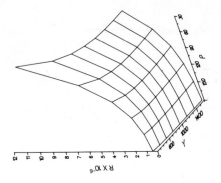

(c)

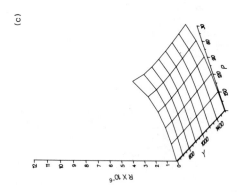

(b)

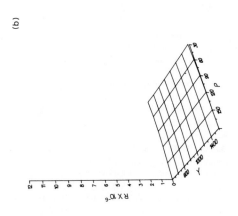

(a)

Figure 9.11: Diagram to illustrate recruitment (R) of *Perca fluviatilis* (at age two years) as a function of temperature, adult biomass (P) and *Esox lucius* year class strength (Y) in Windermere, England. Three temperatures have been selected: (a) 150 (b) 350 and (c) 500 degree days over 14°C. Values were derived from Equation 9.2.

of population size probably are cyclic and regular in the long-term, as described in the Lake Tyulen example for perch. In the short-term these fluctuations may not appear to be regular. Year class strengths of walleye in West Blue Lake, Canada, vary greatly and it is suggested that abundance of the year class depends on spawning success (Kelso & Ward 1977). In the long-term this unexploited population has low egg to fry survival and in the short-term, seasonal abundance is regulated by mortalities in the autumn. Intensive fishing can upset the self-regulating mechanisms (Chapter 10). A classic example is the blue pike population in Lake Erie. These fish were abundant from about 1860 (time of commencement of records) to the early-1900s but then numbers began to fluctuate widely. Regier *et al.* (1969) suggest that these fluctuations were due to over-intensive fishing which eventually upset the self-stabilising mechanisms of the blue pike population. The changes which occurred and reasons for the changes are very similar in some respects to those of the perch population in Windermere, England. A reduction in adults led to a population explosion and then the production of very poor year classes due to excessive cannibalism by the older fish. As these older fish died out another population explosion would occur. Eventually these oscillations would be expected to dampen out as in the Windermere perch. However the oscillations in the blue pike population indicated that the main controls were not only cannibalism but the predators themselves, which were oscillating in numbers due to the fishery (Parsons 1967). A continuation of intensive fishing even when they were scarce resulted in the extinction of blue pike in Lake Erie.

Competition

Competition (emulous striving for the same object) and predation control the structure of fish communities. Predation is much easier to measure than competition. Competition may be intraspecific as well as interspecific. For example, large populations of perch are usually slow growers and a reduction in their numbers results in improved growth (Alm 1946; Le Cren 1958). One way in which competition may arise is in pursuit of the same food supply. One species may be more successful at

competing for this food supply than another. For
example it was shown by Hanson and Leggett (1985)
that yellow perch and pumpkinseed, *Lepomis
gibbosus* (Linnaeus), kept separately in enclosures
in the littoral zone of Lake Memphremagog, Quebec-
Vermont, Canada-USA border, gained weight at low
densities and lost weight at high densities.
Yellow perch and pumpkinseed feed on similar food
items in the littoral zone of lakes. When yellow
perch and pumpkinseed were placed in the enclosures
together growth of yellow perch was suppressed but
pumpkinseeds grew at the same rate as if they had
been on their own. It would appear that the
pumpkinseed was superior to yellow perch in
competing for the food. The authors used this
finding to explain the increase in pumpkinseed
growth and decline in yellow perch abundance in a
ten year period in the lake.

Although different species may be feeding on
the same food source, in some situations, they may
be separated into different habitats in time or
space. Or they may use the same habitat but feed
on different prey. A proportional similarity
factor was used to compare the use of food and
thermal habitat by five species of fish in Lake
Michigan, USA (Crowder, Magnusson & Brandt 1981).
It was derived from:

$$C_{xy} = \sum_i \min (P_{xi} \cdot P_{yi}) \qquad \text{Equation 9.3}$$

where P_{xi} was the proportional contribution of
resource i to the total resource used by species x
and P_{yi} was the proportional contribution of
resource i to the total resource used by species
y. Figure 9.12 illustrates the resource partitioning between the species. During the day, spottail shiners, young-of-the-year alewives and yellow
perch used the same thermal habitat but fed on
different prey. Alewives and rainbow smelt,
Osmerus mordax (Mitchill), were introduced into
Lake Michigan. Alewives were first noted in the
lake in 1949 (Miller 1957) and rainbow smelt
appeared sometime in the 1920s (Crowder *et al.*
1981). The species which declined as a result of
these introductions were those which had both the
same food and habitat requirements as the introduced fish.

Observations of species dominance and
community structure have been extensive both in the
natural state and in artificial situations such as
species removal or introductions or in man-made

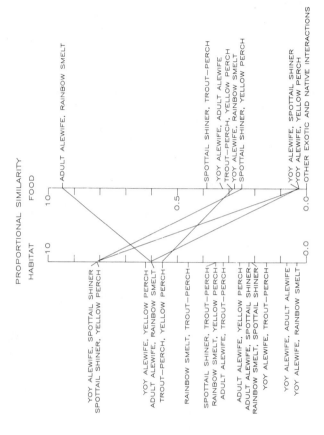

Figure 9.12: Daytime proportional similarity in food and thermal habitat use by Lake Michigan, USA, fishes. Fish were caught by bottom trawls in September 1977. Proportional similarity was based on equation 9.3. (After Crowder *et al.* 1981).

water bodies such as reservoirs. However the causal mechanisms underlying species dominance in most cases have not been explained quantitatively. A survey of Swedish lakes was made to study the interspecific dominance in fish communities (Svärdson 1976). The perch is the most widely distributed fish in Sweden but its populations do not always compete favourably with other species. Where perch and whitefish, *Coregonus* sp. Lacépède, compete the perch is more successful than the whitefish in small lakes where the littoral area is large in relation to the open water. However the whitefish is a better plankton feeder than the perch and is more successful in large oligotrophic lakes. The whitefish is better adapted also in colder lakes since its physiological optimum temperature is lower than that of perch. The zander prefers warmer temperatures than other percids and has been successfully introduced into the warm eutrophic lakes of Sweden. In these lakes it competes against perch and pike and causes a decline in these two species. The zander may be more successful because it is a 'wandering' predator making use of both the pelagic and benthic habitats. The perch is less successful as a pelagic fish and the pike tends to stay in the littoral zone where it stalks its prey.

The competition between perch and roach has received considerable attention. The roach spread throughout Sweden during the Pleistocene period but its distribution was less extensive in Norway as mountains formed a barrier to its distribution. In addition to preferring warmer water than the perch, the roach is not very tolerant of low oxygen concentrations or extremes of water hardness or low pH. It cannot reproduce below pH 5.5. When lakes containing perch and roach are subjected to increased acidification the roach may be eliminated and the perch population may increase in size, both in numbers and growth of individuals. However, where roach lives sympatrically with perch it dominates. The roach is very plastic in its feeding habits. When food is in short supply in one habitat it can alter its behaviour and feed in another habitat. For example it will feed on algae and detritus when other foods are limited and can become a pelagic algal eater. In some of the small eutrophic lakes in Sweden the available space is very homogeneous and competition for the space is fierce and often food is limited. In this situation the roach is able to turn to alternative

food sources and the perch is not (Persson 1983b).
Thus, although the two species are not competing
for the same food, they are competing for the
available space, an example of interactive segregation. In this situation the roach is more
successful and can reach a population size ten
times that of the perch population. In the Klicava
Reservoir, Czechoslovakia, the roach eventually
replaced the perch as the dominant species
(Pivnička & Švátora 1977). The reasons for the
decline were considered by Holčik (1977) to be
cannibalism, predation by the zander and competition with the roach.

Yellow perch and walleye can thrive in the
same lake as was illustrated for Oneida Lake (this
chapter) and has been shown in West Blue Lake,
Canada (Kelso & Ward 1977). When sauger are
present there is usually a reduction in the
proportion of yellow perch and walleye in the
community (Clady 1978). Species diversity appears
to be negatively related to the importance of
yellow perch and positively related to the number
of sauger. Species diversity does not appear to be
related to the relative abundance of walleye.
Sauger tend to inhabit more southerly lakes than
the yellow perch and these waters contain more
diverse fish faunas. However indications are that
where yellow perch exists in North American lakes
and rivers it competes very well against other
species.

In northern Canadian lakes walleye commonly
coexist with pike. In a study of Ontario lakes the
existence and composition of four common species
was determined (Johnson, Leach, Minns & Olver
1977). The most common combination was walleye and
pike. Walleye combinations with lake trout,
Salvelinus namaycush (Walbaum), and smallmouth
bass, *Micropterus dolomieui* Lacépède, were extremely rare. Walleye and pike tend to feed on the
same prey (Figure 9.13) but their habitat is
different since pike is a daytime feeder and
walleye is a twilight and night feeder. Thus they
are able to live sympatrically. In small lakes
walleye are less common and the only predatory fish
is usually the pike.

Evidence suggests that fish populations are
limited by food availability and species within a
water body must compete for that available food.
Percids seem to be quite successful and labile as
is illustrated by their common occurrence and high
biomass in many bodies of water. However, their

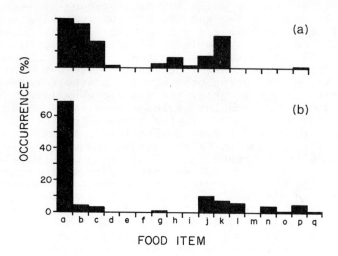

Figure 9.13: The occurrence of prey items in the stomachs of (a) *Esox lucius* and (b) *Stizostedion vitreum* from Wolf Lake, Canada. (a) = Empty, (b) = *Perca flavescens*, (c) *Notropis hudsonius*, (d) = *Coregonus clupeaformis*, (e) = *Catostomus commersoni*, (f) = *Pimephales promelas*, (g) = *Lota lota*, (h) = *Esox lucius*, (i) = *Couesius plumbeus*, (j) = fish remains, (k) = dragonfly nymphs, (l) = damselfly nymphs, (m) = dipteran larvae, (n) = dipteran pupae, (o) = leech, (p) gammarid and (q) = vegetation. (After Craig & Smiley 1986).

requirements are fairly specific and perturbations to their niche can alter their balance in the ecosystem. As mentioned earlier it is difficult to calculate the direct effect of competition. It is probably best to carry out precise controlled experiments in future investigations rather than observing gross changes in natural situations.

Chapter 10

FISHERIES AND ECONOMIC IMPORTANCE

Introduction

Biological production is the change in biomass with
time and includes reproductive products which may
be released during the period under study (Figure
5.1). It can be described by:
    P=C-F-U-R   (see equation 5.3 where P $= \Delta B$)
or
    $P = G\hat{B}$
where production, P, depends on instantaneous rate
of increase in weight, G, and mean biomass, $\hat{B}$,
during time Δt. Production is normally higher
during the juvenile stages than in adults (Figure
10.1). For example, in only one year class (1959)
did perch adult production exceed that of juveniles
in Windermere, England, and on average adult production was 61% of that of juveniles. Yield is the
part of production used by man. Over about the
last 50 years management of both inland and marine
fisheries has been based on the maximum sustainable
yield (MSY) of populations of single species.
    Consider a simple model relating fish stocks,
commercial fishing effort and annual yield (Figure
10.2). At a low level of fishing (A), the yield
will be small and the stocks will remain high (A^1)
as the population makes adjustments to this added
mortality. Point C is the level of MSY. At this
point annual yield is balanced with stock abundance
and the ability of the population to sustain
itself. If fishing increases past this point, the
yield (E) and the stocks (E^1) will be reduced, the
latter possibly to a point of collapse. Fisheries
have a tendency to exceed MSY. This may be explained in the following economic terms. At a low
level of fishing the cost of production, including

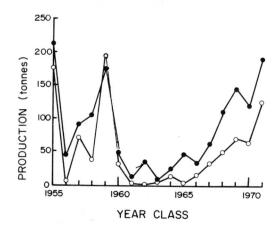

Figure 10.1: Year class production for juvenile (●), aged 0 to 2 y, and adult (o) *Perca fluviatilis* from 1955 to 1971 in Windermere, England. (After Craig 1980a).

profit, is below the return and a super profit or economic rent is generated. This encourages the existing fishermen to expand operations and other fishermen to enter the fishery. If the fishery was operated by a single fisherman, expansion would continue until a point was reached (B) where the costs of production was still marginally below the revenue generated. At this level of fishing the stocks would still be capable of responding to the mortality imposed on them. However individual fishermen, including both commercial and recreational, compete against each other and individually only consider their own costs and returns. No consideration is given to the overall yield, fishing effort and cost of production and fishing increases until costs equal revenue (D). If governments subsidise the fishery, effort will increase to point E and the possible collapse of the fishery. Management policy aims to control fishing effort to point B. At this level the excess profits are extracted as payment for the resource. This type of policy applies equally well to recreational and commercial fisheries. Methods used to control fishing effort will be discussed later in this chapter.

In 1976 the concept of an optimum yield was

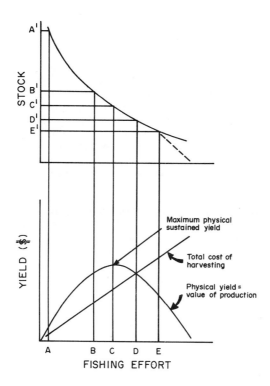

Figure 10.2: Diagram to show relationships of fish stocks and yields to fishing effort. (Figure kindly provided by D. Cauvin).

formalised in Canada and the United States (Healey 1984). It takes into account biological, economic and social factors. For example, as well as considering the conservation of the fished species, the maximum net income of the fisherman and the maximum employment of people in the industry are also used in determining the yield from the fisheries.

MSY has been based on the production model of Schaefer (1954; 1957) or the analytical model of Ricker (1958; 1975) and Beverton and Holt (1957). In the latter case the production of the population is determined by the net effect of growth, reproduction and mortality of individuals in the population. The yield (Y) in weight can be expressed by:

$$Y=F \int_{t_r}^{t_{max}} RW_t e^{-z(t-t_r)} dt$$

where F is the instantaneous rate of fishing, t_{max} is the maximum age reached by the fish, t_r is the age of recruitment, R is the number of recruits entering the fishery at age t_r, W_t is the weight at age t based on the Von Bertalanffy equation (Beverton & Holt 1957). This model can be illustrated (Figure 10.3) by considering the potential yield of walleye in Wolf Lake, Canada (Craig & Smiley 1986). The weight of production per individual is negligible below an age of recruitment of six years regardless of the fishing intensity. Above this age the yield increases rapidly. The type of yield curves produced will depend on the population and will be particularly dependent on growth.

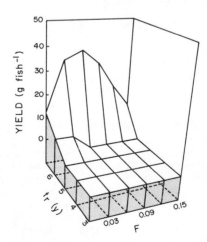

Figure 10.3: Diagram to show the simulated relationships of fish yield to fishing effort (instantaneous fishing mortality, F) and age of recruitment (t_r) to the fishing gear (gillnets) for *Stizostedion vitreum*, from Wolf Lake, Canada. (After Craig & Smiley 1986).

Fisheries and Yields

Remains of percids have been discovered in archeological excavations of human habitations. *P. fluviatilis* and *S. lucioperca* were fished along the south coast of the Baltic Sea 6,000 to 3,000 years BP (Tsepkin 1984a). The mean size of the zander caught in the fishery at that time was greater than the present day average. Perch and zander remains have also been found in excavations of human sites in the upper regions of the Dnieper River, USSR. Fossils there date between 2,700 and 400 years BP (Tsepkin 1984b). Indians in North America made use of fish stocks including percids in inland waters, but it was probably not until the invasion of European settlers that demands on these fish stocks became significant.

The main commercial fishing gears of economic importance used to catch percids include gill nets, trammel nets, seines, trawls, portable traps, fyke nets and hook and line for perch, gill nets, pound nets and trap nets for walleye and sauger and gill nets, fyke nets, trawls, seines, artificial lures and hook and line for zander (Figure 10.4). A discussion on the efficiency and selectivity of these gears will be given later in this chapter.

Worldwide yields of commercial catches of *P. fluviatilis, P. flavescens, S. vitreum* and *S. lucioperca* are given in Table 10.1 for the period 1980 to 1983. Finland has the highest perch catches and in 1983 this was the second most important species by weight landed in Finland. The highest yields of zander are caught in the USSR but in 1983 this only represented 0.2% of the total fish landed in the USSR. In an inland country, such as Switzerland, the yield of perch makes up to 48% of the total fish landings. The importance of these species must be considered in a more local context. Inland areas will rely more heavily on fresh water fisheries than coastal areas. Yellow perch and walleye fished in Canada have their biggest market in the central USA. The largest commercial catches of walleye are landed in Canada. In the USA most walleye are caught by recreational fishermen and thus are not listed in Table 10.1.

In the past there has been insufficient attention paid to fisheries used for recreation. In economic terms they are extremely important. This importance can be demonstrated by considering the fisheries of central Canada including Ontario,

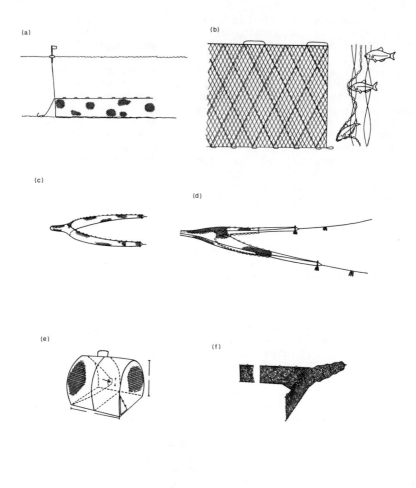

(a)

(b)

(c)

(d)

(e)

(f)

(g)

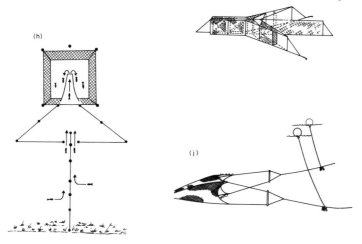

Figure 10.4: Fishing gears used in commercial fisheries for *Perca fluviatilis*, *P. flavescens*, *Stizostedion lucioperca* and *S. vitreum*. (a) Bottom set gill net, (b) trammel net, (c) beach seine, (d) bottom trawl, (e) wire mesh trap, (f) fyke net, (g) hook and line, (h) pound net, (i) trap net and (j) midwater trawl. (After Dahm 1980, Craig 1980b, von Brandt 1984).

Manitoba, Saskatchewan, Alberta and the Northwest Territories (Table 10.2). The fisheries resources are used by commercial fishermen, by natives for domestic use and by recreational fishermen. The total commercial catch of fresh water fish (about 100 species) from this region of Canada represents over 95% of Canada's fresh water fish harvest and landed value. The recreational fisheries provide about 47.5 million days of fishing, producing an annual harvest which is greater than the commercial harvest. Ontario has the largest and most valuable recreational fishery resource in Canada. It attracts 650,000 non-resident anglers and employs between 10,000 and 15,000 people.

The local economic importance of percids can be illustrated by three examples, the yellow perch fishery of Lake Erie, the walleye fishery of Manitoba and the zander fishery of Lake Balaton.

Indians living near the shores of Lake Erie used fish as a main source of food but their impact on the fish population was small. The early European settlers caught fish to supplement their diet but fishing was confined to inshore areas. The first commercial hook and line fishery began in eastern Lake Erie in 1795 (Regier *et al.* 1969). Then after the war of 1812, a commercial fishery using seines was established in western Lake Erie. During the nineteenth century, sauger, walleye and

Table 10.1. World yields in tonnes of *P. fluviatilis*, *P. flavescens*, *S. vitreum* and *S. lucioperca* by country from 1980 to 1983. Also given in brackets for the year 1983 is the percentage of the species represented in the total annual catch for all species (marine and fresh water) in that country (* data not available; ●represents commercial catch from Great Lakes only). (From FAO 1984, Ontario Ministry of Natural Resources for *S. vitreum* data for Canada and the United States Department of the Interior for *S. vitreum* data for USA).

Species: *P. fluviatilis*

	1980	1981	1982	1983
Finland	10,931	10,459	10,112	10,030 (6.4)
Switzerland	1,711	1,781	1,870	1,880 (48.0)
Netherlands	625	848	711	631 (0.1)
German D R	496	678	809	682 (0.3)
Romania	*	364	353	347 (0.1)
Poland	124	146	121	811 (0.1)
Denmark	*	*	35	40 (0.1)
Sweden	*	*	*	*
Nominal world catch	13,887	14,393	14,130	14,537

Species: *P. flavescens*

	1980	1981	1982	1983
Canada	6,526	5,042	5,223	5,000 (0.4)
USA●	2,296	2,024	1,983	1,245 (<0.1)
Nominal world catch	8,822	7,066	7,206	6,245

Species: *S. vitreum*

	1980	1981	1982	1983
Canada	5,533	6,214	6,857	5,991 (0.4)
USA	38	33	38	41 (<0.1)
Nominal world catch	5,571	6,247	6,895	6,032

Species: *S. lucioperca*

	1980	1981	1982	1983
USSR	15,583	15,982	14,057	15,604 (0.2)
Turkey	1,590	1,770	1,461	1,429 (0.2)
Finland	1,124	844	718	676 (0.4)
Romania	*	502	464	569 (0.2)
German DR	465	473	406	808 (0.3)
Poland	227	217	264	578 (0.1)
Netherlands	139	65	73	167 (<0.1)
Sweden	101	172	131	99 (<0.1)
Bulgaria	86	40	48	negligible
Nominal world catch	19,315	20,065	17,622	19,930

Table 10.2. Recreational fisheries including number of anglers, numbers of fish retained and direct expenditures (Canadian $) and commercial harvest including number of fishermen, harvest (tonnes) and landed value (Canadian $) for Provinces and Territories in the central region of Canada during the year 1982-3.

Recreational Fisheries

Province/ Territory	Number of Anglers $X10^{-3}$	Number of Fish Retained $X10^{-3}$	Direct Expenditure ($) $X10^{-3}$
Alberta	368	10,560	62,570
Saskatchewan	221	5,596	42,933
Manitoba	196	5,582	48,155
NWT	15	229	9,789
Ontario	2,389	97,675	516,824
Total	3,189	119,642	680,271

Commercial Fisheries

Province Territory	Number of Fishermen	Harvest (tonnes)	Landed Value ($) $X10^{-3}$
Alberta	516	1,106	834
Saskatchewan	1,156	3,801	2,686
Manitoba	3,709	15,454	15,508
NWT	215	1,613	1,674
Ontario	2,700	34,110	36,788
Total	8,296	56,084	57,490

smallmouth bass, were the main species caught. The
most desired species were lake trout, cisco,
Coregonus artedii Lesueur, and lake whitefish, *C.
clupeaformis* (Mitchill). The lake sturgeon,
Acipenser fulvescens Rafinesque, was at first considered a nuisance since it became caught and tore
nets set for desirable species. As many as
possible were removed. It was not until the 1860s
that the sturgeon became commercially important and
by that time its numbers had declined considerably.
The fisheries and the intensity of fishing increased during the second half of the 1800s due to
improved transportation (canals, lake, rail and
road), improved preservation techniques and
increases in the human population of the area.
Fishing was made easier by the introduction of
steam boats in the 1880s which also meant that the
central region of the lake could be fished. Not
only were the fish stocks subjected to heavy
fishing pressure but they were also exposed to a
number of other perturbations caused by man's activities. These included eutrophication, introduction of non-indigenous species (such as the sea
lamprey, *Petromyzon marinus* Linnaeus, through the
Welland Canal in about 1921, and the rainbow smelt
in 1931), tributary and shoreline development
including drainage of wetlands, an increase in
siltation and turbidity and the release of toxic
materials including biocides from industry, vessels
and vehicles (Regier`& Hartman 1973).
    The early development of the Lake Erie
fisheries took place in the USA. In the 1880s when
catches of lake whitefish and cisco were at their
highest, the landings in Canada were only 10%
of the total catch. However, in the early-1900s
the Canadian fisheries gradually increased and in
the last 40 years the commercial fish catches have
been dominated by Canada. The main reasons for
this include lower labour costs, government price
supports producing price stabilisation, a more
innovative industry, greater stocks of marketable
fish in Canadian waters and a greater use in the
USA of the lake as a sport fishery (Regier *et al*.
1969). The USA buys fish in Canadian ports and the
fish are transported overland. Yellow perch are
marketed in the form of fillets and breaded and
cooked products. The fisheries of Lake Erie have
always come under the jurisdiction of the four
border states in the USA, Michigan, Ohio,
Pennsylvania and New York, and the province of
Ontario in Canada. The regulatory powers of the

fisheries have been jealously guarded by these authorities. The great pressures put on the fish stocks in the Great Lakes in general led to the formation of the Great Lakes Fishery Commission in 1955. Its mandate was to implement a programme of sea lamprey control (the fish has never been a major problem in Lake Erie), formulate and co-ordinate research programmes and advise governments on measures to improve fish stocks. However actual fishery regulations remained with the individual states and provinces.

From 1927 to 1936 landings of yellow perch from Lake Erie averaged 5,700 tonnes and most fish came from the USA. The decline in cisco led to increased pressure on the yellow perch by American trap netters. In the 1950s, the introduction of nylon gill nets resulted in a two or threefold increase in the efficiency of the nets over cotton or linen nets and a rapid decline was evident in the walleye and blue pike fisheries (Figure 10.5). The latter species has now become extinct (Chapter 8). At this time increased pressure was placed on the yellow perch populations and Canada became the chief producer. The highest catch of yellow perch was recorded in 1969 at 13,546 tonnes and this declined to about 5,000 tonnes in the mid-1970s. Further pressure was placed on the yellow perch at this time by the partial ban on white bass, *Morone chrysops* (Rafinesque), and a complete ban on walleye. The catches of yellow perch have been strongly influenced by year class strengths (Chapter 9). Strong year classes were recorded in 1952, 1954, 1956, 1959, 1962 and 1965 (Nepszy 1977). Relatively strong year classes were recorded in 1970 and 1975. The 1959 year class was particularly strong and was represented in large numbers during the late-1960s. The year classes of yellow perch in Lake Erie appear to be influenced by similar factors to those of walleye, in parti-cular the spring temperature in the year of hatch (Chapter 9). The great fluctuations in year class strengths and the increased pressures put on the yellow perch populations was considered to indicate that they were under stress and were likely to deteriorate. In 1975 the Yellow Perch Committee was established under the Great Lakes Fishery Commission to closely monitor the yellow perch populations. From 1980 to 1984 the Canadian commercial catch of yellow perch in Lake Erie varied from 2,564 to 5,731 tonnes with a mean of 4,071 tonnes. Over the time period the yellow

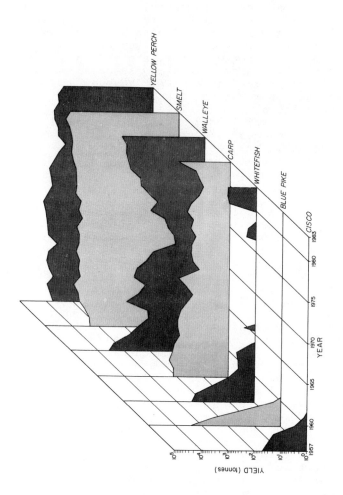

Figure 10.5: Plots of annual commercial yields of the major species of fish from 1957 to 1983 for the Canadian waters of Lake Erie. (Data kindly provided by the Ontario Ministry of Natural Resources).

perch represented 55.5% of the value of all fish landed in Canada from Lake Erie. The largest landings continued to be of the less valuable smelt. Although catches of white bass and walleye were much lower than historic levels they made a significant contribution to the value of the Lake Erie landings due to the demand put upon them by the consumer. In the early-1980s walleye catches have increased significantly. Stocks of Lake Erie walleye recovered after a ban was placed on them due to mercury contamination in the early-1970s and recently a international management quota system has been applied. Lake Erie is an example of a lake which has undergone extensive perturbations with the resultant changes in the nature of the fisheries both in species composition and yields.

Manitoba is the chief producer of *S. vitreum* in Canada. Large scale commercial fishing (not including domestic use of walleye for animal consumption) started in the 1880s after the construction of the Canadian Pacific Railway and the arrival of Icelandic immigrants on the west shore of Lake Winnipeg (Gislason, MacMillan & Craven 1982). Up to 1900 fishing was carried out in the summer, mainly with gill nets, although some pound nets and trap nets were also used. With the invention of the jigger (Figure 10.6) gill nets could be fished under the ice and winter fisheries started in many of the Manitoba lakes. Other important developments included the introduction of petrol driven boats in the 1920s. In some of the large lakes, boats were used with net lifters for the first time in the 1940s and this brought about a reduction in crew numbers. In the 1950s nylon nets replaced cotton nets.

The viability of a commercial fishery is dependent on transport from source to consumer. Initially lake whitefish, goldeye, *Hiodon alosoides* (Rafinesque), and sturgeon were the most important species. The whitefish kept well when salted and stored in barrels. With the development of railways and roads and improvement in preservation techniques, including refrigeration, walleye became more important to the commercial fisheries. Today walleye caught in northern lakes are flown to places which have good ground transport to Winnipeg where the fish are processed.

In the later part of the nineteenth century restrictions were introduced to protect future stocks. These included closed seasons and area, gear, mesh size, and licence restrictions.

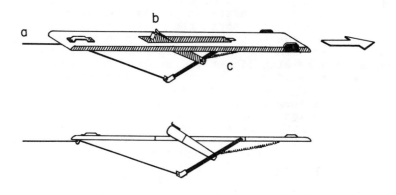

Figure 10.6: Sketch of a jigger for setting gill nets under the ice. When rope a is pulled, the metal claw b pushes against the ice and moves the jigger in the direction of the arrow. When a is released, the spring c takes the claw back ready for the next pull. (After Hamley 1980).

Initially the fisheries were operated by private individuals of three types, owner operators, renters who rented equipment from fish companies and fishing labourers who were paid wages by a fish company or a owner operator or a renter. This system resulted in a number of complications including duplicity of services by existing fish companies, fishermen's lack of bargaining power, lack of a basic price for fish and poor quality of fish produced. These problems and the need to coordinate transportation led to the formation of the Freshwater Fish Marketing Corporation (FFMC) in 1969. FFMC has exclusive jurisdiction over interprovincial and export trade in fresh water fish for a region extending from northwestern Ontario to Alberta and north to the Northwest Territories.

In the 1982-3 season Manitoba fishermen harvested 70% by weight and 90% by value of the fish in the FFMC area. These fish were chiefly walleye, sauger and whitefish. The walleye landed weight of 4,237 tonnes represented 27% of the Manitoba catch. These walleye had a landed value of Canadian $6,316,000, 49% of the total Manitoban catch and a market value of Canadian $13,050,000.

During this period a total of 3,700 people were involved with the harvest of Manitoba fish. This very important fishery needs careful management if it is to be sustained.

Lake Balaton in Hungary has been fished by man since 7,000 BP (Sági 1974). Records show that the fishery rights were given to religious orders by the monarchy in the 1000s and since then the lake has been fished extensively by seines and gill nets (Biró 1977). Further records show that the fishery yields declined during the 150 years of the Turkish occupation in the 1500 to 1600s. In the 1800s flood control measures were implemented and many zander spawning areas were destroyed. The intensity of fishing increased and, by 1880, 20,000 gill nets were in use in Lake Balaton. The regulation of the fisheries was effectively started in 1884 with the formation of the Balaton Fishery Co-operative, which was replaced in 1900 by the Balaton Fishery Corporation. These bodies rented the lake until it was taken over by the Hungarian Government in 1948. The Corporation was responsible for the collection of fishing data, the modernisation of gear, the protection of spawning sites and the introduction of a number of new species. These included the catfish, *Ictalurus nebulosus* (Lesueur), largemouth bass, *Micropterus salmoides* (Lacépède), and the pumpkinseed, from North America, carp, vendace, eel, and others. Large numbers of eels were stocked during the 1960s. With increased human development, the nutrient loading of the lake increased and by 1930 the lake was becoming eutrophic. In the 1950s, the use of artificial fertilisers increased the eutrophication and biocides also entered the food chains. A large kill of 500 tonnes of fish, including 200 tonnes of zander, in 1965 was linked to biocides. A further large fish kill was recorded in 1975 caused by deoxygenation due to the collapse of an algal bloom, a further sign of cultural eutrophication (Figure 10.7).

Today, zander are fished commercially by 1,000 m long seines with a cod-end mesh size of 35-40 mm (Biró 1985). The annual yield of zander increased from about 80 tonnes in the early-1900s to about 160 tonnes by the late-1920s to 1940 (Figure 10.7). After the state took the fishery over there was increased fishing pressure and the yield soon fell to about 120 tonnes. In the early-1970s, the landings of zander represented 6-12% of the total, while 78%

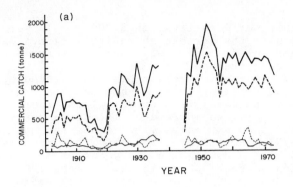

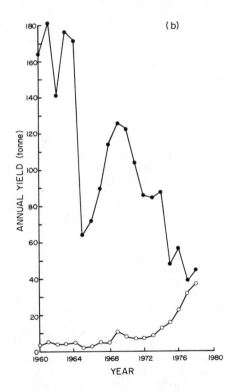

Figure 10.7: Plots of (a) annual commercial catches of major fish species from 1902 to 1973 (━━━ = total fish, ━ ━ = *Abramis* sp., --- = *Pelecus cultratus* and ━━ = *Stizostedion lucioperca*) (after Biró 1977) and (b) annual catches of *Stizostedion lucioperca* from commercial ● and sport ○ fisheries from 1960 to 1978 (data from Biró 1985) for Lake Balaton, Hungary.

of the catch was bream, *Abramis brama* (Linnaeus).
In recent years there has been an increase in the
catch of less valuable species such as bream and a
decrease in the valuable zander and also a decrease
in the perch. Since the late-1960s there has been
an increase in the yield of zander to the
recreational fishery. In 1978 the weight of zander
caught by sports fishermen was only slightly less
than the commercial fishery. Reduction in the
yields to commercial fishermen brought about by
over-fishing Lake Balaton may make commercial
fishing uneconomic in the future. It may be more
economic to run the fishery for recreation only.

Perch are a prized food in Finland. It is of
secondary importance in the USSR and Europe and in
many countries it is fished for sport only. In
many salmonid lakes and rivers it is considered to
be a nuisance and several methods are used to try
and eradicate it. Therefore records of yields of
perch and yellow perch are not very extensive. In
a number of cases the yields of perch and yellow
perch have shown considerable variation with time
as has already been illustrated in yellow perch
catches from Lake Erie. In Lake Constance
(Bodensee) bordered by Switzerland, West Germany
and Austria the yield of perch from 1914-19 to
1966-74 rose from 0.6 to 16.0 kg ha^{-1} y^{-1} in the
upper lake and from 3.0 to 12.0 kg ha^{-1} y^{-1} in the
lower lake. This was attributed to increased
eutrophication (Hartman & Numann 1977). In Lake
Ijssel, Netherlands, the yield of perch increased
from 0.8 to 2.4 kg ha^{-1} y^{-1} during the periods
1949-69 to 1970-75 (Willemsen 1977b). These
variations are understandable since the biological
production within a population can be so variable.
The changes in growth and population size in
Windermere, England, after exploitation ceased,
resulted in a range of adult production from 2 to
15 kg ha^{-1} yr^{-1} during the period 1961-72 (Craig
1980a).

Although yields of walleye show extensive
variation between and within lakes, some general
conclusions can be drawn. This is, in part,
allowed by better records of yields having been
kept as opposed to the case with perch and yellow
perch. The average annual yields of walleye in
North America range from 0.04 to 3.06 kg ha^{-1} y^{-1}
(Carlander 1977).

Zander usually produce higher yields in
brackish water than fresh water. In Poland the
average yields from brackish water during the

period 1948–75 were 5.4 kg ha^{-1} y^{-1} for the Firth of Vistula and 6.5 kg ha^{-1} y^{-1} for the Firth of Szczecin (Nagieć 1977). This compared to yields ranging from 1.0 to 8.3 kg ha^{-1} y^{-1} from seven Polish lakes with an average of 3.8 kg ha^{-1} y^{-1} over approximately the same time period.

A number of attempts have been made to produce predictive models to determine potential sustainable yields for percids given certain environmental factors. For example, Mikulski (1964) found an inverse correlation between mean depth and zander yields. Ryder (1965) described the potential for fish production in north temperate lakes by the morphoedaphic index, MEI:

$$MEI = \frac{TDS}{\overline{Z}}$$

where TDS = total dissolved solids and $\overline{Z}$ is the mean depth. Data from 23 intensively fished lakes in Canada and the northern USA were used to relate MEI to sustainable yield (SY) of walleye by Schlesinger and Regier (1983). The relationship was:

$$Log_{10}SY = 1.3829 \, (log_{10}MEI) \, -1.8136$$

Over 69% of the variation in yield was explained by the equation. Others have used factors such as total biological phosphorus to determine fish yields (Hanson & Leggett 1982). However in the recent paper by Schlesinger and Regier (1983) the effect of long-term temperature (TEMP) conditions appears most crucial in determining sustainable yields. This is not surprising considering the controlling and limiting influence of temperature (Chapter 3). Percids are mesotherms and produce highest yields slightly to the north of the midway point between the Arctic and Tropics (Figure 10.8). The relationship between SY and TEMP was described by:

$$Log_{10} \, SY=0.3866 \, (TEMP) - 0.0558 \, (TEMP^2) - 0.0105$$

$$(TEMP^3) + 0.011 \, (TEMP^4) - 0.4478 \qquad \text{Equation 10.1}$$

The model explained 73% of the variance. Equation 10.1 is represented in Figure 10.9 and illustrates that the theoretical maximum yield is produced at about 2°C, the 2°C isotherm is in the

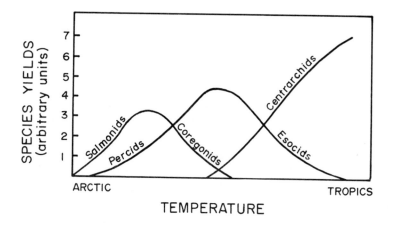

Figure 10.8: Diagram to illustrate hypothetical relationships between potential fish yields and environmental temperatures in subartic and temperate zones. Fish yield units are arbitrary. (After Schlesinger & Regier 1983).

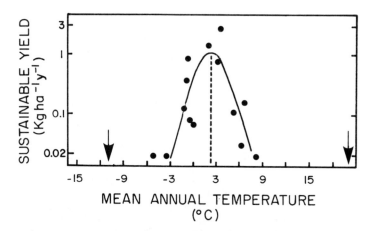

Figure 10.9: Plots to illustrate the relationship between sustainable yields of *Stizostedion vitreum* and long-term mean annual air temperatues. Arrows indicate the approximate temperature range for native populations of walleye. (After Schlesinger & Regier 1983).

northerly part of the walleye range.

A major factor determining the size both in numbers and length (and/or condition) of the catch is the nature of the fishing gear. Most commercial fishing gear is passive and relies on the behaviour of the fish (gill nets, traps and hook and line) as compared to active gear which is moved through the water to catch the fish (trawls and seines). Mesh size will determine minimum size of the fish caught in both types of gear. In a survey carried out with Lake Winnipeg fishermen (Gislason *et al.* 1982), a number of characteristics about gill nets used to catch walleye were recorded. Green and blue nets caught more fish than white ones and brightly coloured nets such as yellow caught even fewer fish. The effect of colour was reduced as the water became more turbid. As has already been described, nylon nets caught more fish than cotton ones. Also the finer the ply of the net material the greater the catch although the finer nets had a shorter life. The position of the net is important. Nets set inshore caught more walleye in Lake Winnipeg than those set offshore as did nets set perpendicular to the shore as compared to those set parallel. Craig and Fletcher (1982) found the position of nets in relation to the shore influenced the size of perch catches. More perch were caught in monofilament gill nets set perpendicular to the shore than those set parallel. The selectivity of gill nets is illustrated in Figure 10.10. The amplitude of selectivity increases with mesh size but smaller mesh sizes are less efficient. Selectivity curves for each mesh size are bimodal. The mode to the left represents walleye that are wedged in the mesh while the mode to the right represents fish that are tangled by teeth, maxillaries, preopercles and opercles. The difference in fatness or condition of the fish and thus size of girth determines the minimum size caught by a mesh size. This size will vary with time of year. Using a range of mesh sizes ensures that representatives of all fish within a certain size range are caught in the gear. Monofilament gill nets of stretched mesh sizes 10, 12.5, 16.5, 22 and 28 mm catch perch in the length range 90-210 mm with 72% efficiency (Linlokken 1984). However commercial nets are usually designed for high selectivity so that large marketable fish are caught and smaller fish are not netted. Factors influencing the number and size of percids caught in traps depend on the location, the length of time

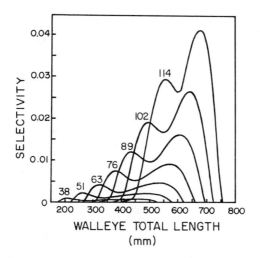

Figure 10.10: Estimated selectivity curves of from 38 to 114 mm mesh gill nets to fish length of *Stizostedion vitreum*. Each curve is the sum of the wedging and tangling curves for that mesh. Selectivity is estimated from $S_{ij} = [R_{ijt} / X_{it}]/T_{jt}$ where S_{ij} is the selectivity of mesh i for size class j, R_{ijt} is the number of marked fish caught in day t by mesh i, X_{it} is effort by mesh i in day t and T_{jt} is the number of marked fish of size-class j alive at the start of day t. (After Hamley & Regier 1973).

the trap is set, the size of the trap entrance, the size of the mesh, the season, the sex and the species (Craig 1980b). The variability in catches between traps is usually very large, as has been demonstrated for Windermere perch traps (Chapter 9) (Bagenal 1972a) and trapnets used for yellow perch in Lake Erie (Hamley & Howley 1985). In the latter case, to obtain a geometric mean with confidence limits within 20-25% would require about 100 lifts of the trapnets.

Anglers tend to remove smaller walleye than commercial fishermen (Craig & Smiley 1986; Serns & Kempinger 1981) and many of these walleye are sexually immature. In Lac des Mille, Canada, during the period 1958-75, anglers removed walleye in the age range 4 to 6 years as compared to commercial fishermen who took 5 to 11 year old fish (Elsey & Thomson 1977). Yields to anglers can also exceed those of commercial fishermen and need to be taken into consideration when management rules are made for a fishery.

Percid fisheries are important. Not only do they produce an economic return but they provide hours of leisure time activity. However, many bodies of water containing percid fishes have and are undergoing significant changes including

increased fishing pressure and increasing productivity. To sustain these fisheries for the future
will require careful management and an appraisal of
past management practices.

Management

The perch and yellow perch adapt very easily
to new habitats within their range. In many areas
attempts are made to suppress these species,
especially when they are in supposed competition
with salmonids. Areas that are affected include
British Columbia, eastern Canada, western and
northeastern states of the USA, Scotland and
Ireland. In contrast in other more inland areas,
for example central Canada and the midwestern and
central USA and central Europe, *Perca* are held in
high regard and are important in the fisheries.
Some attempts, in most cases unsuccessful, have
been made to manage perch and yellow perch
fisheries by quota, minimum size and minimum mesh
size. These policies are also applied to
commercial fisheries for walleye. In the USA,
walleye are extensively fished for sport and control measures include closed seasons, bag limits
and minimum sizes.

The management of fish stocks has a long
history. It is also very political and the degree
to which the recommendations of biologists are
taken into consideration depends on the local
jurisdiction. The managers of the resource have to
consider the users who in many cases are the voters
who put the law makers in office. The manager of a
fishery has six basic options to control the
fishery. These are gear control, season control,
limited entry, pricing the right to fish and non-
transferable and transferable quotas. Control of
fishing gear, for example stipulating the mesh size
to be used, is intended to permit sufficient
escapement of young fish so that they may later be
recruited to the adult population and sustain the
stocks. They are also used to control fishing
effort, for example, in the number of nets set per
day. Closed seasons, closed areas and shortened
seasons aim to protect fish during critical periods
in their life cycle such as spawning periods and
also to control fishing effort. However these
measures only reduce the time in which the fish may
be harvested and usually increase the fishing
effort. This is uneconomic as fishermen invest in

more equipment to intensify fishing effort during a
shorter period of time. The net effect is to
increase harvesting, storage, processing and
marketing costs. Limiting entry to a fishery may
be a viable management option. Reduction in the
number of boats usually leads to sophistication of
the gear and vessels in the residual fleet exploi-
ting the fishery. This system of management may be
used in conjunction with a rental. In this way the
beneficiaries of the resource pay for the benefits
and these revenues can be used in the costs of
management. Experience has shown that the use of
quotas may be the best method of controlling the
level of harvest and also in controlling invest-
ments commensurate with the value of the individual
quota production. The major weakness of a non-
transferable quota is its inflexibility in
permitting the fishery to adjust to changing
markets, costs and technology. The industry cannot
consolidate quotas and rationalise the size of the
fleet. These problems are overcome by an
individual transferable quota system.

The removal of predators often results in an
increase in smaller forage fish. This has already
been illustrated in the Lake Erie fishery where the
removal of blue pike, sauger and walleye led to an
increase in yellow perch, smelt and white bass.
Alternatively an increase in predatory fish causes
a decrease in overall yields as has been
demonstrated in a number of Polish lakes (Bonar
1977) and in Lake Vortsjarv, USSR (Pihu & Maeemets
1982). In Lake Vortsjarv the total yield in the
early-1970s was about 300 tonnes y^{-1} of which
80-90% was ruffe or small perch (Pihu & Maeemets
1982). The yield in 1979 declined to 184 tonnes
but the proportion of zander had gone up and they
and eels represented 50-60% of the catch. The
value of the total catch had risen by a factor of
two to three. The changes were brought about by
careful management, including the introduction of
elvers, thus increasing the predatory pressure on
forage fish. The use of a fine meshed trawl which
caused high mortality of young stages of zander was
banned. Also a closed season during spawning, a
ban on fishing at spawning sites throughout the
year and size limits were introduced. This is an
example of effective management.

A limited walleye gill net fishery was established in the 1950s in the New York state waters of
Lake Erie (Wolfert 1981). During the period
1950-78 four very large year classes were produced,

229

1959, 1962, 1964 and 1971. When a strong year class was produced fishing intensity increased and small mesh, 70 or 76 mm stretched mesh, nets were used; 46% of the landings contained one year old walleye and thus many fish were removed before they could spawn. If the small gill nets had not been used but fishing had been restricted to large mesh nets, 121 or 127 mm, the fishery yields would have increased by 35% and many walleye would have reached the age of sexual maturity. In this example the fishery probably could have been better managed from a biological perspective.

An interesting experiment was performed on the sport fishery of Escanaba Lake, USA (Churchill 1957). No restrictions were placed on hook and line fishing for any species and there was no evidence of depletion of fish stocks after ten years. In the period about 97,000 fish were angled of which about 80% were yellow perch or walleye. The fishing pressure was low during the spawning period due to the remote location of the lake so the effect of no closure at this time could not be evaluated. It was calculated that fishing regulations would have brought about a 50% reduction in the catch and minimum size limits would have more effect than bag or season limits.

Restrictions on size limits are intended to maximise the yield, increase the catch of larger fish and protect potential spawners. However in many cases an increase in size limits has resulted in a decrease in the yield of large fish, and an increase in the number of young and smaller sized fish (Serns 1978). Taylor (1981) used a simple simulated model to determine the effect of size limits on the sport fishery for walleye in Lake McConaughy, USA. His model used the basic equation:

$$N_{t+1} = N_t - N_t(u+v) + f(g) + r \qquad \text{Equation 10.2}$$

where N_t and N_{t+1} are the numerical sizes of the population at the start and end of the time period (usually one year), u and v are the expectations of death from fishing and natural causes respectively, $f(g)$ is a growth function and r is the number of recruits during the time period t to t+1. Equation 10.2 was applied to each year class since values of u, v, g and r change with age. The long-term results of size limits on the walleye population illustrated that an increase in size limits resulted in an increase in the population but a

decrease in the angler harvest (Table 10.3).
    Stocking is a common management practice and
can be of three types. The first type is
introductory, in other words the species stocked is
new in the habitat. The second type is maintenance
stocking where the fish present do not reproduce
naturally or if they do it is very limited. The
third type is supplementary stocking to augment
natural reproduction of existing fish. In a study
of walleye stocking in 125 bodies of water in the
last 100 years, Laarman (1978) found that stocking
success was very low. In type one there was 48%
success, 32% in type two and only 5% in type
three. Type one situations included stocking of
newly formed reservoirs and in areas extending
outside the species range, providing conditions
were still within the physiological range of the
species. Type two included lakes which underwent
occasional winterkills or where there was little
spawning habitat. These stockings were often the
basis for 'put and take' sport fisheries. Percids
are normally fecund enough to produce large numbers
of eggs at low population levels. Thus if
conditions are optimum for a good year class the
planting of further larvae or fingerlings (type
three) will make very little contribution to the

Table 10.3. Estimated response of the Lake McConaughy, USA, walleye
population to various length limits. (After Taylor 1981).

Length limit (mm)	Population		Angler harvest			No. ha^{-1} caught and released
	No. ha^{-1}	Kg ha^{-1}	No. ha^{-1}	Kg ha^{-1}	Kg (fish)$^{-1}$	
None	31.7	9.2	6.7	3.8	0.57	1.3
300	31.7	9.2	6.7	3.8	0.57	1.3
325	31.8	9.3	6.6	3.8	0.58	1.4
350	33.4	9.9	6.2	3.8	0.63	2.3
375	37.0	11.7	4.8	3.6	0.79	4.7
400	39.4	12.9	3.6	3.3	0.92	6.7
425	40.1	13.2	3.3	3.1	0.96	7.1
450	45.2	15.2	2.2	2.6	1.21	9.2

total year class strength. Consider examples of
mortality of reared walleyes as compared to native
walleyes (Figure 10.11). The object of stocking is
to rear the fish to overcome an unfavourable period
(high mortality) that they would naturally
experience and time their introduction into a water
body when conditions are at an optimum. Thus a
strong year class would be produced when a
naturally produced year class would be weak. The
chances of success must be weighed against the
chance of selecting the optimum time to introduce
the fish (later conditions may make the plantings a
failure anyway), and the cost of rearing.

Oneida Lake, USA, has a natural population of
walleye. Stocking with larvae influenced the
initial abundance of the year class but this
influence did not persist to age one year and thus
stocking of walleye larvae did not necessarily mean
an increase in year class strengths in subsequent
years (Forney 1976). The success of stocking
larger walleye was measured in Michigan lakes by
using fin clips as marks (Laarman 1981). Walleye
were reared to a length of 110-170 mm, the average
length of walleye in the lakes at the end of the
first year and stocked at a rate of 25 ha^{-1}. The
total (natural and fishing) annual mortality from

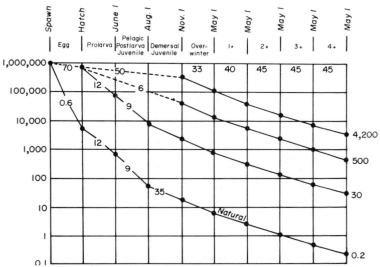

Figure 10.11: The effect of different mortality rates (assuming an initial
stock of one million eggs) on natural and cultured *Stizostedion vitreum*. The
lower line represents a heavily exploited natural population which would collapse under the mortality rates shown. The three upper lines represent populations cultured to various stages (--). Numbers given are the percentage
survival for the given period. (After Mathias in preparation).

one to two years was 74% and from two to eight
years was 56% for both native and stocked fish.
The exploitation rate by anglers ranged from 3 to
35% with a mean of 17% but only 3.5% of the stocked
fish were harvested by the anglers. The cost-
benefit of stocking walleye was calculated in
Claytor Lake, USA, by introducing walleye which
were genetically distinct from the indigenous stock
using the MDH alleles (Chapter 8) (Murphy *et al.*
1983). Walleye were stocked in alternate years,
1977 and 1979 at a size of 25-45 mm. The stocked
fish contributed about 67% to recruitment of the
year class to which they were added. The cost of
rearing a juvenile walleye was US $0.46 and the
average stocking costs were US $21,528 y^{-1}. The
returns by anglers in the period of study indicated
that the cost of each walleye harvested was about
US $27. The cost of stocking must also be related
to income from the fishery. Such a high cost as
the one given in the example would not be practical
for commercial fishing but may be for a sport
fishery where much of the income is secondary in
nature. Thus not only is income derived from
selling licences but is also derived from the sale
of fishing equipment and hotel and travel costs.
At present little is still known about the benefits
of stocking with larvae as compared to fingerlings.
Indications are that unless conditions are suitable
the exercise will be useless but this has not de-
terred many authorities from spending vast quantities of money in rearing fish for stocking. The
success of walleye stocking to produce a self-
sustaining population appears to depend on environmental and biological conditions of the water
bodies rather than the numbers or sizes of walleye
introduced. The most important of these are
probably water temperature at spawning time, amount
of potential spawning area and the biomass of
potential predators feeding on the walleye. These
examples provided for walleye are equally
applicable to perch, yellow perch and zander,
although conditions for success may vary.

Culture

With an increase in demand for percids both
for eating and for sport, and the resulting strains
put on natural populations, there is a need for
artificial production of these species. Unfortunately information on husbandry, economics,

disease, genetics, nutrition and physiology of percids is not very extensive. Artificial production
of percids includes the rearing of larvae and
fingerlings for stocking and the rearing of large
fish for consumption. The farming of table sized
fish has mainly been confined to yellow perch.

Collection and Fertilisation

Perch, yellow perch and walleye can be
stripped for artificial fertilisation. Perch,
yellow perch and walleye are caught from a wild
stock during the spring by traps or gill nets.
They may be held for a few days until they ripen.
A future development may be the production of a
brood stock of female percids which have been
treated with 17α -methyltestosterone. Female yellow
perch treated in this way produced viable sperm and
when this was used to fertilise eggs the offspring
were all female (Malison *et al.* 1986; Chapter 4).
The advantage of rearing females is that in percids
they grow to a larger size than males. Fish for
stripping are selected when slight pressure on the
abdomen results in the extrusion of eggs or sperm.
Usually fertilisation is achieved by the dry
method. The eggs are extruded into a stainless
steel dish and sperm are added. The eggs and sperm
are then stirred with a feather and after thorough
mixing, water is slowly added. The fertilised eggs
are washed with several changes of water. Eggs of
walleye are adhesive, so to avoid clumping the eggs
have to be stirred until they are water hardened.
This takes about one hour. Sometimes tannin is
added to the fertilised eggs to prevent clumping.
Fertilised eggs of perch and yellow perch may also
be obtained by placing artificial spawning substrates such as bundles of twigs into a small pond
or lake which contains a dense population of fish.
The eggs are collected and incubated in the same
way as artificially fertilised eggs. Artificial
methods of fertilisation are not used for zander as
pond spawning of brood stock has been adequate
(Huet 1970). Brood stocks of zander are reared and
held in carp ponds. Eggs of zander are usually
collected by placing artificial nests made of old
netting in small spawning ponds. They are placed
at a depth of about one metre at a density of one
per 5 m^2 and pairs of zander equal to the number of
nests are introduced. After spawning these nests
may be raised and the eggs artificially incubated

or the nests are distributed to other ponds at a density of one per hectare.

Incubation

Yellow perch eggs have been incubated by a number of methods. These include trays, normally used for trout, and Zoug jars (Figure 10.12). Just before hatching the ribbons of eggs are transferred to troughs or introduced to ponds where they are placed on submerged branches to stop them falling into the mud. Walleye eggs are incubated in jars (Figure 10.12). Water is gently circulated through the jars and dead eggs rise and are discharged over the top. Survival at this stage can be as good as 75-80%. When the larvae have hatched they are introduced to rearing ponds or directly into the lake or river where stocking is required. Recently a mobile hatchery has been developed at the Freshwater Institute, Winnipeg, Canada. This hatchery can be moved beside a lake or river where stocking is required. As the larvae hatch they move to the top of the jars and into a trough and from the trough they can enter the water body. The whole process avoids handling and transportation of the sensitive embryos or larvae. Artificial nests containing zander eggs are hung in rooms kept at constant temperature of 14-15°C and a fine spray of water from an atomiser is sprayed into the room (Woynarovich 1960). This method has been very successful. Only small quantities of water are required, the oxygen supply to the eggs is good, the maintenance of a constant temperature is easy and fungal growth is avoided. Just before hatching the eggs are immersed in water. They still stick to the fibres of the nest at this stage. Eyed eggs of zander are very hardy and can be transported over long distances. In the USSR the zander eggs are often put in ponds beside rivers so that when the young reach about a size of 30-40 mm they can be liberated directly into the river (Zhdonova 1961; Dmitrieva 1960).

Rearing

There has been little success feeding larval percids with artificial foods and live food is required during early development. Table 10.4 illustrates the progression of zooplankters

(a) (b)

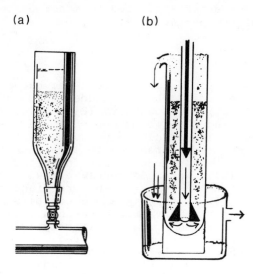

Figure 10.12: Sketches of (a) a Zoug jar for hatching *Perca fluviatilis* eggs (after Huet 1970) and (b) a jar for hatching *S. vitreum* eggs. Water flows out through the top in both jars.

Table 10.4: The composition (%) of main food items and daily consumption (% body weight) by young zander held in rearing ponds. (After Zhmurova 1982).

Fish Length (mm)	Copepods Small	Copepods Large	Cladocera Small	Cladocera Large	Chironomid Larvae	Daily Consumption
7	95					32
11	64		36			21
12	28			64		14
18		19		76		14
31				86	12	13

selected by zanders in pond culture. The progression from small copepods to large cladocerans is also followed by perch, yellow perch and walleye. The importance of abundant small zooplankters at the commencement of exogenous feeding is emphasized by the daily consumption of 32% body weight. This percentage declines as the fish grow. High mortality of larval walleye is caused by insufficient food density at commencement of feeding, the optimum is about 100 small crustaceans per litre (Li & Mathias 1982). Fish density and culture volume also influence walleye mortality. The larval density should be less than one fish per litre. Increase in density of walleye causes an increase in cannibalism which has a significant influence on the mortality of the cohort and thus the year class strength.

The best growth rates, lowest mortality and best physiological condition are obtained when zander are reared in 6‰ salinity (Zhmurova & Somkina 1976). There may be advantages in rearing perch, yellow perch and walleye at this salinity to reduce osmotic stress at a critical period of development. This still has to be tested.

Larval *Perca* have been fed with invertebrates collected from sewage lagoons (Raisanen & Applegate 1983) but in most cases invertebrate production has been promoted within the fish pond by fertilisation methods. Hay has been added to yellow perch rearing ponds for the production of infusoria. In walleye ponds alfalfa meal has been successfully used for promoting zooplankton numbers. Other organic fertilisers used include sheep manure and brewers' yeast. In some experimental ponds in Manitoba alfalfa meal at a rate of 187 kg ha^{-1} is applied weekly over four weeks in May. Larval walleye are stocked into the ponds at a density of 70,000 ha^{-1} in early June. Ponds used for zander production are also fertilised. Postlarval fish can feed on prey up to 50% of their length. Walleye reaching a size of 55-65 mm and zander reaching a size of 40 mm need to be fed on forage fish fry otherwise they become cannibalistic. The switch in diet may be influenced by the development of the tapetum lucidium and the resulting change in feeding behaviour (Walker & Applegate 1976; Mathias personal communication).

Yellow perch yield from a stocked pond fertilised with hay was 68 kg ha^{-1} (West & Leonard 1978). This consisted of 35,789 fingerlings from a 0.2 hectare pond, each weighing approximately 0.38 g harvested in early July. The production of walleye from fertilised ponds is similar, usually about 60 kg ha^{-1}. In Manitoba ponds the fish are harvested as fingerlings weighing about 2 g (30,000 ha^{-1}) in late July or they are reared to a larger size in the autumn of about 6.7 g (9,000 ha^{-1}). Zander production in carp ponds is about 50 kg ha^{-1} (Steffens 1960). About 20,000 ha^{-1} are produced at an average weight of 2.5 g and this number declines as the weight of fish increases.

Fingerling yellow perch can be trained to accept dry food and do so more readily than walleye (Ketola 1978). Calbert and Huh (1976) reared yellow perch from fingerling to 150 g in 9-11 months on pelleted food. Water was kept at 21°C, circulated through the rearing tanks and then through a filter. In this way it was used about 20 times. The yellow perch were kept in light for 16 h per day. An 8 h photoperiod significantly reduced yellow perch growth but changes in photoperiod had no significant effect on walleye growth (Huh, Calbert & Stuiber 1976). Fish, both yellow perch and walleye, grow best at a ration of about three per cent body weight per day. Fish less than 15 g should be given at least four meals per day but this can be reduced to two or three meals for larger fish (Huh 1976). The conversion efficiency of pelleted food is about 67% for yellow perch and 42% for walleye. A number of different formulations for artificial food have been developed. The nutritional requirements are as follows (Milliken 1982): Dietary protein ranging from 30-55%. Essential amino acids include arginine, histidine, isoleucine, leucine, lysine, methionine, phenylalanine, threonine, trptophan and valine. Dietary lipid in the range 12-24% with the essential fatty acid, linoleic acid. Vitamins required are thiamine, riboflavin, pyridoxine, niacine, pantothenic acid, ascorbic acid, choline, folic acid, cyanocobalamin, biotin, insitol, vitamin A, cholecalciferol, vitamin E and vitamin K. Minerals needed are phosphorus, magnesium and trace amounts of manganese, zinc, copper, iron, iodine and selenium. Percids are capable of utilising carbohydrates and fibre is essential in the diet formulation. The use of animal fat in place of vegetable fat may improve growth and is also cheaper (Heck & Calbert 1977). The formulation used at the University of Wisconsin, where most of the development of yellow perch cultivation has been carried out, is shown in Table 10.5.

Table 10.5: Composition and proximate analysis of food used in the cultivation of yellow perch (After Garber 1983).

Composition	%	Proximate analysis	%
Fish meal	50	Protein	52.1
Soybean flour	10	Fat	18.9
Blood flour	5	Moisture	4.7
Brewers' yeast	5	Ash	8.5
Whey	5	Crude carbohydrate	15.8
Fish solubles	10	Calorific content	5.1 Kcal g^{-1}
Oil	9		
Vitamin supplements	6		

Gastric evacuation of pelleted food and thus the rate of food passage is unaffected by size of fish or by the amount of moisture although it is affected by the meal size (Garber 1983).

At present the rearing of yellow perch in ponds or in tanks to a size that they can be processed for consumption is barely economic. The cost of producing a fingerling at US $0.05-0.10 rises to only US $0.30-0.40 for the table size fish. Similarly the cost of fish production of about US $2.50 kg^{-1} is high compared to the market price of lake fish which can range from US $1.70 – 2.80 kg^{-1}. The fate of yellow perch and possibly walleye fish farming will depend on demand and the viability of the natural stocks. The management of these stocks has already been discussed. The final part of this chapter will be devoted to pollutants which may significantly affect the environment of percid stocks.

Pollutants

Many bodies of water have elevated levels of substances harmful to fish and often to man if the fish are eaten. These increases are usually due to the impact of man. The toxicants can be heavy metals such as mercury, cadmium, lead, zinc, arsenic and copper, organic pollutants such as chlorinated insecticides and effluent from paper and pulp mills and coal mines. Many other substances produced in industrial processes can be liberated into fresh waters inhabited by percids such as chlorine in cooling water from power plants and accidental spills of radioactive materials. On a positive note, control or ban on some of these substances has brought about a reduction in the tissue concentration in perch, yellow perch, walleye and zander (Armstrong & Scott 1979; Frank, Van Hove Holdrinet, Desjardine & Dodge 1978; Pfeifer, Ponyi & Nagy 1979) and often an improvement to the stocks (Weinbauer, Thiel, Kaczynski & Martin 1980). Contamination may be brought about indirectly. After the creation of a reservoir on the Churchill River, Canada, mercury concentrations in walleye muscle rose from $0.2 - 0.3$ μg g^{-1} prior to flooding in 1978 to $0.5 - 1.0$ μg g^{-1} in the period 1978 to 1982 (Bodaly, Hecky & Fudge 1984). Most of the mercury in the walleye was in the organic (methylated) form. There is no industrial development in this area and mercury was derived from the flooded terrestrial area by bacterial methylation of mercury occurring naturally in the soil. Bodaly *et al.* (1984) related the concentration of mercury to the area of land flooded.

Heavy metals affect oxygen uptake, osmoregulation, carbohydrate metabolism and haematology. Exposed animals suffer from various pathological alterations in gill tissues. Some metals exist in several forms depending on pH and the toxicity of different forms may vary substantially. Often fish are more susceptible to the metals in acidic waters. In addition, synergism between acid and metal may occur. Perch living in the effluent from a sulphide ore smelting plant accumulated metal residues in liver and muscle (Larsson, Haux, Sjoebeck & Lithner 1984). They showed signs of anaemia, hypocalcemia, increase in muscle water content and reduced liver size all of which were of transcient nature and disturbed chloride balance and hyperglycemia which were more persistent. Of interest was their reduced resistance to withstand stress compared to controls. Stress may increase the toxic nature of heavy metals.

Cadmium concentrates in the gills, kidney and liver of percids (Edgren & Notter 1980) as compared to mercury which is mainly deposited in the muscle (von Hegi & Geiger 1979). In the contaminated River Emaan, Sweden, perch exposed to cadmium had 40-100% more lymphocytes than controls, an indication of a stimulated immune system response. Contaminated fish showed signs of slight anaemia, changes in blood ion concentrations and disturbed carbohydrate metabolism. The physiological disturbance was not so great in perch from the river compared to laboratory fish. This indicates that the perch were able to develop resistance to cadmium in the natural situation or the cadmium was less 'available' in the river, in other words it was bound or complexed (Sjoebeck, Haux, Larsson & Lithner 1984) or the laboratory fish were more stressed than the river fish. At sublethal levels cadmium can affect growth rate in natural populations of perch (Kearns & Atchison 1979). Copper can also reduce growth rate in perch and at concentrations above 22 μg l^{-1} of copper, food conversion efficiency is reduced (Collvin 1985). This is attributed to increased standard metabolism required for the detoxification of the copper. Unfertilised perch eggs also increase their respiratory rate when exposed to copper but in this case the copper dissipates an oxygen permeability barrier located at the chorion (Akberali & Earnshaw 1984). Perch are fairly insensitive to zinc (Ball 1967) and show little change in growth when exposed naturally to sublethal levels (Kearns & Atchison 1979).

Pulp and paper mill effluent adversely affects perch and walleye. Perch held in Kraft pulp mill waste water exhibited an inability to compensate in a rotary flow test when exposed to levels of 2 or above V/V concentrations (Lehtinen & Oikari 1980). Symptoms noted were: in the liver, hepatocytes with pycnotic nuclei, particularly near the central veins, increased cytoplasmic granularity and occasional swollen secondary lamellae and parasitic cysts were noted between the secondary lamellae. These were not observed in the controls.

Experiments with conifer groundwood fibre on walleye fingerlings showed that fish were shorter in length and lighter compared to controls when exposed to 50 μg l^{-1} and higher concentrations of fibre (Smith, Kramer & Oseid 1966). As for many other pollutants the standard metabolic rate went up, at 150 μg l^{-1} of effluent it increased by 18% and the active metabolism went down 15%, compared to controls. The number of mucous cells also went

down and at 150 μg l^{-1} were 38% less than controls.
Percids may be more vulnerable at certain life
stages to pollutants. The eggs of perch are less
affected by the insecticide mexacarbate than
juvenile or adult fish (Mauck, Olson & Hogan 1977).
The eggs of yellow perch are the most resistant to
cyanide ions whilst the juveniles are the most sensitive especially at low temperatures and low
oxygen concentrations (Smith, Broderius, Oseid,
Kimball & Koenst 1978). This may be the result of
increased demands on the respiratory system to deal
with the toxicant. Cyanide ions interfere with
oxygen utilisation and the lowered oxygen available
in the water may be an additional stress.
    Perca exposed to chlorinated insecticides
accumulate them in the body tissues. The main
storage areas in the body for PCBs (polychlorinated
biphenyls) which are soluble in lipids are the viscera. The skin, scales and skeletal muscle are
only minor sites (Guiney & Peterson 1980). Many
organic toxicants are concentrated in lipid. When
lipid stores are saturated, toxicants may be released and cause stress. Usually the concentration
of the chemical increases with size of fish
(Mathews & Dolan 1983) and in perch found in heated
discharges the concentration is often higher than
in perch found in cooler areas (Edgren, Olsson &
Reutergardh 1981). This may indicate the effect of
bioaccumulation in the food chain and faster food
uptake in warmer water. Perch and yellow perch are
able to break down several insecticides in the
liver. These include carbaryl (Chin, Sullivan &
Eldridge 1979) and malathion (Gantverg & Rozengart
1984). At high concentrations (5.0 mg l^{-1})
malathion inhibits the cholinesterase activity in
the brain of perch (Gantverg & Perevoznikov 1983).

Conclusions

    As this chapter has illustrated, man has
influenced and will continue to influence the
abundance and quality of percid fishes. Many fish
communities and stocks are depressed, collapsed, or
extinct as a result of severe stresses brought
about directly or indirectly by man (Loftus 1976).
Discrete stocks of percids in the same body of
water have evolved over thousands of years and some
of these stocks are now being lost. Loftus (1976)
believes the main reasons for this are: (1) excessive exploitation; (2) incidental catches by

gears directed at adjacent stocks; (3) genetic drift imposed by selective fishing gear, often removing early maturing and/or fast growing individuals from the stock; (4) hatchery plantings may survive to mature and mix with the native stock thus diluting the gene pool of the well adapted stock (often plantings are not successful because they are not well adapted to the new environment); and (5) environmental change may force the breakdown of segregation between formerly discrete stocks.

Rehabilitation of percid stocks can be achieved but further research is required in many areas including hatching, rearing, selective breeding, exploitation control and the precise determination of water productivity and quality. Only careful management, conservation and control of the fishes' environment may halt the decline in percid stocks.

Chapter 11

OTHER PERCINI

In addition to *Perca* species, the Percini contain
two other genera confined to Eurasia, *Gymnocephalus* and *Percarina* (Chapter 1). These two
genera probably evolved from a basic *Perca* species
(Collette and Bănărescu 1977).

The four species of *Gymnocephalus*, *G. cernua*
(ruffe), *G. acerina* (Don ruffe), *G. schraetzer*
(striped ruffe) and *G. baloni* (Balon's ruffe) are
illustrated in Figure 11.1. They resemble the
perch with the distinction that their dorsal fins
are partially united. The ruffe is greenish brown
in colour along the dorsal surface. The sides and
belly of the fish are yellowish. The body is
marked with numerous dark flecks. The Don ruffe is
slightly lighter and the striped ruffe is lemon
coloured. The striped ruffe is distinguished, as
its name implies, by more or less distinct broken
dark stripes lengthwise along its flanks. The head
and body of Balon's ruffe is yellowish brown in
colour, darker on the flanks and yellow on the
belly. Along the back there are four to six spots
which continue downwards and lose their intensity
as in the perch (Holčik & Hensel 1974). Balon's
ruffe is most closely related to the ruffe and both
have short and deep bodies as compared to the Don
and striped ruffes which have more elongate bodies.
The species (apart from distinguishing between *G.
cernua* and *G. baloni)* can be identified by the
number of lateral line scales and spines in the
anterior dorsal fins (Table 11.1).

G. cernua is found in lakes and slow flowing
rivers throughout most of Europe and northern Asia
(Figure 1.4). It is a poor swimmer and lives close
to the bottom. Its lateral line system is well developed for this mode of life allowing detection of
prey and predators (Disler & Smirnov 1977) and

244

it can live in very turbid water. *G. baloni* is found only in the Danube River basin. It lives in fast flowing water. *G. acerina* inhabits the drainage basins of rivers emptying into the north of the Black Sea including the Don, Dniester and Dnieper. Like the ruffe, it lives in slow flowing water or in lakes. *G. schraetzer* is found in the Danube basin including the estuary into the Black Sea and normally lives in deep water over a substrate of sand or gravel.

G. cernua rarely grows to a length >250 mm (400 g). *G. acerina* grows to about 180 mm and *G. schraetzer* to 200 mm. There are no recorded data for growth of *G. baloni*. There is some evidence that ruffe grow more slowly and live to a greater age the further north they are located. Female ruffe grow faster, grow to a greater ultimate length and live longer than males (Figure 11.2).

Table 11.1: The number of lateral line scales and anterior dorsal fin spines in the four species of *Gymnocephalus*.

Species	Lateral line scales	Anterior dorsal fin spines
G. cernua	35–40	11–16
G. baloni	35–39	14–16
G. acerina	50–55	17–19
G. schraetzer	55–62	17–19

Gymnocephalus species feed actively through the day usually with a peak towards the evening. At night they lie close to the bottom. They feed on insects and Crustacea and sometimes small fish. *G. cernua* and *G. schraetzer* also feed extensively on molluscs and the latter species eats fish eggs when they are available.

Ruffe mature at two to three years of age at a length of 110–120 mm. In some warmer lakes they can mature earlier. For example in Lake Ijssel, the Netherlands, 50% mature at age one year at a size of 65–70 mm (Willemsen 1977b). Spawning normally occurs in all species between April and June although it can be extended over a longer period of time in colder areas. The ruffe undergoes spawning migrations from winter habitats which are deep

(a)

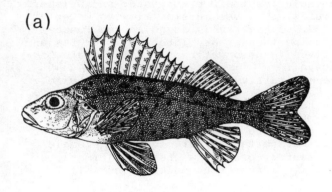

(b)

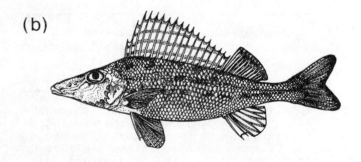

(c)

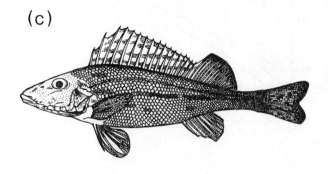

(d)

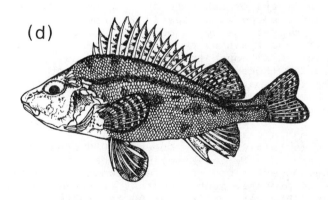

Figure 11.1: The external appearance of (a) *Gymnocephalus cernua*, (b) *G. acerina*, (c) *G. schraetzer* and (d) *G. baloni*. (After Holčík & Hensel 1974).

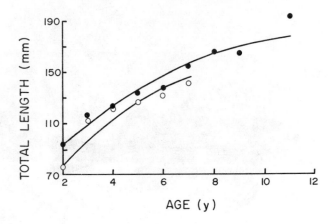

Figure 11.2: Total length against age for male (o) and female (●)
Gymnocephalus cernua from the Nadym River, USSR. Males and females lived to 7
and 11 years respectively. (Data from Kolomin 1977).

areas in rivers or lakes to shallow areas which are
stony and covered with aquatic macrophytes. The
spawning migrations commence at a temperature of
about 4°C and spawning can occur at temperatures of
6.0 to 8.0°C although the normal range is
11.6-18.0°C (Hokanson 1977). The number of eggs
laid by the female depends on its size. In the
Nadym River, USSR, the average number of eggs laid
by the ruffe is 17,800 per female (Kolomin 1977).
The striped ruffe also spawns over stones and
vegetation in shallow water but usually where the
current is fairly rapid. About 10,000 eggs per
female are laid by this species. There are no
recorded observations of ruffe spawning behaviour
but it is probably much like that of *Perca*
species. However, unlike perch, the ruffe is an
intermittent spawner and usually the eggs are laid
in two or more batches. The first batch of eggs
are larger and have more yolk than those laid
later. The eggs are deposited individually and are
adhesive, sticking to stones and submerged
vegetation. The average diameter of the egg is 1
mm. At a water temperature of 10-15°C the larval
ruffe hatch in 8-10 days. After the absorption of
the yolk the larval ruffe feed on rotifers and

small Crustacea. The optimum temperature for growth of the larvae is in the range 25-30°C (Hokanson 1977). Species of *Gymnocephalus* have little economic importance. In eastern Europe the ruffe is fished locally for sport and sometimes commercially. It is used in the production of 'ruffe soup'! It may be important as a forage fish for more economically valuable fish such as the zander. However, in other situations it may conflict with other, more valuable food fish in sharing the same niche.

Percarina is monotypic represented by the species *P. demidoffi*. The two dorsal fins are well separated in this species (Figure 11.3) and the anterior dorsal fin has 9-11 spines. The body is yellow in colour and there is a row of black spots on the dorsal surface. The fish is found in the northern area of the Black Sea, in the Sea of Azov and in the lower reaches of rivers entering these seas (Figure 1.5). It is salinity tolerant. Little is known of the ecology of *P. demidoffi*. It reaches a length of 60-90 mm in three to four years and has a maximum length of about 100 mm. Sexual maturity is reached by most individuals in one year. It feeds on invertebrates and small fish,

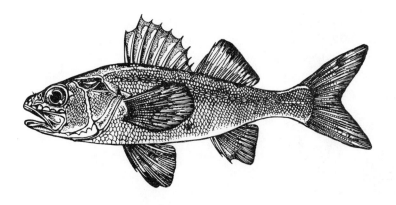

Figure 11.3: The external appearance of *Percarina demidoffi*. (After Maitland 1977).

particularly Copepoda, Cladocera, Mysidae and Gammaridae (Mikhman 1978).

The percarina spawns in June and July in shallow water which can be fresh, brackish or sea water. The fecundity of the female is about 3,000 eggs. Eggs are laid over sand and silt and hatch very quickly, normally within three days. The larval fish begin exogenous feeding on the young stages of Crustacea.

The percarina has little economic importance except in some local net fisheries.

Chapter 12

ETHEOSTOMATINI

The Etheostomatini or darters are indigenous to North America. They are represented by three genera, *Percina, Ammocrypta* and *Etheostoma* (Figure 12.1). However, within these genera there are over 150 species making up over 20% of the 750 fresh water species in North America north of Mexico (Page & Swofford 1984).

Percina, the most primitive of the darters, have one or more large and heavily toothed scales between the pelvic fins. The male usually has a row of enlarged, toothed scales along the ventral midline or belly but in the female this area is usually partly naked. The lateral line of *Percina* species is complete and extends to the base of the caudal fin. The anal fin has two spines.

Ammocrypta species are very slender and covered with fine scales which in some species are restricted to certain parts of the body. The body is often translucent, a feature not found in the other two genera. The anal fin has only one spine.

Species of *Etheostoma,* like *Ammocrypta,* have no enlarged toothed scales between the pelvic fins. The scales along the ventral midline are normal or in some species this area is naked. There usually are two anal fin spines in *Etheostoma* but some species have only one. Interrupted head canals are found in many specialised species.

Within the three genera the number of lateral line scales ranges from 33 in *E. microperca* Jordan and Gilbert to 90 in *P. aurantiaca* (Cope) and the number of dorsal spines from 6 in *E. microperca* to 16 in *P. burtoni* Fowler (Page 1983). The darters are varied in both coloration and marking and readers should consult the beautifully illustrated handbooks of Page (1983) and Kuehne and Barbour (1983) for further details.

251

(a)

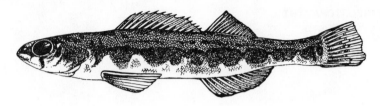

(b)

(c)

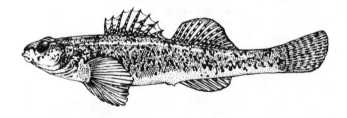

Figure 12.1: The external appearance of (a) *Percina maculata,* (b) *Ammocrypta pellucida* and (c) *Etheostoma nigrum.* (After Page 1983).

Darters are found in rivers, lakes, swamps and springs from Arctic Canada to the mountain streams of northern Mexico (Figure 1.6). The numbers of each species found in the main drainage basins are shown in Table 12.1. They are not found in the northeast USA, eastern Canada, the lower reaches of streams entering the Arctic Ocean and the Pacific side of the Rocky Mountains except where they have been introduced by man. The range of habitats where they are found is illustrated in Table 12.2. The darters have evolved to live in shallow riffles and wave-washed beaches and thus the more advanced forms are small and have either lost their swim bladder or it is considerably reduced. Riffles are free of most predators and there is a plentiful supply of food under the stones. During periods of flood, extreme drought and extreme cold the young darters move to pools but here they are subjected to heavier predation. The young live in pools until they are big enough to expend sufficient energy to remain in currents. The advanced forms living in riffles usually distribute themselves in different parts of the stream at different times of the year. There is a prespawning upstream movement to the spawning habitat which normally has a fast current. After spawning the fish are found in shallow riffles where they feed before moving downstream to a relatively deep area for overwintering. Some movements may be density dependent (Mundahl & Ingersoll 1983). Most species of darters have specific habitat requirements. In the same stretch of the River Thames, Ontario, Canada, *E. caeruleum* and *E. blennioides* Rafinesque live in riffles, *E. nigrum* and *P. maculata* live in pools and raceways and *E. flabellare* lives in both riffles and raceways (Englert & Seghers 1983). Although found in the same habitat *E. nigrum* (johnny darters) and *P. maculata* (blackside darters) may be partitioned vertically (Smart & Gee 1979). The johnny darter is benthic while the blackside darter lives in midwater and has a well developed swim bladder. The two species differ in other morphological features (Figure 12.1) such as the position of the mouth and eyes, protrusibility of the premaxilla, retinal acuity and number and morphology of the gill rakers. During low water flows the spatial separation may be broken down and there is more competition between the species.

Temperature can influence the spatial distribution of darters. For example the fantail darter, *E. flabellare*, which lives in riffles selects

Table 12.1: Numbers of described species of darters native to, endemic to and shared by each of the major drainages of North America. (After Page 1983).

| | Drainages | | | | | |
---	Hudson Bay	Great Lakes	Mississippi River	Gulf of Mexico*	Atlantic	Pacific
No. species	5	17	87	48	28	0
No. endemic species	0	0	54	21	18	0
(Endemics as percentage of total)	(0%)	(0%)	(62%)	(44%)	(64%)	(0%)
No. species shared by drainages:						
Hudson Bay		4	4	3	2	0
Great Lakes			18	9	8	0
Mississippi River				24	14	1
Gulf of Mexico					7	0
Atlantic						0

*excluding Mississippi River

cooler temperatures in summer and winter than the johnnny darter, a pool dweller. However, when the fish are placed together they try to avoid each other overriding thermo-regulation (Ingersol & Claussen 1984).

Darters show variable tolerance to oxygen concentrations among species (Table 12.3). *E. rufilineatum* is restricted to fast or torrential water and is intolerant to hypoxia. *E. flabellare* and *E. duryi* live in fast water but can tolerate periods of hypoxia. *E. squamiceps* and *E. boschungi* inhabit slow streams with low oxygen concentrations although they can live in fast streams as well. *E. fusiforme* is found in still water with low oxygen concentrations.

The more specialised species of *Etheostoma* are smaller than the more primitive *Percina* (Figure 12.2). *P. sciera* with a maximum length of about 110 mm is the largest darter and *E. fonticola* with a maximum length of 35.5 mm is the smallest. The larger darters have a longer life expectancy (over four years) than the smaller species (about one year). Males tend to be the oldest and largest members of a population (Figure 12.3). After an initial high mortality at the larval stage the

Table 12.2: The habitats of various species of Etheostomatini.

Species	Habitat
E. fonticola (Jordan & Gilbert)	Springs which are maintained at a constant temperature (21°C).
A. pellucida (Putnam)	Sand bottomed areas in streams and rivers and sandy shoals in lakes. It sometimes buries itself in the sand with only its eyes exposed.
E. caeruleum Storer	Clear streams in glaciated regions which have gravel or rubble bottoms.
E. flabellare Rafinesque	Small shallow streams which have gravel or boulder bottoms and have slow to moderate currents. Deeper regions downstream are required for overwintering.
E. exile (Girard)	Clear, slowly moving or still water of rivers and lakes. The bottom is usually covered wth organic debris, peat or sand and has extensive growths of aquatic macrophytes.
P. maculata (Girard)	Medium sized gravelly streams. It normally lives at mid-depths in pools and is less benthic than other species.
P. shumardi (Girard)	In moderately fast currents of large rivers which are boulder strewn. May live in quite turbid river tributaries and lakes.
P. caprodes (Rafinesque)	Slow moving rivers and lakes.
E. nigrum (Rafinesque)	Tolerant of a wide range of habitats.

darters have a fairly constant death rate through life until advanced age when the rate increases sharply.

Darters are diurnal feeders relying on sight for prey capture. Thus the movement of the prey is important. Olfaction appears to be of minor significance in feeding (Daugherty, Daugherty & Blair 1976) and has a more important role in escaping predators. The chemical stimuli from injured fish reduces the activity of other darters and they become quiescent on the bottom (Smith 1979; Smith 1982). Some species show peaks of activity through the day. *E. vitreum* (Cope) is active at dawn and dusk and *P. nigrofasciata* (Agassiz), *E. caeruleum* and *E. flabellare* are active early in the morning and late in the afternoon (Mathur 1973; Adamson

Table 12.3: The oxygen concentration (±2 S.E.) (mg l⁻¹) at death for six species of *Etheostoma* held at a water temperature of 20°C. (After Ultsch, Boschung & Ross 1978).

Species	Oxygen Concentration (mg l⁻¹)
E. rufilineatum (Cope)	3.6 ± 0.6
E. flabellare	1.0 ± 0.3
E. duryi (Henshall)	1.1 ± 0.3
E. squamiceps Jordan	1.0 ± 0.5
E. boschungi Wall and Williams	0.8 ± 0.2
E. fusiforme (Girard)	0.8 ± 0.3

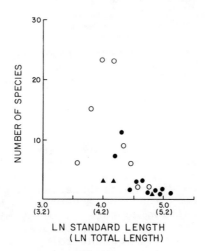

Figure 12.2: Diagram to illustrate the relationship between number of species for each genera of darters (● = *Percina*, ▲ = *Ammocrypta* and ○ = *Etheostoma*) and fish length (expressed as a natural logarithm). (After Page & Swofford 1984).

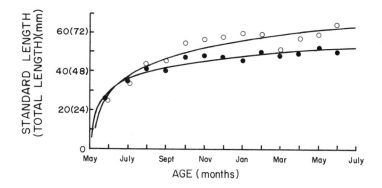

Figure 12.3: Plots of length with age (in months) of male (o) and female (●) *Etheostoma perlongum* from Lake Waccamaw, USA. (After Shute, Shute & Lindquist 1982).

& Wissing 1977). Juvenile darters feed on clado-cerans, copepods and ostracods while adults prefer chironomids, simulids, ephemeropterans and tricop-terans. Large darters, for example *E. sqamiceps* and *P. macrocephala* (Cope), feed on amphipods, isopods and crayfishes (Page 1978). Although species of darter may feed on the same food items, the separation of their niches prevents competition. This is also the case in their relationships with minnows. There are over 220 species of minnows in North America but these fish tend to be mid-water forms.

Darters exhibit some degree of sexual dimor-phism. This takes the form of differences in growth rate, genital papillae, nuptial coloration and modifications in the fins. The genital papilla of male *E. perlongum* (Hubbs and Raney), for example, is suboval and bilobed (Figure 12.4). The anterior portion of each lobe is pigmented and the gonopore is situated at the posterior junction of the lobes. The female genital papilla is also bilobed and is highly pigmented at the lateral edges. The gonopore is located midway between the posterior end of the papilla and the anus. The papilla of the female is much larger than the male and is used in the tactile searching for a suitable

(a)

(b)

Figure 12.4: Genital papillae of breeding (a) male and (b) female *Etheostoma perlongum* . (After Lindquist *et al*. 1981).

spawning site (Lindquist, Shute & Shute 1981). The
male is usually more brightly coloured than the
female. This is especially the case in species of
Etheostoma.
     Most darters become sexally mature as one year
olds. In some species the more northerly populations mature later than southern populations.
Females of *P. aurantiaca* and females and males
of *E. rubrum* Raney and Suttkus mature after two
years (Howell 1972; Raney & Suttkus 1966). Ova of
female darters are small and white in late summer
(Figure 12.5) but by late autumn and early winter a
proporton become larger and yellower. In late
winter and early spring the ovary contains both
these white and yellow ova and additionally large
orange ova that prior to spawning become transparent except for the yolk. Only one clutch of ova
mature each year and fecundity amongst darters
ranges from 100 to 750 eggs per female. The number
of eggs increases exponentially with increase in
length (Page 1983). The majority of darter species
spawn from February to June, with spawning
occurring later in more northern areas. *E.
fonticola*, which lives in constant temperature
springs, spawns all the year round, although peaks

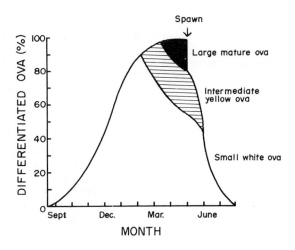

Figure 12.5: The annual cycle of ova differentiation in darters. (After Page 1983 from Page & Smith 1970).

of activity occur in August and early spring (Schenck & Whiteside 1977). *E. ditrema* Ramsey and Suttkus also lives in constant temperature spring water and spawns from March to September (Seesock, Ramsey & Seesock 1978). Sex ratios at spawning are normally one to one. The size of the egg does not vary with the size of the fish but differences in egg size can be related to the type of spawning behaviour. Spawning of darters is basically of three types. The first involves burying the eggs in the substrate. The most primitive species spawn in this way including all *Percina* and some *Etheostoma* species, for example *E. variatum* Kirtland. During spawning the female partially buries her body, including the genital papilla, in loose gravel and sand. The male mounts the female and eggs and sperm are released into the substrate. In the second type of spawning eggs are attached to plants and rocks and abandoned. The *E. blennioides* female selects a suitable object for egg attachment and swims above it. The male mounts the female and the two fish vibrate. Gametes are released and the one to three eggs produced during each act are pushed by the female onto a plant or rock where they stick. In the third type of spawning the darter

259

places eggs in clusters under a stone or rock and then the developing embryos are guarded by the male until hatching occurs. The *E. nigrum* male establishes a territory in the spring which include cavities beneath larges stones. The male leaves the cavity to court the female. The female of *E. nigrum* tends to select the most aggressive male, the male which will move out furthest from his nest (Grant & Colgan 1983). A male of this type, with increased fitness may better be able to defend the eggs and the survival of the progeny will be increased. When the female is ready to spawn, she rolls to one side and presses up against the underside of the stone. The male positions himself beside the female and the pair vibrate. Eggs and sperm are released and the adhesive eggs stick to the stone. The female of *E. squamiceps* is an intermittent spawner but *E. nigrum* continues laying eggs until she is spent. This can take up to two hours. The males of both species may spawn with other females. The eggs of *E. nigrum* are laid in a single layer while those of *E. maculatum* Kirtland are stacked. The spawning behaviour of *Ammocrypta* species has not been observed.

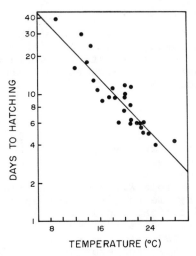

Figure 12.6: Plots of embryo development time (fertilisation to hatching) in relation to temperature for darters. (After Page 1983).

(a)

⌐ I mm ⌐

(b)

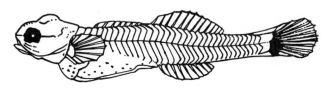

⌐ I mm ⌐

Figure 12.7: Late yolk sac larvae of (a) *Percina caprodes* and (b) *Etheostoma flabellare*. (After Cooper 1978 & 1979).

The eggs of species guarded by males tend to be bigger than those of unguarded species. The incubation of the eggs is linked to water temperature (Figure 12.6). Freshly hatched pro-larvae are 3 to 7.5 mm in length and have a large yolk sac. The larvae of many *Etheostoma* species are better developed at hatching than the more primitive *Percina* species (Figure 12.7). The eggs of the smallest darters, *E. proeliare* (Hay), *E. fonticola* and *E. microperca* produce eggs which have deep indentations on one side (Burr & Ellenger 1980). This is an unique feature in fresh water fish although it is found in some marine species. However, it has no effect on post-fertilisation development and the egg assumes a spherical shape.

Darters have no economic importance. They may play an important role as forage fish for more

valuable species such as walleye. They have
received considerable attention because of their
diversity and the adaptability they show to various
environmental conditions. They have evolved and
exploited ecological niches to a far wider range
than any other group of percids.

Chapter 13

ROMANICHTHYINI

The Romanichthyini evolved in the River Danube which may be the origin of percids in general. A common ancestor gave rise to *Romanichthys* and *Zingel*. Neither genera has any economic importance and their biology and ecology is not well understood.

The asprete, *R. valsanicola* (Dumitrescu, Bănărescu & Stoica 1957) (Figure 13.1) was first described in 1957. It is similar in build to the bullhead, *Cottus gobio* Linnaeus, and like the bullhead, the eyes are positioned dorsally on the head. It lives in the same habitat as the bullhead and often may have been confused with it. The asprete is commonly called the Rumanian bullhead perch. The two dorsal fins are well separated and the posterior fin is larger than the anterior fin. The fish is brown in colour and the belly is lighter than the rest of the body. As an adaptation to living in fast flowing water, the asprete has no swim bladder.

R. valsanicola was found in the Arges, Vilsan, Riul and Doamnei rivers in the Danube basin in Rumania but has become extinct (Stanescu 1971) except in the Vilsan River (Figure 1.8). It is probably nocturnal in habit and feeds on insect larvae, chiefly Plecoptera, and small fishes. It normally grows in length to 80-120 mm with a maximum of 130 mm. Little is known about its reproduction. During the breeding season it develops breeding tubercles. Eggs probably are adhesive and hidden among stones.

Species of *Zingel* have slender, rounded bodies and the mouths are ventral in position (Figure 13.2). The two dorsal fins are well separated in all three species. Scales cover the gill flaps. The fish have brown backs with dark mottling and

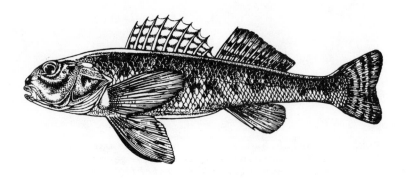

Figure 13.1: The external appearance of *Romanichthys valsanicola*. (After Maitland 1977).

blotches. The sides and belly are yellowish in colour. In *Z. zingel* (zingel) and *Z. asper* (apron) the caudal peduncle is shorter than the base of the posterior dorsal fin, in *Z. streber* (streber) it is longer. The zingel has 13-15 spines and 18-20 rays in the anterior and posterior dorsal fins respectively. Both the streber and the apron have 8-9 and 12-13 rays in the anterior and posterior dorsal fins respectively.

Zingel species, like *Romanichthys*, have no swim bladder and all three species are found in shallow, fast-running water. They are bottom living rather inactive fish with flattened bellies and rather streamlined bodies which adapt them to their habitat. The zingel is found in the basin of the River Danube and in the River Dniester. The streber also inhabits the Danube and is found in the Vardar River which flows into the Aegean Sea (Figure 1.8). Probably an ancestor of *Z. streber* entered the Rhône River and gave rise to *Z. asper* which is found there now.

The zingel is the largest of the three species growing in length to 150-300 mm, streber grows to about 150-200 mm and the apron to about 120-150 mm.

Zingel species are active at night and during

(a)

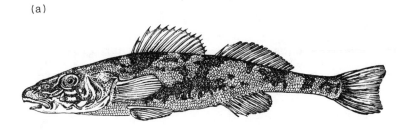

(b)

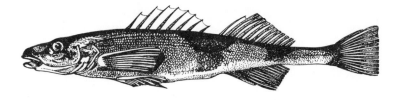

(c)

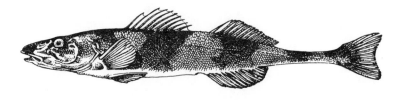

Figure 13.2: The external appearance of (a) *Zingel zingel*, (b) *Z. asper* and (c) *Z. streber* . (After Muns & Dahlstrom 1971).

the day they remain hidden and camouflaged between
stones. They feed on benthic invertebrates and
small fishes. The apron also feeds on fish eggs
and fry.

All three species spawn from March to May, and
lay adhesive eggs amongst stones in fast flowing
water. A female zingel may lay as many as 5,000
eggs. The Romanichthyini have no economic importance but are of biological interest in their
adaptation to fast flowing water and their limited
distribution.

BIBLIOGRAPHY AND AUTHOR INDEX

The pages where authors are cited in the text are given in bold type.

Abdu-Nabi, A.H. (1983). Factors related to selection of fish scales for growth studies of yellow perch, *Perca flavescens*. *Diss. Abstr. Int. B. Sci. Eng. 44* (6), 1703. **51**

Adamson, S.W. & Wissing, T.E. (1977). Food habits and feeding periodicity of the rainbow, fantail and banded darters in Four-Mile Creek. *Ohio J. Sci. 77*, 164-169. **255**

Ahlbert, I.B. (1969). The organisation of the cone cells in the retinae of four teleosts with different feeding habits *(Perca fluviatilis* L., *Lucioperca lucioperca* L., *Acerina cernua* L., *Coregonus albula* L.). *Ark. Zool. 22*, 445-481. **42**

Akberali, H.B. & Earnshaw, M.J. (1984). Copper-stimulated respiration in the unfertilized egg of the Eurasian perch, *Perca fluviatilis*. *Comp. Biochem. Physiol. 78C* (2), 349-352. **241**

Aksiray, F. (1961). About sudak *(Lucioperca sandra* Cuv. and Val.) introduced into some of the lakes of Turkey. *Proc. gen. Fish. Counc. Medit. 6*, 335-343. **76,177**

Akster, H.A. (1981). Ultrastructure of muscle fibres in head and axial muscles of the perch *(Perca fluviatilis* L.): A quantitative study. *Cell Tissue Res. 219* (1), 111-131. **27**

Akster, H.A. & Osse, J.W.M. (1978). Muscle fibre types in head muscles of the perch, *Perca fluviatilis* L., Teleostei. A histochemical and electromyographical study. *Neth. J. Zool. 28* (1), 94-110. **27**

Albers, C. (1970). Acid-base balance. In: *Fish Physiology. IV.* (Eds W.S. Hoar & D.J. Randall). 173-208. Academic Press. New York. **128**

Ali, M.A. & Anctil, M. (1968). Corrélation entre la structure rétinienne et l'habitat chez *Stizostedion vitreum vitreum* et *S. canadense. J. Fish. Res. Board Can. 25* (9), 2001-2003. **42**

Ali, M.A. & Anctil, M. (1977). Retinal structure
and function in the walleye *(Stizostedion
vitreum vitreum)* and sauger *(S. canadense)*. *J.
Fish. Res. Board Can. 34* (10), 1467-1474. **42**

Ali, M.A., Ryder, R.A. & Anctil, M. (1977). Pho-
toreceptors and visual pigments as related to
behavioural responses and preferred habitats
of perches *(Perca* spp.) and pikeperches
(Stizostedion spp.). *J. Fish. Res. Board
Can. 34* (10), 1475-1480. **42**

Alm, G. (1946). Reasons for the occurrence of
stunted fish populations with special regard
to the perch. *Medd. Statens Unders.
Foerrsoekoanst. Soettvattenfish.* (25), 1-146.
59,65,201

Amin, O.M. (1979). Lymphocystis disease in
Wisconsin fishes. *J. Fish. Dis. 2,* 207-217.
146

Anderson, D.P. (1974). *Fish Immunology.* T.F.H.
Publications, Inc. Ltd. Neptune City. N.J.
239 pp. **172**

Andrews, C.R. (1977). The biology of the parasitic fauna of perch *(Perca fluviatilis* L.) from
Llyn Tegid, North Wales. *Ph.D. thesis.* University of Liverpool. **166**

Armstrong, F.A.J. & Scott, D.P. (1979). Decrease
in mercury content of fishes in Ball Lake,
Ontario, since imposition of controls on mercury discharges. *J. Fish. Res. Board Can.
36* (6), 670-672. **240**

Avedikova, T.M. & D'Yakova, G.P. (1979). Produktivnost' populyatsij poluprokhodnykh rob pri
menyayushchemsya rezhimе Azovskogo Morya.
*Vliyanie sovremennykh vodokhozyajstvennykh
meropriyatij na biologicheskuyu produktivnost'
Azovskogo i Kaspijskogo Morej.* (Ed. E.A.
Yablonskaya). *Tr. Vniro.* Moskua. *133,*
70-83. **128**

Babaluk, J.A. & Campbell, J.S. (In press). Pre-
liminary results of tetracycline labelling for
validating annual growth increments in opercula of walleye. *N. Am. J. Fish. Manage. 7*
(2), In press. **51**

Bagenal, T.B. (1972a). The variability in numbers
of perch, *Perca fluviatilis* L., caught in
traps. *Freshwat. Biol. 2,* 27-36. **193,227**

Bagenal, T.B. (1972b). The variability of the
catch from gillnets set for pike, *Esox lucius*
L. *Freshwat. Biol. 2,* 77-82. **193**

Bagenal, T.B. & Braum, E. (1978). Eggs and early
life history. In: *Methods for Assessment of
Fish Production in Fresh Waters*. I.B.P. Handbook No. 3 3rd Ed. (Ed. T.B. Bagenal). 165-
201. Blackwell Scientific Publications.
Oxford. **72**

Bagenal, T.B. & Tesch, F.W. (1978). Age and
growth. In: *Methods for Assessment of Fish
Production in Fresh Waters*. I.B.P.Handbook
No. 3. 3rd Ed. (Ed. T.B. Bagenal). 101-136.
Blackwell Scientific Publications. Oxford.
50,54

Baker, B.I. & Wigham, T. (1979). Endocrine as-
pects of metabolic coordination in teleosts.
In: *Fish Phenology*. (Ed. P.J. Miller). *Symp.
Zool. Soc. Lond.* No. 44, 89-103. Academic
Press. London. **43,49**

Ball, I.R. (1967). The relative susceptibilities
of some species of freshwater fish to poisons.
II. Zinc. *Water Res. 1,* 777-783. **241**

Ball, J.N. (1969). Prolactin (fish prolactin or
paralactin) and growth hormone. In: *Fish Physiology*. *II*. (Eds W.S. Hoar & D.J. Randall).
207-240. Academic Press. London. **126**

Balon, E.K. (1956). Mezdidruhová hybridiźacia
dunajských ryb. 1. Oplodenie ikier ostrieza
dunajského spermion zubača obyčajného *(Perca
fluviatilis* infraspecies *vulgaris* (Schäffer
1759) Pokrovskij 1951 x *Lucioperca
lucioperca* (Linnaeus 1758)). *Polnohospo-
dárstvo, Bratisl. 3* (5), 581-592. **180**

Balon, E.K. (1975). Reproductive guilds of
fishes: a proposal and definition. *J. Fish.
Res. Board Can. 32,* 821-864. **80**

Bangham, R.V. (1955). Studies on fish parasites
of Lake Huron and Manitoulin Island. *Am.
Midl. Nat. 53* (1), 184-194. **158,160**

Bannister, L.H. (1965). The fine structure of the
olfactory surface of teleostean fishes.
Quart. J. Microscop. Sci. 106, 333-342. **39**

Bauer, O.N. (1962). Ecology of the parasites of
freshwater fish. Interrelationships between
the parasite and its habitat. *Israel Program
Sci. Transl. Cat.* No. 622.
149,166,168,169,170

Bauer, O.N., Musselius, V.A. & Strelkov, Yu. A.
(1973). Diseases of pond fishes. *Israel
Program Sci. Transl. Cat.* No. 60118.
146,148,165

Belanger, S.E. & Hogler, S.R. (1982). Comparison
   of five ageing methodologies applied to walleye *(Stizostedion vitreum)* in Burt Lake,
   Michigan. *J. Great Lakes Res. 8* (4), 666-671.
   51
Belyi, N.D. (1972). Downstream migration of pike-
   perch *Lucioperca lucioperca* and its feeding in
   the lower reaches of the Dnieper during early
   stages of development. *J. Ichthyol. 12* (3),
   465-472. **91,92,94**
Berg, L.S. (1905). *Ryby Turkestana.* St.
   Petersburg. 280 pp. **177**
Berg, L.S. (1949). *Ryby presnykh vod SSSR. i
   Sopredelnykh stran. III,* 929-1382. **177**
Berg, L.S. (1965). Freshwater fishes of the USSR
   and adjacent countries. *Israel Program Sci.
   Transl. Cat.* No. 743. **14,17,18,26**
Bertalanffy, L. von. (1938). A quantitative
   theory of organic growth. *Human Biol. 10,*
   181-213. **56**
Berzins, B. (1949). On the biology of the Latvian
   perch *(Perca fluviatilis* L.). *Hydrobiologia
   2,* 64-71. **127**
Beverton, R.J.H. & Holt, S.J. (1957). On the
   dynamics of exploited fish populations.
   *Fish. Invest. Ser. II Mar. Fish. G.B.
   Minist. Agric. Fish. Food. 19,* 533
        p. **209,210**
Biró, P. (1973). The food of pikeperch,
   Lucioperca lucioperca in Lake Balaton. *Ann.
   Inst. Biol. (Tihany) Hung. Acad. Sci.
   40,* 159-183. **99**
Biró, P. (1977). Food consumption, production and
   energy transformation of pikeperch
   (Stizostedion lucioperca (L))population in
   Lake Balaton. *Acta Biol. Iugosl. Ser. E.
   Ichthyol. 9* (1), 47-60. **221,222**
Biró, P. (1985). Dynamics of the pikeperch,
   Stizostedion lucioperca (L.), in Lake
   Balaton. *Int. Rev. ges. Hydrobiol. 70* (4),
   471-490. **60,221,222**
Blaxter, J.H.S. (1968). Light intensity, vision
   and feeding in young plaice. *J. Exptl. Marine
   Biol. Ecol. 2,* 293-307. **42**
Bodaly, R.A. (1980). Pre- and post-spawning move-
   ments of walleye, *Stizostedion vitreum,* in
   Southern Indian Lake, Manitoba. *Can. Tech.
   Rep. Fish. Aquat. Sci.* No. 931, 35 pp. **78**

Bodaly, R.A., Hecky, R.E. & Fudge, R.J.P. (1984). Increases in fish mercury levels in lakes flooded by the Churchill River diversion northern Manitoba, Canada. *Can. J. Fish. Aquat. Sci. 41* (4), 682-691. **240**

Bonar, A. (1977). Relations between exploitation, yield, and community structure in Polish pikeperch *(Stizostedion lucioperca)* lakes, 1966-71. *J. Fish. Res. Board Can. 34* (10), 1576-1580. **229**

Botsjarnikowa, A.W. (1952). Dannye no biologiirasmnozheniya i razvitiya kubanskogo sudako. *Zool. Zh. 31* (1), 122. **80**

Brandt, A. von. (1984). *Fish Catching Methods of the World.* 3rd Ed. Fishing News (Books) Ltd. Farnham. xiv + 418 pp. **213**

Breder, C.M., Jr. (1959). Studies on social groupings in fishes. *Bull. Am. Mus. Nat. Hist. 117*, 393-483. **139**

Brett, J.R. (1971). Satiation time, appetite and maximum food intake of sockeye salmon *(Oncorhynchus nerka). J. Fish. Res. Board Can. 28*, 409-415. **116**

Brett, J.R. (1979). Environmental factors and growth. In: *Fish Physiology. VIII.* (Eds W.S. Hoar, D.J. Randall & J.R. Brett). 599-675. Academic Press. New York. **47**

Brett, J.R., Shelbourn, J.E. & Shoop, C.T. (1969). Growth rate and body composition of fingerling sockeye salmon, *Oncorhynchus nerka*, in relation to temperature and ration size. *J. Fish. Res. Board Can. 26*, 2363-2394. **116**

Brunelli, G. & Rizzo, L. (1928). Chizndala esocrina, ovario impari ed ermafroditismo nella, *"Perca fluviatilis". Atti R. Acad. Naz. Lincei Cl. Sci. Fis. Mat. Nat. Rend. 7*, 865-867. **36**

Brunet, M.R. (1957). Le sandre et le brochet. *Rivieres et Forets 6*, 33-38. **177**

Bryuzgin, V.L. (1963). O metodah izucheniya rosta ryb po cheshue, kostiam i otolitam. (Methods of studying growth of fish using scales, bones and otoliths). *Vopr. Ikhtiol. 3* (27), 347-365. (F.R.B. trans. No. 553). **53**

Bucke, D., Cawley, G.D., Craig, J.F., Pickering, A.D. & Willoughby, L.G. (1979). Further studies of an epizootic of perch, *Perca fluviatilis* L., of uncertain aetiology. *J. Fish Dis. 2* (4), 297-311. **147**

Budd, J., Schroder, J.D. & Dukes, K.D. (1975).
Tumours of the yellow perch. In: *The Patho-
logy of Fishes*. (Eds W.E. Ribelin & G.
Migaki). 895-906. The University of
Wisconsin Press. Wisconsin. **145**

Bulkowski, L. & Meade, J.W. (1983). Changes in
phototaxis during early development of walleye. *Trans Am. Fish. Soc. 112* (3), 445-447.
92

Burkhardt, D.A. & Hassin, G. (1983). Quantitative
relations between colour-opponent response of
horizontal cells and action spectra of cones.
J. Neurophysiol. 49 (4), 961-975. **42**

Burr, B.M. & Ellinger, M.S. (1980). Distinctive
egg morphology and its relationship to development in the percid fish, *Etheostoma
proeliare*. *Copeia* (3), 556-559. **261**

Bykhovskaya-Pavlovskaya, I.E., Gusev, A.V.,
Dubinina, M.N., Izyumova, N.A., Smirnova,
T.S., Sokolovskaya, I.L., Shtein, G.A.,
Shul'man, S.S. & Epshtein, V.M. (1964). Key
to Parasites of Freshwater Fish of the USSR.
Israel Program Sci. Transl. Cat. No. 1136.
**149,150,151,152,153,154,155,156,157,158,159,
160,161,162**

Cadwallader, P.L. & Backhouse, G.N. (1983). *A
Guide to the Freshwater Fish of Victoria*.
Victorian Government Printing Office.
Melbourne. **146**

Calbert, H.E. & Huh, H.T. (1976). Culturing yellow perch *(Perca flavescens)* under controlled
environmental conditions for the upper Midwest
market. *Proc. World Maricult. Soc. 7*, 137-
144. **238**

Campbell, A.D. (1974). The parasites of fish in
Loch Leven. *Proc. R. Soc. Edinburgh (B). 74*,
347-364. **149,160,161**

Campbell, G. (1970). Autonomic nervous systems.
In: *Fish Physiology. IV*. (Eds W.S. Hoar &
D.J. Randall). 109-132. Academic Press. New
York. **40**

Campbell, J.S. & Babaluk, J.A. (1979). Age determination of walleye, *Stizostedion vitreum
vitreum* (Mitchill), based on the examination
of eight different structures. *Can. Tech.
Rep. Fish. Mar. Serv.* No. 849, 27 pp. **51**

Cannon, L.R.G. (1973). Diet and intestinal helminths in a population of perch, *Perca
flavescens*. *J. Fish Biol. 5*, 447-458.
167,171

Carlander, K.D. (1961). Variations on rereading
walleye scales. *Trans Am. Fish. Soc. 90* (2),
230-231. **51**

Carlander, K.D. (1977). Biomass, production and
yields of walleye *(Stizostedion vitreum
vitreum)* and yellow perch *(Perca flavescens)*
in North American Lakes. *J. Fish. Res. Board
Can. 34* (10), 1602-1612. **223**

Carlander, K.D. & Cleary, R.E. (1949). The daily
activity patterns of some freshwater fishes.
Am. Midl. Nat. 41 (2), 447-452. **141**

Chevey, P. (1922). Observation sur une perche
hermaphrodite *(Perca fluviatilis* Linn).
Bull. Soc. Zool. Fr. 47, 3-4. **36**

Chiasson, R.B. (1966). *Laboratory Anatomy of the
Perch.* Wm. C. Brown Company Publishers.
Dubluque. 53 pp. (2nd Ed. 1980. 67 pp).
21,30,33,37,38

Chin, B.H., Sullivan, L.J. & Eldridge, J.E.
(1979). In vitro metabolism of carbaryl by
liver explants of bluegill, catfish, perch,
goldfish and kissing gourami. *J. Agric. Food
Chem. 27* (6), 1395-1398. **242**

Chirkova, Z.N. (1955). O raspredelenii i roste
segoletkov okunya v Rybinskom vodokhranili-
shche. *Tr. Biol. Stn. Borok. 2,* 191-199.
92

Chubb, J.C. (1964). Observations on the
occurrence of the plerocercoids of
Triaenophorus nodulosus (Pallas, 1781)
(Cestoda: Pseudophyllidea) in the perch, *Perca
fluviatilis* L., of Llyn Tegid (Bala Lake),
Merionethshire. *Parasitology 54,* 481-491.
169

Chubb, J.C. (1977). Seasonal occurrence of helminths in freshwater fishes. Part I.
Monogenea. *Adv. Parasitol. 15,* 133-199.
151,167

Chubb, J.C. (1979). Seasonal occurrence of helminths in freshwater fishes. Part II. Trematoda. *Adv. Parasitol. 17,* 141-313.
151,153,154,156,167

Chubb, J.C. (1980). Seasonal occurrence of helminths in freshwater fishes. Part III. Larval Cestoda and Nematoda. *Adv. Parasitol.
18,* 1-120. **158,159,167**

Chubb, J.C. (1982). Seasonal occurrence of hel-
minths in freshwater fishes. Part IV. Adult
Cestoda, Nematoda and Acanthocephala. *Adv.
Parasitol. 20,* 1-292. **159,166,167**

Churchill, W.S. (1957). Conclusions from a ten-year creel census on a lake with no angling restrictions. *J. Wildl. Manage. 21* (2), 182-188. **230**

Cĭhăr, J. (1975). Geographical and ecologic variability of perch *(Perca fluviatilis* L.) and history of its distribution from Eurasia to North America. *Acta Musei Natl. Prague Ser. B. Hist. Nat. 31* (1-2), 5-89. **176,177**

Clady, M.D. (1978). Structure of fish communities in lakes that contain yellow perch, sauger and walleye populations. In: *Selected Coolwater Fishes of North America.* (Ed. R.L. Kendall). *Am. Fish. Soc. Spec. Publ.* (11), 100-108. **205**

Clady, M. & Hutchinson, B. (1975). Effect of high winds on eggs of yellow perch, *Perca flavescens,* in Oneida Lake, New York. *Trans Am. Fish. Soc. 104* (3), 524-525. **88**

Clayton, J.W., Harris, R.E.K. & Tretiak, D.N. (1973). Identification of supernatant and mitochondrial isozymes of malate dehydrogenase of electropherograms applied to the taxonomic discrimination of walleye *(Stizostedion vitreum vitreum),* sauger *(S. canadense)* and suspected interspecific hybrid fishes. *J. Fish. Res. Board Can. 30* (7), 927-938. **180**

Clayton, J.W., Harris, R.E.K. & Tretiak, D.N. (1974). Geographic distribution of alleles for supernatant malate dehydrogenase in walleye *(Stizostedion vitreum vitreum)* populations from Western Canada. *J. Fish. Res. Board Can. 31* (3), 342-345. **179**

Clayton, J.W., Tretiak, D.N. & Kooyman, A.H. (1971). Genetics of multiple malate dehydrogenase isozymes in skeletal muscle of walleye *(Stizostedion vitreum vitreum). J. Fish. Res. Board Can. 28* (7), 1005-1008. **179**

Clugston, J.P., Oliver, J.L. & Ruelle, R. (1978). Reproduction, growth and standing crops of yellow perch in southern reservoirs. In: *Selected Coolwater Fishes of North America.* (Ed. R.L. Kendal). *Am. Fish. Soc. Spec. Publ.* (11), 89-99. **75**

Colby, P.J., McNicol, R.E. & Ryder, R.A. (1979). Synopsis of biological data on the walleye, *Stizostedion v. vitreum* (Mitchill 1818). *FAO Fish. Synop.* No. 119, 139 pp. **56,62,78,81,87, 88,93,98,105,107,136,143**

Colby, P.J. & Nepszy, S.J. (1981). Variation
among stocks of walleye *(Stizostedion vitreum
vitreum)*: management implications. *Can. J.
Fish. Aquat. Sci. 38* (12), 1814-1831. **57,61**
Coles, T.F. (1981). The distribution of perch,
Perca fluviatilis L., throughout their first
year of life in Llyn Tegid, North Wales. *J.
Fish Biol. 18* (1), 15-30. **92**
Collette, B.B. (1963). The subfamilies, tribes,
and genera of the Percidae (Teleostei).
Copeia. (4), 615-623. **7**
Collette, B.B. & Bănărescu, P. (1977). Systema-
tics and zoogeography of the fish family Percidae. *J. Fish. Res. Board Can. 34* (10),
1450-1463. **5,8,10,11,175,176,177,244**
Collvin, L. (1985). The effect of copper on
growth, food consumption and food conversion
of perch, *Perca fluviatilis,* offered maximal
food rations. *Aquat. Toxicol. (Amsk.) 6* (2),
105-114. **241**
Cook, F.A. (1959). *Freshwater fishes in
Mississippi.* Mississippi Game and Fish
Commission. Jackson. Miss. 239 pp. **76**
Cooper, C.L., Ashmead, R.R. & Crites, J.L.
(1977). Prevalence of certain endoparasitic
helminths of the yellow perch from Western
Lake Erie. *Proc. Helminthol. Soc. Wash. 44*
(1), 96. **171**
Cooper, J.E. (1978). Eggs and larvae of the logperch, *Percina caprodes* (Rafinesque). *Am.
Midl. Nat. 99* (2), 257-269. **261**
Cooper, J.E. (1979). Description of eggs and larvae of fantail *(Etheostoma flabellare)* and
rainbow *(E. caeruleum)* darters from Lake Erie
tributaries. *Trans Am. Fish. Soc. 108* (1),
46-56. **261**
Craciun, V., Craciun, M., Neacsu, I & Trandafirescu, I. (1982). Na super (+) - K super
(+) pump activity in the zander during acclimatisation to salinity conditions in the Black
Sea. *Cercet. Mar. Rech. Mar. 15,* 227-233.
127
Craig, J.F. (1973). The population dynamics of
perch *(Perca fluviatilis* L.) in Slapton
Ley. *M.Phil. Thesis.* University of London.
191 pp. **139**
Craig, J.F. (1974a). Population dynamics of
perch, *Perca fluviatilis* L., in Slapton Ley,
Devon. 1. *Freshwat. Biol. 4,* 417-431.
97,141,169

Craig, J.F. (1974b). Population dynamics of
    perch, *Perca fluviatilis* L., in Slapton Ley,
    Devon. 2. *Freshwat. Biol. 4,* 433-444.
    50,51,53,54,74,77

Craig, J.F. (1975). Seasonal variation in the
    catching power of traps used for perch, *Perca
    fluviatilis* L. *Freshwat. Biol. 5,* 183-187.
    193

Craig, J.F. (1977a). The body composition of
    adult perch, *Perca fluviatilis* L., in
    Windermere, with reference to seasonal changes
    and reproduction. *J. Anim. Ecol. 46,* 617-632.
    55,59,66,121

Craig, J.F. (1977b). Seasonal changes in the day
    and night activity of adult perch, *Perca flu-
    viatilis* L. *J. Fish Biol. 11* (2), 161-166.
    77,102,140

Craig, J.F. (1978). A study of the food and feed-
    ing of perch, *Perca fluviatilis* L., in
    Windermere. *Freshwat. Biol. 8* (1), 59-68.
    97,102,104,105,111,112,113,120

Craig, J.F. (1979). Some aspects of the feeding,
    growth and population dynamics of perch, *Perca
    fluviatilis* L., in Windermere. *Ph.D. Thesis.*
    University of Lancaster. 85 pp. **111**

Craig, J.F. (1980a). Growth and production of the
    1955 to 1972 cohorts of perch, *Perca fluviati-
    lis* L., in Windermere. *J. Anim. Ecol. 49* (1),
    291-315. **53,57,64,208,223**

Craig, J.F. (1980b). Sampling with traps. In:
    *Guidelines for Sampling Fish in Inland
    Waters.* (Eds T. Backiel & R.L. Welcomme).
    EIFAC Tech. Pap. No. 33, 55-70. **213,227**

Craig, J.F. (1982). Population dynamics of
    Windermere perch. *Annu. Rep. Freshwat. Biol.
    Ass.* No. 50, 49-59. **64,197**

Craig, J.F. (1985). Aging in fish. *Can. J.
    Zool. 63,* (1) 1-8. **62,65**

Craig, J.F. & Fletcher, J.M. (1982). The variabi-
    lity in the catches of charr, *Salvelinus
    alpinus* L., and perch, *Perca fluviatilis* L.,
    from multi-mesh gillnets. *J. Fish Biol. 20*
    (5), 517-526. **226**

Craig, J.F. & Kipling, C. (1983). Reproduction
    effort versus the environment: case histories
    of Windermere perch, *Perca fluviatilis* L., and
    pike, *Esox lucius* L. *J. Fish Biol. 22* (6),
    713-727. **60,63,195,198,199**

Craig, J.F., Kipling, C., Le Cren, E.D. &
McCormack, J.C. (1979). Estimates of the
numbers, biomass and year-class strengths of
perch *(Perca fluviatilis* L.) in Windermere
from 1967 to 1977 and some comparisons with
earlier years. *J. Anim. Ecol. 48* (1), 315-
325. **63,193,195**

Craig, J.F., Sharma, A. & Smiley, K. (1986). The
variability in catches from multi-mesh gill
nets fished in three Canadian lakes. *J. Fish
Biol. 28,* 671-678. **193**

Craig, J.F. & Smiley, K. (1986). Walleye
(Stizostedion vitreum) and northern pike
(Esox lucius) populations in three Alberta
lakes. *J. Fish Biol. 29,* 67-85. **204,210,227**

Cross, S.X. (1938). A study of the fish parasite
relationships in the Trout Lake region of
Wisconsin. *Trans. Wisc. Acad. Sci. 31,*
439-456. **156**

Crowder, L.B., Magnuson, J.J. & Brandt, S.B.
(1981). Complementarity in the use of food
and thermal habitat by Lake Michigan fishes.
Can. J. Fish. Aquat. Sci. 38 (6), 662-668.
202,203

Dahm, E. (1980). Sampling with traps. In: *Guide-
lines for Sampling Fish in Inland Waters.*
(Eds T. Backiel & R.L. Welcomme). *EIFAC
Tech. Pap.* No. 33, 71-89. **213**

Danzmann, R.G. (1979). The karyology of eight
species of fish belonging to the family
Percidae. *Can. J. Zool. 57,* 2055-2060. **44**

Daugherty, C.H., Daugherty, L.B. & Blair, A.P.
(1976). Visual and olfactory stimuli in the
feeding behavior of darters, *Etheostoma,* inhabiting clear and muddy water. *Copeia* (2),
380-382. **255**

Day, F. (1880). *The Fishes of Great Britain and
Ireland.* Vol. 1. William and Norgate.
London. 366 pp. **176**

Day, F. (1886). On the hybridisation of
Salmonidae at Howietown. *Rep. Br. Assoc.
Adv. Sci. 55,* 1059-1063. **177**

Dechtiar, A.O. (1972a). Parasites of fish from
Lake of the Woods, Ontario. *J. Fish. Res.
Board Can. 29* (3), 275-283. **152,160,162**

Dechtiar, A.O. (1972b). New parasite records for
Lake Erie fish. *Tech. Rep. Great Lakes Fish.
Comm.* (17), 20 pp. **162**

Dechtiar, A.O. & Loftus, K.H. (1965). Two new hosts for *Cyathocephalus truncatus* (Pallas 1781) (Cestoda, Cyathocephalidae) in Lake Huron. *Can. J. Zool. 43*, 407-408. **156**

Deelder, C.L. (1951). A contribution to the knowledge of the stunted growth of perch *(Perca fluviatilis* L.) in Holland. *Hydrobiologia 3*, 357-378. **104**

Deelder, C.L. & Willemsen, J. (1964). Synopsis of biological data on pikeperch, *Lucioperca lucioperca* (Linnaeus) 1758. *FAO Fish. Synop.* No. 28, 52pp. **76,79,81,87**

Dence, W.A. (1938). Hermaphroditism in a walleyed pike *(Stizostedion vitreum). Copeia.* (2), 95. **36**

Derback, B. (1947). The adverse effect of cold weather upon the successful reproduction of pickerel, *Stizostedion vitreum*, at Heming Lake, Manitoba in 1947. *Can. Fish-Cult. 2* (1), 22-23. **76**

Deufel, J. (1961). Barschsterben im Bodensee. *Allg. Fischereiztg. 86* (16), 1 p. **153,156**

Disler, N.N. (1950). Development of the lateral line sense organs in perch and ruff. *Tr. Inst. Morfol. Zhivotn. Akad. Nauk, SSSR. 2*, 85-139. (In Russian). **42**

Disler, N.N. & Smirnov, S.A. (1977). Sensory organs of the lateral-line canal system in two percids and their importance in behaviour. *J. Fish. Res. Board Can. 34* (10), 1492-1503. **42,244**

Dmitrieva, E.N. (1960). Sravnitel'nyi analiz etapov razvitiya sudaka, *Lucioperca lucioperca* (Linné), Volgi, Dona i Kubani. *Trud. Inst. Morfol. Zhivotn. Akad. Nauk, SSSR. 25*, 99-136. **235**

Dodd, J.M. & Kerr, T. (1963). Comparative morphology and histology of the hypothalamo-neurohypophysial system. *Symp. Zool. Soc. Lond.* (9), 5-27. **37**

Dolinin, V.A. (1974). Effect of environmental conditions on the main parameters of the respiratory function in fish having different mobility and oxyphily. *J. Ichthyol. 14* (1), 122-132. **132,133,134**

Donaldson, E.M. Fagerlund, U.H.M., Higgs, D.A. & McBride, J.R. (1979). Hormonal enhancement of growth. In: *Fish Physiology. VIII.* (Eds W.S. Hoar, D.J. Randall & J.R. Brett). 456-598. Academic Press. New York. **45**

Dorr, J.A. (1982). Substrate and other environmental factors in reproduction of the yellow perch *(Perca flavescens)*. *Diss. Abstr. Int. B - Sci. Eng.* *43* (6), 1703. **77**

Driver, E.A. & Garside, E.T. (1966). Meristic numbers of yellow perch in saline lakes in Manitoba. *J. Fish. Res. Board Can.* *23*, 1815-1817. **126**

Dukravets, G.M. & Biryukov, YU.A. (1976). Ichthyo-fauna of the Nura River Basin in the Central Kazakh-SSR, USSR. *J. Ichthyol.* *16* (2),271-276. **176**

Dumitrescu, M., Bănărescu, P. & Stoica, N. (1957). *Romanichthys valsanicola* nov. gen. nov. sp. (Pisces, Percidae). *Trav. Mus. Hist. Natur. "Grigore Antipa."* *1*, 225-244. **263**

Duncan, K.W. (1980). On the back-calculation of fish lengths; modifications and extensions to the Fraser-Lee equation. *J. Fish Biol.* *16* (6), 725-730. **53**

Economon, P.P. (1978). Myofibrogranuloma, a muscular dystrophy-like anomaly of walleye *(Stizostedion vitreum vitreum)*. In: *Selected Coolwater Fishes of North America.* (Ed. R.L. Kendall). *Am. Fish Soc. Spec. Publ. No.* (11), 226-234. **145**

Edgren, M. & Notter, M. (1980). Cadmium uptake by fingerlings of perch *(Perca fluviatilis)* studied by Cd-115M at two different temperatures. *Bull. Environ. Contam. Toxicol.* *24* (5), 647-651. **240**

Edgren, M., Olsson, M. Reutergardh, L. (1981). A one year study of the seasonal variations of SDDT and PCB levels in fish from heated and unheated areas near a nuclear power plant. *Chemosphere.* *10* (5), 447-452. **242**

EIFAC. (1971). *European Inland Water Fish.* A multilingual catalogue. Fishing News (Books) Ltd. London. 24 pp. + illust. **12**

Einhouse, D. & Winter, J. (1981). Movement patterns and habitat utilisation of radio-tagged walleye in Chautauqua Lake, New York. *Underwat. Telem. Newsl.* *11* (2), 1-3. **141**

Elliott, J.M. (1975a). Weight of food and time required to satiate brown trout, *Salmo trutta* L. *Freshwat. Biol.* *5*, 51-64. **116**

Elliott, J.M. (1975b). Number of meals in a day,
maximum weight of food consumed in a day and
maximum rate of feeding for brown trout, *Salmo
trutta* L. *Freshwat. Biol. 5*, 287-303. **116**

Elliott, J.M. (1975c). The growth of brown trout
(Salmo trutta L.) fed on maximum rations.
J. Anim. Ecol. 44, 805-821. **116**

Elliott, J.M. (1976a). Body composition of brown
trout *(Salmo trutta* L.) in relation to temperature and ration size. *J. Anim. Ecol. 45*,
273-289. **116**

Elliott, J.M. (1976b). Energy losses in the waste
products of brown trout *(Salmo trutta* L.).
J. Anim. Ecol. 45, 561-580. **116**

Elliott, J.M. (1979). Energetics of freshwater
teleosts. In: *Fish Phenology*. (Ed. P.J.
Miller). *Symp. Zool. Soc. Lond*. No. 44,
29-61. Academic Press. London. **115,118**

Elliott, J.M. & Mann, K.H. (1979). A key to the
British freshwater leeches. *Freshwat. Biol.
Assoc. Spec. Publ.* No. 40, 72 pp. **168**

Elliott, J.M. & Persson, L. (1978). The
estimation of daily rates of food consumption
for fish. *J. Anim. Ecol. 47* (3), 977-991.
111

Ellis, D.V. & Giles, M.A. (1965). The spawning
behaviour of the walleye, *Stizostedion
vitreum* (Mitchill). *Trans Am. Fish Soc.
94* (4), 358-362. **78,79**

Elsey, C.A. & Thomson, R.T. (1977). Exploitation
of walleye *(Stizostedion vitreum vitreum)* in
Lac des Mille Lacs, northern Ontario, by commercial and sport fisheries, 1958-75. *J. Fish
Res. Board Can. 34* (10), 1769-1773. **227**

Elshoud.- Oldenhave, M.J.W. (1979). Prey capture
in the pikeperch, *Stizostedion lucioperca*
(Teleostei, Percidae): A structural and functional analysis. *Zoomorphologie. 93* (1),
1-32. **107,108**

Englert, J. & Seghers, B.H. (1983). Predation by
fish and common mergansers on darters (Pisces:
Percidae) in the Thames River watershed of
southwestern Ontario. *Can. Field-Nat. 97* (2),
218-219. **253**

Epple, A. (1969). The endocrine pancreas. In:
Fish Physiology. II. (Eds W.S. Hoar & D.J.
Randall). 275-319. Academic Press. New
York. **43**

Erickson, C.M. (1983). Age determination of Manitoban walleyes using otoliths, dorsal spines, and scales. *N. Am. J. Fish. Manage.* *3* (2), 176- 181. **51**

Eriksson, L - 0. (1978). A laboratory study of diel and annual activity rhythms and vertical distribution in the perch, *Perca fluviatilis*, at the Arctic Circle. *Environ. Biol. Fishes.* *3* (3), 301-307. **102,140**

Eschmeyer, P.H. (1950). The life history of the walleye, *Stizostedion vitreum vitreum* (Mitchill), in Michigan. *Bull. Mich. Dep. Conserv.*, *Inst. Fish. Res.* (3), 99 pp. **36,67,69,70,78,79,93**

Eslami, A. & Mokhayer, B. (1977). Nematode larvae of medical importance found in market fish in Iran. *Pahlavi Med. J. 8* (3), 345-346. **158**

Fabricius, E. (1956). Hur abborren leker. *Zool. Revy. 18*, 48-55. **77**

Fänge, R. & Grove, D. (1979). Digestion. In: *Fish Physiology. VIII.* (Eds W.S. Hoar, D.J. Randall & J.R. Brett). 162-260. Academic Press. New York. **114**

Fänge, R. & Holmgren, S. (1982). Choline acetyl-transferase activity in the fish swimbladder. *J. Comp. Physiol. B. 146* (1), 57-61. **139**

FAO. (1984). Yearbook of fishery statistics. 1983 catches and landings. *FAO Fisheries Series. 56*, ix+393 pp. **214**

Farmer, G.J. & Beamish, F.W.H. (1969). Oxygen consumption of *Tilapia nilotica* in relation to swimming speed and salinity. *J. Fish Res. Board Can. 26*, 2807-2821. **124**

Fedorova, G.V. & Drozzhina, K.S. (1982). Daily feeding rhythm of pikeperch, *Stizostedion lucioperca*, and perch, *Perca fluviatilis*, from Lake Ladoga. *J. Ichthyol. 22* (2), 52-60. **107**

Filatov, G.P. & Duplakov, S.N. (1926). Materialen zur kenntuiss der fische des Aral Seas. *Bul. Univ. Asie Cent. Tachkent. 14*, 203-230. **76**

Fischthal, J.H. (1952). Parasites of northwest Wisconsin fishes III. The 1946 survey. *Trans. Wisc. Acad. Sci. 41*, 17-58. **151**

Fish, G.R. (1960). The comparative activity of some digestive enzymes in the alimentary canal of tilapia and perch. *Hydrobiologia. 15*, 161-179. **113,114**

Fitter, R.S.R. (1959). *The Ark is Our Midst*.
Collins. London. 178

Flock, A. (1971). The lateral line organ mechano-
receptors. In: *Fish Physiology*. V. (Eds W.S.
Hoar & D.J. Randall). 241-263. Academic
Press. New York. 42

Forney, J.L. (1963). Distribution and movement of
marked walleyes in Oneida Lake, New York.
Trans Am. Fish. Soc. 92 (1), 47-52. 142

Forney, J.L. (1966). Factors affecting first-year
growth of walleyes in Oneida Lake, New York.
N.Y. Fish Game J. 13 (2), 146-167. 59

Forney, J.L. (1967). Estimates of biomass and
mortality rates in a walleye population.
N.Y. Fish Game J. 14 (2), 176-192. 63,78

Forney, J.L. (1976). Year-class formation in the
walleye *(Stizostedion vitreum vitreum)*
population of Oneida Lake, New York, 1966-73.
J. Fish. Res. Board Can. 33 (4), 783-792.
93,232

Forney, J.L. (1977a). Evidence of inter and
intra-specific competition as factors
regulating walleye *(Stizostedion vitreum
vitreum)* biomass in Oneida Lake, New York.
J. Fish. Res. Board Can. 34 (10), 1812-1820.
185,186

Forney, J.L. (1977b). Reconstruction of yellow
perch *(Perca flavescens)* cohorts from examination of walleye *(Stizostedion vitreum
vitreum)* stomachs. *J. Fish. Res. Board Can.
34*, 925-932. 187,188

Forney, J.L. (1977c). Population dynamics of wal-
leye and yellow perch in Oneida Lake. US
Federal Aid in Fish Restoration. Report No.
F-17-R. New York State. 19pp. 187,189

Frank, R., Van Hove Holdrinet, M., Desjardine,
R.L. & Dodge, D.P. (1978). Organochlorine
and mercury residues in fish from Lake Simcoe,
Ontario 1970-76. *Environ. Biol. Fishes.
3* (3), 275-285. 240

Fry, F.E.J. (1947). Effects of environmental factors on animal activity. *Univ. Toronto Stud.
Biol. Ser. 55. Publ. Ont. Fish. Res. Lab. 68*,
64pp. 46

Fry, F.E.J. (1957). Aquatic respiration of fish.
In: *The Physiology of Fishes*. *I*. (Ed. M.E.
Brown). 1-63. Academic Press. London.
131,133

Fryer, G. (1982). The parasitic Copepoda and
Branchiura of British freshwater fishes.
Freshwat. Biol. Assoc. Spec. Publ. No. 46, 87
pp. **165**

Fujii, R. (1969). Chromatophores and pigments.
In: *Fish Physiology. III.* (Eds W.S. Hoar &
D.J. Randall). 307-353. Academic Press. New
York. **19**

Furnass, T.I. (1979). Laboratory experiments on
prey selection by perch fry, *Perca
fluviatilis. Freshwat. Biol. 19* (1), 33-43.
100,101

Gagne, J.L. (1977). *Le sandre et sa piscicul-
ture.* Toulouse Univ. 161 pp. **178**

Gantverg, A.N. & Perevoznikov, M.A. (1983). Cholinesterase inhibition in the brain of the
perch, *Perca fluviatilis* L. (Percidae), and
carp, *Cyprinus carpio* L. (Cyprinidae), exposed
to malathion. *J. Ichthyol. 23* (4), 174-175.
242

Gantverg, A.N. & Rozengart, V.I. (1984).
Carbophos decomposition rate in fish liver
in-vitro. *J. Ichthyol. 24* (5), 161-162.
242

Garber, K.J. (1983). Effect of fish size, meal
size and dietary moisture on gastric evacuation of pelleted diets by yellow perch, *Perca
flavescens. Aquaculture. 34* (1-2), 41-49.
239

Gee, J.H., Machniak, K. & Chalanchuk, S.M.
(1974). Adjustment of buoyancy and excess
internal pressure of swimbladder gases in some
North American freshwater fishes. *J. Fish.
Res. Board Can. 31,* 1139-1141. **139**

Gee, J.H., Tallmann, R.F. & Smart, H.J. (1978).
Reactions of some Great Plains fishes to pro-
gressive hypoxia. *Can. J. Zool. 56* (9), 1962-
1966. **135**

Gelman, A., Mokady, S. & Cogan, U. (1984). The
effect of seasonal changes on the activity of
intestinal alkaline phosphatase of pikeperch,
Lucioperca lucioperca, and of bream, *Abramis
brama. J. Fish Biol. 25* (2), 207-212. **115**

Gislason, G.S., MacMillan, J.A. & Craven, J.W.
(1982). *The Manitoba Commercial Freshwater
Fishery: an Economic Analysis.* University of
Manitoba Press. Manitoba. 311 pp. **219,226**

Goetz, F.W. & Bergman, H.L. (1978). The *in vitro* effects of mammalian and piscine gonadotropin and pituitary preparations on final maturation in yellow perch *(Perca flavescens)* and walleye *(Stizostedion vitreum)*. *Can. J. Zool. 56* (2), 348-350. **75**

Goetz, F.W. & Theofan, G. (1979). *In vitro* stimulation of germinal vesicle breakdown and ovulation of yellow perch *(Perca flavescens)* oocytes. Effects of 17α - hydroxy - 20β- dihydroprogesterone and prostoglandins. *Gen. Comp. Endocrinol. 37,* 273-285. **75**

Golovanenko, L.F., Shuvatova, T.F., Putina, Ye.P., Fedorova, L.S. & Arakelova, A.L. (1970). A physiological and biochemical description of Don pikeperch females at different stages of the sexual cycle. *J. Ichthyol. 10,* 260-267. **76**

Grabda-Kazubska, B. (1974). *Clinostomum complanatum* (Rudolphi, 1819) and *Euclinostomum heterostomum* (Rudolphi, 1809)(Trematoda, Clinostomatidae), their occurrence and possibility of acclimatisation in artificially heated lakes in Poland. *Acta Parasitol. Pol. 22,* 285-293. **166**

Grant, J.W.A. & Colgan, P.W. (1983). Reproductive success and mate choice in the johnny darter, *Etheostoma nigrum* (Pisces:Percidae). *Can. J. Zool. 61* (2), 437-446. **260**

Greenwood, P.H. (1975). *A History of Fishes.* 3rd Ed. Ernest Benn. London. 467 pp. **19**

Griffiths, W.E. (1976). Feeding and gastric evacuation in perch *(Perca fluviatilis* L.). *Mauri Ora. 4,* 19-34. **109**

Grinstead, B.G. (1971). Reproduction and some aspects of the early life history of walleye, *Stizostedion vitreum* (Mitchill), in Canton Reservoir, Oklahoma. *Spec. Publ. Am. Fish. Soc.* (8), 41-51. **78**

Gripp, K. & Beyle, M. (1937). Das interglazial von billstedt (Öjendorf). *Mitt. Geol. Staatsinst. Hamburg. 16,* 19-36. **175**

Guiney, P.D. & Peterson, R.E. (1980). Distribution and elimination of a polychlorinated biphenyl after acute dietary exposure in yellow perch and rainbow trout. *Arch. Environ. Contam. Toxicol. 9* (6), 667-674. **242**

Guma'a, S.A. (1978a). On the early growth of 0+ perch, *Perca fluviatilis,* in Windermere. *Freshwat. Biol. 8* (3), 213-220. **56**

Guma'a, S.A. (1978b). The effects of temperature on the development and mortality of eggs of perch, *Perca fluviatilis*. *Freshwat. Biol.* *8* (3), 221-227. **85,87,88**

Guma'a, S.A. (1978c). The food and feeding habits of young perch, *Perca fluviatilis*, in Windermere. *Freshwat. Biol. 8* (2), 177-187. **92,94,96,99,101,102**

Guma'a, S.A. (1982). Retinal development and retinomotor responses in perch, *Perca fluviatilis* L. *J. Fish Biol. 20* (5), 611-618. **41**

Gunn, J.M. (1982). Acidification of lake trout *(Salvelinus namaycush)* lakes near Sudbury, Ontario. In: *Acid Rain/Fisheries.* (Ed. R.E. Johnson). p. 351. American Fisheries Soc. Bethesda. MD (USA). Northeastern Div. **129**

Gunther, A. (1859). *Catalogue of the Acanthopterygian fishes in the collection of the British Museum. I.* London. xxxi + 548 pp. **176**

Guseva, T.V. (1974). The ecology of spawning and embryonic development of the sea zander, *Lucioperca marina. Izv. Akad. Nauk Turkmenskoi SSR, Ser. Biol. Nauk. 2,* 87-91. (In Russian). **80,92**

Hamley, J.M. (1980). Sampling with gillnets. In: *Guidelines for sampling fish in inland waters.* (Eds T. Backiel & R. Welcomme). *EIFAC Tech. Rep.* 33, 37-53. **193,220**

Hamley, J.M. & Howley, T.P. (1985). Factors affecting variability of trapnet catches. *Can. J. Fish. Aquat. Sci. 42* (6), 1079-1087. **227**

Hamley, J.H. & Regier, H.A. (1973). Direct estimates of gillnet selectivity to walleye *(Stizostedion vitreum vitreum). J. Fish. Res. Board Can. 30* (6), 817-830. **227**

Hanson, J.M. & Leggett, W.C. (1982). Empirical prediction of fish biomass and yield. *Can. J. Fish. Aquat. Sci. 39,* 257-263. **224**

Hanson, J.M. & Leggett, W.C. (1985). Experimental and field evidence for interspecific and intraspecific competition in two fresh water fishes. *Can. J. Fish. Aquat. Sci. 42* (2), 280-286. **202**

Hara, T.J. (1971). Chemoreception. In: *Fish Physiology. V.* (Eds W.S. Hoar & D.J. Randall) 79-120. Academic Press. New York. **37**

Hartig, J.H. & Jude, D.J. (1984). Opportunistic cyclopoid predation on fish larvae. *Can. J. Fish. Aquat. Sci.* 41 (3), 526-532. **91**

Hartman, J. & Numann, W. (1977). Percids of Lake Constance, a lake undergoing eutrophication. *J. Fish. Res. Board Can.* 34 (10), 1670-1677. **223**

Hasler, A.D. and Bardach, J.E. (1949). Daily migrations of perch in Lake Mendota, Wisconsin. *J. Wildl. Manage.* 13 (1), 40-51. **140,141**

Hasler, A.D. & Villemonte, J.R. (1953). Observations on the daily movements of fishes. *Science.* (Wash. D.C.) *118*, 321. **103,139**

Healey, M.C. (1984). Multiattribute analysis and the concept of optimum yield. *Can. J. Fish. Aquat. Sci. 41*, 1393-1406. **209**

Heck, N.E. & Calbert, H.E. (1977). Use of animal fat in formulated diets for yellow perch *(Perca flavescens). Proc. World Maricult. Soc. 8*, 787-794. **238**

Hegi, H.R. von & Geiger, W. (1979). Schwermetalle (Hg, Cd, Cu, Pb, Zn) in lebern und muskulatur des flussbarsches *(Perca fluviatilis)* aus Bielersee und Walensee. *Schweiz. Z. Hydrol. 41* (1), 94-107. **241**

Heisler, N. (1984). Acid-base regulation in fishes. In: *Fish Physiology. XA.* (Eds W.S. Hoar & D.J. Randall). 315-401. Academic Press. Orlando. Florida. **128**

Helfman, G.S. (1979). Twilight activities of yellow perch, *Perca flavescens. J. Fish. Res. Board Can. 36* (2), 173-179. **102,103**

Helfman, G.S. (1984). School fidelity in fishes: the yellow perch pattern. *Anim. Behav. 32* (3), 673-689. **140**

Hergenrader, G.L. (1969). Spawning behaviour of *Perca flavescens* in aquaria. *Copeia.* 839-841. **77**

Hergenrader, G.L. & Hasler, A.D. (1966). Diel activity and vertical distribution of yellow perch *(Perca flavescens)* under the ice. *J. Fish. Res. Board Can. 23*, 499-509. **140**

Hergenrader, G.L. & Hasler, A.D. (1967). Seasonal changes in swimming rates of yellow perch in Lake Mendota as measured by sonar. *Trans Am. Fish. Soc. 96*, 373-382. **137,138**

Hergenrader, G.L. & Hasler, A.D. (1968). Influence of changing seasons on schooling behaviour of yellow perch. *J. Fish. Res. Board Can. 25*, 711-716. **140**

Hickman, C.P. & Trump, B.F. (1969). The kidney. In: *Fish Physiology. I.* (Eds W.S. Hoar & D.J. Randall). 91-239. Academic Press. New York. **34,125**

Hinegardner, R.T. (1968). Evolution of cellular DNA content in teleost fishes. *Am. Nat. 102*, 517-523. **175**

Hinegardner, R.T. & Rosen, D.E. (1972). Cellular DNA content and the evolution of teleostean fishes. *Am. Nat. 106*, 621-644. **175**

Hirji, K.N. (1983). Observations on the histology and histochemistry of the oesophagus of the perch, *Perca fluviatilis* L. *J. Fish Biol. 22* (2), 145-152. **33**

Hirji, K.N. & Courtney, W.A.M. (1979). Pear-shaped cells in the digestive tract of the perch, *Perca fluviatilis* L. *J. Fish Biol. 15* (4), 469-472. **33**

Hoar, W.S. & Randall, D.J. (Eds). (1969). *Fish Physiology. II.* Academic Press. New York. xiv + 446 pp. **43**

Hoar, W.S. & Randall, D.J. (Eds). (1978). *Fish Physiology. VII.* Academic Press. New York. xviii + 576 pp. **137**

Hoestlands, H. 1979. Namisme de la perche en France est-il un mythe? *Bull. Cent. Etud. Rech. Sci., Biarritz 12* (3), 453-470. **59**

Hoffman, G.L. (1967). *Parasites of North American Freshwater Fishes.* University of California Press. Berkeley. vii + 486 pp. **149,150,151, 152,153,154,155,156,157,158,159,160,161,162**

Hokanson, K.E.F. (1977). Temperature requirements of some percids and adaptations to the seasonal temperature cycle. *J. Fish. Res. Board Can. 34* (10), 1524-1550. **46,48,75,76,91,116, 117,248,249**

Hokanson, K.E.F. & Kleiner, C.F. (1974). Effects of constant and rising temperatures on survival and developmental rates of embryonic and larval yellow perch, *Perca flavescens* (Mitchill). In: *The Early Life History of Fish.* (Ed. J.H.S. Blaxter). 437-448. Springer-Verlag. New York. **56,85**

Holčik, J. (1977). Changes in the fish community of Klicava Reservoir with particular reference to Eurasian perch *(Perca fluviatilis).* 1957-72. *J. Fish. Res. Board Can. 34* (10), 1734-1747. **205**

Holčik, J. & Hensel, K. (1974). A new species of
    Gymnocephalus (Pisces: Percidae) from the
    Danube, with remarks on the genus. *Copeia*
    (2), 471-486. **8,244,247**
Holčik, J. & Mihalik, J. (1970). *Freshwater
    Fishes*. 3rd Ed. Hamlyn Publishing Group Ltd.
    London. 128 pp. **17,18**
Holloway, H.L. Jr. & Smith, C.E. (1982). A
    myopathy in North Dakota walleye, *Stizostedion
    vitreum* (Mitchell). *J. Fish Dis. 5* (6),
    527-530. **145**
Holt, C.S., Grant, G.D.S., Oberstar, G.P., Oakes,
    C.C. & Bradt, D.W. (1977). Movement of wal-
    leye *Stizostedion vitreum,* in Lake Bemidji,
    Minnesota, as determined by radio-
    biotelemetry. *Trans Am. Fish. Soc. 106* (2),
    163-200. **141**
Houde, E.D. (1969a). Distribution of larval wal-
    leyes and yellow perch in a bay of Oneida Lake
    and its relation to water currents and zoo-
    plankton. *N.Y. Fish Game J. 16,* 184-205.
    92
Houde, E.D. (1969b). Sustained swimming ability
    of larvae of walleye *(Stizostedion vitreum
    vitreum)* and yellow perch *(Perca flavescens)*.
    J. Fish. Res. Board Can. 26 (6), 1647-1659.
    138
Howell, J.F. (1972). The life history, behaviour
    and ecology of *Percina aurantiaca* (Cope).
    Diss. Abstr. Int. B. Sci. Eng. 32, 6354.
    258
Hubbs, C.L. (1926). A check-list of the fishes of
    the Great Lakes and tributary waters, with
    nomenclatorial notes and analytical keys.
    Univ. Mich. Mus. Zool. Misc. Publ. 15, 1-77.
    177
Hubbs, C. (1971). Survival of intergroup percid
    hybrids. *J. Ichthyol. 18* (2), 65-75. **180**
Hubert, W.A. & Sandheinrich, M.B. (1983). Pat-
    terns of variation in gill-net catch and diet
    of yellow perch in a stratified Iowa lake.
    N. Am. J. Fish. Manage. 3 (2), 156-162. **102**
Huet, M. (1970). *Textbook of Fish Culture -
    Breeding and Cultivation of Fish*. Eyre and
    Spottiswoode Ltd. Margate. 435 pp. **234,236**
Hughes, G.M. (1984). General anatomy of gills.
    In: *Fish Physiology XA*. (Eds W.S. Hoar & D.J.
    Randall). 1-72. Academic Press. Orlando.
    30

Huh, H.T. (1976). Bioenergetics of food conversion and growth of yellow perch *(Perca flavescens)* and walleye *(Stizostedion vitreum vitreum)* using formulated diets. *Diss. Abstr. Int. B. Sci. Eng. 36* (11), 5393. **238**

Huh, H.T., Calbert, H.E. & Stuiber, D.A. (1976). Effects of temperature and light on growth of yellow perch and walleye using formulated feed. *Trans Am. Fish. Soc. 105,* 254-258. **238**

Hulsman, P.F., Powles, P.N. & Gunn, J.M. (1983). Mortality of walleye eggs and rainbow trout yolk-sac larvae in low-pH waters of the La Cloche Mountain area, Ontario. *Trans Am. Fish. Soc. 112* (5), 680-688. **88**

Hurley, D.A. (1972). Observations on incubating walleye eggs. *Prog. Fish-Cult. 34* (1), 49-54. **88**

Ingersoll, C.G. & Claussen, D.L. (1984). Temperature selection and critical thermal maxima of the fantail darter, *Etheostoma flabellare,* and johnny darter, *E. nigrum,* related to habitat and season. *Environ. Biol. Fishes. 11* (2), 131-138. **254**

Isaia, J. (1984). Water and nonelectrolyte permeation. In: *Fish Physiology. XA.* (Eds W.S. Hoar & D.J. Randall). 1-38. Academic Press. Orlando. **122**

Ivlev, V.S. (1955). Iksperimentalnaya ekologiya pitaniya ryb. *Pishchepromizdat.* Moscow. 252 pp. **182**

Jansson, B-O. & Olsson, R. (1960). The cytology of the caecal epithelial cells of *Perca. Acta Zool.* (Stockh). *41,* 267-276. **115**

Jarvis, R.S., Klodowski, H.F. & Sheldon, S.P. (1978). New Method of quantifying scale shape and an application to stock identification in walleye *(Stizostedion vitreum vitreum). Trans Am. Fish. Soc. 107* (4), 528-534. **20**

Jastrzebski, M. (1984). Polymorphism of flagellates, *Trypanosoma,* occurring in blood of crucian carp, *Carassius auratus gibelio,* perch, *Perca fluviatilis,* and stone perch, *Acerina cernua. Wiad. Parazytol. 30* (2), 172-182. **150**

Jellyman, D.J. (1976). Hermaphrodite European perch, *Perca fluviatilis* L. *N.Z. J. Mar. Freshwat. Res. 10* (4), 721-723. **36**

Jezierska, B. (1974). The effect of various types of food on the growth and chemical composition of the body of perch *(Perca fluviatilis* L.) in laboratory conditions. *Pol. Arch. Hydrobiol. 21*, 467-479. **121**

Johnson, M.G., Leach, J.H., Minns, C.K. & Olver, C.H. (1977). Limnological characteristics of Ontario lakes in relation to associations of walleye *(Stizostedion vitreum vitreum)*, northern pike *(Esox lucius)*, lake trout *(Salvelinus namaycush)*, and smallmouth bass *(Micropterus dolomieui)*. *J. Fish. Res. Board Can. 34* (10), 1592-1601. **205**

Johnson, T. & Müller, K. (1978). Different phase position of activity in juvenile and adult perch. *Naturwissenschaften. 65*, 392. **140,141**

Jones, D.R., Kiceniuk, J.W. & Bamford, O.S. (1974). Evaluation of the swimming performance of several fish species from the MacKenzie River. *J. Fish. Res. Board Can. 31* (10), 1641-1647. **137,139**

Jones, D.R. & Randall, D.J. (1978). The respiratory and circulatory systems during exercise. In: *Fish Physiology. VII.* (Eds W.S. Hoar & D.J. Randall). 425-501. Academic Press. New York. **131,132**

Jones, J.R.E. (1964). *Fish and river pollution.* Butterworths. London. 203 pp. **133**

Jordon, D.S. & Gilbert, C.H. (1877). On the genera of North American freshwater fishes. *Proc. Acad. Nat. Sci. Phila. 29*, 83-104. **177**

Jovanovic, M. (1970). Comparative life histories of the North American and European walleyes. *Mich. Dep. Nat. Resources Res. Dev. Rep.* (201), 1-71. **107**

Kammerer, P. (1907). Bastardierung von flussbarsch *(Perca fluviatilis* L.) und kaulbarsch *(Acerina cernua* L.). *Arch. Entwicklungsmech. Org. 23*, 511-551. **180**

Kapoor, B.G., Smit, H. & Verighina, I.A. (1975). The alimentary canal and digestion in teleosts. *Adv. Mar. Biol. 13*, 109-239. **31**

Kayes, T.B. & Calbert, H.E. (1979). Effects of photoperiod and temperature on the spawning of yellow perch *(Perca flavescens)*. *Proc. World Maricult. 10*, 306-316. **76**

Kearns, P.K. & Atchison, G.J. (1979). Effects of trace metals on growth of yellow perch *(Perca flavescens)* as measured by RNA-DNA ratios. *Environ. Biol. Fishes. 4* (4), 383-387. **241**

Kelly, R.K. & Miller, H.R. (1978). Characterisation of a fish cell line from walleye *(Stizostedion vitreum vitreum)*. Abstract. *In Vitro. 14,* 389. **145**

Kelly, R.K., Nielsen, O., Mitchell, S.C. & Yamamoto, Y. (1983). Characterisation of *Herpesvirus vitreum* isolated from hyperplastic epidermal tissue of walleye, *Stizostedion vitreum vitreum* (Mitchill). *J. Fish. Dis. 6,* 249-260. **146**

Kelso, J.R.M. (1972). Conversion, maintenance and assimilation for walleye, *Stizostedion vitreum vitreum,* as affected by size, diet and temperature. *J. Fish. Res. Board Can. 29* (8), 1181-1192. **116**

Kelso, J.R.M. (1976). Diel movement of walleye, *Stizostedion vitreum vitreum,* in West Blue Lake, Manitoba, as determined by ultrasonic tracking. *J. Fish. Res. Board Can. 33* (9), 2070-2072. **140**

Kelso, J.R.M. & Ward, F.J. (1977). Unexploited percid populations of West Blue Lake, Manitoba, and their interactions. *J. Fish. Res. Board Can. 34* (10), 1655-1669. **201,205**

Kennedy, C.R. (1974). A checklist of British and Irish freshwater fish parasites with notes on their distribution. *J. Fish Biol. 6,* 613-644. **149,150,152,153,154,155,156,157,158,159,160, 161**

Kennedy, C.R. (1981). Long term studies on the population biology of two species of eyefluke *Diplostomum gasterostei* and *Tylodelphys clavata* (Digenea: Diplostomatidae), concurrently infecting the eyes of perch, *Perca fluviatilis. J. Fish Biol. 19* (2), 221-236. **151,170**

Ketola, H.G. (1978). Nutritional requirements and feeding of selected coolwater fishes: a review. *Prog. Fish-Cult. 40* (4), 127-132. **94,238**

Keup, L. & Bayless, J. (1964). Fish distribution at varying sediments in Neuse River Basin, North Carolina. *Chesapeake Sci. 5,* 119-123. **127**

Kipling, C. (1957). The effect of gillnet selec-
    tion on the estimation of weight-length re-
    lationships. *J. Cons. int. Explor. Mer. 23*,
    51-63. **193**
Kipling, C. (1976). Year class strengths of perch
    and pike in Windermere. *Rep. Freshwat. Biol.
    Assoc.* 44, 68-75. **76**
Kipling, C. (1984). A study of perch *(Perca
    fluviatilis* L.) and pike *(Esox lucius* L.) in
    Windermere from 1941 to 1982. *J. Cons int.
    Explor. Mer. 41*, 259-267. **194,196**
Kipling, C. & Frost, W.E. (1970). A study of the
    mortality, population numbers, year class
    strengths production and food consumption of
    pike, *Esox lucius* L., in Windermere from 1944
    to 1962. *J. Anim. Ecol. 39*, 115-157. **193**
Kipling, C. & Le Cren, E.D. (1984). Mark-
    recapture experiments on fish in Windermere,
    1943-1982. *J. Fish Biol. 24*, 395-414. **141**
Kirsipuu, A. (1967). Differences in the protein
    composition of the blood serum in two forms of
    perch in the lake Vortsjarv. *Eesti NSV Tead.
    Aked. Toim. Biol. 16* (1), 37-40. (In Russian
    with English summary). **178**
Kirsipuu, A. (1971). Some physiological processes
    and environmental conditions affecting the
    protein composition of the blood serum in
    fish. *Rapp. P-V. Reun. Cons. Int. Explor.
    Mer. 161*, 154-157. **178**
Kitchell, J.F., Stewart, D.J. & Weininger, D.
    (1977). Applications of a bioenergetics model
    to yellow perch *(Perca flavescens)* and wal-
    leye *(Stizostedion vitreum vitreum)*. *J.
    Fish. Res. Board Can. 34* (10), 1922-1935.
    115,116,117,118,119,120
Knight, R.L., Margraf, F.J. & Carline, R.F.
    (1984). Piscivory by walleyes, *Stizostedion
    vitreum vitreum*, and yellow perch, *Perca fla-
    vescens*, in Western Lake Erie, USA. *Trans
    Am. Fish. Soc. 113* (6), 677-693. **99**
Koenig, S.D., Kayes, T.B. & Calbert, H.E. (1978).
    Preliminary observations on the sperm of yel-
    low perch. In: *Selected Coolwater Fishes of
    North America*. (Ed. R.L. Kendall). *Am. Fish.
    Soc. Spec. Publ.* (11), 177-186. **69,70**
Kokurewicz, B. (1969). The influence of temper-
    ature on the embryonic development of the
    perches: *Perca fluviatilis* L. and *Lucioperca
    lucioperca* (L.). *Zool. Pol. 19* (1), 47-66.
    88

Kolomin, Yu. M. (1977). The Nadym River ruffe, *Acerina cernua*. *J. Ichthyol*. *17* (3), 345-349. **248**

Konstantinov, K.G. (1957). Sravitelnyi analiz morfologii i biologii okunya, sudaka i bersha na raznykh etapakh razritiya. *Tr. Inst. Morfol. Zhivotn. Akad. Nauk, SSSR*. *16*, 181-236. **55**

Kudrinskaya, O.M. (1970). Food and temperature as factors affecting the growth, development and survival of pikeperch and perch larvae. *J. Ichthyol*. *10*, 779-788. **112**

Kuehne, R.A. & Barbour, R.M. (1983). *The American Darters*. University Press of Kentucky. Lexington. 177 pp. **8,251**

Kukuradze, A.M. (1974). A description of the spawning stock and reproduction of the pike-perch *Lucioperca lucioperca*, of the Danube Delta and waters in the Danubian Region. *J. Ichthyol*. *14* (3), 385-392. **94,99**

Kuzmina, V.V. (1984a). Relative enzyme activity of the fish intestinal lumen and mucosa. *J. Ichthyol*. *24* (3), 140-144. **114**

Kuzmina, V.V. (1984b). Effect of temperature on pH - function of phosphatases active in fish intestine. *J. Icthyol*. *24* (1), 136-142. **115**

Kuznetsov, V.A. (1982). Vliyanie uslovij nagula na plodovitost' i kachestvo irky bersha, *Stizostedion volgensis* (Gmelin) (Percidae), Kujbyshevskogo Vodokhtanilishcha. *Vopr. Ikhtiol*. *22* (4), 599-607. **74**

Laarman, P.W. (1978). Case histories of stocking walleyes, *Stizostedion vitreum vitreum*, in inland lakes, impoundments and the Great Lakes - 100 years with walleyes. In: *Selected Coolwater Fishes of North America*. (Ed. R.L. Kendall). *Am. Fish. Soc. Spec. Publ*. (11), 254-260. **231**

Laarman, P.W. (1981). Vital statistics of a Michigan fish population, with special emphasis on the effectiveness of stocking 15-cm walleye fingerlings. *N. Am. J. Fish. Manage*. *1* (2), 177-185. **232**

Lang, I. (1981). Electron microscopic and histochemical study of the postovulatory follicles of *Perca fluviatilis* L. (Teleostei). *Gen. Comp. Endocrinol*. *45*, 219-233. **67**

Langdon, J.S., Humphrey, J.D., Williams, L.M.,
    Hyatt, A.D. & Westbury, H.A. (1986). First
    virus isolation from Australian fish: an
    iridovirus-like pathogen from redfin perch,
    Perca fluviatilis L. *J. Fish Dis. 9*,
    263-268. **146**
Lapkin, V.V., Svirskij, A.M. & Golovanov, V.K.
    (1981). Vozrastnaya dinamika izbiraemykh i
    letal 'nykh temperatur ryb. *Zool. Zh.*
    60 (12), 1792-1801. (In Russian). **46**
Larsson, A., Haux, C., Sjoebeck, M.-L. & Lithner,
    G. 1984. Physiological effects of an
    additional stressor on fish exposed to a simu-
    lated heavy-metal-containing effluent from a
    sulphide ore smeltery. *Ecotoxicol. Environ.*
    Saf. 8 (2), 118-128. **240**
Lartseva, L.V. & Zubkova, L.A. (1981). Kul' tivi-
    rovanie odnoslojnykh kletochnykh kul'tur iz
    kozhi i plavnikov karpa i sudaka. In: *Bolezni*
    ryb i Vodnaya Toksikologiya. (Eds V.A.
    Musselius & I.S. Shesterin). *Originsb.*
    Nauch. T.R. Vniiprkh. Collatvol. 32, 25-32.
    145
Lauder, G.V. (1983). Functional design and evolu-
    tion of the pharyngeal jaw apparatus in eute-
    leostean fishes. *Zool. J. Linn. Soc. 77* (1),
    1-38. **27**
Laurent, P. (1984). Gill internal morphology.
    In: *Fish Physiology. XA.* (Eds W.S. Hoar &
    D.J. Randall). 73-183. Academic Press.
    Orlando. **35**
Lawler, G.H. (1969). Aspects of the biology of
    Triaenophorus nodulosus in yellow perch,
    Perca flavescens, in Heming Lake, Manitoba.
    J. Fish. Res. Board Can. 26, 821-831. **169**
Leary, R. & Booke, H.E. (1982). Genetic stock
    analysis of yellow perch from Green Bay and
    Lake Michigan. *Trans Am. Fish. Soc. 111* (1),
    52-57. **179**
Lebedev, V.D. (1952). Fishes from alate-
    paleolithic settlement at Murzak-Koba in
    Crimea. *Bull. Soc. Nat. Hist. Moscow. 51*
    (6), 46-51. (In Russian). **175**
Le Cren, E.D. (1947). The determination of the
    age and growth of the perch *(Perca*
    fluviatilis) from the opercular bone. *J.*
    Anim. Ecol. 16, 188-204. **50,53**
Le Cren, E.D. (1951). The length-weight relation-
    ship and seasonal cycle in gonad weight and
    condition in the perch *(Perca fluviatilis).*
    J. Anim. Ecol. 20, 201-219. **53,54**

Le Cren, E.D. (1958). Observations on the growth of perch *(Perca fluviatilis* L.) over twenty-two years with special reference to the effects of temperature and changes in population density. *J. Anim. Ecol. 27,* 287-334. **57,201**

Le Cren, E.D. (1965). Some factors regulating the size of populations of freshwater fishes. *Mitt. Internat. Verein. Limnol. 13,* 88-105. **76**

Le Cren, E.D., Kipling, C. & McCormack, J.C. (1977). A study on the numbers, biomass and year-class strengths of perch *(Perca fluviatilis* L.) in Windermere from 1941 to 1966. *J. Anim. Ecol. 46,* 281-307. **193**

Leeuwen, J.L. Van & Müller, M. (1984a). Optimum sucking techniques for predatory fish. *Trans Zool. Soc. Lond. 37* (2), 137-170. **107**

Leeuwen, J.L. Van & Müller, M. (1984b). The recording and interpretation of pressures in prey sucking fish. *Neth. J. Zool. 33* (4), 425-475. **107**

Lehtinen, K.-J. & Oikari, A. (1980). Sublethal effects of kraft pulp mill waste water on the perch, *Perca fluviatilis,* studied by rotary-flow and histological techniques. *Ann. Zool. Fenn. 17* (4), 255-259. **241**

Leino, R.L. (1982). Rodlet cells in the gill and intestine of *Catostomus commersoni* and *Perca flavescens:* a comparison of their light and electron microscopic cytochemistry with that of mucous and granular cells. *Can. J. Zool. 60* (11), 2768-2782. **30,33**

Lessman, C.A. (1978). Effects of gonadotropin mixtures and two steroids on inducing ovulation in the walleye. *Prog. Fish-Cult. 40* (1), 3-5. **75**

Letichevskii, M.A. (1946). K voprosu o plodovitosti ryb yuga Aralskogo morya. *Zool. Zh. 25* (4), 351-356. **126**

Li, S. & Mathias, J.A. (1982). Causes of high mortality among cultured larval walleyes. *Trans Am. Fish. Soc. 111* (6), 710-721. **89,90,91,92,237**

Lind, E.A., Ellonen, T., Keranen, M., Kukko, O. & Tenhunen, A. (1973). Advenen pyydystettävyyden vuorokauden ajat talvella ja Kesällä. *Kalamies. 3,* 3. **140**

Lindquist, D.G., Shute, J.R. & Shute, P.W. (1981).
Spawning and nesting behaviour of the Waccamaw
darter, *Etheostoma perlongum*. *Environ. Biol.
Fishes.* 6 (2), 177-191. **257,258**

Lindroth, A. (1947). Time of activity of freshwater fish spermatazoa in relation to temperature. *Zool. Bidr. Upsala. 25*, 165-168. **77**

Linfield, R.S.J. & Rickards, R.B. (1979). The
zander in perspective. *Fish. Manage. 10* (1),
1-16. **19,178**

Linlokken, A. (1984). Gill-net selectivity for
perch, *Perca fluviatilis*. *Fauna. Oslo.
37* (3), 112-116. **226**

Loftus, K.H. (1976). Science for Canada's fisheries rehabilitation needs. *J. Fish. Res.
Board Can. 33*, 1822-1857. **242**

Lowenstein, O. (1971). The labyrinth. In: *Fish
Physiology. V.* (Eds W.S. Hoar & D.J.
Randall). 207-240. Academic Press. New
York. **39**

Lutz, P.L. (1972). Ionic and body compartment
responses to increasing salinity in the perch,
Perca fluviatilis. *Comp. Biochem. Physiol.
42A*, 711-717. **126,127**

Lynch, W.E., Jr., Johnson, D.L. & Schell, S.A.
(1982). Survival, growth and food habits of
walleye x sauger hybrids (saugeye) in ponds.
N. Am. J. Fish. Manage. 2 (4), 381-387. **180**

Lyons, J. (1983). Olfactory organ morphology and
histology in the yellow perch *Perca flavescens*, and golden shiner, *Notemigonus
crysoleucas*. *Can. J. Zool. 61* (12),
2987-2990. **39**

Mackay, W.C. & Craig, J.F. (1983). A comparison
of four systems for studying the activity of
pike *(Esox lucius* L.) and perch *(Perca
fluviatilis* L. and *Perca flavescens*
(Mitchill)). *Proceedings of 4th International
Wildlife Biotelemetry Conference.* Halifax.
Canada. (Ed. D.G. Pincock). 22-30. **141,142**

Maclean, N.G., Teleki, G.C. & Polak, J. (1982).
Ultrasonic telemetry studies of fish activity
near the Nanticoke thermal generating station.
J. Great Lakes Res. 8 (3), 495-504. **48**

Maitland, P.S. (1977). *The Hamlyn Guide to Freshwater Fishes of Britain & Europe*. Hamlyn.
London. 256 pp. **249,264**

Malison, J.A., Kayes, T.B., Best, C.D., Amundson, C.H. & Wentworth, B.C. (1986). Sexual differences and use of hormones to control sex in yellow perch *(Perca flavescens)*. *Can. J. Fish. Aquat. Sci. 43*, 26-35. **66,67,234**

Mansueti, A.J. (1964). Early development of the yellow perch, *Perca flavescens*. *Chesapeake Sci. 5*, (1-2), 46-66. **70,81,83,89**

Manteifel, B.P., Girsa, I.I., Leshcheva, T.S. & Pavlov, D.S. (1965). Sutochnye ritmy pitaniya i dvigatelnoi aktivnosti nekotorykh presnovodnykh khishchnykh ryb. In: *Pitanie khishchnykh ryb*. (Ed. B.P. Manteifel). 3-81. Nauka. Moscow. **103**

Margolis, L & Arthur, J.R. (1979). Synopsis of the parasites of fishes of Canada. *Bull. Fish. Res. Board Can.* 199, 1-269. **149,150,151,152,153,154,155,156,157,158,159, 160,161,162**

Margolis, L., Esch, G.W., Holmes, J.C., Kuris, A.M. & Shad, G.A. (1982). The use of ecological terms in parasitology (report of an ad hoc committee of the American Society of Parasitologists). *J. Parasitol. 68*, 131-133. **167**

Markevich, A.P. (1963). Parasitic Fauna of Freshwater Fish of the Ukrainian SSR. *Israel Program Sci. Transl. Cat.* No. 884. **149,150,151,152,153,154,155,157,158,159, 160,161,162**

Matei, V.E. (1984). Comparative analysis of the gill epithelium ultrastructure in the perch, *Perca fluviatilis*, from basins with different ion composition. *Tsitologiya* 26 (7), 778-782. (In Russian). **30,31**

Mathews, S.H. & Dolan, D.M. (1983). Polychlorinated biphenyls (PCBs) in Saginaw Bay yellow perch, 1977-1980. In: *Proceedings of the 26th Conference on Great Lakes Research*. Abstract. p. 36. Oswego. New York. **242**

Mathias, J.A. & Li, S. (1982). Feeding habits of walleye larvae and juveniles: comparative laboratory and field studies. *Trans Am. Fish. Soc. 111* (6), 722-735. **94,97,107**

Mathur, D. (1973). Food habits and feeding chronology of the black-banded darter, *Percina nigrofasciata*, in Halawakee Creek, Alabama. *Trans Am. Fish. Soc. 102* (1), 48-55. **255**

Mauck, W.L., Olson, L.E. & Hogan J.W. (1977).
Effects of water quality on deactivation and
toxicity of mexacarbate (Zectran) to fish.
Arch. Environ. Contam. Toxicol. 6 (4),
385-393. **242**

Mawdesley-Thomas, L.E. (1972). Some tumors of
fish. In: *Diseases of Fish* (Ed. L.E.
Mawdesley-Thomas). *Symp. Zool. Soc. Lond.*
No. 30, 191-283. **145**

Menshutkin, V.V. & Zhakov, L.A. (1964). Opyt
matematicheskogo opredeleniya kharaktera dina-
miki chislennosti okunya v zadannykh ekologic-
heskikh usloviyakh. In: *Ozera karelskogo
Peresheika*. (Eds I.I. Nikolaev & E.A. Popov).
140-155. Nauka. Moscow-Leningrad. **182,184**

Metcalfe, A.L. (1966). Fishes of the Kansas river
system in relation to zoogeography of the
Great Plains. *Univ. Kansas Publ. Mus. Nat.
Hist. 17*, 23-189. **176**

Mezhnin, F.I. (1972). Interrenal and chromaffin
tissue of freshwater fish. *J. Ichthyol. 12*,
671-684. **43**

Mezhnin, F.I. (1977). Interrenalovaya i suprare-
nalovaya zheleze i tel'tsa stanniusa okunya v
nerestovyj period. *Biol. Nauki*. (Mosc.).
(No. 11), 62-69. **44**

Mezhnin, F.I. (1978). Development of the sex
cells in the early ontogeny of the common
perch, *Perca fluviatilis*. *J. Ichthyol. 18*
(1), 71-86. **67**

Mezhnin, F.I. (1979). Morphology and topography
of interrenal and suprarenal glands of bony
fishes. *Nauchnye Dokl. vyssh. shk. Biol.
Nauki*. (3), 33-38. (In Russian). **44**

Mikhailov, V. (1951). Stadialnosi rozwoju nictor-
ych tasiemcow (Cestoda). *Ann. Univ. Mariae
Curie Skladowska. Sect. C. 6* (3). **167**

Mikhman, A.S. (1978). Pitanie i pishchevye
potrebnosti lichinok perkariny *Percarina
demidoffi* Nordmann v vostochnoj chasti
Taganrogskogo zaliva. *Vopr. Ikhtiol. 18* (2),
366-370. **250**

Mikulski, J. (1964). Some biological features of
pikeperch lakes. *Verh. int. Ver. Limnol.
15*, 151-157. **224**

Miller, L.W. (1967). The introduction, growth,
diet and depth distribution of walleye,
Stizostedion vitreum (Mitchill), in El
Capitan Reservoir, San Diego County. *Admin.
Rep. Calif. Resour. Agency, Dep. Fish Game,
Inland Fish. Br.* (67-10), 1-14. **75**

Miller, R.R. (1957). Origins and dispersal of the alewife, *Alosa pseudoharengus*, and gizzard shad, *Dorosoma cepedianum*, in the Great Lakes. *Trans Am. Fish. Soc. 86*, 97-111. **202**

Milliken, M.R. (1982). Qualitative and quantitative nutrient requirements of fishes: a review. *Fish. Bull. 80*, (4), 655-686. **94,238**

Mills, E.L., Confer, J.L. & Ready, R.C. (1984). Prey selection of young yellow perch, *Perca flavescens*, the influence of capture success, visual acuity and prey choice. *Trans Am. Fish. Soc. 113* (5), 579-587. **100**

Mills, E.L. & Forney, J.L. (1981). Energetics, food consumption and growth of young yellow perch in Oneida Lake, New York. *Trans Am. Fish. Soc. 110* (4), 479-488. **113,118**

Mitchill, S.L. (1818). Memoir on ichthyology. The fishes of New York described and arranged. *Am. Month. Mag. Crit. Rev.* 1817-1818(2), 241-8, 321-8. **176**

Molnar, K., Hanek, G. & Fernando, C.H. (1974). Parasites of fishes from Laurel Creek, Ontario. *J. Fish Biol. 6*, 717-728. **149,150,153,156,157,159**

Moore, G.A. (1944). The retinae of two North American teleosts with special reference to their tapeta lucida. *J. Comp. Neurol. 80* (3), 369-379. **42**

Moravec, F. (1979). Occurrence of the endoparasitic helminths in pike *(Esox lucius* L.) from the Mácha Lake fishpond system. *Věst. Česk. Spol. Zool. 43*, 174-193. **164**

Müller, M. & Osse, J.W.M. (1984). Hydrodynamics of suction feeding in fish. *Trans Zool. Soc. Lond. 37* (2), 51-136. **107**

Muncy, R.J. (1962). Life history of the yellow perch, *Perca flavescens*, in estuarine waters of Severn River, a tributary of Chesapeake Bay, Maryland. *Chesapeake Sci. 3* (3), 143-59. **127**

Mundahl, N.D. & Ingersoll, C.G. (1983). Early autumn movements and densities of johnny *(Etheostoma nigrum)* and fantail *(E. flabellare)* darters in a southwestern Ohio stream. *Ohio J. Sci. 83* (3), 103-108. **253**

Muns, B.J. & Dahlstrom, P. (1967). (1971 English translation). *Collins Guide to the Freshwater Fishes of Britain and Europe*. Wm. Collins & Co. Ltd. London. 222 pp. **265**

Murphy, B.R., Nielson, L.A. & Turner, B.J. (1983).
Use of genetic tags to evaluate stocking
success for reservoir walleyes. *Trans Am.
Fish. Soc. 112* (4), 457-463. **179,233**

McAllister, D.E. (1970). Rare or endangered
Canadian fishes. *Can. Field-Nat. 84* (1),
124-125. **177**

McCarthy, D.M. (1975). Fish furunculosis caused
by *Aeromonas salmonicida var. achromogenes.
J. Wildlife Dis. 11,* 489-493. **147**

McConville, D.R. & Fossum, J.D. (1981). Movement
patterns of walleye *(Stizostedion v. vitreum)*
in Pool 3 of the upper Mississippi River as
determined by ultrasonic telemetry. *J.
Freshwat. Ecol. 1* (3), 279-285. **140,141**

McElman, J.F. & Balon, E.K. (1979). Early ontogeny of walleye, *Stizostedion vitreum,* with
steps of saltatory development. *Environ.
Biol. Fishes. 4* (4), 309-348. **82,84,85,86**

McWilliams, P.G. (1982). A comparison of physiological characteristics in normal and acid exposed populations of the brown trout, *Salmo
trutta. Comp. Biochem. Physiol. 72A.* (3),
515-522. **129**

Nagieć, M. (1977). Pikeperch *(Stizostedion
lucioperca)* in its natural habitats in Poland.
J. Fish. Res. Board Can. 34 (10), 1581-
1585. **224**

Nakashima, B.S. & Leggett, W.C. (1978). Daily
ration of yellow perch *(Perca flavescens)* from
Lake Memphremagog, Quebec-Vermont, with a comparison of methods for *in situ* determinations.
J. Fish. Res. Board Can. 35 (12), 1597-
1603. **113**

Natochin, Y.V. & Lavrova, E.A. (1974). The influence of water salinity and stage of life
history on ion concentration of fish blood
serum. *J. Fish Biol. 6,* 545-555. **126**

Neacsu, I., Craciun, V. & Craciun, M. (1981).
L'equiliere hydro-mineral chez le sandre
(Stizostedion lucioperca (L.)) transfere de
l'eau douce en milieux mixo-mesohalins et in-
versement. *Cercet. Mar. Rech. Mar.* (14),
201-215. **127**

Neill, W.H. & Magnuson, J.J. (1974).
Distributional ecology and behavioural thermo-
regulation of fishes in relation to heated
effluent from a power plant at Lake Monona,
Wisconsin. *Trans Am. Fish. Soc. 103,* 663-710.
48,49

Nelson, J.S. (1984). *Fishes of the World*. 2nd Ed.
John Wiley & Sons, Inc. New York. xv + 523
pp. **1,2,4**

Nelson, W.R. (1968). Embryo and larval characteristics of sauger, walleye and their reciprocal
hybrids. *Trans Am. Fish. Soc. 97* (2),
167-174. **90**

Nepszy, S.J. (1977). Changes in percid populations and species interactions in Lake Erie.
J. Fish. Res. Board Can. 34 (10), 1861-1868.
217

Neuhaus, E. (1934). Studien über das Stettiner
Haff und seine Nebengewaser. Untersuchungen
uber den Zander. *Z. Fisch.* (32), 599-634.
107

Newsome, G.E. & Leduc, G. (1975). Seasonal
changes of fat content in the yellow perch.
J. Fish. Res. Board Can. 32, 2214-2221. **74**

Newton, E.T. (1908). Note relative à des
fragments fossiles de petite vertébrés trouvés
dans les dépôts pliocènes de Tegelen sur-
Meuse. *Bull. Soc. Belg. Geol. 21,* 591-596.
175

Ney, J.J. (1978). A synoptic review of yellow
perch and walleye biology. In: *Selected Coolwater Fishes of North America*. (Ed. R.L.
Kendall). *Am. Fish. Soc. Spec. Publ.* (11),
1-12. **99**

Niimi, A.J. & Morgan, S.L. (1980). Morphometric
examination of the gills of walleye,
Stizostedion vitreum vitreum (Mitchill), and
rainbow trout, *Salmo gairdneri* Richardson.
J. Fish Biol. 16 (6), 685-692. **30,32**

Noaillac-Depeyre, J. & Gas, N. (1978). Ultra-
structural and cytochemical study of the
gastric epithelium in a fresh water teleostean
fish *(Perca fluviatilis)*. *Tissue & Cell.
10* (1), 23-37. **33**

Noaillac-Depeyre, J. & Gas, N. (1979). Structure
and function of the intestinal epithelial
cells in the perch *(Perca fluviatilis* L.).
Anat. Rec. 195 (4), 621-639. **33**

Noaillac-Depeyre, J. & Gas, N. (1982). Ultrastructure of endocrine cells in the stomach of
two teleost fish, *Perca fluviatilis* L. and
Ameiurus nebulosus L. *Cell Tissue Res. 221*
(3), 657-678. **33**

Noble, R.L. (1970a). Parasites of yellow perch in
Oneida Lake, New York. *N.Y. Fish Game J. 17*
(2), 95-101. **151,171**

Noble, R.L. (1970b). Evaluation of the Miller high-speed sampler for sampling yellow perch and walleye fry. *J. Fish. Res. Board Can.* *27* (6), 1033-1044. **187**

Noble, R.L. (1972). A method of direct estimation of total food consumption with application to young yellow perch. *Prog. Fish-Cult.* *34*, 191-194. **101,103**

Nonnotte, G. (1981). Cutaneous respiration in six freshwater teleosts. *Comp. Biochem. Physiol.* *70A* (4), 541-543. **131**

Nordstrom, P.R., Bailey, J.L. & Heaton, J.R. (1960). A bacterial disease of yellow perch *(Perca flavescens)*. *Trans Am. Fish. Soc.* *89*, 310-312. **147**

Nyberg, P. (1979). Production and food consumption of perch, *Perca fluviatilis* L., in two Swedish forest lakes. *Rep. Inst. Freshwat. Res. Drottningholm*. (58), 140-157. **113**

Nygren, A., Edlund, P., Hirsch, U. & Ahsgren, L. (1968). Cytological studies in perch *(Perca fluviatilis* L.), pike *(Esox lucius* L.), pike-perch *(Lucioperca lucioperca* (L.)) and ruffe *(Acerina cernua* L.). *Hereditas.* *59*, 518-524. **44**

Oliver, D.R. (1960). The macroscopic bottom fauna of Lac la Ronge, Saskatchewan. *J. Fish. Res. Board Can.* *17* (5), 607-624. **160,161**

Olson, D.E., Schupp, D.H. & Macins, V. (1978). An hypothesis of homing behavior of walleyes as related to observed patterns of passive and active movement. In: *Selected Coolwater Fishes of North America.* (Ed. R.L. Kendall). *Am. Fish. Soc. Spec. Publ.* (11), 52-57. **142**

Orlova, E.L. (1976). Feeding habits of predatory fishes in the outer delta of the Volga. *Hydrobiol. J.* *12* (2), 41-47. **113**

Oseid, D.M. & Smith, L.L. Jr. (1971). Survival and hatching of walleye eggs at various dissolved oxygen levels. *Prog. Fish-Cult.* *33* (2), 81-85. **135,136**

Osse, J.W.M. (1969). Functional morphology of the head of the perch *(Perca fluviatilis* L.): an electromyographic study. *Neth. J. Zool.* *19* (3), 289-392. **21,29,107,108**

Page, L.M. (1978). Redescription, distribution, variation and life history notes on *Percina macrocephala* (Percidae). *Copeia.* (4), 655-664. **257**

Page, L.M. (1983). *Handbook of Darters*. T.F.H. Publications, Inc. Ltd. New Jersey. 271 pp. **12,251,252,254,258,259,260**

Page, L.M. & Smith, P.W. (1970). The life history of the dusky darter, *Percina sciera* in the Embarras River, Illinois. *Ill. Nat. Hist. Surv. Biol. Notes*. No. 69, 15 pp. **259**

Page, L.M. & Swofford, D.L. (1984). Morphological correlates of ecological specialisation in darters. *Environ. Biol. Fishes*. *11* (2), 139-159. **251,256**

Parsons, J.W. (1967). Contributions of year-classes of blue pike to the commercial fishery of Lake Erie, 1943-59. *J. Fish. Res. Board Can*. *24* (5), 1035-1066. **201**

Pauly, D. (1980). On the inter-relationships between natural mortality, growth parameters and mean environmental temperatures in 175 fish stocks. *J. Cons. Int. Explor. Mer*. *39*, 175-192. **65**

Payan, P., Girard, J.P. & Mayer-Gostan, N. (1984). Branchial ion movements in teleosts: the roles of respiratory and chloride cells. In: *Fish Physiology*. *XB*. (Eds W.S. Hoar & D.J. Randall). 39-64. Academic Press. Orlando. **124**

Pearson, A.A. (1936). The acoustic-lateral nervous sytem in fishes. *J. Comp. Neurol*. *64*, 235-273. **43**

Persson, L. (1979). The effects of temperature and different food organisms on the rate of gastric evacuation in perch, *Perca fluviatilis*. *Freshwat. Biol*. *9* (2), 99-104. **110**

Persson, L. (1981). The effects of temperature and meal size on the rate of gastric evacuation in perch *(Perca fluviatilis)* fed on fish larvae. *Freshwat. Biol*. *11* (2), 131-138. **109,110**

Persson, L. (1983a). Food consumption and competition between age classes in a perch, *Perca fluviatilis*, population in a shallow eutrophic lake. *Oikos*. *40* (2), 197-207. **113**

Persson, L. (1983b). Effects of intra- and inter-specific competition on dynamics and size structure of a perch, *Perca fluviatilis*, and a roach, *Rutilus rutilus*, population. *Oikos*. *41*, 136-132. **205**

Peter, R.E. & Nagahama, Y. (1974). A light and electron microscope study of the structure of the nucleus preopticus and nucleus lateral tuberis of the goldfish, *Carassius auratus*. *Can. J. Zool. 54*, 1423-1437. **50**

Petrosky, B.R. & Magnuson, J.J. (1973). Behavioural responses of northern pike, yellow perch, and bluegill to oxygen concentrations under simulated winterkill conditions. *Copeia* (1), 124-133. **135**

Petrushevskii, G.K. (Ed.). (1963). Parasites and Diseases of Fish. *Israel Program Sci. Transl. PST Cat.* No. 105. **149,150,155,159,160**

Pfeifer, G., Ponyi, J.E. & Nagy, Z. (1979). Pesticide residues in Lake Balaton. In: *Human impacts of life in freshwaters*. (Eds P. Biro & J. Salanki). 21-26. Akademiai Kiado. Budapest. **240**

Pickford, G.E. & Atz, J.W. (Eds). (1957). *The Physiology of the Pituitary Gland of Fishes*. N.Y. Zool. Soc. New York. XXIV + 613 pp. **19**

Pihu, E. & Maeemets, A. (1982). The management of fisheries in Lake Voertsjaerv. *Hydrobiologia. 86* (1-2), 207-210. **229**

Piironen, J. & Hyvaerinen, H. (1983). Composition of the milt of some teleost fishes. *J. Fish Biol. 22* (3), 351-361. **69,77**

Pitt, C.E. & Grundman, A.W. (1957). A study into the effects of parasitism on the growth of yellow perch produced by the larvae of *Ligula intestinalis* (Linnaeus, 1758) Gmelin, 1790. *Proc. Helminthol. Soc. Wash. 24*, 73-80. **144**

Pivnička, K. & Švátora, M. (1977). Factors affecting the shift in predominance from Eurasian perch *(Perca fluviatilis)* to roach *(Rutilus rutilus)* in the Klicava Reservoir, Czechoslovakia. *J. Fish. Res. Board Can. 34* (10), 1571-1575. **205**

Pokrovskii, V.V. (1951). Materialy po issledovaniyu v nutrividovoi izmenchivosti okunya- *(Perca fluviatilis* L.). *Tr. Kärelo-Finsk. Vses. Nauchno-Issled. Inst. Ozern. Rechn. Rybn. Okeanogr. Khoz. 3*, 95-149. **177**

Poole, B.C. & Dick, T.A. (1985). Parasite recruitment by stocked walleye, *Stizostedion vitreum vitreum* (Mitchill), fry in a small boreal lake in central Canada. *J. Wildlife Dis. 21* (4), 371-376. **169,173**

Poole, B.C. & Dick, T.A. (1986). *Raphidascaris acus* (Bloch, 1779) in northern pike, *Esox lucius* L., walleye, *Stizostedion vitreum vitreum* (Mitchill), and yellow perch, *Perca flavescens* (Mitchill), from central Canada. *J. Wildlife Dis.* 22 (3), 435-436. **163**

Popova, O.A. & Sytina, L.A. (1977). Food and feeding relations of Eurasian perch *(Perca fluviatilis)* and pikeperch *(Stizostedion lucioperca)* in various waters of the USSR. *J. Fish. Res. Board Can.* 34 (10), 1559-1570. **100**

Priegel, G.R. (1964). Early scale development in the walleye. *Trans Am. Fish. Soc.* 93 (2), 199-200. **20,90**

Puke, C. (1952). Pikeperch studies in Lake Vänern. *Rep. Inst. Freshwat. Res. Drottning.* 33, 168-78. **143**

Pycha, R.L. & Smith, L.L., Jr. (1955). Early life history of the yellow perch, *Perca flavescens.* (Mitchill) in the Red Lakes, Minnesota. *Trans Am. Fish. Soc.* 84, 249-260. **90**

Rahel, F.J. (1983). Population differences in acid tolerance between yellow perch, *Perca· flavescens,* from naturally acidic and alkaline lakes. *Can. J. Zool.* 61 (1), 147-152. **129**

Raisanen, G.A. & Applegate, R.L. (1983). Selection of live food by captive yellow perch larvae. *Prog. Fish-Cult.* 45 (3), 172-174. **237**

Randall, D.J. (1970). The circulatory system. In: *Fish Physiology.* IV. (Eds W.S. Hoar & D.J. Randall). 133-172. Academic Press. New York. **33**

Randall, D. & Daxboeck, C. (1984). Oxygen and carbon dioxide transfer across fish gills. In: *Fish Physiology.* XA. (Eds W.S. Hoar & D.J. Randall). 263-314. Academic Press. Orlando. **131**

Raney, E.C. & Suttkus, R.D. (1966). *Etheostoma rubrum,* a new percid fish of the subgenus *Nothonotus* from Bayon Pierre, Mississippi. *Tulane Stud. Zool.* 13, 95-102. **258**

Rankin, J.C. & Bolis, L. (1984). Hormonal control of water movement across the gills. In: *Fish Physiology XB.* (Eds W.S. Hoar & D.J. Randall). 177-201. Academic Press. Orlando. **126**

Rao, G.M.M. (1968). Oxygen consumption of rainbow trout *(Salmo gairdneri)* in relation to activity and salinity. *Can. J. Zool.* 46, 781-785. **124**

Rask, M. (1984). The effect of low pH on perch,
    Perca fluviatilis L. 3. The perch popula-
    tion in a small, acidic, extremely humic
    forest lake. *Ann. Zool. Fenn. 21* (1), 15-22.
    88,129
Rawson, D.S. (1946). Successful introduction of
    fish in a large saline lake. *Can. Fish Cult.*
    1 (1), 5-8. **128**
Rawson, D.S. (1957). The life history and ecology
    of the yellow walleye, *Stizostedion vitreum*,
    in Lac la Ronge, Saskatchewan. *Trans Am.*
    Fish. Soc. 86, 15-37. **161**
Regier, H.A. & Hartman, W.L. (1973). Lake Erie's
    fish community: 150 years of cultural
    stresses. *Science*. (Wash. D.C.). *180*,
    1248-1255. **216**
Regier, H.A., Applegate, V.C. & Ryder, R.A.
    (1969). The ecology and management of the
    walleye in Western Lake Erie. *Tech. Rep.*
    Great Lakes Fish. Comm. (15), 101 pp.
    177,201,213,216
Reighard, J. (1890). The development of the wall-
    eyed pike *(Stizostedion vitreum)*. A popular
    introduction to the development of bony
    fishes. *Mich. Fish. Comm. Bull.* (1), 66 pp.
    91
Reynolds, W.W. & Casterline, M.E. (1979). Be-
    havioural thermoregulation and locomotor acti-
    vity of *Perca flavescens*. *Can. J. Zool. 57*,
    2239-2242. **49**
Ricker, W.E. (1954). Stock and recruitment. *J.*
    Fish. Res. Board Can. 11, 559-623. **188**
Ricker, W.E. (1958). Handbook of computations for
    biological statistics of fish populations.
    Bull. Fish. Res. Board Can. (119), 300 pp.
    209
Ricker, W.E. (1975). Computation and interpreta-
    tion of biological statistics of fish popula-
    tions. *Bull. Fish. Res. Board Can.* (191),
    xviii + 382 pp. **62,188,209**
Riley, L.M. & Carline, R.F. (1982). Evaluation of
    scale shape for the identification of walleye
    stocks from Western Lake Erie. *Trans Am.*
    Fish. Soc. 111, (6), 736-741. **20**
Romer, A.S. (1966). *Vertebrate Paleontology*. 3rd
    Ed. University of Chicago Press. Chicago.
    468 pp. **4**
Ross, J., Powles, P.M. & Berrill, M. (1977).
    Thermal selection and related behavior in lar-
    val yellow perch *(Perca flavescens)*. *Can.*
    Field-Nat. 91 (4), 406-410. **92**

Ross, M.J. & Siniff, D.B. (1980). Spatial distribution and temperature selection of fish near the thermal outtall of a power plant during fall, winter and spring. *U.S. Environ. Protect. Agency. Ecol. Res. Series. EPA-600/3-80-009*, 129 pp. (PB80-148703). **48**

Ross, M.J. & Siniff, D.B. (1982). Temperatures selected in a power plant thermal effluent by adult yellow perch *(Perca flavescens)* in winter. *Can. J. Fish. Aquat. Sci. 39* (2), 346-349. **48**

Rottiers, D.V. & Lemm, C.A. (1985). Movement of underyearling walleyes, *Stizostedion vitreum,* in response to odour and visual cues. *Prog. Fish-Cult. 47* (1), 34-41. **101**

Runn, P., Johansson, N. & Milbrink, G. (1977). Some effects of low pH on the hatchability of eggs of perch, *Perca fluviatilis* L. *Zoon. 5* (2), 115-125. **88**

Ryan, P.M. & Harvey, H.H. (1980). Growth responses of yellow perch, *Perca flavescens* (Mitchill), to lake acidification in the La Cloche Mountain lakes of Ontario. *Environ. Biol. Fishes 5* (2), 97-108. **129,130**

Ryder, R.A. (1965). A method for estimating the potential fish production of north-temperate lakes. *Trans Am. Fish. Soc. 94* (3), 214-218. **224**

Ryder, R.A. (1968). Dynamics and exploitation of mature walleyes, *Stizostedion vitreum vitreum,* in the Nipigon Bay region of Lake Superior. *J. Fish. Res. Board Can. 25* (7), 1347-1376. **143**

Ryder, R.A. (1977). Effects of ambient light variation on behaviour of yearling, subadult, and adult walleyes *(Stizostedion vitreum vitreum)*. *J. Fish. Res. Board Can. 34* (10), 1481-1491. **49,105,106**

Sachs, T.R. (1878). Transportation of live pike-perch *(Lucioperca zanda)* in Germany called zander. *Land and Water. 25,* 476. **178**

Sagi, K. (1974). A Balaton-vidék történelme és régeszeti emléki. In: *Balaton Monográfia.* (Ed. K. Toth). 337-356. Panoráma. Budapest. **221**

Samokhvalova, L.K. (1982). Osobennosti pitaniya sudaka v kurshskom zalive Baltijskogo Morya v osennij period. In: *Pitanie i pishchevye otnosheniya ryb i bespozvonochnykh Atlantischeskogo Okeana.* 67-74. Atlantniro. Kaliningrad. **99**

Sandstroem, O. (1983). Seasonal variations in the swimming performance of perch *(Perca fluviatilis* L.) measured with the rotatory-flow technique. *Can. J. Zool. 61* (7), 1475-1480. **137**

Schaefer, M.B. (1954). Some aspects of the dyna-mics of populations important to the management of the commercial marine fisheries. *Bull. Inter-Am. Trop. Tuna Comm. 1* (2), 27-56. **209**

Schaefer, M.B. (1957). A study of the dynamics of the fishery for yellowfin tuna in the eastern tropical Pacific Ocean. *Bull. Inter-Am. Trop. Tuna Comm. 2,* 247-268. **209**

Schat, K.A. & Carlisle, J.C. (1980). Susceptibi-lity of walleye fry to infection by IHN and IPN viruses. Abstract only. *Proc. Joint 4th Biennial Fish Health Section & Fish Disease Workshops.* Seattle. Washington. p.26. **146**

Schenck, J.R. & Whiteside, B.G. (1977). Reproduc-tion, fecundity, sexual dimorphism and sex ratio of *Etheostoma fonticola,* Osteichthyes, Percidae. *Am. Midl. Nat. 98* (2), 365-375. **259**

Scherer, E. (1971). Effects of oxygen depletion and of carbon dioxide buildup on the photic behaviour of the walleye *(Stizostedion vitreum vitreum). J. Fish. Res. Board Can. 28* (9), 1303-1307. **135**

Scherer, E. (1976). Overhead-light intensity and vertical positioning of the walleye, *Stizostedion vitreum vitreum. J. Fish. Res. Board Can. 33* (2), 289-292. **105**

Schlesinger, D.A. & Regier, H.A. (1983). Re-lationship between environmental temperature and yields of subarctic and temperate zone fish species. *Can. J. Fish. Aquat. Sci. 40* (10), 1829-1837. **224,225**

Schmitt, D.N. & Hubert, W.A. (1982). Comparison of cleithra and scales for age and growth analysis of yellow perch. *Prog. Fish-Cult. 44* (2), 87-88. **51**

Schott, E.F., Kayes, T.B. & Calbert, H.E. (1978). Comparative growth of male versus female yellow perch fingerlings under controlled en-vironmental conditions. In: *Selected Cool-water Fishes of North America.* (Ed. R.L. Kendall). *Am. Fish. Soc. Spec. Publ.* (11), 181-186. **59**

Schweigert, J.F., Ward, F.J. & Clayton, J.W.
    (1977). Effects of fry and fingerling intro-
    ductions on walleye *(Stizostedion vitreum
    vitreum)* production in West Blue Lake,
    Manitoba. *J. Fish. Res. Board Can. 34* (11),
    2142-2150. **179**
Scott, D.B.C. (1979). Environmental timing and
    the control of reproduction in teleost fish.
    In: *Fish Phenology.* (Ed. P.J. Miller). 105-
    132. *Symp. Zool. Soc. Lond.* (44). Academic
    Press. London. **50**
Scott, D.C. (1955). Activity patterns of perch,
    Perca flavescens, in Rondeau Bay of Lake
    Erie. *Ecology. 36* (2), 320-327. **103**
Scott, W.B. & Crossman, E.J. (1973). Freshwater
    fishes of Canada. *Bull. Fish. Res. Board
    Can.* (184). 966 pp. **18,26,56,76,80,81,177**
Seesock, W.E., Ramsey, J.S. & Seesock, F.L.
    (1978). Life and limitation of the coldwater
    darter *(Etheostoma ditrema)* in Glencoe Spring,
    Alabama. *ASB (Assoc. Southeast Biol.) Bull.
    25,* 26. **259**
Serns, S.L. (1978). Effects of a minimum size
    limit on the walleye population of a northern
    Wisconsin lake. In: *Selected Coolwater Fishes
    of North America.* (Ed. R.L. Kendall). *Am.
    Fish. Soc. Spec. Publ.* (11), 390-397. **230**
Serns, S.L. (1982). Influence of various factors
    on density and growth of age-0 walleyes in
    Escanaba Lake, Wisconsin, 1958-1980. *Trans
    Am. Fish. Soc. 111* (3), 299-306. **59**
Serns, S.L. & Kempinger, J.J. (1981). Relation-
    ship of angler exploitation to the size, age
    and sex of walleyes in Escanaba Lake,
    Wisconsin. *Trans Am. Fish. Soc. 110* (2),
    216-220. **227**
Shute, P.W., Shute, J.R. & Lindquist, D.G. (1982).
    Age, growth and early life history of the
    Waccamaw darter, *Etheostoma perlongum.
    Copeia* (3), 561-567. **257**
Shuter, B.J. & Koonce, J.F. (1977). A dynamic
    model of the Western Lake Erie walleye
    (Stizostedion vitreum vitreum) population.
    J. Fish. Res. Board Can. 34 (10), 1972-1982.
    189,190,191
Shuter, B.J., Koonce, J.F. & Regier, H.A. (1979).
    Modelling the Western Lake Erie walleye popu-
    lation: a feasibility study. *Tech. Rep. Great
    Lakes Fish. Comm.* No. 32, 40 pp. **190**

Siefert, R.E. & Spoor. W.A. (1974). Effects of
reduced oxygen on embryos and larvae of the
white sucker, coho salmon, brook trout and
walleye. In: *The Early Life History of
Fish*. (Ed. J.H.S. Blaxter). 487-495.
Springer-Verlag. New York. **88,91**

Simkiss, K. (1974). Calcium metabolism of fish in
relation to ageing. In: *Ageing of Fish* (Ed.
T.B. Bagenal). 1-12. Unwin Bros Ltd. Old
Woking. **19**

Sjoebeck, M.-L., Haux, C., Larsson, A. & Lithner,
G. (1984). Biochemical and haematological
studies on perch, *Perca fluviatilis* from the
cadmium-contaminated River Emaan. *Ecotoxicol.
Environ. Saf. 8* (3), 303-312. **241**

Skorping, A. (1980). Population biology of the
nematode, *Camallanus lacustris* in perch, *Perca
fluviatilis* L., from an oligotrophic Lake in
Norway. *J. Fish Biol. 16* (5), 483-492. **167**

Smart, H.J. & Gee, J.H. (1979). Coexistence and
resource partitioning in two species of darters (Percidae), *Etheostoma nigrum* and *Percina
maculata*. *Can. J. Zool. 57* (10), 2061-2071.
253

Smith, C.L. (1954). Pleistocene fishes of the
Berends fauna of Beaver County, Oklahoma.
Copeia (4), 282-289. **176**

Smith, H.M. (1892). Report on an investigation of
the fisheries of Lake Ontario. *Bull. U.S.
Fish. Comm. 10* (1890), 177-215. **177**

Smith, L.L., Jr., Broderius, S.J., Oseid, D.M.,
Kimball, G.L. & Koenst, W.M. (1978). Acute
toxicity of hydrogen cyanide to freshwater
fishes. *Arch. Environ. Contam. Toxicol. 7*
(3), 325-337. **242**

Smith, L.L., Jr., & Koenst, J. (1975). Temperature effects on eggs and fry of percoid
fishes. *U.S. Environ. Protect. Agency Proj.
18050 PAB*, 99 pp. **91**

Smith, L.L. Jr., Kramer, R.H. & Oseid, D.M.
(1966). Longterm effects of conifer-
groundwood paper fiber on walleyes. *Trans
Am. Fish. Soc. 95* (1), 60-70. **241**

Smith, O.H. & Van Oosten, J. (1939). Tagging experiments with lake trout, whitefish and other
species of fish from Lake Michigan. *Trans Am.
Fish. Soc. 69*, 63-84. **141**

Smith, R.J.F. (1979). Alarm reaction of Iowa and
johnny darters *(Etheostoma*, Percidae, Pisces)
to chemicals from injured conspecifics. *Can.
J. Zool. 57* (6), 1278-1282. **255**

Smith, R.J.F. (1982). Reaction of *Percina nigro-fasciata, Ammocrypta beani* and *Etheostoma swaini* (Percidae, Pisces) to conspecific and intergeneric skin extracts. *Can. J. Zool. 60* (5), 1067-1072. **255**

Smyly, W.J.P. (1952). Observations on the food of the fry of perch *(Perca fluviatilis* L.) in Windermere. *Proc. Zool. Soc. Lond. 122,* 407-416. **91,94**

Solomon, D.J. & Brafield, A.E. (1972). The energetics of feeding, metabolism and growth of perch *(Perca fluviatilis* L.). *J. Anim. Ecol. 41,* 699-719. **116**

Spanovskaya, V.D. & Grygorash, V.A. (1977). Development and food of age-0 Eurasian perch *(Perca fluviatilis)* in reservoirs near Moscow, USSR. *J. Fish. Res. Board Can. 34,* 1551-1558. **113**

Stacey, N.E. (1984). Control of the timing of ovulation by exogenous and endogenous factors. In: *Fish Reproduction: Strategies and Tactics.* (Eds G.W. Potts & R.J. Wooton). 207-222. Academic Press. London. **74,75**

Stanescu, G. (1971). *Romanichthys valsanicola,* Pisces, Percidae, and its distribution in Romania and the causes of its extinction. *Vestn. Cesk. Spol. Zool. 35* (2), 132-135. **13,263**

Starmach, J. 1983. Electrophoretic separation of blood plasma of perch, *Perca fluviatilis,* living in the Rybnik and Goczalkowice reservoirs, Poland. *Acta Hydrobiol. 24* (3), 283-288. **178**

Steffens, W. (1960). Ernahrung und Wachstum des jungen Zanders *(Lucioperca lucioperca* (L.)) in Teichen. *Z. Fisch. 9* (3/4), 161-272. **107,238**

Steindachner, F. (1878). Ichthyologische Beitrage (VII). X. *Perca fluviatilis,* Lin. Sitzungsber. Akad. Wissensch. Wien. *78* (1), 398. **176**

Sterba, G. (1962). *Freshwater Fishes of the World.* Vista Books. London. 878 pp. **177**

Sterns, S.L. (1981). Occurrence of accessory checks on the scales of walleye fingerlings stocked in mid-August. *Prog. Fish-Cult. 43* (1), 46-47. **51**

Suriano, D.M. & Beverley-Burton, M. (1981).
Urocleidus aculeatus (Van Cleave and Mueller,
1932) (Monogenea: Ancyrocephalinae) from
Stizostedion vitreum (Mitchill)(Pisces:
Percidae) in eastern North America: anatomy
and systematic position. *Can. J. Zool.* *59*,
240-245. **156**

Svärdson, G. (1976). Interspecific population
dominance in fish communities of Scandinavian
lakes. *Inst. Freshwat. Res. Drottningholm.
Rep.* No. 55. **204**

Svetovidov, A.N. & Dorofeeva, E.A. (1963). Syste-
matics, origin and history of the distribution
of the Eurasian and North American perches and
pikeperches (Genera *Perca, Lucioperca* and
Stizostedion). Vopr. Ikhtiol. *3* (4), 625-
651. (In Russian). **175**

Svirskii, A.M., Malinin, L.K. & Ovchinnikov, V.I.
(1976). On the diel rhythm of motor activity
in perch. *Inf. Byull. Biol. Vnutr. Vod.* (30),
12-14. (In Russian). **140**

Swenson, W.A. & Smith, L.L., Jr. (1973). Gastric
digestion, food consumption, feeding periodicity and food conversion efficiency in walleye *(Stizostedion vitreum vitreum). J. Fish
Res. Board Can.* *30* (9), 1327-1336.
110,113,116

Swenson, W.A. & Smith, L.L., Jr. (1976). Influence of food, competition, predation, and
cannibalism on walleye *(Stizostedion vitreum)*
and sauger *(Stizostedion canadense)* populations in Lake of the Woods, Minnesota. *J.
Fish. Res. Board Can.* *33* (9), 1946-1954.
97,112

Swift, D.R. & Pickford, G.E. (1965). Seasonal
variations in the hormone content of the
pituitary gland of the perch, *Perca
fluviatilis* L. *Gen. Comp. Endocrinol.* *5*, 354-
365. **45**

Sychevskaya, E.K. & Devyatkin, E.V. (1960). Per-
vyje nachodky ryb iz neogenovych i nizne cet-
verticnych otlozenij. *Gornogo. Altaja. Dokl.
Akad. Nauk. SSSR.* *142* (1), 175. **175**

Taylor, M.W. (1981). A generalized inland fishery
simulator for management biologists. *N. Am.
J. Fish. Manage.* *1* (1), 60-72. **230,131**

Tedla, S. & Fernando, C.H. (1969). Observations
on the biology of *Ergasilus* spp. (Cyclopoidea:
Copepoda) infesting North American freshwater
fishes. *Can. J. Zool.* *47* (3), 405-408.
148,165

Teichmann, H. (1954). Vergleichende untersuchungen an der nase der fische. *Z. Morphol. Oekol. Tiere. 43,* 171-212. **39**

Theofan, G. & Goetz, F.W. (1983). The in vitro synthesis of final maturational steroids by ovaries of brook trout *(Salvelinus fontinalis)* and yellow perch *(Perca flavescens). Gen. Comp. Endocrinol. 51* (1), 84-95. **75**

Thorpe, J. (1977). Synopsis of biological data on the perch, *Perca fluviatilis* Linnaeus, 1758 and *Perca flavescens* (Mitchill, 1814). *FAO Fish. Synop.* No. 113, vii + 138 pp. **9,72,76,81,82,103,109,113,140,177,182,184**

Treasurer, J.W. (1981). Some aspects of the reproductive biology of perch *Perca fluviatilis* L. Fecundity, maturation and spawning behaviour. *J. Fish Biol. 18,* 729-740. **77**

Treasurer, J.W. (1983). Estimates of egg and viable embryo production in a lacustrine perch, *Perca fluviatilis. Environ. Biol. Fishes. 8* (1), 3-16. **88**

Treasurer, J.W. & Holliday, F.G.T. (1981). Some aspects of the reproductive biology of perch, *Perca fluviatilis* L. A histological description of the reproductive cycle. *J. Fish Biol. 18* (3), 359-376. **68,69**

Troitskiy, S.K. & Tsunikova, Ye. P. (1976). The time of spawning migrations and spawning of the pikeperch, *Lucioperca lucioperca,* in the Azov-Kuban Region. *J. Ichthyol. 16* (4), 592-598. **79**

Tsepkin, E.A. (1984a). Fish remains from ancient settlements on the Baltic Sea coast. *Byull. Mosk. O-va Ispyt. Prir. Otd. Biol. 89* (2), 50-58. (In Russian). **211**

Tsepkin, E.A. (1984b). History of the commercial ichthyofauna in the Upper Dnieper River USSR. *Biol. Nauki (Mosc.). 10* (7), 48-52. (In Russian). **211**

Turner, C.L. (1927). A case of hermaphroditism in the perch. *Anat. Rec. 37* (2), 186. **36**

Ultsch, G.R., Boschung, H. & Ross, M.J. (1978). Metabolism, critical oxygen tension and habitat selection in darters *(Etheostoma). Ecology. 59* (1), 99-107. **256**

Uthe, J.F., Roberts, E., Clarke, L.W. & Tsuyuki, H. (1966). Comparative electropherograms of representatives of the families Petromyzontidae, Esocidae, Centrarchidae and Percidae. *J. Fish. Res. Board Can. 23* (11), 1663-1671. **179**

Uthe, J.F. & Ryder, R.A. (1970). Regional variation in muscle polymorphism in walleye *(Stizostedion vitreum vitreum)* as related to morphology. *J. Fish. Res. Board Can. 27* (5), 923-927. **179**

Utrecht, W.L. van. (1979). Remarks of the anatomy and ontogeny of scales of teleosts. *Aquaculture. 17* (2), 159-174. **20**

Vivier, P. (1951). Poissons et crustacés d'eau douce acclimatés en France en eaux libres depuis le debut du siecle. *Terre Vie.* (2), 57-82. **178**

Volodin, V.M. (1980). Plodovitost, okunya *Perca fluviatilis* L., Rybinskogo Vodokhranilishcha. *Vopr. Ikhtiol. 19* (4), 672-679. **73,74**

Walker, R. (1969a). Virus associated with epidermal hyperplasia in fish. *Natl. Cancer Inst. Monogr. 31,* 195-207. **145**

Walker, R. (1969b). Epidermal hyperplasia in fish: two types without visible virus. *Natl. Cancer Inst. Monogr. 31,* 209-213. **146**

Walker, R.E & Applegate, R.L. (1976). Growth, food and possible ecological effects of young-of-the-year walleyes in a South Dakota prairie pothole. *Prog. Fish-Cult. 38,* 217-220. **237**

Walker, R. & Weissenberg, R. (1965). Conformity of light and electron microscopic studies on virus particle distribution in lymphocystis tumor cells of fish. *Ann. N.Y. Acad. Sci. 126* (1), 375-385. **146**

Ward, F.J. & Robinson, G.G.C. (1974). A review of the research on the limnology of West Blue Lake, Manitoba. *J. Fish. Res. Board Can. 31,* 977-1005. **103**

Weatherley, A.H. (1963). Thermal stress and interrenal tissue in the perch, *Perca fluviatilis* (Linnaeus). *Proc. Zool. Soc. Lond. 141,* 527-555. **48**

Webb, P.W. (1975). Hydrodynamics and energetics of fish propulsion. *Bull. Fish. Res. Board Can.* (190), 1-159. **137**

Webb, P.W. (1978). Fast-start performance and body form in seven species of teleost fish. *J. Exp. Biol. 74,* 211-226. **136**

Weiler, W. (1933). Die Fischreste aus dem Ober-
    pliocän von Willershausen. *Arch. Hydrobiol.*
    25, 291-304. **175**
Weinbauer, J.D., Thiel, D.A., Kaczynski, V.W. &
    Martin, C.S. (1980). Receiving stream
    fisheries studies relative to secondary
    treated pulp and paper mill effluents.
    Tappi. 63 (10), 121-125. **240**
Weinfurter, E. (1950). Die oberpannonische Fisch-
    fauna vom Eichkogel bei Mödling.
    Sitzungsber. *Österr. Akad. Wiss. (Math.*
    Naturwiss. Kl.) 159 (1-5), 37-50. **175**
Weissenberg, R. (1965). Fifty years of research
    on the lymphocystis virus disease of fishes
    (1914-1964). *Ann. N.Y. Acad. Sci. 126* (1),
    362-374. **146**
West, G. & Leonard, J. (1978). Culture of yellow
    perch with emphasis on development of eggs and
    fry. In: *Selected Coolwater Fishes of North*
    America. (Ed. R.L. Kendall). *Am. Fish. Soc.*
    Spec. Publ. (11), 172-176. **237**
Wheeler, A. & Maitland, P.S. (1973). The scarcer
    freshwater fishes of the British Isles. I.
    Introduced species. *J. Fish Biol. 5*, 49-68.
    178
Whiteside, M.C., Swindoll, C.M. & Doolittle, W.L.
    (1985). Factors affecting the early life his-
    tory of yellow perch, *Perca flavescens.*
    Environ. Biol. Fishes. 12 (1), 47-56. **92,94**
Willemsen, J. (1977a). Influence of temperature
    on feeding, growth and mortality of pikeperch
    and perch. *Verh. int. ver. Limnol. 20* (3),
    2127-2133. **48**
Willemsen, J. (1977b). Population dynamics of
    percids in Lake Ijssel and some smaller lakes
    in the Netherlands. *J. Fish. Res. Board Can.*
    34 (10), 1710-1719. **190,223,245**
Willoughby, L.G. (1970). Mycological aspects of a
    disease of young perch in Windermere. *J. Fish*
    Biol. 2, 113-116. **148**
Winberg, G.G. (1956). Rate of metabolism and food
    requirements of fishes. Belorussian State
    University. Minsk. *Fish. Res. Board Can.*
    Transl. Ser. No. 194, 1-253. **118**
Wolfert, D.R. (1969). Maturity and fecundity of
    walleyes from the eastern and western basins
    of Lake Erie. *J. Fish. Res. Board Can. 26*
    (7), 1877-1888. **73**

Wolfert, D.R. (1981). The commercial fishery for walleyes in New York waters of Lake Erie, 1959-1978. *N. Am. J. Fish. Manage. 1* (2), 112-126. **229**

Wolfert, D.R. & Van Meter. H.D. (1978). Movements of walleyes tagged in Eastern Lake Erie. *N.Y. Fish Game J. 25* (1), 16-22. **143**

Wong, B. & Ward, F.J. (1972). Size selection of *Daphnia pulicaria* by yellow perch *(Perca flavescens)* fry in West Blue Lake, Manitoba. *J. Fish. Res. Board Can. 29* (12), 1761-1764. **100**

Woodbury, L.A. (1942). A sudden mortality of fishes accompanying a supersaturation of oxygen in Lake Waubesa, Wisconsin. *Trans Am. Fish. Soc. 71*, 112-117. **131**

Woynarovich, E. (1960). Aufzucht der zanderlarven bis sum raubfischalter. *Z. Fisch. 9* (1/2), 73-83. **56,235**

Woynarovich, E. (1962). Die kunstliche erbrutung des zanders. *Z. Fisch. 10* (8-10), 677-680. **106**

Yakovlev, V.N. (1960). O sistematicheskom polozhenii presnovodnykh ryb is zeogena Zapadnoi Sibiri. *Paleontol. Zh. 3*, 102-108. **175**

Yakovlev, V.N. (1961). Rasprostranenie presnovodnykh ryb neogena Golarktiki i zoogeographicheskoe raionirovanie. *Vopr. Ikhtiol. 1* (2), 209-220. **176**

Yakovleva, A.S., Amstislavskiy, A.Z., & Baymuratov, A. (1976). Features of the relative growth of some internal organs in the perch, *Perca fluviatilis. J. Ichthyol. 16* (3), 419-426. **178**

Yamamoto, T., Kelly, R.K. & Nielsen, O. (1985). Morphological differentiation of virus-associated skin tumors of walleye *(Stizostedion vitreum vitreum). Fish Pathol. 20* (2/3), 361-372. **145,146**

Yamamoto, T., MacDonald, R.D., Gillespie, D.C. & Kelly, R.K. (1976). Viruses associated with lymphocystis disease and dermal sarcoma of walleye. *J. Fish. Res. Board Can. 33* (11), 2408-2419. **145**

Young, J.Z. (1962). *The Life of Vertebrates.* Oxford University Press. Oxford. XVI + 820 pp. **25**

Zelenkov, V.M. (1982). Early gametogenesis and sex differentiation in the perch, *Perca fluviatilis. J. Ichthyol. 21* (2), 124-130. **67**

Zhdanova, N.N. (1961). Ves molodi sudaka, vypus-
kaemoi iz Donskikh nerestovo-vyrastnykh kho-
zyaisty. *Rybn. Khoz.* (10), 19-22. **235**
Zhmurova, Ye. K.H. (1982). Daily food ration of
pikeperch in spawning and breeding farms on
the Don. *Hydrobiol. J. 18* (4), 97-98. **236**
Zhmurova, Ye. K.H. & Somkina, N.V. (1976). The
effect of salinity on the early development
stanzas of the walleye *(Lucioperca
lucioperca)*. *J. Ichthyol. 16* (3), 511-514.
128,237
Zyznar, E.S. & Ali, M.A. (1975). An interpre-
tative study of the organization of the visual
cells and tapetum lucidum of *Stizostedion*.
Can. J. Zool. 53, 180-196. **42**

Abramis brama 190,222, 223
abundance (see also population dynamics) 100,169,170,171,182,185, 186,187,190,191,192,201, 202, 205,207,242
Acanthcephalus lucii 160,164
Achlya 147
acidity 114
Acipenser fulvescens 216,219
Actheres percarum *162*, 165
activity (see movements)
Aeromonas hydrophila 147
A. salmonicida 147
ageing (see also operculum) 50,51
    age at maturity 50, 59,61,72,180,182,197, 230,245,249,258
    fins 51
    validity (verification) 50,51,53
alewife see *Alosa pseudoharengus*
algal blooms 131,140,221
allometric 53
Alosa pseudoharengus 99,202,203
Ammocrypta 5,8,12,251, 256,260
    distribution 10,12
A. pellucida 252,255
anchovy see *Engraulis encrasicolus*
Anguilla anguilla 190, 192,221,229

A. rostrata 185
Aphanomyces 147
Apophallus brevis 151, 171
apron see *Zingel asper*
Argulus foliaceus 147, 162,165,166,168
Argulus sp. 169
Artemia sp. 101
Asellus 97,98
A. aquaticus 164
asprete see *Romanichthys valsanicola*
Atherina presbyter 99
ATPase 27,124,127

back calculation 53,57
bacteria 145,146,147, 172,240
    furunculosis 147
Balkhush perch see *Perca schrenki*
Balon's ruffe see *Gymnocephalus baloni*
Bayou darter see *Etheostoma rubrum*
benthos (benthic organisms) 94,103,266
biomass 186,187,188,194, 196,197,198,199,200,205, 207,233
blackbanded darter see *Percina nigrofasciata*
blackside darter see *Percina maculata*
blackside snubnose darter see *Etheostoma duryi*
Blicca bjoerkna 99
blotchside logperch see

318

Percina burtoni
blue pike see
Stizostedion vitreum glaucum
Bosmina obtusirostris 96
Bothriocephalus sp. 156, 167,171
bream see *Abramis brama*
broad whitefish see *Coregonus nasus*
brown trout see *Salmo trutta*
buccal cavity 22,23,43, 89,107,108
bullhead see *Cottus gobio*
Bunodera lucioperca 152, 166,167,171
B. sacculata 152,167
burbot see *Lota lota*
Bythotrephes longimanus 96,98

Caenis 96
calcium 19,40,44
Camallanus lacustris 158,167
C. oxycephalus 158,171
cannibalism 91,97,107, 181,182,183,184,186,187, 190,192,194,198,199,201, 205,237
Carangidae 2,3
Carassius carassius 99
carp see *Cyprinus carpio*
Caspian roach see *Rutilus rutilus caspicus*
catch per unit effort see fishing
catfish see *Ictalurus nebulosus*
Catostomus catostomus 139
C. commersoni 139,206
Cenozoic 175
Centropomidae 2,3
Chaetodon ocellatus 175

Chaetodontidae 3,175
chain pickerel see *Esox niger*
Chaoborus sp. 97,110
charr see *Salvelinus alpinus*
chemoreception 37
chromatophores 19,40,81, 85,89
    melanophores 66,81, 82,84,85
chromosomes 44
Chydorus ovalis 96
Cichlidae 2,3
circulatory system 33-34,35,85
    duct of Cuvier 34,86
    heart 31,32,33,38,40, 82,84,85,155,156,168
    plasma 124,125,126, 127,128,129
cisco (lake herring) see *Coregonus artedii*
Clinostomum complanatum 152,166
C. marginatum 152,171
Clupeonella sp. 97
coldwater darter see *Etheostoma ditrema*
competition 59,62,170, 177,185,186,187,190,199, 201-206,253,257
    proportional, similarity factor 202,203
condition 54,193,226
copper (see also pollutants) 238
Coregonus albula 99,100, 221
C. artedii 216,218
C. clupeaformis 139,206, 216,218,219,220
C. nasus 139
Coregonus sp. 100,204
Corixa 97
Coryphaenidae 2,3
Cottus gobio 263
Couesius plumbeus 206
Crangonyx pseudogracilis 96,98
Crepidostomum cooperi

152,167,171
crucian carp see
Carassius carassius
Crustacea (see also
parasites and diseases)
14,97,114,164,167,168,
237,245,249,250
culture (see also
rearing) 173,232,233–239
   artificial
   fertilisation 234
   artificial foods
   235,238
   hatchery 235
   incubation 234,235
   Zoug jars 235,236
Cyclops bicuspidatus
163
cypress darter see
Etheostoma proeliare
Cyprinidae 165,172,175
257
cyprinodont 126
Cyprinus carpio 46,75,
218,221,238
cytology 44

*Dactinitoides cotylo-
phora* 158,167,171
Daphnia hyalina 96,98,
100,101,102
D. pulex 100,113
D. pulicaria 100
Daphnia sp. 101,113
darters see *Ammocrypta,
Etheostoma* and *Percina*
density see population
dynamics
development 80–91,92,
148,166,167,168,237,260,
261
   blastula 81,83,87
   cleavage 81,82,84
   embryo 80,81,83,84,
   85,86,87,88,129,164,
   166,180,235,260
   gastrula 81,83,87
   hatching 20,81,82,83,
   85,86,87,88,89,92,93,
   135,165,166,174,180,
   182,194,198,199,217,

235,236,243,250,260
   incubation (see also
   culture) 81,85,87,88,
   91,261
Diacyclops thomasi 91
Diaptomus gracilis 96
D. minutus 100
digestion 94,110,111,
113–115,169
   absorption 33,115
   bile 114
   pinocytosis 33,115
   stomach (gastric)
   evacuation 103,109,
   110,111,239
Diphyllobothrium latum
156,166,167
Diplostomum gasterostei
153,169,170
D. spathaceum 153,163
DNA 175
Don ruffe see *Gymno-
cephalus acerina*
Dorsoma cepedianum 99
dusky darter see
Percina sciera

eastern sand darter see
Ammocrypta pellucida
eel see *Anguilla
anguilla* and *A. ros-
trata*
egestion 112,115,117,118
   faeces 116,125,163
egg see gametes
electrophoresis 59,179
embryogenesis 46
emerald shiner see
Notropis atherinoides
enclosures 202
endocrine system 34,
43–44
   hormones 19,43,45,46,
   49,66,67,74–75,125,
   126,166,168,169
   ovary see gonads
   pineal body (organ)
   37,43
   pituitary 37,39,43,
   45,46,49,74,125,126
   testes see gonads

urophysis 37,43
energetics (see also
metabolism) 115-121
  catabolic 59,66,128,
  185
  energy content 54,55,
  120,121
  energy intake
  (supply) 72,94,111,
  115,116,121,137
  gross efficiency
  116,118
  net efficiency
  116,118
Engraulis encrasicolus
99
enzymes 114,115,128
  lipase 114
  phosphatase 115
  protease 114
Epinephelus 1
Ergasilus luciopercarum
162,173
E. sieboldi 162,164,166
Erpobdella octoculata
98
Esox lucius 46,136,139,
140,147,163,164,169,185,
190,192,193,194,195,196,
197,198,199,200,204,205,
206
E. niger 185
estuaries
  Firth of Szczecin 224
  Firth of Vistula 224
Etheostoma 5,8,12,175,
251,254,256,258,259,261,
  distribution 10,12
E. blennioides 253,258
E. boschungi 254,256
E. caeruleum 253,255
E. ditrema 259
E. duryi 254,256
E. exile 255
E. flabellare 253,254,
255,256,261
E. fonticola 254,255,
258,261
E. fusiforme 254,256
E. maculatum 260
E. microperca 251,261

E. nigrum 252,253,254,
255,260
E. perlongum 257,258
E. proeliare 261
E. rubrum 258
E. rufilineatum 254,256
E. spectabile 180
E. squamiceps 254,256,
257,260
E. variatum 258
E. vitreum 255
Etheostomatini 5,8,251-
262
  genital papillae 257,
  258,259
  spatial distribution
  253
Eudiaptomus gracilis
100
Eustrongylides tubifex
158,171
excretion (see also
ionic and water balance;
kidneys) 47,95,112,115,
117,128,129
  ammonia 116,117,118,
  124,129
excretory and
reproductive systems
34-36

fantail darter see
Etheostoma flabellare
fathead minnow see
Pimephales promelas
feeding 45,46,49,57,89,
90,91,94,101,102,103,
104,105,106,107,108,136,
141,143,169,172,187,192,
202,204,235,237,250,253,
255,257,266
  consumption 94,104,
  109-113,117,120,183,
  186,187,188,236,237,
  239
  diet 59,100,169,185
  food selection 99-108
  gape 99,100,101
  mechanics of 107-108
  period 103,143
  prey 94,96,97,98,99,

100,101,104,106,107,
108,110,112,113,174,
177,182,183,185,186,
187,192,202,204,205,
206,237,244,255
ration
100,109,113,116,118,
119,183,184,187,188,
238
fins 2,14,18,24,26,
27,30,79,80,83,85,89,92,
108,146,149,150,
152,153,154,156,161,
162,164,232,244,245,
249,251,263,264
fishing (see also
mortality)
169,177,201,207,208,209,
213,216,219,221,229,230
   angling (sports;
   recreational)
   63,105,106,185,192,
   208,211,213,215,216,
   222,223,227,228,230,
   231,233,249
   catch per unit effort
   58,105,189,228
   commercial 63,182,
   189,192,193,196,201,
   207,208,209,211,213,
   214,215,216,217,218,
   219,221,222,223,227,
   228,233,249,250
   domestic 213,216
  fishing gear 63,193,
  210,211,213,221,226,
  228,229,243
   efficiency 211,217,
   226
   fyke nets 211,213
   gill net 185,192,
   193,210,211,213,217,
   219,220,221,227,229,
   230,234
   hook and line 211,
   213,226,230
   jigger (ice) 219,220
   Miller sampler 187
   plumb-line 192
   pound net
   192,193,211,213,219

   seines 211, 213, 221,
   226
   selectivity 211,226,
   227
   trammel net 211,213
   trap 191,211,213,217,
   219,226,227,234
   trawl 187,203,211,
   213,226,229
   variability 227
fountain darter see
Etheostoma fonticola
fry 46,80,82,91,93,94,
97,100,103,113,129,146,
172,182,184,185,187,188,
201,237,266
Fundulus heteroclitus 46
fungi 145,147,148,172,
235

gametes 19,74,259
   number of sperm 69
   oocytes (eggs;ova)
   36,66,67,68,69,74,75,
   76,77,79,80,81,85,86,
   88,129,135,136,142,
   148,163,165,166,167,
   169,174,181,184,196,
   197,198,201,231,232,
   234,235,241,242,245,
   248,250,258,259,260,
   261,263,266
   spermatozoa (sperm)
   36,69,70,74,77,79,
   80,81,234,259,260
Gammarus lacustris 96
G. pulex 98,110
gills 22,30-31,33,37,
38,40,44,82,89,90,108,
116,122,123,124,126,128,
129,130,131,132,135,148,
149,150,151,152,153,154,
156,161,162,164,165,240
   chloride cells 30,122
   circulatory system 35
   gill rakers 2,31,90,
   91,253
   lamellae 30,31,122,
   131,241
gizzard shad see
Dorosoma cepedianum
glassy darter see

Etheostoma vitreum
Gobiomorphus cotidanus
109
goldeye see *Hiodon alosoides*
gonads 31,66,70,112,120, 121
    gonadectomies 66
    hermaphrodites 36
    ovary 32,36,43,66,67, 68,69,70,74,80,121, 145,159,258
    oviduct 36,66
    testes 34,36,43,44, 66,69,70,71,121,145
grayling see *Thymallus thymallus*
great crested grebe see *Podiceps cristatus*
Great Lakes Fishery Commission 217
greenside darter see *Etheostoma blennioides*
growth 20,45-65,66,72, 91,94,95,100,115,116, 120,128,129,135,144,174, 180,181,185,186,188,189, 190,194,196,199,201,202, 204,209,210,223,230,235, 237,238,241,245,249,257, 263,264
    genetic differences 59
    growth rates 50,57, 59,65,118,119,128
    logistic curve 56
    scope for growth 45, 116
gut (viscera) 1,31-33, 36,89,90,91,125,148,152, 153,154,156,157,158,159, 163,168,172,242
    circulatory system 34,35
    endocrine cells 33
    gall bladder 31,89, 114,149,152,153
    intestinal (pyloric) caecae 31,32,33,91, 115,152,153,155,156, 157,163

intestine 31,33,40, 90,109,113,114,115, 149,150,151,152,153, 154,155,156,157,158, 159,160,161,163,164, 167
liver 31,32,34,85,89, 126,149,152,155,157, 158,159,163,240,241, 242
mucosa 31,33,114,115
oesophagus 31,32,108
pancreas 31,32,43,114
spleen 31,32,150,155
stomach 31,32,33,40, 89,90,91,99,100,101, 102,104,109,110,111, 113,151,153,155,158, 159,160,187,206
Gymnocephalus 5,8,244, 245,249
    coloration 244
G. acerina 8,9,244,245, 247
G. baloni 8,9,244,245 247
G. cernua 8,9,99,100, 146,190,229,244,245, 247,248
G. schraetser 8,9,180, 244,245,247,248

habitat 170
Haemulidae 2,3
hermaphrodites see gonads
Herpesvirus vitreum 145,146
Hiodon alosoides 219
Hirudinea (see also parasites and diseases) 97,98,164,168,172,206
homogenetic sex 67
humpback whitefish see *Coregonus clupeaformis*
hybridisation 176,177, 180
Hydrachna 162,165
Hydroporus 97

Ictalurus nebulosus 221

*Icthyophthirius
multi-filiis* 148,149,
166,167,168,169
immunology 172-173
inconnu see *Stenodus
leucichthys*
internal and external
factors (see also
endocrine system) 47,136
    acid stress 129
    carbon dioxide 128,
    129,131,135
    critical thermal
    maximum 46,48
    day lengths 45
    genetical 64,65
    incipient lethal
    temperatures 46,48
    light 49,92,105,106,
    107,135,140,144,167,
    168,238
    oxygen (see also res-
    piration) 88,91,118,
    122,124,126,130,131,
    132,133,135,136,144,
    167,168,172,174,176,
    181,204,235,240,241,
    242,254,256
    pH 27,88,113,114,115,
    128,129,130,144,167,
    168,174,204,240
    pheromones 75
    photoperiod 49,50,
    75,76
    salinity 47,79,122,
    126,127,128,129,144,
    167,168,176,237,249
    temperature 45,46,47,
    48,49,57,59,60,61,64,
    65,75,76,78,79,80,81,
    85,87,88,91,92,109,
    110,112,113,116,117,
    118,119,120,128,130,
    132,133,134,135,136,
    137,138,140,144,147,
    166,167,172,174,181,
    182,188,189,190,192,
    194,196,197,198,199,
    200,204,217,224,225,
    233,235,242,248,249,
    253,255,258,259,260,

    261
    water velocity
    (current speed)
    79,80,137,139,144,
    167,176
interrenal tissue see
kidney
iodine 43
ionic and water balance
34,44,122-130,172
    acid-base equilibrium
    124,128,129
    bicarbonate 124,125,
    128,129
    calcium 124,125,127
    chloride 114,124,125,
    126,127,240
    hydrogen ion 124,128,
    129
    hypophysectomy 126
    osmoregulatory 37,
    124,240
    osmotic pressure 122
    potassium, 124,125,
    127,129
    sodium 114,124,125,
    126,127,129
Iowa darter see
Etheostoma exile
iridocytes 19

johnny darter see
Etheostoma nigrum
juvenile 62,90,91,98,
113,117,140,141,166,207,
208,233,242,257

kidneys 31,32,34,43,44,
122,123,124,125,155,240
    circulatory system
    34,35
    head kidney 34,35,43,
    44,48,125,126
    nephrons 34,125
    renal action (see
    also ionic and water
    balance) 124
    trunk kidney 34,44

lake chub see *Couesius
plumbeus*

lake sturgeon see
Acipenser fulvescens
lake trout see
Salvelinus namaycush
lake whitefish see
Coregonus clupeaformis
lakes and rivers
  Arges River 13,263
  Bigland Tarn 142
  Buffalo-Niagara River
  143
  Canton Reservoir 78
  Cazenovia Lake 140
  Churchill River 240
  Claytor Lake 233
  Dailey Lake 147
  Danube Delta 99
  Danube River 12,245,
  263,264
  Dauphin Lake 72
  Dniester River 245,
  264
  Don River 76,245
  Doubs River 178
  Elbe River 177
  Escanaba Lake 59,230
  Estang du Vaccares
  178
  Great Ouse Relief
  Channel 178
  Heming Lake 76,169,
  173
  Keyes Lake 179
  Klicava Reservoir 205
  Kolyma River 176
  Kubon River 79
  Lac des Mille 227
  Lake Baikal 126
  Lake Balaton 59,60,
  213,221-223
  Lake Champlain 179
  Lake Constance
  (Bodensee) 223
  Lake Erie 20,72,73,
  98,99,120,143,171,
  177,189,190,191,201,
  213-219,223,227,229
  Lake Gogebic 62,69,
  93
  Lake Ijssel 48,72,
  190-192,223,245

Lake Ladoga 107
Lake McConaughy 230,
231
Lake Memphremagog
113,202
Lake Mendota 138
Lake Michigan 76,77,
179,202,203
Lake Monona 48
Lake of the Woods 97,
113
Lake Ontario 177
Lake Opeongo 167,171
Lake Superior 142
Lake Tyulen 182-185,
201
Lake Vortsjarv 229
Lake Waccamaw 257
Lake Waubesca 131
Lake Winnipeg 219,226
Lesser Slave Lake 176
Llyn Tegid 92,169
Loch Leven 113
Mackenzie River 176
Mississippi River
176,254
Mozhaisky Reservoir
113
Nadym River 148
Neuse River 127
Oneida Lake 56,59,63,
88,92,93,100,101,103,
112,118,142,145,171,
185-189,192,205,232
Pearl River 76
Pskov-Chudskoy Lake
100
Rhine River 177,178
Rhône River 12,178,
264
Riul-Doamnei River
13,263
River Angeran 140
River Bug 178
River Dneiper 178,
211,245
River Emaan 241
River Thames 253
Rybinsk Reservoir 72,
73,100
Sâone River 178

Shebandowan Lake 106
Slapton Ley 50,54,77,
97,170,193
Southern Indian Lake
78
Sövdeborgssjön 113
Syam Lake 100
Uchinsky Reservoir
113
Vardar River 12,264
Vilsan River 13,263
Volga Delta 100,113
Volga River 126
Wapun Lake 51,61
Welland Canal 216
West Blue Lake 100,
140,201,205
Windermere 51,52,53,
54,55,56,57,58,60,63,
64,66,72,76,92,94,95,
97,98,100,101,102,
103,104,105,111,112,
113,120,121,139,141,
147,148,178,186,192-
201,207,208,223,227
Wolf Lake 206,210
Lampsilis radiata 161,
164
largemouth bass see
Micropterus salmoides
larvae 79,88,89,91,92,
94,96,110,112,135,136,
138,142,148,163,164,165,
166,167,168,173,174,
180,184,231,232,233,
234,235,237,248,249,
250,254,261
lateral line (see also
nervous system)
number of scales
along 20,244
least darter see
Etheostoma microperca
leeches see Hirudinea
Lee's phenomenon 53
length-weight relation-
ships 53
Lepomis gibbosus 202,221
Leptodora kindti 96,98
Leptolegnia 147
Leptomitus 147

Leptorhynchoides
thecatus 160,167,171
Lernaea cyprinacea 162,
165,166
light see internal and
external factors
Ligula intestinalis 144,
157,166,169
logperch see *Percina*
caprodes
longevity 45,50,64-65,
166
longhead darter see
Etheostoma macrocephala
longnose sucker
see *Catostomus*
catostomus
Lota lota 139,206
Luciopercinae 5,8
Luciopercini 5,8
Lutjanidae 2,3
Lymnaea peregra 170

malate dehydrogenase
(MDH) 179,180,233
management 171,208,219,
221,227,228-233,239,243
bag limits 228,230
closed seasons 219,
228
quota 219,228,229
size limits (minimum)
228,229,230
stocking 177,179,
231-233,234,235,237
maturity see ageing –
age at maturity
mesenteries 152,154,155,
156,158,159,160,161
metabolism 94,112,115,
118,124,130,174,240,241
aerobic 130,168
anaerobic 27,168
assimilation 95
metabolic 43,49,128,
174
metabolic rate 47,241
specific dynamic
action 47,115,116
Micropterus dolomieui
205,216

M. salmoides 221
milt see gametes
minnows see Cyprinidae
Miocene 175
Mollusca 161,164,168
Morone americana 186
M. chrysops 217,219,229
morphoedaphic index
(MEI) 224
mortality 45-65,88,128,
135,147,148,171,172,
173,174,181,183,187,
190,196,201,207,208,
209,229,232,237,254,256
    fishing 181,190,196,
    210,230,232
    mortality rates 62,
    63,64,130,255
    natural 63,172,183,
    196,230,232
    of fertile eggs 88
    predation 62,140,172
movements 46,76,77,78,
91,92,101,107,115,118,
130,133,134,135,136-
143,164,165,166,167,
175,253,255,259
    acceleration rate 136
    cruising 131,141
    diel 49,77,140
    homing 78,142,143
    migration 76,77,78,
    79,142,143,163,245,
    248
    motor activity 134
    school fidelity 140
    shoaling 101,104,106,
    136,137,138,139,140
    swimming speed 77,
    136,137,138
mucous 19,30,31,33,39,
172,241
musculature 27-30,145,
147,151,152,153,154,155,
156,157,158,159
    adductor mandibulae
    27,28,29
    circulatory system 34
    cranial 27,29
    eye - moved by 41
    intestine 33

myotomes 27,30,82
    of the submucosa 31
    red muscle 27
    stomach 33
    white muscle 27,179

Nematistiidae 2,3
nervous system 36-43
    autonomic 36,37,40
    brain 33,36,39,43,
    74,83,84,153,178,242
    cranial and spinal
    nerves (peripheral)
    36,37,38,39,43
    ear 36,38,39,41
    eye 14,36,38,41,81,
    83,84,85,87,89,148,
    150,153,154,163,169,
    170,172,253,263
    lateral line 1,8,36,
    38,42,43,90,244,245,
    251
    nose (snout) 36,38
    semi-circular canals
    see skeleton
    spinal cord 27,36,37
    visual acuity 41,42
Notropis atherinoides 99
N. hudsonius 99,202,203,
206

oestradiol 17β 66
operculum (opercular
bone) 22,23,25,27,29,30,
50,51,52,53,57,89,107,
108,130,146,226
orangethroat darter see
Etheostoma spectable
Osmerus eperlanus 99,
100,190
O. mordax 202,203,216,
218,219,229
otoliths 40,41,51,84,85

parasites and diseaes
    abiotic and biotic
    factors 165-171
    Acanthocephala 160-
    161,164,167,171
    Acarina 162,165
    Cestoda 156-157,163,

167,171
Crustacea 162,164,167
epizootic 148,166,172
genetic defect 145
Hirudinoidea 161,164
host 144,148,163,164,
165,166,167,169,170,
171,172
Limnaeidae 163
Monogenea
148,151-156, 166,167
Myxosporida 148,149-
151
Nematoda 158-160,163,
167
Protozoa 148,149-151,
167,172
Trematoda 148,151-
156,166,167,171
tumours 145,146
zooparasites 148,149-
162
Pelecus cultratus 222
Perca 5,8,13,20,21,22,
24,25,26,27,31,34,36,41,
42,43,44,46,48,50,51,57,
59,67,69,74,75,76,77,78,
80,82,89,91,92,94,97,
101,102,103,106,114,126,
129,130,136,139,140,144,
174,175,176,228,237,242,
244,248
    coloration 14
    hatch at a length of
55
P. flavescens 8,20,21,
26,31,32,33,35,37,38,39,
44,46,48,49,55,59,61,64,
66,67,69,70,74,75,76,77,
81,83,85,88,89,91,92,93,
97,98,99,100,101,103,
113,115,117,118,119,
120,126, 127,129,130,
131,133,135,136,137,138,
139,140,141,144,145,146,
147,148,149,150,151,152,
153,154,155,156,157,158,
159,160,161,163,164,167,
169,171,173,175,176,177,
179,180,185,186,187,188,
188,189,202,203,205,206,
211,213,214,216,217,218,
219,223,227,228,229,230,
233,234,235,237,238,239,
240,242
    distribution 8,9
P. fluviatilis 8,20,21,
23,26,28,29,33,35,39,41,
42,43,44,45,46,48,50,51,
52,53,54,55,56,57,58,59,
60,61,63,64,65,66,67,68,
69,71,72,73,74,76,77,81,
85,87,88,90,94,95,97,98,
99,100,101,102,103,104,
105,107,108,109,110,111,
112,113,114,115,116,120,
121,126,127,129,133,137,
139,140,141,142,146,147,
148,149,150,151,152,153,
154,155,156,157,158,159,
160,161,163,164,165,167,
168,169,170,175,176,177,
178,180,182,183,184,186,
190,192,193,194,195,196,
197,198,199,200,201,204,
205,207,208,211,213,214,
223,226,227,228,229,233,
234,236,237,240,241,242,
244,248
    distribution 8,9
    external appearance
    of 15
P. schrenki 8,20,26,176
    coloration 14
    distribution 8,9
percarina see *Percarina
demidoffi*
Percarina demidoffi 5,8,
244,249,250
    coloration 249
    distribution 8,10
    external appearance
    of 249
perch see *Perca
fluviatilis*
Percichyidae 2,3
Percidae 1,2,3,4,13,19,
27,31,34,37,39,40,43,45,
46,48,49,55,64,66,93,94,
99,109,112,113,115,116,
118,120,122,125,133,135,
145,146,148,163,164,165,

168,172,173,174,175,178,
180,182,185,190,199,204,
205,211,213,224,225,226,
227,231,233,234,235,238,
239,240,242,243,262,263
    radiographs of 6-7
    subfamilies, tribes
    and genera 5
percids see Percidae
Perciformes 1,2
Percina 5,8,12,244,251,
254,256,259,261
    distribution 10,12
P. aurantiaca 251,258
P. burtoni 251
P. caprodes 255,261
P. macrocephala 257
P. maculata 252,253,255
P. nigrofasciata 255
P. sciera 180,254
P. shumardi 255
Percinae 5,8
Percini 5,8,244-250
Percoidei 1,2,3,175
    families of 3-4
Percopsis omiscomaycus
99,203
pericardial cavity 31,
33,155
peritoneal cavity 31,34,
36,147,155,159
Petromyzon marinus 216,
217
pharynx 30,31,37,153
Philometra cylindracea
159,171
pike see *Esox lucius*
Pimephales promelas *206*
Piscicola geometra 161,
164,168,169
Pleistocene 175,176,204
Pliocene 175
Podiceps cristatus 170
pollutants 239-242
    heavy metals 219,
    240-241
    organic 240,241-242
Polyphemus pediculus 96
population dynamics 62,
181-206
    density 57,60,170,

181,182,183,185,187,
189,192,196,199,202,
237,253
    of parasites 165
    recruitment 170,173,
    177,182,185,186,188,
    189,190,191,192,197,
    198,200,210,228,230,
    233
predation, 62,95,181,
187,188,190,192,198,199,
201,205,253
predators 80,91,95,97,
98,101,104,107,108,110,
111,112,136,147,169,175,
177,182,183,185,187,192,
201,204,229,233,244,253,
255
production 94,95,174,
186,199,201,207,208,209,
210,223,234,237,238,239
Proteocephalus pearsei
157,167,171
Proteocephalus sp. 157,
171
Pseudomonas 147
pumpkinseed see *Lepomis
gibbosus*
Pythiopsis 147

rainbow darter see
Etheostoma caeruleum
rainbow smelt see
Osmerus mordax
rainbow trout see *Salmo
gairdneri*
Raphidascaris acus *159*,
163,173
rearing 172,232,233,234,
235-239,243
redline darter see
Etheostoma rufilineatum
reproduction (see also
gonads; gametes) 46,49,
164,231
    courtship 79,121
    fecundity 71,72,73,
    74,174,180,184,231,
    250,258
    fertilisation (see
    also culture) 81,88,

174,260,261
maturation 69,75
oogenesis
(gametogenesis) 67,74
oviposition 74
ovulation 75,75,77
reproduce 128,136,204
spawn (spawning) 18,
54,63,74,75,76,77,78,
79,80,129,141,142,
143,146,170,171,174,
175,188,189,190,193,
197,201,221,228,229,
230,231,233,234,245,
248,250,253,258,259,
260,266
spermatogenesis
(gametogenesis) 66,
67,74
spermiation 74,75
vitellogenesis 66,67
yolk sac 45,85,89,
136,261
reproductive cycle 44,
74,75
reservoirs see lakes and
rivers
respiration 89,95,117,
130-136,241,242
coefficient of oxygen
uptake 132,133,134
ventilation volume
132,133,134
respiratory movements
27,39,132,133,134
river darter see
Percina shumardi
roach see *Rutilus*
rutilus
rodlet cells 30,33
Romanichthyini 5,8,263-
266
Romanichthys 5,8,12,263,
264
R. valsanicola 13,263
coloration 263
distribution 12,13,
263
external appearance
of 264

rudd see *Scardinius*
erythropthalmus
ruffe see *Gymnocephalus*
cernua
Rutilus rutilus 97,99,
100,104,190,204,205
R. rutilus caspicus 100

Salmo gairdneri 46,235
S. trutta 116,192
salmonids 94,115,116,
146,147,172,223,225,228
Salvelinus alpinus 139,
192,194
S. namaycush 205,216
Sanguinicola occiden-
talis 148,155,163
Saprolegnia 147
S. ferax 148
sauger see *Stizostedion*
canadense
scad see *Trachurus*
trachurus
scales 15,89,172,178,
242,244,251,263
ageing 20,51
circuli 19,20
ctenoid 1,15,19
cycyloid 1,19
development of 19,20
layers 19,20
Scardinius
erythropthalmus 97,99
schooling see shoaling
sea lamprey see
Petromyzon marinus
sea pikeperch see
Stizostedion marina
seas
Aegean Sea 264
Aral Sea 76,126,177
Arctic Ocean 253
Atlantic Ocean 254
Baltic Sea 99,126,
168,177,211
Bering Sea 176
Black Sea 8,177,178,
245,249
Caspian Sea 80,177,
178

Chesapeake Bay 127
Gulf of Mexico 254
Hudson Bay 254
Pacific Ocean 176
Sea of Azov 8,79,128, 249
senescence 61,74
Serranidae 1,3,175
Sialis 97,98
silverside see *Atherina presbyter*
skeleton 21-27
  branchial arches 22, 23,25,27,29,30,31, 33,108
  branchiocranium 23
  branchiostegal 2,22, 23,24,108,130
  cleithra 2,51
  dermal 21,23,24
  endochrondral 21,23
  hyoid 22,29,108
  interhaemal bone 6,7, 8
  jaws 21,22,27,29,89, 107,108,145,146
  Meckel's cartilage 21
  neurocranium 22,23, 107,108
  notochord 24,82
  pectoral girdle 22, 23,37,108
  pelvic girdle 24,37
  pterygiophore 24,30
  rays 24,26,30,90,264
  retro-articular process 22
  semi-circular canals 22,39
  skull 2,21,24,25,29
  spinal cord 27
  spines 8,14,18,24,26, 30,90,107,177,244, 245,249,251,264
  suspensorium 22,27, 30,107,108
  urostyle 27
  vertebrae 24,27,37, 51
skin 18-19,22,30,38,42, 130,145,147,148,149,150,

151,152,153,154,156,161, 162,163,164,172,242
slackwater darter see *Etheostoma boschungi*
smallmouth bass see *Micropterus dolomieui*
smelt see *Osmerus*
eperlanus and *O. mordax* (rainbow smelt)
Spinitectus gracilis 159,167,171
spottail darter see *Etheostoma squamiceps*
spottail shiner see *Notropis hudsonius*
spotted darter see *Etheostoma maculatum*
sprat see *Sprattus sprattus*
Sprattus sprattus 99
Stenodus leucichthys 139
Stizostedion 5,8,12,13, 20,22,24,26,36,41,42,43, 44,46,48,50,51,57,59,67, 69,75,82,89,91,92,94, 101,106,139,144,174, 175,176
  coloration 14
  tapetum lucidum 14, 42,106,107,237
S. canadense 26,46,48, 85,91,180,205,211,213, 220,229
  coloration 18
  distribution 11,12
  external appearance of 17
  hatches at a length of 56
S. lucioperca 20,26,31, 42,43,44,46,48,59,60,61, 64,72,76,79,80,81,85,87, 88,91,92,97,99,100,106, 107,108,112,113,114,115, 127,128,132,133,134,139, 143,145,148,149,150,151, 152,153,154,155,156,157, 158,159,160,163,164,165, 168,174,175,177,178,180, 190,204,205,211,213,214, 221,222,223,229,233,234,

235,236,237,238,240,249
   coloration 14
   cteni number 19
   distribution 11,12
   external appearance
    of 16
   hatches at a length
    of 56
S. marina 26,31,80,178
   coloration 18
   distribution 11,12
   external appearance
    of 16
S. vitreum 20,26,30,31,
32,42,44,46,48,51,56,57,
59,61,62,63,64,67,69,72,
73,75,76,77,78,79,80,81,
82,84,85,86,87,88,89,90,
91,92,93,97,98,99,101,
104,105,106,107,110,111,
112,113,115,116,128,129,
131,132,135,136,137,138,
139,140,141,142,143,145,
146,148,149,150,151,152,
153,154,155,156,157,158,
159,160,161,163,164,173,
174,175,177,179,180,185,
186,187,188,189,190,191,
201,205,206,210,211,213,
214,217,218,219,220,223,
225,226,227,228,229,230,
231,232,233,234,235,236,
237,238,240,241,262
   coloration 18,90
   distribution 11,12,
   98
   external appearance
    of 17
   hatches at a length
    of 56
S. vitreum glaucum 177,
201,217,218,229
S. vitreum vitreum 177
S. volgensis 22,26,31,
44,74,178
   coloration 18
   distribution 11,12
stocks 20,59,78,143,
173,178,179,180,186,
188,189,190,192,197,

198,199,207,208,209,
211,216,217,219,228,
230,234,239,240,242,
243
streber see *Zingel
streber*
striped ruffe see
*Gymnocephalus
schraetser*
survival see mortality
swamp darter see
Etheostoma fusiforme
swim bladder 1,31,32,36,
40,68,84,92,137,139,155,
159,168,253,263,264
   pneumatic duct 31,32
swimming see movements

tangerine darter see
Percina aurantiaca
tapetum lucidum see
Stizostedion
teeth 22,23,89,108,226
telemetry 48
temperature see internal
and external factors
Tertiary 176
Tetracotyle sp. 155,171
tetracycline antibiotic
51
Thymallus thymallus 139
Trachurus trachurus 99
Triaenophorus crassus
157,168
T. nodulosus 163,166,
167,168,169,171
trout-perch see
Percopsis omiscomaycus
Tylodelphys clavata 156,
169,170
T. podicipina 156,169,
170

urinary system (see also
kidney) 148
   ureter (Wolffian
   duct) 34,44,150,154
   urinary bladder 34,
   36,40,85,145,149,150,
   153,154,155
Urocleidus adspectus

148,156,171

variegate darter see
Etheostoma variatum
vendace see *Coregonus*
albula
viruses (see
also *Herpesvirus*
vitreum) 145,146,172
   dermal sarcoma 145,
   146
   epidermal hyperplasia
   145,146
   infectious
   haematopoietic
   necrosis virus 146
   infectious pancreatic
   necrosis virus 146
   lymphocystis 145,146
   Nillahcootie redfin
   virus 146
Volga pikeperch see
Stizostedion volgensis

Waccamaw darter see
Etheostoma perlongum
walleye see
Stizostedion vitreum
white bass see *Morone*
chrysops
white bream see *Blicca*
bjoerkna
white perch see *Morone*
americana
white sucker see
Catostomus commersoni
whitefish see *Coregonus*
sp.

year class 51,52,55,57,
58,59,60,61,63,64,182,
185,186,187,188,189,
190,192,194,196,197,
198,199,201,207,208,
217,229,230,231,232,233,
237
yellow perch see *Perca*
flavescens
yield (see also mor-
tality; production) 189,

207,208,209,210,211–228,
230,237
   optimum yield 208
   sustainable yield
   207,208,209,224,225
zander see Stizostedion
lucioperca
ziege see *Pelecus*
cultratus
zinc (see also
pollutants)238
Zingel 8,12,263,264
   coloration 263–264
zingel see *Zingel*
zingel
Z. *asper* 12,264,266
   distribution 12
   external appearance
   of 265
Z. *streber* 12,264
   distribution 12
   external appearance
   of 265
Z. *zingel* 12,264,266
   distribution 12
   external appearance
   of 265
zooplankton 94,97,101,
104,106,110,112,174,182,
235,237